From Jesus to Constantine:
A History of Early Christianity

Bart D. Ehrman, Ph.D.

THE
GREAT
COURSES

PUBLISHED BY:

THE GREAT COURSES
Corporate Headquarters
4840 Westfields Boulevard, Suite 500
Chantilly, Virginia 20151-2299
Phone: 1-800-832-2412
Fax: 703-378-3819
www.thegreatcourses.com

Bart D. Ehrman, Ph.D.

Professor, Department of Religious Studies
The University of North Carolina at Chapel Hill

Bart Ehrman is The James A. Gray Professor and Chair of the Department of Religious Studies at the University of North Carolina at Chapel Hill. With degrees from Wheaton College (B.A.) and Princeton Theological Seminary (M.Div. and Ph.D., *magna cum laude*), he taught at Rutgers for four years before moving to UNC in 1988. During his tenure at UNC, he has garnered numerous awards and prizes, including the Students' Undergraduate Teaching Award (1993), the Ruth and Philip Hettleman Prize for Artistic and Scholarly Achievement (1994), the Bowman and Gordon Gray Award for excellence in teaching (1998), and the James A. Gray Chair in Biblical Studies (2003).

With a focus on early Christianity in its Greco-Roman environment and a special expertise in the textual criticism of the New Testament, Professor Ehrman has published dozens of book reviews and more than 20 scholarly articles for academic journals. He has authored or edited 12 books, including *The Apostolic Fathers* (Loeb Classical Library; Cambridge, Mass: Harvard University Press, 2003); *Lost Christianities: The Battles for Scripture and the Faiths We Never Knew* (New York: Oxford University Press, 2003); *Jesus: Apocalyptic Prophet of the New Millennium* (Oxford University Press, 1999); *The New Testament: A Historical Introduction to the Early Christian Writings* (Oxford, 1997; 3rd ed. 2004); *After the New Testament: A Reader in Early Christianity* (Oxford, 1999); *The New Testament and Other Early Christian Writings: A Reader* (Oxford, 2nd ed. 2004); and *The Orthodox Corruption of Scripture* (Oxford, 1993). He is currently at work on a new commentary on several non-canonical Gospels for the *Hermeneia Commentary* series, published by Fortress Press.

Professor Ehrman is a popular lecturer, giving numerous talks each year for such groups as the Carolina Speakers Bureau, the UNC Program for the Humanities, the Biblical Archaeology Society, and select universities across the nation. He has served as the President of the Society of Biblical Literature, SE Region; book review editor of the *Journal of Biblical Literature*; editor of the Scholar's Press Monograph Series *The New Testament in the Greek Fathers*; and co-editor of the E.J. Brill series *New Testament Tools and Studies*. Among his administrative responsibilities, he has served on the executive committee of the Southeast Council for the Study of Religion and has chaired the New Testament textual criticism section of the Society of Biblical Religion, as well as serving as Director of Graduate Studies and Chair of the Department of Religious Studies at UNC.

Table of Contents

From Jesus to Constantine:
A History of Early Christianity

Table of Contents

From Jesus to Constantine:
A History of Early Christianity

From Jesus to Constantine:
A History of Early Christianity

Scope:

The Christian church has been the most powerful religious, political, social, cultural, economic, and intellectual institution in the history of Western civilization, from late antiquity, to the Middle Ages, the Renaissance, the Reformation, and on into modern times. It continues to assert enormous influence on the history and shape of our culture today as the largest of the world's religions (with two billion adherents). Yet the Christian movement did not start out as a culturally significant phenomenon; it began in a remote part of the Roman Empire as a small, lower-class group of followers of a Jewish apocalyptic preacher, crucified as an enemy of the state. For more than a century, the Christian church was virtually unknown among the political and cultural leaders of the Western world. How did Christianity grow into such an enormously influential institution from such humble beginnings? That is the overarching question of this course.

Following two lectures that introduce the topic, explain the issues that we address, and set the context for the emergence of Christianity among the other (pagan and Jewish) religions of the Roman world, the course divides itself up into six major sections. Section 1 deals with the "Beginnings of Christianity." There, we will consider the figures and traditions that lie at the foundation of the emerging Christian religion. We will begin by exploring what can be known about the life, teachings, and death of Jesus of Nazareth, the Jewish prophet who became the object of worship for Christians throughout the world, based on a belief in his Resurrection from the dead as a sign of God's divine favor and of his own unique standing before God. We will then consider the traditions about Jesus that began to circulate after his death, leading to the writing, some decades later, of the Christian Gospels—some of which came to be included in the New Testament. Finally, we will consider the life and teachings of the apostle Paul, who was, beyond doubt, the most important figure for the development of early Christianity apart from Jesus.

Section 2 considers "Jewish-Christian Relations." Christianity began as a sect within Judaism, originally composed of Jewish followers of a Jewish teacher of the Jewish Law; yet within a century, it had become an anti-Jewish religion. How did this happen? In three lectures, we will explore the rise of anti-Judaism within the Christian church and the emergence of Christianity as a religion distinct from and in opposition to the Jewish religion from which it emerged.

Section 3 consists of two lectures on the spread of Christianity throughout the Mediterranean, beginning with the missionary work of the apostle Paul and continuing with the Christian mission of the second and third centuries. Here, we will consider the message the Christians proclaimed and their approaches to winning converts, asking what they said or did that convinced people to abandon the worship of their own gods to accept the God of the Jews and put their faith in Jesus as his son.

In section 4, we examine the hostile reactions to the Christian mission from among those who were not persuaded to convert, but who considered Christianity to be a dangerous, or at least an anti-social, religion, leading to the persecutions of the second and third centuries. In the process, we will explore, not only the historical information about when and where persecutions erupted, but the even more intriguing question of why pagan crowds, and eventually imperial officials, most of whom were themselves religious persons and generally tolerant of religious diversity, decided to attack Christians in an attempt to force them to recant.

Section 5 moves from the external opposition to the religion to conflicts that occurred within its ranks, as Christians with divergent understandings of the faith engaged in struggles to determine what the "true" faith involved and what Christians everywhere should believe. In four lectures, we will consider the wide range of Christian belief in evidence in the first and second centuries, held by various groups. All these groups believed that they were "right" and the others were "wrong." Moreover, all had authoritative texts that supported their views, books allegedly written by apostles, but most of which were, in fact, forged. We will then examine several of these forged works that happen to have been discovered in modern times.

Finally, in the five lectures of section 6, we will explore the factors that led to the formation of traditional Christianity, that is, Christianity as it developed into the Middle Ages and down into modern times, with its canon of New Testament Scriptures, its set creeds, its liturgical practices (such as baptism and the Eucharist), and its church hierarchy.

The final lecture will bring together the various issues we have discussed and consider the state of Christianity at the beginning of the fourth century, when the Roman emperor Constantine converted to the faith. We will conclude by seeing how this conversion played such an enormous role in the history of Western civilization, as it propelled the Christian church from being a persecuted minority to becoming a sanctioned religion. Eventually, by the end of the fourth century, it was to be declared the official religion of the Roman Empire.

Lecture One
The Birth of Christianity

Scope: Christianity has been, by far, the most important religious, social, and cultural phenomenon in Western civilization and continues to be the largest religion in the world, with some two billion adherents. In this course, we will consider how it all began, starting with the historical Jesus himself and moving through the critical first 300 years of Christianity, up to a key moment, the conversion of the Roman emperor Constantine in the early fourth century.

This lecture introduces some of the essential issues: How did Christianity develop away from its Jewish roots to become an anti-Jewish religion? How did it win converts throughout the Roman Empire? Why and how was it persecuted in its early years? How diverse was it internally, with various "heretical" groups claiming to represent the true teachings of Jesus? And how did the creeds, the canon of the New Testament, and the church hierarchy all develop out of its earlier diversity? How, in the end, did this religion conquer the Roman Empire to become the most important religion of our civilization?

Outline

I. Christianity is without a doubt the most significant religious movement in the history of Western civilization.

    A. Throughout the history of the West, the most important institution of any kind—not just religiously but also politically, economically, socially, and culturally—has been the Christian church, from late antiquity, to the Middle Ages, the Renaissance, the Reformation, and on into modern times.

    B. Despite the central importance of other great religious traditions—Islam, Judaism, Buddhism, Hinduism—Christianity remains the largest religion in the world, with some two billion adherents.

    C. Yet it was obviously not always that way. Christianity, in fact, began as a small and inauspicious sect within Judaism; its earliest adherents were a tiny group of uneducated and illiterate Jewish peasants in a remote and unsavory corner of the Roman Empire. They followed a virtually unknown Jewish teacher who was executed for treason against the state.

II. The basic question we will deal with in this course is how we got from one to the other, how Christianity could have such a stunning impact after such an unpromising beginning.

    A. We will not cover the entirety of the Christian religion, but only its first three centuries—from the time of Jesus of Nazareth, in the first century A.D., to the time of the Roman emperor Constantine, in the early fourth century.

    B. Jesus of Nazareth was, of course, the founder and foundation of the Christian religion.

        1. After his day, Christianity moved by fits and starts through the Roman Empire, usually slowly, even if steadily.

        2. For centuries, though, it was a small, unfavored, and even persecuted splinter group from Judaism.

    C. Constantine was the first Roman emperor to convert to become a follower of Jesus.

        1. Once he accepted the Christian message, everything changed. Before his conversion, the church had grown from being a mere handful of Jewish followers of Jesus to being something like five percent of the empire.

        2. After Constantine's conversion, though, the religion took off in a big way; by the end of the fourth century, it could claim something like half of the empire's population and, in fact, was declared the empire's official religion.

    D. What happened in those intervening years between Jesus and Constantine? How did the religion start? How did it relate to its mother religion, Judaism? How did it grow? How was it received by the masses? By the empire? Why was it persecuted? How did it develop and change internally?

    E. These are the questions we will explore in this course. I will begin, in this lecture, by explaining some of the intriguing questions that we will address in the lectures to follow.

III. Most people who converted to Christianity, of course, were former pagans—polytheists adhering to various religions of the Roman Empire.

A. Thus, we need to begin by seeing what these religions were like, what kinds of gods their adherents worshipped, why they worshipped them, and how they did so.

B. We will consider whether there are any points of contact between the Christian's belief in one true God who created all things and was sovereign over all and the pagan's beliefs in many gods who influenced every aspect of life. Was Christianity *completely* different from these other religions?

C. Christianity started out, of course, as a sect of Judaism. Jesus himself was a Jewish teacher, and his followers were Jewish peasants. We will need to consider, then, what Judaism was like in the ancient world, how it was like and unlike the pagan religions that were predominant at the time.

IV. After reflecting on the religious milieu of Jesus and his earliest followers, we will examine the beginnings of Christianity itself.

A. We will start with the historical Jesus, beginning with why it is so difficult to know what Jesus himself actually said and did, despite the several sources we have that describe his life.

B. We will then consider how modern historians have tried to reconstruct the life of the historical Jesus and show why it appears that he is best understood as a Jewish prophet who devoted his ministry to calling Jews of his day to repent in light of the coming judgment of God.

C. Christians have understood Jesus as much more than that, of course. Thus, we will consider how the religion of Jesus (that is, the one he preached) became the religion about Jesus (that is, the one that preached him.) Here, we will focus especially on the apostle Paul to see how he helped to transform Jesus's message into a new religion based on Jesus's death and Resurrection.

V. Once Christianity became a new religion, separate from Judaism, there is obviously the question of how Christians related to Jews in the early centuries. In the next section of the course, we will consider the historically significant issue of how Christianity started as a sect within Judaism, yet became a virulently anti-Jewish religion in the span of just over a century.

VI. Christians, of course, had to relate not just to Jews and Judaism but to the larger Roman world. In the next section of the course, we will consider issues involving Christianity and empire.

    A. We will start by asking how Christianity managed to win converts in the empire from among pagans.

        1. What did Christians preach that proved so convincing to others that they renounced their former religion to follow the teachings of Christ?

        2. What missionary strategies did Christians use? How successful were they?

    B. How was Christianity received by those who did not accept the religion? Here, we will consider the intriguing historical questions of when, where, and how Christians were persecuted by non-Christian masses and imperial authorities, sometimes to the point of death.

VII. While Christianity was spreading and interacting with both Jews and pagans, of course, it was also developing internally.

    A. Some of the most intriguing aspects of early Christianity involve its widely diverse character, as different people claiming to be Christian adhered to all sorts of beliefs and practices, asserting that their views were true and that other Christians with other beliefs were wrong.

    B. We will consider some of the internal battles among Christians to decide what was *orthodoxy* (that is, "right belief") and what was *heresy* (that is, "false belief").

        1. In this context, we will see how various Christian groups adhered to different written authorities for their views—books allegedly written by apostles.

        2. Many of these books, however, were forged. We still have a number of these forgeries today, because of recent archaeological discoveries.

        3. It was out of this set of conflicts that the New Testament as a collection of authoritative books emerged. How did we get this set of books, and why do we have these books instead of others?

C. We will conclude the course by considering the formation of early Christianity to become the kind of religion with which people today are familiar.

   1. This religion includes a canon of Scripture; a creed that expresses the "correct" theological beliefs, such as the doctrine of the Trinity; practices of worship that include such rites as baptism and the Eucharist; and a kind of church structure that includes clerical offices, such as priests, bishops, and eventually, a pope.

   2. Christianity did not always have these things, of course, which means that we will address the question of how they all developed.

VIII. In a final wrap-up lecture, we will consider the internal and external success of Christianity, as it developed over its first 300 years to become a religion that would eventually convert, then dominate the religious, political, social, and cultural world of the Roman Empire and be transmitted down to us today as the most important institution in the history of our form of civilization.

Essential Reading:

Henry Chadwick, *The Early Church.*

Bart Ehrman, *After the New Testament*, chapter 1.

Supplementary Reading:

Everett Ferguson, *Encyclopedia of Early Christianity* (articles on sundry topics).

W. F. C. Frend, *The Rise of Christianity.*

Questions to Consider:

1. Before we begin to explore the historical record, it might be useful for you to reflect on your own about the success of early Christianity. Come up with as many reasons as you can for why Christianity might have proved "successful" in establishing itself as a major religion. In your opinion, does the success of a religion (Christianity or any other) indicate anything about its truth claims? In other words, if it succeeded, does that indicate that it is right?

2. Try to imagine ways that the Christianity you may be familiar with today—whether by personal commitment or any other experience—might be different from Christianity in its early years. Is it possible that the religion of the earliest followers of Jesus might have been radically different from the Christianity you have been exposed to in the modern world? How would we know?

Lecture One—Transcript
The Birth of Christianity

I'd like to welcome you to this course, in which we study the history of early Christianity, from Jesus to Constantine. As we'll see early on, our topic is one of the most important subjects for anyone interested in religion, Western civilization, or the history of the Western world.

At the same time, this is a widely neglected area, little known or understood among otherwise highly educated people. Many people have vague ideas about early Christian history, some notion that Christians were a small, persecuted minority, hiding out in catacombs to avoid arrest, but a group that grew rapidly because of their fervent convictions and willingness to die for their faith.

In this course, we will be examining the real history of the early Christian movement, exploring some of the common myths about it, while highlighting just how important this history was for us today. The fact is that whether we ourselves are Christian or not, this history of early Christianity has had a profound impact on our form of civilization, our social world, our beliefs, values, assumptions, worldviews, all of which would be radically different if things had turned out differently.

I'd like to begin with a very brief statement of why the history of early Christianity is such an important topic, and then spend the rest of this particular lecture indicating different aspects of the topic that we will be covering during the course of lectures. As I hope you'll see, these matters are not only important, but fascinating as well. Yet, they are little known outside of the world of scholarship.

First, the importance of the topic. Christianity is, without a doubt, the most significant religious movement in the history of Western civilization. Throughout the history of the West, the most important institution of any kind, not just religiously, but also politically, economically, socially, and culturally, has been the Christian church, from late antiquity, to the Middle Ages, to the Renaissance, to the Reformation, and on into modern times. None of these historical movements would have been anything like the same had Christianity not been the dominant religion of the West—not the fall of the Roman Empire, or the Middle Ages, or the European Renaissance, or the Reformation, or the movement into the modern world.

Without Christianity, what would our world have looked like in all of these periods? What would have happened, and how would we all be different today, despite the great importance of other central religious traditions in our world, such as Islam, Judaism, Buddhism, Hinduism? Christianity remains the largest religion in the world, with some two billion adherents today, and yet, it was not always that way.

Christianity began as a small, inauspicious sect within Judaism. Its earliest adherents were a tiny group of uneducated and illiterate peasants in a remote, unsavory corner of the Roman Empire, who followed a virtually unknown teacher; this teacher was executed for treason against the state. The basic question we will be dealing with in this course is how we got from one to the other, how Christianity could have had such a stunning impact on our world after having such an unpromising beginning.

We will not cover the entirety of the Christian religion in this set of lectures, but only its first three centuries, the highly formative years from the time of Jesus of Nazareth in the first century A.D. to the time of the Roman Emperor Constantine in the early fourth century.

To begin, I should say a word about these two historic figures, to provide the nodal points for our discussion: Jesus at the beginning, and Constantine at the end.

Jesus of Nazareth was, of course, the founder, and the foundation, of the Christian religion. I can give something, briefly, of his life here. We are going to spend an entire lecture on the life of Jesus, but briefly, to set the context for our reflections in this lecture, Jesus was born around the year 4 B.C. That seems a little bit odd that Jesus would be born four years before Christ, but in fact, that probably is when he was born. The person who came up with our calendars in the Middle Ages, a monk named Dionysius Exiguous, was a bit confused about some of the dates of Roman history, and he had King Herod dying in what we now know was before B.C. When he came up with our calendar, if Jesus were actually born during the reign of King Herod, then he was born four years before Christ. That's how people today generally think about things. Jesus was born around 4 B.C.

He lived until around the year 30 A.D. His public ministry, if it lasted for three years, then would have lasted between 27 and 30 A.D. His ministry consisted of a proclamation that he made, of the coming kingdom of God. Jesus was a Jewish prophet, proclaiming a coming kingdom to people in rural areas in Galilee and then in Judea, in Israel.

He was reputed to be a miracle worker and healer. At the end of his life, he went to Jerusalem in order to make his proclamation there, and there, in Jerusalem, he was arrested, put on trial, and crucified for claiming to be the king of the coming kingdom that he proclaimed.

After Jesus's day, Christianity moved by fits and starts throughout the Roman Empire, usually quite slowly but steadily. The disciples of Jesus came to believe that after his crucifixion, God had vindicated Jesus by raising him from the dead. They believed he really was the king of this coming kingdom, and so they called him "the Messiah." "The Messiah" in a new sense, the king of Israel, the king, in fact, of the world. "The Messiah" who had died for the sins of the world.

For centuries, these followers of Jesus continued to be a small, favored, and even persecuted splinter group from Judaism, but they steadily expanded over the years as they converted other people to come to the belief in Jesus as the Messiah. They converted, principally, Gentiles to this faith; Gentiles, non-Jews, were the principal converts of these Christians, over the years, especially after the beginning of Christianity in the early first century.

Looking at the other end of our time period, Constantine was the first Roman emperor to convert, to become a follower of Jesus. Once the emperor of Rome converted to Christianity—that changed everything. Prior to Constantine's conversion, the Christian church had grown slowly, from being a mere handful of Jesus's followers, to becoming something like five or maybe seven percent of the Roman Empire by the beginning of the fourth century. Constantine's conversion is usually dated to around the year 312 A.D. Once that conversion happened, the Christian religion took off in a big, major way, so that by the end of the fourth century, it could claim something like half of the empire's entire population. And in fact, by the end of the fourth century, Christianity was declared to be the empire's official religion.

Thus, we have the inauspicious beginnings with Jesus and his followers in a remote part of the empire in the beginning of the first century. By the fourth century, we have a major world religion that's destined to become, then, the official religion of the Roman Empire. We are interested, in this course, in the intervening years.

What happened in the years between Jesus and Constantine? How did the religion start? How did it relate to its mother religion, Judaism? How did it grow? How was it received by the masses? How was it received by imperial authorities? Why was it persecuted, and how did it develop and change internally, so that the religion that Constantine converted to, in fact, was different from the religion that Jesus started? How was it different, and how did it move from point A to point B?

These questions we will be addressed in this course. For the rest of this particular lecture, I would like to lay out in a bit more detail the nature of some of the issues that we will be addressing.

Issue number one: Most people who converted to Christianity in the first three centuries, as I have pointed out, were Gentiles (non-Jews), which means that in terms of religion, they were pagans. Now, I should clarify this term, since I will be using it throughout the course. What I use the term "pagan" in this course, I'm not using it in a derogatory way, the way we might use it today, as when I'm referring to my next-door neighbor, who's a "real pagan" because he throws his Budweiser cans out in the yard, doesn't mow his lawn, and such. It's not a derogatory term when used by historians to refer to the ancient world. The word "pagan" simply refers to anyone who was an adherent of any of the polytheistic religions throughout the empire. "Pagan," then, simply refers to a polytheist: one who worships many of the gods.

Most of the people who converted to Christianity were pagans over the three centuries that we will be looking at, polytheists adhering to various religions of the Roman Empire. To begin the course, then—this is our first issue—we need to begin by seeing what these religions were like, these polytheistic religions adhered to by the vast majority of adherents in the ancient world. We have to consider what kinds of gods these people worshipped, why they worshipped them, and how they went about doing so. We will see that polytheists in the ancient world thought, of course, that their understanding of religion was correct. Today, people think of monotheism as the one option, and so, people might ask somebody, "Do you believe in God?"

Well, in the ancient Roman world, that sort of question wasn't asked, both because belief itself was not that big of an issue, as odd as this may seem to us today (belief in God wasn't that much of an issue, it was taken for granted), but it was also because most pagans, virtually all pagans, believed not just in one superior god, but they believed in lots of gods. These "lots of gods" had all kinds of functions in people's lives, and they resided in all sorts of places. There were great gods who were in charge of the states, the empire. There were lower gods below them; there were less significant gods much closer to us, gods for all kinds of places and all kinds of functions.

We need to consider what this religious environment was all about, and we need to look at points of contact between the Christians' belief in the "one true God" who created all things, and was sovereign over all things, and the pagans' beliefs in many gods who influenced every aspect of life. What are the connections between what Christians were saying about their God and Jesus as his son, and what pagans were saying about the multiplicity of gods?

I will be arguing that, in fact, there are connections between these two kinds of religion, that Christianity would not have succeeded if it hadn't been able to show that there are connections between its understanding of the divine realm and the pagan understanding of the divine realm. If Christianity had been preaching something completely different from what pagans were saying, it would not have made sense to anybody, and so we need to consider what these points of contact were. That's issue number one.

At the same time, Christianity started out as a sect within Judaism. Jesus was a Jewish teacher. His followers were Jewish peasants, and so, we need to consider what Judaism was like in the ancient world, how it was unlike the pagan religions that were dominant at the time; for in fact, Judaism was quite different from anything else in the world. There were lots of religions throughout the empire that were—all of these religions were polytheistic, except Judaism, which was monotheistic, believing that there was only one God who deserved to be worshipped. Jews maintained that this one God was their God, who had called them, the "children of Israel," to be his people. They maintained that God had made a covenant with them, had given them his Law that they were to follow, since they were his people.

Christianity started out as a sect of Judaism, because Jesus and his followers were Jewish, and so, in order to understand the development of Christianity, we need understand something more about the Jewish religion. That will be our second issue.

Issue number three: After reflecting on the religious milieu of Jesus and his earliest followers, we will begin to examine the beginnings of Christianity itself. We will start, naturally enough, with the historical Jesus, and we will begin by seeing why it is so difficult for historians today to know what Jesus himself actually said and did. This may be counterintuitive to many people today, that it's hard to know much about Jesus. It may seem counterintuitive, because it seems that everybody knows everything about Jesus. Turn on the TV on any Sunday morning and you'll find all sorts of people who seem to know a lot about Jesus. Well, how do they know what they know? How do we know what we know?

As it turns out, scholars have recognized that, in fact, it's very difficult to know about what Jesus himself actually said and did, with the difficulty residing in the nature of our sources. As it turns out, we don't have very many or very good sources for knowing about the historical Jesus. We have very few sources outside of the New Testament, and the sources within the New Testament don't say very much about the historical Jesus except for the four Gospels. We have four Gospels in the New Testament, and those books themselves are somewhat problematic for engaging in historical research about Jesus. I'm not saying that they are problematic for people who are, themselves, Christian, who read these books for their theological insights, for their belief in Jesus, but for historians, these books can be problematic, as we will see in a later lecture. Thus, our third issue will be dealing with the very beginnings of Christianity, with Jesus himself.

The fourth issue: We will then move to consider how the religion that Jesus himself proclaimed turned into the religion about Jesus. How the religion that Jesus proclaimed turned into the religion about Jesus, for Christianity, in fact, is much more than the proclamation of the historical Jesus himself. Christianity is a religion that is rooted in the belief in Jesus's death and Resurrection for the salvation of the world. How did we get from one to the other? How did we get from the religion "of Jesus" to the religion "about Jesus"?

In this section of the course, we will be focusing our attention especially on the apostle Paul, to see how he helped transform Jesus's message into religion based on Jesus's own death and Resurrection. The apostle Paul is a very important figure for the beginning of Christianity. He started out, originally, as an opponent of Jesus's followers, but then he converted, and began to proclaim Jesus's message. We have several writings by the apostle Paul within the New Testament, which can help us understand his proclamation of Jesus. That, then, will be issue number four: How the religion *of* Jesus became the religion *about* Jesus.

Issue number five: Once Christianity became a new religion separate from Judaism, there is obviously the question of how Christians related to Jews in these early centuries—the fascinating topic of early Jewish-Christian relations. Our next section of the course, then, will consider the historically significant issue of how Christianity started out as a sect within Judaism, and yet became a virulently anti-Jewish religion, all within the course of just over a century; how Christianity moved from being a sect within Judaism, to becoming strongly anti-Jewish.

The earliest Christians were, themselves, Jews who worshipped the Jewish God, read the Jewish Scriptures, and understood Jesus to be the Jewish Messiah, sent in fulfillment of the Jewish prophecies to the Jewish people. How did Christianity move from being that kind of religion to a religion that condemned Jews for being "Christ killers" within one hundred years? That will be the fifth issue that we will be looking at in this course of lectures.

Issue number six: Christians, of course, had to relate not just to Jews and Judaism, but to the larger Roman world. In the next section of the course, we will then consider issues involving the relationship of Christianity and empire. We will begin this section of the course by asking how Christianity managed to win converts in the empire from among pagans. It's actually a fairly interesting question that many people haven't thought very much about. If Christians are converting Jews to believe in Jesus, then, it's not that complicated conceptually. These are people who believe in the one God of the Jews, and Christians are trying to convince them that Jesus is the son of that God, that Jesus is the Messiah of that God. The assumption is that everybody agrees that there is one God, and that he gave the Jewish Law and made the Jewish covenant. What Christians were then saying was that this was the fulfillment of that covenant, that law.

Conceptually, that's not difficult, but what about when Christians were trying to convert pagans? Pagans didn't believe in the one Jewish God, so for Christians to convert a pagan to Christianity, first they had to convert them to an understanding of the "one true God," the Jewish God. This is involved, though, because in fact, the Christians did not portray themselves as Jews. They were then trying to convince people to believe in the Jewish God, and yet, they were not trying to convince them to become Jewish. This ended up being a rather tricky affair. We will therefore need to consider how this actually worked.

How did it happen? How did Christians actually convert pagans to worship the Jewish God? What did they say to them to convince them, and what did they say to convince them that Jesus was the son of this Jewish God who died for the sins of the world? What could they possibly say to somebody who was a polytheist to convince them? The reason it is a pressing question is because the Christians were remarkably successful at this, but how did they go about doing it? That's one of the issues we will be looking at in this course of lectures: What Christians preached that proved convincing to others so that they not only started worshipping the Jewish God, but gave up worshipping their old gods. They gave up being pagans to become Christians, worshipping the Jewish God without themselves being Jewish.

What missionary strategies did these Christians use? Did they have revival meetings? Did they preach in large theaters and have masses come forward? Did they have massive conversions? Did they engage in door-to-door evangelism? What did they do in order to convince others?

This, then, leads naturally to issue number seven: How was Christianity received by those who were the subjects of the proclamations? How was Christianity received by both Jews and pagans? As we will see, of course, there were some people who accepted the religion. One of the things that we will observe is that, in fact, Christianity does not appear to have had massive conversions. It appears that people converted one at a time, often simply by word-of-mouth, that somebody converted their spouse, who converted the next-door neighbor, who converted his or her spouse, who converted his or her children, and went by word-of-mouth rather than by massive campaign.

How was Christianity received? Sometimes it was accepted. A lot of time, it was ignored by people in the Roman Empire, but on other occasions, Christianity was opposed, and so this is our seventh issue: How was Christianity opposed within the empire? Within this section of the course, we will be considering the intriguing historical questions about Christian persecution. We will look at when, where, and how Christians were persecuted by non-Christian masses and by imperial authorities, sometimes to the point of death. We will see that it's not at all the case that Christianity was "the" illegal religion in the empire. People have this idea that Christianity was illegal, so that you were breaking the law to become a Christian. In fact, that's not true.

Christianity was not illegal, in fact. There was no legislation against Christianity, and there were no empire-wide persecutions of Christians for 200 years. The first time any emperor condemned Christianity and tried to force everybody in the empire to stop being a Christian wasn't until the year 249, over 200 years after Jesus.

Before that, Christianity wasn't considered to be illegal, but it was sometimes persecuted. Why would one be put on trial, and sometimes be put to death, if their religion was not illegal? Well, that's a very interesting historical question. That's one of the things that we will be trying to understand at that point in our course. That is our issue number seven, the persecution of Christians.

Issue number eight: While Christianity was spreading and interacting with both Jews and pagans, of course, it was also developing internally, changing within itself, so that the religion by the fourth century was quite different from the religion of the first century. Some of the most intriguing aspects of early Christianity involved its widely diverse character, as different people, claiming to be Christian, adhered to all sorts of beliefs and practices, asserting that their views were true, but that views of other Christians were false. Christianity became a highly diverse—and I want to show in this course of lectures, nearer the end of it, why it became such a diverse religion. Some scholars have begun to talk not about ancient Christianity, but about "ancient Christianities," it was so diverse.

We want to consider some of the internal battles, especially at internal battles that focused on issues of orthodoxy and heresy. "Orthodoxy" meaning "correct belief;" that's the technical meaning of orthodoxy. It comes from two Greek words that mean "correct belief" and "heresy." The word "heresy" comes from a Greek word that means "choice," and so a "heretic" is somebody who chooses not to believe the right beliefs.

Well, within early Christianity, we have issues of orthodoxy and heresy as Christians battled it out over what point of view was correct, what beliefs were correct, and we will see that there was a remarkable diversity among Christians, many Christians holding points of view that today, nobody would say were Christian. In the early centuries, though, there were people who called themselves Christian, who said they were followers of Jesus, who said that they were adhering to the writings of the apostles, and who said, for example, that there was not one God, but two gods. Some people who called themselves Christian said that there were 30 gods. We have some Christians on record claiming that there were 365 gods. These were Christians; they called themselves Christians. They said that they followed Jesus. Well, how could that possibly be?

Well, because, in fact, early Christianity was quite diverse, and Christianity had internal battles to decide which set of beliefs was correct, and which set of beliefs was heretical. The heretical beliefs got wiped out, so that today, the kind of Christianity that we have inherited is one form that came down from these early decades, these early centuries.

In this context, we will look not only at what different people believed among Christians, but we will also see that they each had different written authorities for their views. Every group of Christians, even those who said there were 365 gods, had books that supported their points of view, and these books all claimed to be written by the apostles of Jesus. That means that a number of these books, probably most of these books, were, in fact, forged. We will consider forgeries.

Many of these forgeries have turned up in modern times, by archaeologists, and sometimes, simply by accident, and we will look at some of these early forgeries in the names of the apostles.

It was out of this set of conflicts over what to believe and which books to read, that the New Testament, as a collection of books, emerged. Well, how did we get these books, these 27 books? Why don't we have other books?

As it turns out, there are other Gospels. Why didn't the other Gospels make it into the New Testament, instead of just Matthew, Mark, Luke, and John? We will be considering all those issues at a later point in the course.

Finally, issue number nine. We will conclude the course by considering the formation of early Christianity to become the kind of religion that people are familiar with today. This religion, that people are familiar with today, includes a canon of Scripture (27 books) that you can buy in any used bookstore today. It included not only a canon of Scripture, but it also included a creed that people still confess today, that expresses the "correct" theological beliefs, such as the belief in the Trinity. We will be seeing how this belief in the Trinity, and the other early Christian beliefs became crystallized by the fourth century.

Christianity today involves practices of worship that include such things as the practice of baptism, and the taking of the Eucharist. Christianity today involves a church structure that includes clerical offices, such as priests and bishops. Eventually, one form of Christianity ended up with a pope. Christianity did not always have these things: the canon, the creed, the clergy, the Eucharist, the baptism, etc. Well, how did they get these things? We will be considering all of that.

In a final wrap-up lecture, the final lecture for the course, we will be considering the internal and external successes of Christianity as it developed over its first 300 years, to become a religion that would eventually convert and then dominate the religious, political, social, and cultural world of the Roman Empire, and so be transmitted down to us today as the most important institution in the history of our form of civilization.

As we move through this course of lectures, I hope that you'll agree with me that the first three centuries of Christianity are critical for anyone; not just those who are Christians, but for anyone who is interested in understanding the history of Western civilization, our own world, and ourselves.

Lecture Two
The Religious World of Early Christianity

Scope: To understand how Christianity became the dominant religion of the Roman world, we need to understand something about religion in that world generally. The first part of this lecture discusses the "pagan," polytheistic religions to which nearly everyone in antiquity adhered, religions that worshipped many gods through acts of prayer and sacrifice to secure divine favor for the hardships of the present life.

The lecture then considers the most important Roman religion for the birth of Christianity: Judaism, the religion of Jesus and his followers. Jews were distinct in the ancient world for worshipping only one God, who was believed to have created this world and to have chosen the Jews to be his people, as evident in the Law he had graciously given them through Moses. It was out of this Jewish matrix in the broader Greco-Roman world that Christianity was born.

Outline

I. To understand the rise of Christianity, we need to situate it in its own historical context in the Greco-Roman world.

  A. The term *Greco-Roman world* refers to the lands around the Mediterranean from roughly the time of Alexander the Great, c. 300 B.C., to the time of the Roman emperor Constantine, c. A.D. 300.

  1. Alexander was the great world military genius who conquered most of the Mediterranean from his native land Macedonia on east, including Egypt, Palestine, and Persia.

  2. As he conquered, he spread Greek religion, language, and culture with him.

  B. The Romans had conquered most of these lands 200 years after Alexander. Their empire eventually reached from Great Britain to Syria, on the southern and northern Mediterranean, including North Africa, Egypt, and Palestine.

II. The vast majority of persons living in the Roman Empire were *pagan*, that is, polytheists who adhered to various local and state religions, or *cults* ("forms of worship").

    A. The belief in many gods was seen as natural and obvious.

        1. These included the "great gods," known to us through ancient Greek and Roman mythology (Zeus, Apollo, Hera, and Aphrodite and their Roman equivalents).

        2. They also included local gods who protected and cared for cities, towns, and villages; even less powerful gods who were localized in forests, rivers, and roads; and family gods who cared for the home.

        3. The gods oversaw every human function and activity, including the crops, the cupboard, the hearth, personal health, childbirth, war, love, and most everything else.

        4. The divine realm was seen, therefore, as a kind of pyramidal hierarchy, with the few great gods near the top and the less powerful but more immediately relevant gods near the bottom.

    B. Religion was not a matter of securing an afterlife but of honoring the gods who could protect and assist mortals in need.

        1. The "fear of the gods" was a motivating factor in ancient religion.

        2. These religions sought, therefore, the "peace of the gods" (*pax deorum*).

    C. The gods were worshipped principally through acts of prayer and, especially, sacrifice.

        1. For the most part, this was a periodic affair, not a matter of constant devotion.

        2. As a result, ethics was not, for the most part, a feature of these religions.

        3. Nor, surprisingly enough for modern people, was correct doctrine central to these religious. There was no such thing as orthodoxy or heresy, right belief or wrong belief, in these religions.

    D. As a partial result, most of these religions were completely tolerant of one another (because there was no sense that only one of them could be "true").

        1. The state gods were expected to be worshipped by all. That only made sense, because these gods had made the state great.

2. Other gods could be worshipped as tradition required and as people wished.
3. Intolerance was reserved only for immoral or socially disruptive forms of worship.

III. Judaism stood out as unique in the context of the Greco-Roman world.

A. Jews made up a small portion of the Roman Empire—possibly around seven percent at the beginnings of Christianity—and were located not just in Palestine but throughout the Mediterranean.

B. The Jewish religion was like other religions in several ways: It, too, stressed prayer and sacrifice to God at specified times and places and on set occasions to secure divine favor and protect against divine wrath.

C. But in other ways, it was distinctive.
1. Jews insisted on worshipping only one God.
2. They maintained that this God had chosen them to be his people.
3. They believed that he had given them his Law (through Moses), which taught them how to worship him and how to live in community together.
4. Ethics was, therefore, a much bigger part of Jewish than pagan religion, as were certain distinctive community "rules," such as circumcision, Sabbath observance, and food laws.

D. We should not think of Judaism as a complete monolith, however, at the beginnings of early Christianity; in fact, there was a wide range of Judaisms.
1. Some Jews emphasized the proper adherence to the temple cult.
2. Others stressed the importance of keeping the Jewish laws as fully as possible in their daily lives.
3. Others emphasized maintaining ritual purity before God.
4. Others insisted on the coming intervention of God to overthrow the forces of evil in the world.

E. Jesus was born in the Roman world into a Jewish home; to understand the beginnings of Christianity, we need to understand the kind of Judaism that he himself embraced and to see how his teachings then came to be developed after his death by his Jewish followers. That will be the subject of the following lecture.

Essential Reading:

David Cartlidge and David Dungan, *Documents for the Study of the Gospels*.

Bart Ehrman, *The New Testament: A Historical Introduction*, chapters 2, 16.

Calvin Roetzel, *The World That Shaped the New Testament*.

Supplementary Reading:

Robin Lane Fox, *Pagans and Christians*.

E. P. Sanders, *Judaism: Practice and Belief*.

Jo-Ann Shelton, *As the Romans Did: A Source Book in Roman Social History*.

Robert Turcan, *The Cults of the Roman Empire*.

Questions to Consider:

1. Explain why it is important to understand the historical "context" of Christianity and reflect on some examples from your own experience in which a misunderstanding has occurred because somebody took a word or action out of context.

2. In what ways were religions in the Greco-Roman world different from what most people today think of as *religion*?

Lecture Two—Transcript
The Religious World of Early Christianity

In our previous lecture, we saw a wide range of fascinating topics that we will be covering in this course on the history of early Christianity. As we saw there, to begin our study, we need to situate the rise of Christianity in its own historical context within the Greco-Roman world.

The term *Greco-Roman world* refers to the lands around the Mediterranean, from roughly the time of Alexander the Great, who died around the year 300 B.C., to the time of the Emperor Constantine, who was ruling around the time of 300 A.D., so from about 300 B.C. to about 300 A.D., the lands around the Mediterranean during this 600-year period.

The period begins with Alexander the Great, who was one of most important figures in the history of Western civilization, arguably the most important person. About 20 years ago now, there was a survey done of college professors who taught political science, history of Western civilization, history more broadly, philosophy—scholars of the liberal arts. The question asked of these scholars was: Who was the most important person for the history of Western civilization?

Now, when I ask my students this in my large undergraduate classes at Chapel Hill, they have an unambiguous response. The most important person for the history of civilization at all was Jesus, Jesus of Nazareth. They are a bit taken aback when I tell them that Jesus, in fact, in this particular survey, tied for fifth, tied with the apostle Paul. Fifth place; as it came out in the survey, scholars thought these two were the cofounders of Christianity.

Well, who was number one, if Jesus tied for fifth? In fact, Alexander the Great. According to the scholars—there's no way of gauging whether they are right or wrong, but in their opinion Alexander the Great was the most important person for the history of Western civilization, because without him, Western civilization would not have happened. Why is that?

Alexander the Great, known sometimes as Alexander of Macedon, was a great military genius, who conquered most of the Mediterranean lands from his native land, Macedonia, in the east, in what we think of as Greece today. He started conquering Macedonia. He then actually conquered Greece to the south, and he conquered the lands around the Mediterranean, including Egypt, Palestine, and Persia.

It wasn't, though, that he was simply a conqueror that made him important. He's important for the history of the West because of what happened in the wake of his conquests. Alexander was enamored with Greek culture and civilization. He had been a student, a pupil, of the Greek philosopher Aristotle, and so when one thinks about genealogical lines, Socrates was the teacher of Plato, Plato was the teacher of Aristotle, and Aristotle was the teacher of Alexander.

Now, unlike these other three, Alexander himself was not a philosopher, but he was enamored of Greek philosophical ways and culture, religion, and language. As he conquered lands around the Mediterranean, all the way east into the Persian Empire, all the way south into Egypt, he spread Greek culture among the places that he conquered. It became a very popular thing for the educated elite in this area to learn how to speak Greek, and to adopt Greek ways, Greek customs, Greek religions.

Cities were built following the Greek pattern, so that throughout this entire area, Greek became something that was known by the upper-class elites, who were kind of in competition with one another to show that they were more sophisticated, more urbane than their neighbors. Well, how would they demonstrate that? By showing that they were more Greek.

In some ways, this land of the Mediterranean, especially eastern Mediterranean, was then unified under Greek culture in a way that it had never been unified in history. This culture brought a kind of unity to this area that had never been seen before, which allowed for all sorts of things, including travel, shared cultural experiences, shared religions, and so forth.

Alexander died as a very young man. He was born in the year 356 B.C., and died in the year 323, as a 33-year-old. The kingdom that he had established by his conquests was then split up among various ones of his generals, so that there were different regions, then, and the empire itself broke up. The Hellenistic culture, though, meaning Greek culture that had started under Alexander, continued on for centuries. Eventually, the Romans conquered most of the lands that Alexander had previously conquered 200 years earlier.

The Roman Empire eventually reached from Great Britain in the West, to Syria in the East. It extended both into the southern and northern Mediterranean. It included North Africa, Egypt, and Palestine. So, when I refer to the "Greco-Roman world," I am referring to this region around the Mediterranean from the time of Alexander up to the Roman Emperor Constantine.

Christianity was born within this Greco-Roman world, at about its midpoint, with the birth of Jesus, probably sometime around the year 4 B.C. It's important for us to understand the birth of Christianity not simply by situating it within the Mediterranean at this time, but also within the context of religion in the Mediterranean at this time. Therefore, we will be devoting this lecture to the Greco-Roman world, specifically around the time of the birth of Christianity.

The vast majority of persons living in the Roman Empire, as I pointed out in the previous lecture, were *pagans*, meaning that they were polytheists who adhered to various local and state religions, or as scholars usually call these religions, *cults*. This is another term that doesn't mean the same thing when scholars of antiquity use it as compared to modern people that use it today. When you speak of a "cult," you think of a kind of marginalized fringe group that is on the edge of sanctioned religion. When historians refer to "cults" in the ancient world, they aren't referring to it in that sense. "Cult" comes from a Latin term, *cultus deorum*, which means "the care of the gods." We have the same root in English when we say "agriculture"; that is, "the care of the fields." The *cultus deorum* is "the care of the gods." Cults are simply forms of ritual worship. The vast majority of people in the empire were polytheists, then, believing in many gods, who participated in one or another of the many state or local cults, forms of worship.

For people living in this ancient world at the time of Christianity's birth, pagans in this world, the idea of worshipping many gods was seen to be both natural and obvious. In our world today it seems natural and obvious that there either is a God, or there's no God. Hardly anybody in our context thinks it would be natural or obvious that there would be many gods, but that's a different commonsense from what you get in the ancient world. The ancient commonsense was that there were many gods. There were virtually no atheists in the way that we define the term today. Interestingly enough, as we will see later this course, Christians who were worshipping one God were called "atheists" by the pagans. They were atheists because they didn't worship the gods, and so one of the charges against Christianity was that they were the atheists. Things have changed quite drastically since those days.

Ancient people knew that there were lots of gods for a lot of places and lots of purposes. Every place had its god: Forests, rivers, streams, plains, fields, homes, places within the home: the hearth, the pantry, the entryway; all of these had gods who were in charge of these various areas. Gods were in charge of everything involving human life. There were gods in charge of the crops that grew, gods in charge of the weather, gods in charge of war, gods in charge of hell. Various gods for various purposes for different places.

Most people in the ancient world would not understand what it would mean to worship just one god. Why would you worship one god? For ancient pagans that would be like saying, "You can have only one friend." Well, why can you only have one friend? There are lots of people. "Well, why can you only worship one god? There are lots of gods." Pagan worship, then, involved a polytheism that seemed natural and obvious.

There were various kinds of gods. They included, of course, the great gods that we know about from Greek and Roman mythology. These great gods were known to the ancient people by stories told about them in the myths, gods, for example such as Zeus, Hera, Aphrodite, or the Roman gods who were their equivalents, such as Jupiter, Juno, and Venus, and many other great gods. These were gods too far beyond us, who, in fact, had very little to do with us here on Earth.

Below the great gods, there were local gods, powerful deities who protected and cared for cities, towns and villages. There were even lesser gods who were localized in forests, rivers, and roads. There were family gods who cared for the home. Lots of gods, a lot of places, with different degrees of power. These gods, as I have indicated, oversaw every human function and activity. They oversaw the crops, the cupboard, the hearth, personal health, childbirth, war, love, and everything else.

The divine realm, was seen, therefore, among most pagans, as a kind of pyramidical structure, in which, at the very top, many pagans thought there was one god who was the chief god, the head god, sometimes thought of as the one supreme being who was purely spirit, who was so far removed from us that we couldn't even imagine what he was like.

Below him, on this pyramid structure, were the great gods. Below the great gods on this pyramid were local deities, and on down. Many pagans believed that there were human beings who had divine aspects to them. There were men who were sometimes called "divine men," thought to have been born of the union of a mortal woman and a god. You get the stories in mythology of a god, maybe Zeus, commonly Zeus, who looks down and sees a beautiful woman whom he can't resist, then comes down in the shape of human, and he has sexual intercourse with her. The child then that is born is divine but also human, half-and-half. Heracles (the god Hercules), in fact, was one such god who was half-mortal and half-immortal.

As you know, in the Roman Empire, the emperor himself was sometimes thought of as being divine, but it's important to understand that when Romans talk about the emperor being "god," they didn't mean the one, chief god, or one of the great gods. They didn't think that he was Zeus, or one of these other gods. He was a divine man, somebody who was far beyond the rest of us in his power and his abilities. How could he be so magnificent, so great? It was because, in fact, he was a divine being. He was a member of the divine realm even though he was here as a human.

This, then, was the divine realm for most pagans, who were polytheists. Religion, for these people, was not a matter of securing the afterlife, the way it is for many people today where I live, in North Carolina, I guess the part of North Carolina I live in is the buckle of the Bible Belt. I have students who come from this region, and most of my students are raised in very conservative Christian environments. I would say that at least for these college students, the principal reason for being religious is to secure the afterlife. They either want to have a heavenly reward, or they want to avoid hellish payment, in which they are forced to pay for their sins in the afterlife. Many of the people I associate with daily, if they are religious, are religious in order to secure the afterlife.

That's not the case in the ancient world. In fact, religion was not a matter of securing the afterlife. Religion was a matter of honoring the gods who could protect and assist mortals now in the present, because of their needs. People in the ancient world, of course, were living fairly close to the edge as a rule, much more so than most of us are today. It was quite common for women to die in childbirth, for example, or for children to die as infants.

In the Roman world, at this time, in order to keep the population constant, every childbearing-aged woman had to have, on average, five children, a very different world from ours. This, of course, was a world in which there wasn't anything like modern medicine. One very common way of dying in the ancient world was by getting a tooth abscess. They had no way of fighting the infection. If somebody got a tooth abscess, quite often, they would die from it.

People couldn't control such things. They couldn't control the drought. They couldn't control illness. They couldn't control crop failure. If you didn't get sufficient rain one season, the next season, your village might have died from starvation.

The worship of the gods was intended to provide for humans that which they could not provide for themselves. The gods were more powerful than we. They were able to provide us with what we needed in order to thrive in this world: rain, health, prosperity, love, and peace.

One of the motivating factors in ancient religion was the fear of the gods. Gods did not actively involve themselves in human affairs very often, or all the time, but gods were to be feared because they could bring calamity if things didn't go well between the humans and the divine in their cultic experiences. If the gods were not worshipped in the way they were supposed to be worshipped, then, in fact, their wrath could be manifested against humans: earthquakes, volcanoes, hurricanes, famine, drought, disease. These were things that the gods could bring if they were not worshipped properly.

Religion, therefore, sought the peace of the gods. This was a technical term in ancient religion, the *pax deorum*, the "peace of the gods." If the gods were at peace both among themselves and with people, then things would go well, and so you wanted to make sure that the gods were on your side. Religion was a way of making sure that that happened. The gods did not demand a lot, in fact. The gods did not demand exclusive devotion. The gods did not insist that you spent all of your time concerned about them, but there were ritual practices that the gods had asked humans to follow, and when humans did this, then things went well. You maintained the peace of the gods.

What were these ritual acts? Well, the gods were worshipped principally through acts of prayer, and especially, sacrifice, sacrifice of animals. Pagans had temples throughout their world. Some were majestic temples to the great gods, some were just small local temples. Even within the home, there might be a small sanctuary, a place dedicated to a god. Sacrifices to the gods were performed in the temples, in the sacred places that had been set up for the purpose.

Often, in local city religion, there would be a particular day set aside for a particular sacrifice, and this was a time of celebration for ancient pagans. Most people in the ancient world didn't eat meat very regularly. Meat would be eaten only during a time of sacrifice, and so this would be a party time. Suppose a city had a particular god, and they had a particular day in which they worshipped this particular god. They would perform a sacrifice in the temple. You would bring an animal to the temple. The priest sacrificed the animal. Then, they didn't destroy the animal. This was how you got your meat. They might have burned some of the inedible portions. Those would be the portions for the god, but then they would cook the meat and have a party. Many of these temples, in fact, had dining rooms as part of the temple, so that the priest would cook the meat, you would have a party there, have friends and family over, and you would celebrate.

We know about this because we found inscriptions on temples that gave rules about how to celebrate the sacrifice. These rules included such things as telling you that only so much wine could be drunk at a particular meal, what to do in case rowdy behavior broke out. In other words, it's pretty clear that these were festive, enjoyable occasions. Pagans, then, worshipped by saying prayers and performing acts of sacrifice.

These were periodic affairs. Gods did not expect any kind of constant devotion, the way that Christians might think of the way they need to relate to the Christian God, but the sacrifice and prayers were done periodically.

It may seem strange, but in fact, ethics were not, for the most part, a feature of ancient pagan religions. Pagan religions were not interested in ethical behavior in terms of how you related to your neighbor, to your family, so much as they were concerned about how you worshipped the gods. It was philosophy in the ancient world rather than religion that was concerned about ethics. I'm not saying that pagans were unethical. In fact, pagans were about as ethical as people are today. Ethics were not a part of the religion, however, they were part of their philosophy, their ways of life.

Nor, interestingly enough for modern people, was correct doctrine an issue in ancient religion. Now, this seems very strange to many Christians, for whom what you believe really matters. In the ancient pagan religions, though, what you believed didn't matter. There were no creeds that were to be said. There was no heresy. There was no orthodoxy. There was no concern with doctrine. These were religions that were concerned with sacrifices to the gods, following set principles and set rituals that had been developed over the years.

Since doctrine was not important to these religions, these religions tended to be highly tolerant of one another, unlike what you might expect. People today might think of the Roman religions as being intolerant; after all, they persecuted the Christians, which is true, but by and large, these religions were highly tolerant of one another, largely because there was no idea that you had to have "correct" doctrine. Nobody thought that if you worshipped this particular god, you couldn't also worship that god. "They are all gods. You should worship them all." Thus, this was a highly tolerant, embracing sort of religion.

The state gods were to be worshipped by all people. If somebody refused to worship the state gods, that could lead to problems for the person. Why not worship the state gods? That would be a political act, choosing not to worship the state gods, but the state gods were to be worshipped along with other gods, who were to be worshipped as tradition required and as people wished. Intolerance within religion was reserved, by and large, only for immoral or socially disruptive forms of worship.

That's what pagan religions were basically like: Many gods, worshipped according to ancient traditions, usually involving prayer and sacrifices in temples with priests, a highly tolerant set of religions. As we will see later in this course, Christianity came along as a major exception. It was quite different, especially in its emphasis on doctrine and an ethics, and in its intolerant relationship to other religions, because Christians maintained that they were right, and since they were right, everyone else was wrong, something that pagans did not claim for themselves.

With the ancient world, of course, there were not only pagan religions; there was also Judaism. Judaism stood out as unique in the context of the Greco-Roman world before Christianity appeared on the scene. Jews made up a small portion of the Roman Empire, possibly something like seven percent at the beginnings of Christianity, seven percent of the empire. Generally, it is thought that there were something like 60 million people in the Roman Empire at this time, and so there might be something like four million Jews in the empire.

Jews were located not only in Palestine, but throughout the entire Mediterranean. The Jewish religion was like other religions in several ways. As in these pagan religions that I spelled out for you, Jews also stressed prayer and sacrifice to God at specific times and places on set occasions. These prayers, these acts of sacrifice, were performed in order to secure divine favor, so that God would look kindly upon his chosen people, and also to protect against divine wrath. Thus, in many ways, the Jewish religion was like other religions. It, too, had a temple, the temple in Jerusalem. Sacrifices were performed there, prayers were performed there, etc.

In other ways, though, Judaism was very distinct within the pagan context of the Roman world in several ways. First, Jews insisted upon worshipping only one God. This made them unusual in the Roman world. Where everybody else believed in the multiplicity of gods, Jews worshipped only one God. That's not to say that the Jews believed in only one God. It is to say that Jews believed you should only worship one God. There's good evidence that at different periods in history, Jews, in fact, believed that there were a multitude of gods.

You can find this even within the Jewish Bible, the Hebrew Scriptures, what Christians call the Old Testament. Within the Ten Commandments: "You shall have no other gods before me," say the Ten Commandments. Well, you need to think about that for a second. "No other gods before me." That presupposes that there are other gods, it's just that they are not to be worshipped before the God of Israel. At that point in the life of Israel, in fact, Jews were not saying, "There is only one God"; they were saying, "There is only one God to be worshipped." That's the difference between what is called *henotheism* and *monotheism*. Henotheism is the idea that you are only to worship one God. Monotheism is the belief that there is only one God. Some Jews were henotheists, some were monotheists. In any event, all Jews agreed that there was only one God to be worshipped, the God of Israel, who was understood to be distinctively the God who had chosen the Jewish people to be his own people.

Jews had ancient traditions that they had written down in which this selection of them as the chosen people was set forth. Jews had Scriptures. This made them somewhat unusual in the ancient world. The other pagan religions didn't have scriptural authorities for their perspectives. Jews, though, did have Scripture, especially books that we might talk of now as the Hebrew Bible, or the Old Testament; in particular, at the time of Jesus, the first five books, the Torah, which means "law." The Law of the Jews in the first five books: Genesis, Exodus, Leviticus, Numbers, and Deuteronomy. These books show forth the traditions of Israel and show forth how God chose Israel to be his people.

The term the Jews used in order to explain the special relationship they had with this one God was the term *covenant*. The Jewish people believed that God had made a covenant with them, his people. The term "covenant," by the way, is a legal term which just means "an agreement." The legal agreement that they had was that God would be their God, who would protect and defend them in exchange for their devotion to him. That was the agreement. God chose this people to be his people, and in exchange, they do the things that he asks as set forth in the Law, the Torah.

This Law, then, taught the children of Israel how to worship this God and how to live together in community. Those are the major overriding points of the Torah: how to worship God in ways appropriate to him and how to live together in community.

I should stress something that many Christians have not understood over the years, that this "Law of God," this Torah, was not thought of by Jews as being a horrendous burden that they had to follow, and that if they couldn't follow it, then they were going to pay the consequences by going to hell. This was not a religion that thought you had to follow these laws, or God would judge you, and then you would have to pay an eternal price. The Jewish Law was not seen as a burden. The Jewish Law was seen as a great gift: "The one God who created the world has chosen us as his people, and has given us his Law that we can follow." There's nothing particularly burdensome about this Jewish Law. It included things like: "You shouldn't murder one another. You shouldn't take somebody else's spouse. You shouldn't bear false witness in court." These are not overly difficult rules to follow.

They included not just ethical rules, but they also included things that made Jews distinctive as a people. There were certain food laws. Jews were not to eat shellfish or pork. There were certain other ritual laws. "You shouldn't work on the Sabbath." That was not seen as a big burden. That meant that one day out of the week, you got a vacation. Nobody else had this. You didn't have to work seven days. You got a day off. This was seen as a great good by Jews, because this was God's gift, his guidance to his people.

The Jewish Law, then, was seen as the way that Jews kept up their part of the covenantal bargain. Ethics were a larger part of Jewish religion than pagan religion, because ethics were embodied in this Law. Thus, Jews understood that there was only one God to be worshipped, who had made a covenant with his people in Israel. The Law was part of that covenant. It was to be followed so that Jews could stay within this right relationship with God.

We should not think the ancient Judaism was a monolith. Judaism, in the time of Jesus, was, in fact, quite diverse, as diverse as Christianity itself was going to become. There were some Jews who emphasized that what God really wanted was for people to adhere properly to the temple cult in Jerusalem, where the sacrifices were to be performed. They therefore emphasized the sacrificial aspects of the Jewish religion.

There were other Jews who stressed the importance of keeping the Jewish Laws as fully as possible within their daily lives, so that the Laws that God gave in the Torah were to be followed down to the great detail. There were some Jews who emphasized that, rather than emphasizing the temple cult. There were some Jews who emphasized the importance of maintaining purity before God, who thought that what really mattered to God wasn't just kind of keeping the laws, or following the temple cult, but keeping personal purity before God. Thus, some Jews went off into monastic-like communities, to maintain their own purity apart from the contaminating influences of society.

There were other Jews who insisted, as the central aspect of the religion, on the coming intervention of God to overthrow the forces of evil in the world. These were apocalyptic Jews, who maintained that God was soon going to intervene, once and for all, for his people, and overthrow the forces of evil.

Jesus himself was born, in the Roman world, into a Jewish home. If we are to understand the beginning of Christianity, we need to understand the kind of Judaism that Jesus himself embraced, and to see how his teachings then came to be developed after his death by his Jewish followers. That will be the subject of the following lecture.

Lecture Three
The Historical Jesus

Scope: This the first of three lectures that will consider the "birth" of Christianity. Here, we will discuss the founder of the Christian religion, Jesus of Nazareth. Historians have come to recognize that our sparse and biased historical sources make it difficult to reconstruct Jesus's life and teachings. In this lecture, we will see how Jesus is referred to in sources outside of the New Testament, then consider the New Testament Gospels themselves to determine what he said and did. The lecture concludes by arguing that Jesus is best understood as an apocalyptic prophet who anticipated that God would soon intervene in the course of history to overthrow the forces of evil and bring in his good Kingdom on Earth. It is this message that eventually led to Jesus's execution as a threat to the state.

Outline

I. Christianity obviously started with the life, teachings, and deeds of Jesus. It is important for us to begin our sketch of the history of Christianity, then, with the life of the founder itself.

   A. Unfortunately, this proves to be a difficult task, because there are numerous understandings of who Jesus really was and what he actually said and did—even among scholars who have devoted their entire lives to the problem.

   1. For those interested in greater detail, I refer you to The Teaching Company's 24-lecture course on the subject, *Historical Jesus*.

   2. In this lecture, we will scratch the surface in a way that will provide the necessary backdrop for the rest of the course.

   B. The major difficulty in reconstructing the life of the historical Jesus has to do with the sources that are available to us.

   C. The non-Christian sources (such as those by enemies or interested bystanders) are practically nonexistent.

   1. There are no contemporary pagan (that is, Roman, Greek, or similar) sources for Jesus's life (c. 4 B.C.–A.D. 30), in fact, no reference to him at all from any such source of the entire first century.

   2.   Only one non-Christian Jewish source (Josephus) even mentions him and, then, only briefly.

D.   As a result, we are left with accounts of Jesus written by his own followers.

   1.   In the first century, these references to Jesus come almost entirely in the New Testament; scarcely any Christian writings outside the New Testament survive from the period.

   2.   Even within the New Testament, stories of Jesus's life are scarcely found anywhere except in the four Gospels: Matthew, Mark, Luke, and John.

E.   The New Testament Gospels are, thus, virtually our only sources for reconstructing the life of Jesus.

   1.   This provides us with a better situation than for most persons from the ancient world: We have four different biographical accounts.

   2.   The difficulty is that these accounts differ from one another, sometimes in minor points of emphasis, sometimes in historical detail, and sometimes in major aspects of Jesus's life.

   3.   At points, some of these differences appear to be flat out contradictory, making it difficult to know which, if any, of the Gospels records historically factual information.

F.   The problem appears to be that the Gospels were not intended to be objective descriptions of historical facts but proclamations of the "good news" of the salvation Jesus brought, written by his followers who wanted to promote faith in him.

   1.   On occasion, these authors convey information that is not historically accurate in order to advance a particular theological view.

   2.   As a result, scholars have had to devise criteria to determine which bits of information in the Gospels are historically accurate and what has been changed to convey the theology of the church.

   3.   Generally, it is thought that the earliest accounts are more historically accurate than the later. For example, the Gospel of

Mark is generally thought of as containing more historically accurate accounts than the Gospel of John.

4. Scholars also look for information conveyed independently in more than one source (because it was, thus, more "common" information), that does not obviously support a theological bias (because then it was not "made up" to promote a particular view), and that fits well into what we know about Jesus's own historical context in first-century Palestine.

II. When all the sources are carefully examined following strict historical criteria, it appears that Jesus is best understood as a first-century Jewish apocalyptic prophet

A. Apocalypticism was a widespread movement in first-century Judaism.
1. We know about it from such sources as the Dead Sea Scrolls.
2. It was a belief that the present age was ruled by forces of evil, which God would soon overthrow in a cataclysmic act of judgment to bring in a utopian kingdom ruled by his own Messiah.
3. It makes sense that Jesus preached in an idiom familiar to his own day; the words and deeds that can be established as authentic all appear to be related to this kind of apocalyptic message.

B. Jesus's teachings were largely about the coming Kingdom of God and the need to prepare for it.
1. The summary of his words by the earliest Gospel, Mark, is probably accurate (Mark 1:15): The Kingdom was soon to come and people needed to repent in preparation.
2. This was a real Kingdom to be brought by God's special messenger, whom Jesus referred to as the Son of Man (Mark 8:38).
3. The coming judgment would involve a destruction of the present order of things and a complete reversal of fortunes for the powerful and the oppressed (Mark 13:26–27; 10:30).
4. People needed to prepare for its coming, by repenting of their wrongdoing, giving up their power and wealth, and living completely for others (Mark 1:15; Mark 10:13–15, 23–30, 42–44; Matt. 13:45–46).

5. What God wanted was for people to follow the very heart of his Law, the Torah, as summed up in the two commands to love God above all else (Deut. 6:4–6) and to love one's neighbor as oneself (Lev. 19:18).

6. The message was urgent, because the coming destruction and the appearance of this Kingdom were imminent (Mark 9:1; 13:30; 14:62).

III. It was this message that got Jesus into trouble with the ruling authorities and eventually led to his execution.

A. He evidently spent his ministry in the northern part of Israel, Galilee, proclaiming his message.

B. But the last week of his life, he went to Jerusalem to celebrate the Passover feast, with thousands of other Jewish pilgrims.

1. He appears to have wanted to take his message of the coming destruction and salvation to the heart of Judaism.

2. In Jerusalem, he offended the religious and civil authorities by proclaiming that this coming destruction would be aimed at them.

3. The leaders of the Jews in Jerusalem, the Sadducees, arranged to have him taken out of the way as a troublemaker—possibly out of fear that his incendiary message would lead to riots in the city.

4. They delivered him over to the Roman governor, Pilate, who had no qualms about getting rid of another rabble-rouser (two others were executed that same day).

5. Pilate ordered Jesus crucified, and the sentence was carried out immediately, on the morning of the Passover, sometime around the year A.D. 30.

C. Unlike all the other apocalyptic prophets of the first century, though, Jesus had followers who later proclaimed that he had not only been right, but that God had vindicated him by raising him from the dead. That proclamation marks the beginnings of Christianity, as we will see in the next lecture.

Essential Reading:

Bart Ehrman, *Jesus: Apocalyptic Prophet*, chapters 9–13.

———, *The New Testament: A Historical Introduction*, chapter 15.

E. P. Sanders, *The Historical Figure of Jesus.*

Supplementary Reading:

Paula Fredriksen, *Jesus of Nazareth.*

John Meier, *A Marginal Jew* (vol. 1).

Albert Schweitzer, *The Quest of the Historical Jesus.*

Geza Vermes, *Jesus the Jew.*

Questions to Consider:

1. How does the understanding of Jesus as an apocalyptic prophet differ from what you've previously thought about Jesus?

2. Does understanding Jesus as an apocalypticist have any bearing on the relevance of Christianity in the modern world?

Lecture Three—Transcript
The Historical Jesus

Now that we have set the milieu of early Christianity and the context of the Greco-Roman world and its religion, we can turn to the figure who marks the beginnings of Christianity. Christianity obviously started with the life, teachings, and deeds of Jesus. It is important for us to begin our sketch of the history of Christianity, then, with the life of the founder himself.

Unfortunately, this proves to be a difficult task, for there are numerous understandings of who Jesus really was, and what he actually sad and did, even among scholars who have devoted their entire lives to the problem, scholars who have learned the ancient languages: Greek, the language of the New Testament; Hebrew, the language of the Jewish Scriptures; Aramaic, the language that Jesus spoke; Latin and Coptic, languages in which traditions about Jesus were circulated. Scholars have learned these languages, and have examined the sources for years and years, different scholars devoting their entire lives to the project, and coming up with radically different understandings of who Jesus was.

Why is it so difficult to know? Well, for those who are interested in greater detail, there already has been produced a 24-lecture course just on this question, on the sources of the historical Jesus, and how these sources can be utilized in trying to construct what he actually said and did. In this one 30-minute lecture, I will be trying to summarize what happened in that 24-lecture course, which itself was a summary of what happens over an entire semester of classes at UNC-Chapel Hill. In this lecture, of course, we will only be able to scratch the surface, but we will do so in such a way that you will see what's necessary for the backdrop of this course on the history of Christianity from Jesus to Constantine.

The major reason scholars disagree on who Jesus was has to do with the difficulty of the sources that are available to us. It is hard to reconstruct Jesus's actual words, and deeds, and experiences, because of the nature of our sources. One would think that somebody who made such a huge impact on the history of our civilization would have a lot of sources written about him in his own day. I think there's no doubt that Jesus is historically the main person behind the Christian religion as it developed historically, much more important than anyone else; more important, of course, than Paul, Peter, or any of the other apostles.

Yet, as it turns out, we have more information about people like Paul than we have about Jesus. Why is that? Because Paul himself wrote letters that we have, and so, we have writings in his name. Jesus left us no writings. All we have are writings about Jesus.

If one wants to know what Jesus said and did, it might be useful to look at sources other than what his followers set about him. It might be useful, for example, to see what his enemies had to say about him, and so, one might go through a library and try to find ancient sources. Did Pontius Pilate say anything about Jesus? How about Caesar Augustus? What kind of birth records do we have? What kinds of accounts of his death do we have? What were his enemies saying about him? His Jewish enemies? His pagan enemies?

When I was teaching at Rutgers University in the 1980s, I had a student who decided he wanted to do a senior thesis, and his idea was that he would go to the library and find old sources that mentioned Jesus that are not found in the New Testament, and he would see what they had to say about him, and he would come up with something new that nobody else had seen before. I had to inform this student that, in fact, this thought had occurred to people, to see what else had been written about Jesus, and I had to tell him that, in fact, he probably wasn't going to find very much.

If we look at the sources on Jesus written by Romans—non-Christian Romans who were neither Jewish nor Christian—if we look at the sources written in the first century, we have hundreds of sources. We have writings of poets, philosophers, religion scholars, natural scientists, personal letters that people sent through the ancient equivalent of the mail system, inscriptions that were put up on buildings. If we examine all of these pieces of literature from the ancient world, from the first century, from the time Jesus died in the year 30 until the year 100—if we examine all of this record from the Roman Empire, we will find that Jesus is never, ever mentioned at all. His name never occurs in any Roman source that's neither Jewish nor Christian, from the first century of the Common Era. What were his enemies saying about him? We have no idea, because they left us no writings.

Why didn't they talk about Jesus? Well, that's an interesting question. I would assume that they didn't talk about Jesus because he didn't make as big of an impact on his world as he has made on ours.

The first time Jesus is ever mentioned by any pagan source is not until the year 112 of the Common Era. The source is a letter written by a Roman governor whose name was Pliny, Pliny the Younger, as he is called. Pliny the Younger was the governor of a province in the Roman Empire, who had a problem in his province that he was governing, because Christians were gathering together illegally. It was not just that Christian gatherings were illegal in his province; all gatherings were illegal in his province. They had passed this law in his province that did not allow social gatherings because they were afraid of political uprisings.

Well, he found out that Christians were gathering together, and so, this was illegal, because groups weren't supposed to gather together. Thus, he wrote a letter back to the Roman emperor at the time, who was Trajan. This was in the year 112, some 80 years after Jesus's death, and he mentioned that there was a group of people called Christians who were gathering together illegally: "They're called Christians because they worship somebody named Christ, whom they worship as a god." That's all he says about Jesus. It is the first reference to Jesus, though, in a Roman source, in the year 112. After that, Jesus's name starts appearing in Roman sources, but if you want to look at Roman sources for what you can find out about what Jesus actually said and did, they simply don't exist.

We do have one non-Christian Jewish source that mentions Jesus from within a hundred years of his death. This source is the writings of Josephus, a Jewish historian, who wrote multi-volume works about the history of Judaism, and on two occasions, actually does mention Jesus of Nazareth. On one occasion, he tells us that Jesus was a person with a great following. He was a teacher who had followers among both Jews and Greeks, but that he got on the bad side of some of the Jewish leaders, who turned him over to Pontius Pilate, who then had him executed. Josephus goes on to say that his followers continue to adore him after his death, and that they continue to worship him down to Josephus's own day. This reference to Jesus was written by Josephus around the year 93 or 94 A.D., so about 60 or 65 years after Jesus's death.

Within the first century A.D., this is the only reference to Jesus outside of Christian sources. As a result, we are more or less left with accounts of Jesus written by his own followers if we want to know what Jesus said and did.

From within the first century A.D., these references by Jesus's own followers come almost entirely to us from the pages of the New Testament. We have scarcely any Christian writings outside the New Testament that survive from the first century A.D., but even within the New Testament, stories of Jesus's life are scarcely found anywhere except for in the four Gospels: Matthew, Mark, Luke, and John. The apostle Paul, for example, says a lot of things about what "Christ is doing now." He says a lot of things about Christ's death and Resurrection, but he says very little about Jesus's own life, the things that he said and did while he was living.

More or less, then, we are restricted to the Gospels of Matthew, Mark, Luke, and John for understanding the life and death of Jesus. Of course, that provides us with a better situation than for most persons from antiquity. We don't have any record of most people from antiquity. In this case, we have four different books, and so, four books for one person is pretty good when dealing with ancient history.

The difficulty is that these sources are problematic for historians for a variety of reasons. Matthew, Mark, Luke, and John are anonymous books. We call them "Matthew," "Mark," "Luke," and "John," because traditionally, they have been ascribed to two of the disciples of Jesus: Matthew, the tax collector; and John, the beloved disciple; and to two of the friends of the apostles: Mark, who was a secretary for the apostle Peter; and Luke, who was a traveling companion of Paul's. Those are the traditional ascriptions of these books, but when you read the books, you'll see that, in fact, the authors are anonymous. They don't give us their names. We continue to call them Matthew, Mark, Luke, and John simply by way of convenience. When you read Matthew, you will never read a passage where Matthew says, "Then Jesus and I, one time, went up to Capernaum," or anything like that. They are written in the third person about the things that Jesus said.

These books, in fact, did not appear to have been written by eyewitnesses. They are written about Jesus and his followers. They are anonymous. They're written in Greek. Jesus and his followers spoke Aramaic. They're written decades after the facts that they narrate. If Jesus died around the year 30 A.D., well, the first Gospel was probably Mark, written around 65 or 70 A.D., so it's 35 or 40 years later. He's the first Gospel that we have. The last Gospel is John, probably written around 90 or 95 A.D., so that is a distance of 60 to 65 years after the events that it narrates.

These are books that are written not by eyewitnesses, and in a different language from Jesus. They're written decades later, and are based largely on oral traditions of Jesus. Where did these authors get their stories from if they were not there to see these things happen? Well, after Jesus died, his followers told stories about him, in order to convert people, in order to educate those who were converted. In order to provide edification for people, stories of Jesus were told day after day, week after week, month after month, year after year, decade after decade, until these Gospel writers, who apparently were living in some other place—they're writing in Greek, not Aramaic (the language of Palestine)—hear these stories, and write them down.

These stories, then, are based on oral traditions. You know what happens to oral traditions that circulate for a long time. As you have probably experienced yourself, stories get changed in the process of retelling, so we have four Gospels written by four individuals who have different emphases, different points they want to emphasize. They cover different aspects of Jesus's life, and they have inherited different oral traditions. Sometimes they've inherited the same traditions, and sometimes they've inherited different ones, but the problem is that these Gospels often differ from one another. Sometimes these differences are significant, and sometimes the differences are minor. Nonetheless, what we have are four sources that are not completely coherent with one another when it comes to describing the events that they all narrate.

Sometimes these differences appear to be flat-out contradictions, making it difficult to know which if any of the Gospels is recording historically factual information. As I say, I don't have time to develop this point in this particular lecture because it would take the entire time. I will simply say, though, that there are differences in the Gospels that sometimes appear to be discrepancies, which means that sometimes, you aren't sure which, if either, of these authors has it historically correct.

The problem appears to be that the Gospels were not intended to be objective descriptions of the historical facts. These books are called "Gospels." The word "gospel" means "good news." These writers are trying to proclaim the good news of the salvation that Jesus brought. They're written by followers of Jesus who wanted to promote faith in Jesus. On occasion, these authors convey information that's not historically accurate so that they can make a theological point.

Because of that, because these are the kinds of sources that we have, scholars have had to devise criteria to help them determine which bits of information in the Gospels are historically accurate, and what in the Gospels has been changed in order to convey the theology of the church. As a general rule, scholars tend to think that the earliest accounts we have are more historically accurate than later accounts, and it is fairly obvious why. If stories get changed in the process of telling and retelling, then, if you have a source that is closer to the events, there's been less time for the story to be changed, fewer opportunities for it to be changed.

Well, the earliest Gospel we have is the Gospel of Mark, and so, in general terms, Mark is probably, in comparison, more accurate than the Gospel of John, which is 30 years after Mark, more time for the stories to be changed. Scholars therefore tend to lean toward the earliest sources, such as Mark, that we have.

Moreover, scholars have developed specific criteria for dealing with all of the sources, early and late. Scholars look for information in the Gospels that is conveyed independently in more than one source, so that if you've got a tradition of Jesus that is found in several different sources, and these sources didn't collaborate with one another, well, then, that is a tradition that's more likely to be authentic than a tradition that is found, say, in only one source. If you have a story that is only found in one source, maybe that source has come up with a story in theory.

Scholars look for independently attested traditions. They look for traditions about Jesus that do not support a theological bias. If you have a saying or deed of Jesus that seems to support the point of view of the author of the Gospel, well then, maybe that tradition has been changed in light of the author's own views. Moreover, scholars look for traditions that fit in well with what we know about Jesus's own historical context in first-century Palestine. We have some traditions of Jesus that don't seem to fit very well in first-century Jewish Palestine. Well, those probably are not authentic traditions, then.

When all the sources are carefully examined, following strict historical criteria, it appears that Jesus is best understood as a first-century, Jewish apocalyptic prophet. Let me say something about apocalypticism in early Judaism. In fact, apocalypticism—this is a modern, scholarly term—was a widespread movement within first-century Judaism that we know about from a number of ancient sources, from near the time of Jesus, including the Dead Sea scrolls. The Dead Sea scrolls, discovered in 1947, a collection of writings by Jews living at about the same time and in about the same place as Jesus, contain a worldview very similar to the worldview of Jesus, the worldview that I'm calling apocalypticism.

Apocalypticism is the belief that the present age we live in now is ruled by forces of evil, by the devil and demons, and other forces of evil such as sin, death, disease, drought, famine, and that they are soon going to be overthrown by God in a cataclysmic act of judgment, in which God would bring in a utopian kingdom ruled by his own Messiah. This was a view supported by a number of Jews in the first century. It seems to be the point of view supported by Jesus himself.

It appears that Jesus preached in an idiom that was familiar to his own day. The words and deeds of Jesus that can be established as authentic, based on the various criteria that scholars have derived, appear to be related to this kind of apocalyptic message, and so I want to talk for a few minutes about the teachings of Jesus as I reconstruct them based upon our surviving sources, which are, again, principally the Gospels of the New Testament, especially the earliest Gospels.

Jesus appears to have taught largely about the coming Kingdom of God and the need to prepare for it. A summary of his words by the earliest Gospel we have, Mark, is probably accurate. Mark, chapter 1, verse 15, records the first words of Jesus in this earliest of our Gospels. Jesus comes back from the wilderness, and he begins his proclamation. He says: "The time has been fulfilled. The Kingdom of God is at hand. Repent and believe the good news!"

"The time has been fulfilled." That's an apocalyptic image. The apocalypticists believed that they were living in an age controlled by evil, but this evil age was going to have an end to it. The time has been filled up, meaning that we are now at the end of this age. The Kingdom of God is at hand. When ancient Jews talked about the Kingdom of God, many of them referred to an actual kingdom. They meant a kingdom, a place where God would be the king.

This kingdom would be a place where people would live. They would eat and they would drink. People could be thrown out of the kingdom. People could be brought into the kingdom. It was an actual entity, this Kingdom of God. Jesus proclaimed the Kingdom of God was at hand. You can translate the same Greek word: "The Kingdom of God has become near." It's near; it's almost here. "Repent and believe in the good news." Jesus seems to have thought that the kingdom was soon to come, and people needed to prepare for it.

In Jesus's teachings, this kingdom that was coming was a real kingdom that would be brought by God's special messenger, whom Jesus referred to as the "Son of Man." This is a complicated phrase in the sayings of Jesus, the "Son of Man," because he uses the term "Son of Man" in a number of different ways in the Gospels. One of the ways he uses the term "Son of Man" is in reference to a cosmic figure who is coming on the clouds of heaven, and judgment will cover the Earth.

This idea of the Son of Man being a cosmic judge was found in the Hebrew Scriptures. In the book of Daniel, which is the final book of the Hebrew Bible to have been written, a prophet is shown a vision of the future for the Earth, in which he has a dream at night, and he sees a wild beast coming up out of the sea who tramples on the Earth, and then, a second beast comes up and destroys the first, and then a third beast, and a fourth beast.

These beasts are horrible. They are responsible for killing and maiming people, especially the holy people of God, of Israel. After the four beasts come, the author then sees "one like a Son of Man coming on the clouds of heaven in judgment." To this "one like a Son of Man" is given power and dominion forever and ever. The beasts' power is taken away. This "one like a Son of Man," then, becomes the ruler over the Earth.

Jesus appears to be alluding to this vision of Daniel in his preaching about the Son of Man, the coming of the Son of Man. In the book of Daniel, this vision of beasts and the "one like a Son of Man" is then interpreted by an angel to the prophet. He is told that these beasts each represent a kingdom that will come, evil kingdoms opposed to God and his people, but the "one like a Son of Man" represents a kingdom that's coming that is going to be given to the people of God.

Jesus talks about not "one like a Son of Man," but he talks about "the Son of Man" as the cosmic figure, coming on the clouds of heaven: "Whoever is ashamed of me and my words in this adulterous and sinful generation," says Jesus, "of that one will the Son of Man be ashamed when he comes on the clouds of heaven in the presence of the holy angels." Mark 8:38. The "Son of Man" was a cosmic figure who was going to come in judgment to bring in God's kingdom according to Jesus. The coming judgment would involve a destruction of the present order of things, and a complete reversal of fortunes for the powerful and the oppressed.

Jesus maintained that there would be a powerful judgment that would come when the Son of Man arrived. Then, according to Mark, chapter 13, verse 26: "Then, they will see the Son of Man coming on the clouds with great power and glory. Then, he will send out his angels and gather his elect from the four winds, from the ends of the earth to the ends of heaven. The Son of Man will come in great power and glory." When that happens, there will be a complete reversal in fortunes. "The first shall be last, the last shall be first."

This wasn't just a kind of cute one-liner that Jesus said. This was something that he actually meant. "People who are in power now are going to be taken out of power. Those who are low, humble, and oppressed now are going to be put into power." There would be a severe reversal of fortunes. Everyone who humbled themselves would be exalted, and all those who were exalted would be humbled.

This "Son of Man," who was overthrowing the forces of evil to bring in the Kingdom of God, then, needed to be expected, because he was going to arrive soon. People needed to prepare for the coming of this kingdom by repenting of their wrongdoing, giving up their power and their wealth, and living completely for others. Jesus sometimes said that "a person must enter into the kingdom of God as a child. Let the little children come to me, for such is the kingdom of heaven." What does that mean?

Well, little children don't have any claims on others. They don't have wealth. They don't have prestige and power. You must give up your power, your prestige, your wealth in order to enter the kingdom. Jesus said that to enter the kingdom, one must be "a slave of others," must be serving others rather than being served, for the Son of Man came not to be served, but to serve. "People must behave like slaves if they are to enter into this coming kingdom."

What God really wanted people to do in preparation for this coming kingdom was to follow the Law that he had given, the Torah, as summed up for Jesus in two of the commandments of the Scriptures: "People should love the Lord their God with all their heart, soul, and strength." Deuteronomy, chapter 6, and: "People should love their neighbors as themselves." Leviticus, chapter 19.

These are not sayings of Jesus that Jesus came up with. This passage that I have just quoted is actually Matthew, but these are the two chief commandments. He's quoting Scripture. This is what the Torah itself says, that "above all, you should love God, and you should love your neighbor as yourself." Those who do these things will have fulfilled the Law.

People must do that. They must repent of their sins, and they must begin acting in these ways if they want to inherit the kingdom that's coming. Only those who do so will enter into the kingdom. Well, when is this kingdom going to come?

Jesus appears to have believed that his message was urgent because the coming destruction and the appearance of God was imminent: "Truly, I tell you, some of you standing here will not taste death before you see the Kingdom of God has come in power." Mark, chapter 9, verse 1. The words of Jesus. "Some of you standing here," he tells his disciples, "won't taste death before the Kingdom of God has come in power."

Mark, chapter 13, verse 30: "This generation will not pass away before all these things take place." It's going to happen soon. It's imminent.

Mark, chapter 14, verse 32. The high priest asks Jesus during his trial: "Are you the Messiah, the son of the blessed?" Jesus says, "I am, and you will see the Son of Man coming on the clouds of heaven." He tells the chief priest, "You will see it happen." Jesus appears to have expected that the end was coming within his own generation.

Jesus is often thought of as being a great moral teacher, and it is absolutely true that he was a great moral teacher, but it is important to understand that his ethics were not taught in the way that we might teach ethics today. Today, we teach ethics because we want people to know how to get along for the long haul. For Jesus, there was no long haul. The end was coming soon, and people needed to prepare for it. His ethical teachings were teachings meant to get people ready for the coming of the kingdom.

It appears that Jesus took this message to the rural areas of Galilee, the northern part of Israel, until the last week of his life, when he decided to take this message to the heart of Judaism, the heart of the Jewish people, the sacred place of the Jews, Jerusalem.

Jesus made a trip to Jerusalem the last week of his life, apparently to make his proclamation there, at the heart of Judaism, and he went there during a Passover feast, when there was an annual festival of the Passover, or Jews gather together to remember how God had saved them from their slavery to their oppressors in Egypt, back in the days of Moses. People would come every year to celebrate the Passover in Jerusalem, and Jesus went his last year as well to celebrate the Passover feast with thousands of other Jewish pilgrims. He appears to have gone to Jerusalem at this time in order to bring his message of the coming destruction and salvation to the heart of Judaism.

When Jesus arrived in Jerusalem, he appears to have offended the religious and civil leaders by proclaiming that this coming destruction would be aimed not just at the Romans, the bad guys, but also at the Jewish authorities. The authorities in Jerusalem at the time were a group of Jews known as the Sadducees. The Sadducees were the Jewish aristocracy, were given the right by the Romans to run the local affairs. Many of these Sadducees were priests in the temple, and it was precisely at the temple and those in charge of it that Jesus directed his ire. Jesus predicted that God's destruction would involve not just the Romans, but these people here who were in charge, the aristocracy of the Jews.

That obviously angered members of the Sadducees. Of course, they didn't want any riots erupting during this critical time, Passover. We have other instances from around Jesus's time of Jews causing disturbances and riots during Passover feast in Jerusalem. What typically happened to these people, according to the Jewish historian Josephus, was that they were taken out of the way, arrested so that they would not cause problems. That's precisely what happened with Jesus. Jesus, predicting the end was imminent and destruction was near, was taken out of the way. The Sadducees, the local leaders, had Jesus arrested.

They delivered Jesus over to the Roman governor, who was in charge of things, and who happened to be there during Passover, Pontius Pilate. Pontius Pilate, the Roman governor, had no qualms at all about getting rid of another rabble-rouser. This was his job. The governor's job, in Palestine or anywhere else in the Roman Empire, was to keep the peace and to raise the taxes. In order to raise the taxes, you had to keep the peace.

These people, these governors, had complete authority over all things of life and death. There was no need for a trial by a jury of one's peers. There was no appeals process. There was nothing that we would think of as due process at all. The Roman governor could find that a person was a troublemaker and have him executed publicly the same day. That's what happened in this particular instance.

Jesus had been turned over to Pilate by the Sadducees. Pilate, probably after a very brief trial and interrogation, decided that Jesus was, in fact, a troublemaker. He ordered him crucified. The sentence was carried out immediately, on the morning of Passover, sometime around the year A.D. 30.

Unlike all the other apocalyptic prophets of the first century, however, Jesus had followers who later proclaimed not only that he had been right, but that God had vindicated him by raising him from the dead. That proclamation of Jesus raised from the dead marks the beginnings of Christianity, as we'll see in our next lecture.

Lecture Four
Oral and Written Traditions about Jesus

Scope: The goal of this lecture is to show how the Gospels came into being. These are our earliest accounts of the words, deeds, death, and Resurrection of Jesus. Not all of the early Gospels made it into the New Testament, however, and many that were once available have since been lost. As we will see, the four New Testament Gospels were all written anonymously: Only later did Christians claim that they had been produced by apostles. None of them, however, appears to be an eyewitness report.

This lecture shows how these four anonymous authors, living decades after Jesus's life, recorded traditions about Jesus that had been circulating orally over the intervening years. It asks whether these traditions faithfully record the events that transpired during Jesus's life and explores the extent to which the traditions had been modified in the retelling.

Outline

I. In the last lecture, we tried to understand the message and mission of the historical Jesus. Christianity, however, is not so much the religion that Jesus proclaimed as the religion that proclaims Jesus.

    A. Traditional Christianity has maintained that it was the death and Resurrection of Jesus that brought about the salvation of the world.

    B. In this lecture, we will begin to discuss how the apocalyptic message of Jesus came to be transformed into the apocalyptic message about Jesus.

    C. This transformation was completely rooted in the Christian belief that Jesus was raised from the dead.

II. The Resurrection of Jesus poses special problems for historians.

    A. There are certain historical "facts" that one can discuss about what happened after Jesus's death (his burial; the discovery of his empty tomb by a group of women).

    B. But there are other aspects that are problematic for historians.

        1. The accounts are hopelessly contradictory in their details.

2. Further, the event of the Resurrection, as a supernatural (trans-historical) occurrence, is beyond the purview of the historian, who can establish only what happened in history.

III. What is certain is that some of Jesus's followers came to *believe* that he had been raised, and that made all the difference in the world.

A. Jesus had talked about a coming resurrection of the dead at the end of the age; his followers came to believe that he was the first to be raised and, therefore, that the end had begun.

B. Jesus talked about the future judgment to be brought by the Son of Man from heaven; his followers came to believe that he had been exalted to heaven and was himself the Son of Man.

C. Jesus talked about the future Kingdom of God to be ruled by his Messiah; his followers came to believe that he was that future Messiah.

D. Jesus talked about God as the father of all and of himself as having a special relationship with God; his followers came to believe that he was the distinctive Son of God and, eventually, they came to maintain that he was himself divine.

E. If Jesus was the divinely appointed Son of God, coming from heaven as the Son of Man in judgment, why was he here in the first place, and why did he die?

1. For his followers, it soon became apparent that Jesus's death was not just a miscarriage of justice. It was the plan of God. Jesus had to die.

2. Because he did nothing to deserve death, he must have died for others who did deserve it. His death soon came to be seen as a sacrifice for the sins of others.

F. Thus begins Christianity. All of this transformation of Jesus's teaching took place within a few short years of his death.

IV. While this theological development was taking place, and long before the Gospels were written, Christianity was spreading throughout the Roman world. Understanding this earliest Christian mission is important for appreciating the nature of the later Gospels that became part of the New Testament.

A. Within 60 years of Jesus's death, Christianity spread into major urban areas throughout the empire.

B. It was spread by word-of-mouth proclamation, by people telling stories about Jesus.

C. The key question is where people derived their stories, and what happened to the stories as they were told by one person to the next, decade after decade, principally among people who had not been there to see any of the things discussed actually happen.

D. It appears that the stories were modified in the processes of retelling, and a good number of stories about Jesus were actually made up.

V. The Gospels came to be written many years after the stories of Jesus had been in circulation throughout the Roman world.

    A. The earliest surviving accounts we have are the New Testament Gospels of Matthew, Mark, Luke, and John.

        1. These books are actually written anonymously.

        2. Their authors were highly educated, Greek-speaking Christians living in different parts of the empire several decades after the death of Jesus (as opposed to the illiterate, Aramaic-speaking disciples of Jesus from Palestine).

        3. They used as their sources earlier accounts they had heard (or read) about Jesus.

        4. They had some sources in common; for example, Mark, our first Gospel, was evidently used as a source by Matthew and Luke.

        5. Each of these accounts is different from the others, sometimes in minor details that are difficult to reconcile (on such issues as which day Jesus was executed, for example), sometimes in major emphases (such as the nature of Jesus's message and mission).

        6. These differences make the Gospels difficult for historians to use to establish what actually happened in Jesus's lifetime.

        7. These books, however, were not meant to be historically objective biographies of Jesus, but proclamations of the good news of the salvation he brought.

    B. Other Gospels were written as well, some of which survive, but the majority of which do not.

        1. Some of the earliest accounts of Jesus have been lost— including the document that scholars call Q, an early collection of Jesus's teachings, available to Matthew and Luke.

2. Of the other Gospels that do survive, some are quite ancient and may record historically accurate information about Jesus, including the famous Gospel of Thomas, a collection of 114 sayings of Jesus, many of them previously unknown, discovered in 1945.

3. These various Gospels also each had their own theological perspectives and understandings of Jesus. In the Gospel of Thomas, for example, what matters for salvation is not Jesus's death but the secret teachings he delivered.

C. All these Gospels were meant as "community books" and were intended to instruct Christian churches in what Jesus said, did, and experienced. Yet they all differed in their messages.

1. Today, we tend to think of Christianity as one thing—even while recognizing that there is a good deal of variety in what Christians believe and practice.

2. In fact, Christianity is and always has been many different things. This is especially true in the earliest Christianity of the first three centuries, as evidenced in the many Gospels that were written, read, and revered as sacred books that revealed the "truth" (in different ways) about what Jesus said, did, and experienced.

Essential Reading:

Bart Ehrman, *Jesus the Apocalyptic Prophet*, chapter 13.

———, *The New Testament: A Historical Introduction*, chapters 4–12, 17.

Paula Fredriksen, *From Jesus to Christ*.

Supplementary Reading:

James Dunn, *Christology in the Making*.

Martin Hengel, *Between Jesus and Paul*.

Questions to Consider:

1. Consider in detail some familiar stories found in more than one of our New Testament Gospels, such as the accounts of Jesus's birth in Matthew and Luke or the accounts of his Resurrection in all four

Gospels, and note the similarities and differences. Are any of the differences irreconcilable? How do you explain that?

2. If one accepts the premise that Christianity is better understood as the religion *about* Jesus rather than the religion *of* Jesus (that is, it is the religion that proclaims him, rather than the one he proclaimed), how might that affect the practice of Christianity in the modern world?

Lecture Four—Transcript
Oral and Written Traditions about Jesus

In the last lecture, we tried to understand the message and mission of the historical Jesus. Christianity, however, is not so much the religion that Jesus himself proclaimed as it is the religion that proclaims Jesus. Traditional Christianity has maintained that it was the death and Resurrection of Jesus that brought about the salvation of the world.

In this lecture, we will begin to discuss how the apocalyptic message of Jesus came to be transformed into the apocalyptic message about Jesus. This transformation was completely rooted in the Christian belief that Jesus was raised from the dead.

The Resurrection of Jesus poses special problems for historians. There are certain historical facts that one can discuss about what happened after Jesus's death, but it's difficult for historians to say that the Resurrection of Jesus is an historical event, for reasons I need to explain.

In the past lecture, we saw that historians have devised criteria for understanding what Jesus actually said, did, and experienced based upon the Gospel traditions that have survived, and so we look for the earliest Gospel stories about Jesus wherever we can find them. We look for accounts of Jesus that are independently attested in several sources. We look for traditions about Jesus that don't coincide, necessarily, with an author's own bias. We look for traditions about Jesus that can be situated within a plausible historical context.

The Resurrection of Jesus lies at the heart of Christian faith. Unfortunately, it is also a tradition about Jesus that historians have difficulty dealing with. As I said, there are a couple things that we can say for certain about Jesus after his death. We say with relative certainty, for example, that he was buried. I say "with relative certainty," because historians do have some questions about the traditions of Jesus's burial. According to the Gospel accounts, there was a wealthy Jew named Joseph of Arimathea who requested Jesus's body after his crucifixion, was given the body, and then was allowed to bury Jesus in his family tomb, which had previously not been used.

There's nothing completely implausible about that, except to say that Romans as a rule did not allow crucified people to be given proper burials.

It may be that in this case an exception was made, although some scholars have suggested in recent times that the story of Joseph of Arimathea burying Jesus is not historically factual, that it was a later tradition that Christians came up with to explain how it was that Jesus, in three days, left an empty tomb. In order to have the account of Jesus leaving behind an empty tomb, you obviously had to have him put into a tomb, and so you had to have some story that explains how it was that he got put into a tomb, when everybody knew that crucified people were not normally put into tombs.

Some scholars have argued that it's more plausible that, in fact, Jesus was placed in a common burial plot, which sometimes happened, or was, as many other crucified people, simply left to be eaten by scavenging animals, which also happened commonly with crucified persons in the Roman Empire.

However, the earliest accounts we have are fairly unanimous in saying that Jesus was, in fact, buried by this fellow Joseph of Arimathea, and so it is relatively reliable that that is what happened.

We also have solid traditions to indicate that women found this tomb empty three days later. This is tested in all of our Gospel sources, early and late, and so it appears to be a historical datum. Therefore, I think we can say that after Jesus's death, probably with some certainty, he was buried, possibly by this fellow Joseph of Arimathea, and that three days later, he appears not to have been in his tomb.

Still, there are other aspects of the accounts of Jesus after his death that are problematic for historians. As it turns out, the accounts we have of Jesus's Resurrection are hopelessly contradictory in their details. One of the exercises that I have my students do at Chapel Hill for my Introduction to New Testament class is I have them read through the Gospels' (Matthew, Mark, Luke, and John) final chapters that discuss Jesus's Resurrection, and have them simply make a list of everything that happens with all four accounts, and then have them see if they can come up with similarities and differences. It's an interesting exercise to do.

I recommend everybody do it, because once one sees these accounts side-by-side in this way, differences emerge all over the map. The accounts don't agree about who went to visit Jesus's tomb on the third day. What did they see once they got there? What were they told when they arrived at the tomb? What did they do as a result of being told to do something? All of these things are different in the Gospels, in ways that are very difficult to reconcile.

Just to give you one example, in the Gospel of Matthew, the women go to the tomb, and at the tomb, they are told to go tell the disciples that they are to go to Galilee to meet Jesus, because he has been raised from the dead and will meet them in Galilee. They go to Galilee, and they see Jesus there, and Jesus has his final discourse with them, the disciples, in which he tells them that they are now to go out and preach the Gospel throughout the world, to make disciples, to baptize them until the end of the age, and then, that is the end of the story. Jesus leaves them. That's Matthew.

In Luke's Gospel, women go to the tomb, and they are told in Luke's Gospel not that the disciples should go to Galilee, but that they should stay in Jerusalem. "Do not leave the city." That same day, they are still in the city, and Jesus comes and appears to them. He takes them outside, then, up on to a hill, he gives them the last instructions, and he ascends to heaven from Jerusalem.

Well, which is it? Were they to go to Galilee to see Jesus, or were they to stay in Jerusalem to see Jesus? I suppose if you worked hard enough at it that you could reconcile these two accounts, but to reconcile them, you have to say that Jesus is going up and down from heaven, back and forth, giving final instructions, going up, coming back down, giving more final instructions, and going back up. You could reconcile the account that way if you wanted to.

For historians, though, it looks problematic, because there are discrepancies. Even apart from the discrepancies, though, the event of the Resurrection itself is a problematic occurrence for historians, not because historians have to be atheists who don't believe in miracles, but the reality is that historians have real trouble when trying to establish the occurrence of miracles in the past. Let me just take a brief moment to explain what the problem is.

Historians, by their very nature, can only establish what probably happened in the past. That's what historians do, and they determine if something is highly probable, virtually certain, if things are fairly probable, if something is probable, if something is possible. They have to rank things according to levels of certitude and probability. Historians can never prove what happens in the past, because once the past happens, it's over and done with. You can't repeat it, and so you can only establish what probably happened in the past. Some things are more probable than others.

Miracles, by their very definition, are highly improbable. If they weren't highly improbable, they wouldn't be miracles. Thus, one might want to talk about miracles being—you might not want to say "violations of natural law," because modern people probably don't talk about natural law as much as they used to in the 18th and 19th centuries. But people do know that nature works in certain ways, and if something happens that violates the way nature happens, and if it really violates the way nature happens, then you might call that a miracle. If we brought in a vat of lukewarm water here, and one of you were actually able to walk across this vat of lukewarm water without sinking, that just doesn't happen. Of the billions of people in the world, I don't think anybody could do it. If you could do it, it would be a miracle. It would be a violation of what normally happens in nature.

Historians have trouble establishing that a miracle happened in the past precisely because a miraculous event is so, so unlikely, and yet, historians can only establish what likely happened. The Resurrection of Jesus would have been a miracle. If it did happen, historians can't prove it happened. They can't even demonstrate that it happened. They can't show that it is highly probable, because it's a miracle, and by definition, it's highly improbable. There is simply a problem then, that historians, as historians establishing what probably happened in the past, can't say exactly what happened with Jesus after his death, as to whether he was raised from the dead or not.

What historians can say, though, with some certainty is that some of Jesus's followers came to believe that he'd been raised from the dead, and that that, in fact, made all the difference in the world. Jesus had talked about a coming resurrection of the dead as part of his proclamation. Jesus proclaimed that there was going to be a future resurrection, and that when the Son of Man arrived, there would be a destruction of things here on Earth, there would be a reversal of fortune, and people who had died would be raised to face judgment.

Jesus preached that while he was living. Afterwards, his disciples said that he had been raised from the dead. Their natural conclusion was that the end had begun, so that they drew conclusions from their belief in the resurrection. The resurrection was to come at the end of this age, Jesus had been raised, and therefore, the end had begun.

Jesus had talked about the future judgment to be brought by the Son of Man from heaven. His followers came to believe that Jesus himself had been exalted to heaven, and that he was coming back in judgment on the Earth. They therefore began to talk about Jesus as the Son of Man.

While living, Jesus had talked about the future Kingdom of God that was to be ruled by God's Messiah. His followers came to believe that he was that future Messiah. Jesus talked about God as the "father of all," and about himself as having a special relationship with God. His followers came to believe after the Resurrection that Jesus was the distinctive Son of God, and eventually, they came to transform that belief even further, to the point at which they began saying that Jesus himself was divine.

Therefore, even if historians can't establish what actually happened with the Resurrection, they can establish the effects of the belief in the Resurrection, which was that we had the development of a religion about Jesus, where Jesus was no longer simply the proclaimer of a future coming kingdom. Jesus was the one who was being proclaimed as the Messiah, as the Son of Man, as the Son of God, as God himself.

Christians who started saying this soon after they began to believe that Jesus was raised, that Jesus was the divinely appointed Son of God, had to explain something else about Jesus's life that didn't make sense: If Jesus is the Son of God, was coming from heaven as the Son of Man in judgment, why did he come here in the first place, and why did he die? Christians today have a number of explanations for why Jesus died for the sins of the world, but you need to understand that the followers of Jesus prior to his death had no expectation that he was going to die. After his death, they began to proclaim that he was the Messiah, the Son of God, who was coming back in judgment.

If he is that, though, or if he is divine, why did he die? For his followers, it soon became apparent that Jesus's death was not simply a miscarriage of justice. It wasn't just that Jesus got on the wrong side of the law. In fact, it was the plan of God; Jesus had to die. Well, why did he have to die?

Well, since Jesus himself, according to his followers, had done nothing to deserve his death, he must have died for others who did deserve it. Soon, Jesus's death came to be seen as a sacrifice for the sins of others. What I am trying to do here is to think backwards, the way the disciples must have had to think backwards, backwards from the Resurrection of Jesus, to its implications for his death.

Today, Christians probably see it as non-problematic that Jesus died and was raised, but if you weren't expecting Jesus to die, and then he did die, and then you came to believe he was raised, you have to figure out: What's the point of the death?

Part of the problem is that in Judaism at the time of Jesus, there was no expectation among any Jew that we have any record of, that the Messiah was going to die. There is no record in any Jewish source that we have, prior to Christianity, of a suffering Messiah. Jews had different expectations of what the Messiah might be like. Many Jews probably didn't believe in or care about a coming Messiah, but those who did believe in or care about a coming Messiah had a variety of ways of explaining what this Messiah would be like.

For most Jews, the Messiah was probably going be some kind of political leader, the son of David, the great king of Israel. This would be a political leader, a great warrior, who would lead Israel in victory over its enemies and establish Israel as a sovereign state in the land. That would be the Messiah. The Messiah was understood, then, to be a successor to King David. The term "Messiah" by itself, by the way, is a technical term. It comes from a Hebrew word that means "anointed one." Well, who was the anointed one in ancient Israel? It was the king.

During the inauguration ceremony in ancient Israel—they had an inauguration ceremony in Israel, just as we do; to swear in a president today, the president puts his hand on a Bible, and swears an oath of office—in the ancient world, they didn't do that; they had an anointing ceremony where oil was poured on the king's head to show God's special favor. This was his anointing. The word "Messiah" comes from the word "anointing." The Greek word that corresponds to that, by the way, is *christos*, so that "Jesus Christ" means "Jesus the Messiah." I tell this to my students so that they recognize that "Christ" is not Jesus's last name, Jesus Christ born to Joseph or Mary Christ, and that, in fact, this is a title that means "the Messiah."

Well, Jews didn't expect a Messiah to suffer and die. Many Jews thought he would be a political leader or warrior. Some Jews thought that this coming Son of Man talked about by Daniel was a Messiah figure, some divine figure who would be Messiah, a leader of people, coming on the clouds of heaven in judgment. Some Jews expected a great priest to arrive who would be an authoritative interpreter of the Jewish Law. There were various understandings of the Messiah among ancient Jews, and one of the things these various understandings had in common was that all of these understandings understood that the coming Messiah would be a great figure, a figure of grandeur and power. We have no Jewish source prior to Christianity that thought that the coming Messiah was going to be somebody who was weak, who was going to be killed, who was going to be crucified—the kind of lowly death reserved for lowlife criminals in the Roman Empire.

How was it, then, that Jesus was crucified if he is the Messiah? Jewish Christians, Christians who were Jews, started reading their Bibles, which they had obviously done all of their lives, but they started reading their Bibles for a specific purpose in order to see how it was that Jesus could have died if he was the Messiah. They knew he had died, and they thought he was the Messiah, but how was that possible?

They came across passages in which there were accounts of the righteous man of God who was suffering. Isaiah, chapter 53: "He was bruised for iniquities, he was wounded for our transgressions; the chastisement for our peace was upon him, by his wounds we were healed."

Now, Isaiah 53 does not mention the term "Messiah," but it is about a man who suffers for the sake of others. Maybe that refers to Jesus. Psalm 22: "My God, my God, why have you forsaken me?" Somebody who seems to be forsaken of God, and yet who at the end of the Psalm acquires God's special favor. Christians started reading the Hebrew Bible, and they found places in which there was a righteous person who suffered, and Christians said, "That person is the Messiah." These passages, even though they don't mention the Messiah, in fact, are talking about him.

Christians started understanding, then, that the death of Jesus was according to the plan of God as predicted in the Hebrew prophets. This, then, is the beginning of Christianity. In one sense, Christianity did not really begin with Jesus's teaching, because Christianity isn't the teaching of Jesus, it is the teaching about Jesus. It didn't begin with Jesus's death, because if it had stopped at Jesus's death, he would have been another righteous prophet who had been killed. It didn't really start with Jesus's Resurrection, because people had to believe in his Resurrection for the religion to begin.

In many respects, Christianity begins with the proclamation of Jesus's Resurrection, a proclamation that transformed Jesus's own teaching, so that the religion begins to be the religion about Jesus, and all of this takes place, of course, within months or possibly years of Jesus's death.

While this theological development was taking place, and long before the Gospels were written, Christianity was spreading throughout the Roman world. Understanding this earliest Christian mission of spreading the Gospel is important for our understanding of how the religion was transformed in these early years. It is especially important for understanding the nature of the later Gospels that came to be parts of the New Testament.

Within 60 years of Jesus's death, Christianity had spread to major urban areas throughout the Mediterranean. It was largely spread by word of mouth, by proclamation, by people telling other people stories about Jesus. We're going to be devoting a couple of lectures to the question about how people spread the word, and what they said in order to convert other people. The question I want to raise at this point is where people got their stories from that they told in order to convert other people to believe in Jesus. Where did they get their stories from?

Well, obviously, a lot of things had happened in Jesus's life, and his followers must have told stories, but when his followers converted people to believe in Jesus, these people were then responsible for telling the stories, and when they converted people, then those people started telling the stories. When those people told the stories, they converted others who told the stories. These were stories that were being passed on by word of mouth, year after year, decade after decade, until somebody bothered to write them down.

It appears that in the process of retelling these stories, a number of the stories got changed, and many stories actually came to be made up. If you have had kids who were playing the party game "Telephone"—where someone is having a birthday party, and you have a group of kids in the living room, the way the game works is that one kid tells the next kid a story, who tells it to the next kid, who tells it to the next kid, and so on. It goes all the way around the circle, until it comes back to the first kid, and it is a different story by the time it gets back to the first kid. That's how it always works. If it didn't work that way, it wouldn't be a party game. There would be no reason to do it.

What happens, though, if you play the game "Telephone" year after year after year, telling the stories in different languages, to different audiences, for different reasons? Well, the stories get changed, and some stories end up getting made up.

The Gospels came to be written many years after the stories of Jesus had been in circulation throughout the Roman world. The earliest accounts we have are the New Testament Gospels of Matthew, Mark, Luke, and John. As I pointed out in the previous lecture, these books were actually written anonymously. Their authors, the authors Matthew, Mark, Luke, and John, were highly educated, Greek-speaking Christians. Highly educated, Greek-speaking Christians, as opposed to Jesus's followers, who were Aramaic-speaking peasants from Galilee. These authors of the Gospels lived in different parts of the empire several decades after the death of Jesus.

Well, where did they get their stories from? They got their stories from the oral traditions that had been in circulation, and they may well have had written sources at their disposal that no longer survive. It is clear that these earliest authors of the Gospels had some sources in common. We know this, because we can compare these Gospels with one another, and in a number of instances, Matthew, Mark, and Luke, at least, tell the same stories in the same sequence, using the same wording. Well, how does that happen, exactly? How can three people independently come up with the same stories, in the same sequence, using the same wording?

The way that happens is that they were all copying the same sources, unless you want to say that it's a divine miracle, which is fine, but if you say it's a divine miracle, you can explain the similarities, but then you have got to explain the massive differences among these accounts.

For over 150 years, scholars have been convinced that these authors all had the same sources at their disposal, specifically that Mark was the first Gospel written, that Matthew and Luke both had access to Mark's Gospel, and copied a number of its stories. That would explain why Matthew and Luke have the same stories in the same sequences as Mark, but when they tell different stories not found in Mark, they occur in different parts of the Gospels, in Matthew and Luke. They used Mark as a source, and then plugged in other sources wherever they felt it was appropriate.

Each of these accounts—Matthew, Mark, Luke, and John—is different from the others, as I have pointed out in the previous lecture, sometimes in minor details that are difficult to reconcile. For example, both Mark and John indicate that Jesus died sometime during the Passover feast. Mark's Gospel is quite explicit that Jesus died the day after the Passover meal was eaten: Mark 14:12 and 15:25. John is also quite explicit about which day Jesus died. In John's Gospel, Jesus died the day before the Passover meal was eaten. John chapter 19, verse 14. He died on the day of preparation for the Passover. This is a minor detail, but they disagree, and one would have to ask, "Why?"

Sometimes the emphases differ in these Gospels. For example, what did Jesus actually preach? Well, in Mark's Gospel, he preaches about the coming Kingdom of God that people need to prepare for. He doesn't talk about himself. In John's Gospel, he doesn't talk about the coming Kingdom of God that people need to prepare for. In John's Gospel, Jesus talks about himself, and that's about the only thing he talks about: Who he is. He is the one who has come from heaven to reveal the truth that will bring salvation. He's the one who has come from above. Well, it's a different emphasis.

Sometimes the different emphases have to do with major points. For example, how did Jesus meet his own death? According to Mark's Gospel, Jesus appears to be quite disturbed, he is in deep passion, he's anxious about his coming death. In Luke's Gospel, Jesus isn't anxious at all. He's calm and in control until the very end. Well, these Gospels had different emphases.

It is precisely these kinds of differences that make the Gospels so difficult for historians to use to establish what actually happened in Jesus's lifetime, as I have said in the previous lecture. As we saw there, though, these books were not meant to be historically objective biographies of Jesus. They were meant to be proclamations of the good news of the salvation that Jesus himself brought.

There were, by the way, other Gospels written as well, some of which still survive, although the majority of them don't. Some of the earliest accounts of Jesus have unfortunately been lost, including a document that scholars have called, since the 19th century, Q. Q is a reference to an early source that no longer survives, but at one time apparently did exist. Matthew and Luke, as I pointed out, borrowed a number of stories from the Gospel of Mark, but they have other stories.

For example, in both Matthew and Luke, Jesus says the Lord's Prayer. It's not found in Mark. Well, where did they get it from? They must have gotten it from some source. Scholars call this other source Q. They call it Q from the German word *Quelle*, which means "source," and so instead of calling it the "source," they simply shorten it by calling it Q. Q, unfortunately, no longer survives, but it was available to Matthew and Luke.

There are other Gospels, though, outside of the New Testament that do survive. Some of them are quite ancient, and some of them may record historically accurate information about Jesus. We will see later in our course, for example, that one of the most famous of these is the Gospel of Thomas, discovered in 1945. The Gospel of Thomas is a collection of 114 sayings of Jesus, many of which were previously unknown. A Gospel that just showed up in 1945, and scholars debate when the Gospel itself had actually been written. Some scholars think it was written earlier than Matthew, Mark, Luke, and John, although the majority opinion seems to be that the Gospel of Thomas was written sometime in the early second century.

All of these Gospels, whether they are in the New Testament canon or outside of it, each has its own personal perspective on the understanding of Jesus. The Gospel of Thomas understands Jesus quite differently from the Gospels of Matthew, Mark, Luke, and John. In the canonical Gospels, Jesus's death is the point of the story. The entire Gospels move toward his death and his Resurrection. Not so the Gospel of Thomas. In the Gospel of Thomas, Jesus's death has no bearing on salvation. The way a person has salvation for the Gospel of Thomas is by being able to interpret the secret sayings that Thomas contains. "These are the secret sayings of the living Jesus," says the Gospel of Thomas. "The one who learns the correct interpretation of these sayings will not taste death." Eternal life comes through correct interpretation of Jesus's secret teachings.

All of these books, the Gospels both within and outside of the New Testament, were meant as community books, intended to teach Christians in the church what Jesus said, did, and experienced. Yet, they all differ in their message. We may think of Christianity today as one thing, even though we recognize that there's a good deal of variety in what Christians believe and practice, but in fact, Christianity is and always has been many different things. The religion about Jesus is many different things. That's especially true in earliest Christianity of the first three centuries, as evidenced in these many Gospels that were written, read, and revered as sacred books that revealed the truth about what Jesus said, did, and experienced.

To sum it up, the religion of Jesus became the religion about Jesus as soon as his followers came to believe that Jesus had been raised from the dead. Then, they began to call him the Son of Man, the Son of God, the Messiah, the Lord, and they told stories about him, stories that changed in the process of transmission, and were eventually written down by different people at different times who had different perspectives.

We have inherited some of these stories in our Gospels, but one of the most important figures in this transformation of the religion of Jesus to the religion about Jesus was not a Gospel writer. He was an early opponent of Christianity who became its leading spokesperson, the apostle Paul. We will discuss Paul's life and teachings in the next lecture.

Lecture Five
The Apostle Paul

Scope: Next to Jesus himself, the most important figure for the development of earliest Christianity was the apostle Paul. Paul was, at first, a Jewish Pharisee who persecuted the Christian church. But based on a visionary experience of the resurrected Jesus, he converted to faith in Jesus and began an intense missionary campaign to win over *Gentiles* (that is, "non-Jews") to faith in Jesus. After starting churches in major urban areas around the Mediterranean, Paul wrote them letters, some of which became books of the New Testament. These writings show a profoundly theological mind, as Paul develops his understanding of the salvation God has provided through Christ's death and Resurrection, which comes to all people, Jew and Gentile, based on faith, not on following the requirements of the Jewish Law. In some ways, Paul marks the beginning of Christianity as a non-Jewish world religion.

Outline

I.   The most important figure for early Christianity apart from Jesus is the apostle Paul, whom some scholars have called the "Second Founder of Christianity."

    A. By this, they mean that Christianity is more than the religion Jesus preached; it is also—possibly even more so—the religion that preaches Jesus.

        1. In this understanding, it was the apostle Paul who developed the religion of Jesus into the religion about Jesus.

        2. Paul did not simply repeat the teachings of Jesus. He maintained that it was Jesus's own death and Resurrection that could bring salvation for the sins of the world.

        3. Because this belief lies at the heart of the Christian religion, some scholars have maintained that without Paul, Christianity would never have been anything other than a sect within Judaism.

    B. Paul is certainly important for understanding the New Testament; 13 of the 27 books of the New Testament claim to be written by him, one other (Hebrews) was accepted into the New Testament because church leaders thought it was written by him, and one other (Acts) is largely written about him.

C. Paul was also instrumental in the early spread of Christianity, because he was one of the main missionaries of the early church, who took the Gospel of Christ into major urban areas of what is now Turkey and Greece.

II. Despite his importance, there are numerous difficulties in trying to understand Paul's life and theology.

A. Several of the letters that claim to be written by him in the New Testament are commonly thought to be pseudonymous, written by his later followers instead of by Paul himself.

B. The Book of Acts, written long after his death, may not present a completely accurate portrayal of his activities and preaching.

III. Still, it is possible to get a reasonably clear idea of some of the most important aspects of Paul's biography and to see how he developed his theology of the importance of Jesus's death and Resurrection.

A. Paul himself indicates that he did not start out as a Christian, but as a Jewish Pharisee who persecuted the Christians for what he considered to be their blasphemous claim that Jesus was the Messiah.

B. Something happened to convert him, though, from being a persecutor of the Christian faith to being its greatest apostle. Paul indicates that he had a visionary experience of Jesus after his death, which convinced him that Jesus had been raised from the dead.

C. That changed everything. If Jesus was really raised from the dead, he was obviously not the one cursed by God, but the chosen one of God. And that must mean that his death was according to the plan of God, which in turn must have meant that Christ did not die for his own sins (because he was the one most favored by God), but for the sins of others.

1. It is important to realize that before Christianity, there were no Jews who expected the Messiah to die for the sins of others. The Jewish Messiah was to be a great and powerful figure who overthrew the enemies of God and established God's rule

on Earth. He was not to be a weak and defenseless person executed for crimes against the state.

2. Christians like Paul, however, transformed the idea of the Messiah. Because Jesus was the Messiah and because he had suffered, it must be that the Messiah was *supposed* to suffer.

3. Such Christian converts found support for their views in passages in the Jewish Scriptures—not the ones that talk explicitly about the Messiah (where there is no talk of suffering and death), but ones that talk about someone else, a righteous man, who suffers for others. These passages were taken, then, to refer to the Messiah, even though they had never been read that way before (for example, Isaiah 53; Psalm 22).

D. Once Paul came to think that Jesus's death and Resurrection were the keys to salvation, he had to rethink his understanding of his own Jewish religion: If Christ is the way of salvation, what about the salvation God had already provided his people through the Law?

1. Paul came to think that the Jewish Law was misunderstood if it was taken to be a way to maintain a right relationship with God.

2. The Jewish Law can tell a person how to live, but it does not provide anyone with the power to do what it demands. It is itself good, then, but it is not able to bring salvation, only condemnation.

3. Everyone is under the cosmic power of sin in this evil world, and as such, no one is able to fulfill the righteous demands of the Law.

4. Christ, though, broke the cosmic powers of sin and death (evidence: he overcame death!). Those who believe in his death and Resurrection can be made right with God (= *justified*)—not by keeping the Jewish Law, but by having faith in the one who triumphed over evil.

E. Because salvation comes apart from the Law, it is available to everyone, both Jew and Gentile, on equal terms. It comes by faith in Jesus, not by joining the Jewish people or by keeping the Jewish Law.

1. Once Paul became convinced of this, he became a missionary to take the "good news" (the literal meaning of *gospel*) to others, understanding himself principally as an apostle to the *Gentiles* (that is, "non-Jews").

2. He went on numerous missionary expeditions, setting up Christian churches in major urban areas in Cilicia, Asia Minor, Macedonia, and Achaia (modern Turkey and Greece) and converting former pagans to belief in the one God of the Jews and Jesus, his Son, whose death brought salvation.

3. Once Paul established a church in one place, he would move on to another, working to convert as many people as he could as quickly as possible, because for him, "The end is near."

IV. With one exception, the surviving writings of Paul are all letters that he wrote to his churches after he left.

A. Problems would arise in these churches, involving questions of what to believe and how to act, and Paul would deal with these questions one by one.

1. Some of the churches had to deal with other Christian missionaries that Paul considered to be "false teachers." For example, in the churches of Galatia, other missionaries taught the Christians that they needed to keep the Jewish Law in order to be right with God.

2. Some others had to deal with ethical problems that arose. For example, in the church of Corinth, some people assumed that because salvation comes apart from the Law, one can, therefore, live lawlessly, leading to all sorts of immoral behavior.

3. Paul dealt with these problems as they came up, writing letters back to the churches to give them instructions on what to believe and how to live.

B. The one exception is Paul's Letter to the Romans, written to a church he did not found and that he had not visited.

1. Paul apparently wrote Romans to explain his view of the Gospel of Christ, to win their support so that he could use them as a base for his missionary work further west, because he wanted to take his gospel all the way to Spain.

2. Given the nature of this letter, it is the best place to turn for a full expression of Paul's understanding of the gospel.

V. In sum, Paul was an extremely important person in the spread of early Christianity and in the development of Christianity into a religion that was more than a sect within Judaism that accepted the teachings of Jesus about the need to repent and follow the Jewish Law in light of the coming end. For Paul, it was not Jesus's teachings but his death and Resurrection that can bring salvation. Paul's writings, then, form the core of the New Testament and stand at the heart of the beginnings of early Christianity as a major world religion.

Essential Reading:

Bart Ehrman, *The New Testament: A Historical Introduction*, chapters 18–21.

Wayne Meeks, ed., *The Writings of St. Paul*.

Calvin Roetzel, *The Letters of Paul: Conversations in Context*.

Supplementary Reading:

James Dunn, *The Theology of Paul the Apostle*.

Wayne Meeks, *The First Urban Christian: The Social World of the Apostle Paul*.

Alan Segal, *Paul the Convert: The Apostolate and Apostasy of Saul the Pharisee*.

Questions to Consider:

1. Compare the teachings of Jesus with the preaching of Paul about Jesus. What are the similarities and differences? In your judgment, do Jesus and Paul represent fundamentally the same or fundamentally different religions?

2. Exercise some historical speculation: What might have been different about Christianity if Paul had never converted?

Lecture Five—Transcript
The Apostle Paul

So far, we have considered the very beginnings of Christianity: The religious context in Roman paganism and ancient Judaism, the life of Jesus, and the oral interpretations in circulation about him prior to the Gospels. We have also see that the Gospels themselves are not objective biographies, but proclamations of the faith made years later, based on surviving stories that had been in circulation in the oral tradition.

We have already begun to see that Christianity was not simply the religion that Jesus proclaimed, some kind of apocalyptic Judaism, but was a religion that proclaimed Jesus. No one was more instrumental in the development of this religion about Jesus than the apostle Paul, whom some scholars have called the "Second Founder of Christianity."

If you recall, in an earlier lecture, I talked about a survey done by professors of Western civilization, political science, philosophy, and so forth, in which they were asked who the most important figure was in the history of Western civilization. The person who ended up with the most votes was Alexander the Great, and in that lecture, I pointed out that Jesus and Paul tied for fifth. Well, why would they tie, exactly?

The reason they tied, in the opinion of the people taking this survey, was because, without Jesus, of course, one would not have Christianity, because Christianity is about Jesus. On the other hand, though, without Paul, you wouldn't have Christianity, because without Paul, you would simply have a sect of Judaism. You would have the religion that Jesus proclaimed, rather than the proclamation of Jesus.

The apostle Paul did not simply repeat the teachings of Jesus. In fact, when you read through Paul's writings, you rarely find quotations of Jesus's teachings at all. Paul's religion was different from that of Jesus, to the extent that he did not repeat Jesus's teachings of religion. He taught about Jesus. Specifically, he taught about Jesus's own death and Resurrection, which in Paul's view was a death and Resurrection that could bring about the salvation of the world.

Since this belief in the death and Resurrection of Jesus lies at the heart of the Christian religion, some scholars have maintained that without Paul, Christianity would never have been anything other than a Jewish sect. Paul, therefore, is commonly understood by scholars to have been a "Second Founder of Christianity."

Now, I am not going to take a position on this particular view. I can see why it is a valid view, but on the other hand, there are some problems with seeing Paul as the "Second Founder of Christianity." For one thing, Paul inherited his understanding of Jesus from those who went before him. Paul was not the first to proclaim the significance of Jesus's death and Resurrection, and so, in one sense, it isn't really quite right to say that Paul was the one who transformed Christianity, but he certainly was central to that transformation, and of course is highly important for understanding the New Testament itself.

Thirteen of the 27 books found in the New Testament claim to have been written by Paul, just to illustrate his importance to the New Testament. Nearly half of the books claim to be written by him. Another book was actually added into the New Testament, the book of Hebrews, because church fathers thought Paul had written it, even though the book itself doesn't claim to be written by Paul.

Another book, the book of Acts, the Acts of the Apostles, is largely written about Paul. Thus, just in terms of the New Testament itself, 15 of the 27 books are, in one way or another, directly connected with Paul, so he is obviously quite important for understanding the New Testament.

He was also important for understanding the spread of Christianity throughout the Roman world. Paul was one of the main missionaries of the early church, one of those who went about founding churches in major urban areas throughout the Mediterranean, especially in what is now Turkey and Greece. In antiquity, these were the areas of Asia Minor, Macedonia, and Achaia. Paul started a number of important churches in these areas, and so he's important not only for understanding the New Testament, but also for recognizing the spread of early Christianity.

He is also important for reasons of theology, pure and simple. The development of Christian theology owes a good deal to Paul, as he was one who developed his understanding of Jesus's life, death, and Resurrection in ways that came to influence Christians down throughout the centuries until today.

Despite Paul's importance, there are numerous difficulties that historians have in trying to understand Paul's life and theology, and I would like to start in this lecture by giving some of the difficulties that we have in understanding Paul.

First, even though we have a number of writings of Paul in the New Testament—and by the way, these are the only writings of Paul that survive; we don't have authentic writings of Paul outside of the New Testament, but only within the New Testament—despite the fact that we have a number writings that claim to be written by Paul in the New Testament, scholars have long recognized that some of these books are probably pseudonymous, meaning that they were written by someone else claiming to be Paul, rather than Paul himself.

It was a common phenomenon in the ancient world for people to write books pseudonymously. It still happens today. It happened even more in the ancient world, where there were fewer means of detecting forgery, writing in someone else's name. We know of numerous instances of pseudonymous writings. The word "pseudonymous," by the way, means "under a false name," but it's a technical term to refer to a book that claims to be written by somebody who's famous, and in fact, did not write the book. We have a number of instances of pseudonymous writings in the ancient world, in pagan circles, in Jewish circles, and also in Christian circles.

A number of writings claiming to be written by Paul were found outside the New Testament, which obviously were not written by him. This includes a book, for example, called 3 Corinthians, which corresponds to 1 and 2 Corinthians in the New Testament, a book that is allegedly written by Paul to the Laodiceans, as a forgery we have from outside the New Testament. But even within the New Testament, there are some books that scholars think, in fact, were not written by Paul, even though they claim Paul as an author.

Scholars have traditionally, since the 19th century, divided the Pauline writings into three groups. There are the pastoral Epistles of 1 and 2 Timothy and Titus in the New Testament, that most scholars think Paul probably did not write, even though they claim to be written by Paul. The reasons for thinking Paul did not write these books are that the vocabulary, the writing style, the theological point of view, and the historical circumstances presupposed by these writings don't appear to coincide with what we know about Paul from his other writings. Thus, the pastoral Epistles are largely considered pseudonymous by critical scholars.

Another group of writings consists of Colossians, Ephesians, and 2 Thessalonians. Scholars debate whether Paul actually wrote them or not, and so they are commonly called the Deutero-Pauline Epistles.

That leaves seven letters: Romans, 1 and 2 Corinthians, Galatians, Philippians, 1 Thessalonians, and Philemon. These seven letters are called the Undisputed Pauline letters.

It is difficult to know about Paul's life and theology because there are some books that claim to be written by Paul that Paul did not write, and so when scholars explore Paul's thought, they tend to restrict themselves to the seven undisputed letters.

Another difficulty in studying Paul has to do with the book of Acts of the New Testament. The Acts of the Apostles is a book that was written by the same author who produced the Gospel of Luke. It is the second volume of a two-volume work, Luke being the first volume. Luke is a Gospel that goes from Jesus's birth through his early life, through his ministry, to his death, Resurrection, and ascension. The second volume, written by the same author, is the book of Acts, which picks up the story starting with the ascension of Jesus.

It deals not with the life of Jesus, but with the life of the early church, especially the spread of Christianity through the Mediterranean world, and the spread of Christianity away from being purely a Jewish religion to being a religion that is also for Gentiles. The main character in the book of Acts, especially in Acts chapters 12 to the end, 28, is the apostle Paul. Acts, though, was written long after Paul's death, was probably written some 20 years after his death, and it may not present a completely accurate account of his activities and preaching.

One interesting excise to undertake is to find places where Acts talks about something Paul said or did, and then compare it with what Paul himself said he said or did in his undisputed letters. When one engages in that kind of exercise, one finds all sorts of discrepancies between what Acts has to say and what Paul has to say about himself, and it is usually assumed that Paul is probably the better authority for his own teachings and life than this book written 20 years later.

Even though we have these problems in studying Paul, it is possible to get a reasonably clear idea of some important aspects of Paul's biography. We can see how he developed his theology of Jesus's death and Resurrection. Unfortunately, in the undisputed letters, Paul is somewhat reticent to say much about his life, about things that have happened to him, but there are couple of instances in his letters where Paul does talk about things that had happened in his life, and we can use those to derive some kind of a biographical understanding of Paul, especially in his letters to the Galatians and the Philippians.

Paul himself indicates that he did not start out as a Christian, but as a Pharisaic Jew who persecuted Christians for what he considered to be their blasphemous claim that Jesus was the Messiah. Paul claims that he had been Jewish, a very religious Jewish person, and in fact, that he had been a Pharisee. I need to clarify one thing about Pharisees, because there is a common misunderstanding about Pharisees in our culture. Today, if you look up the term "Pharisee" in a dictionary, it will often describe Pharisees as a first-century group of Jews, but when you get to the second- or third-level definition of "Pharisee," he will often find, as a definition of Pharisee, "hypocrite."

This is an interesting definition of a religious group, "hypocrite," because it would be like 2,000 years of having a dictionary that defined "Episcopalian" as "drunkard," or "Baptist" as "adulterer." There probably are alcoholics among the Episcopalians, and probably are adulterers among the Baptists, but to say that that is their definition is a little bit strange, and is kind of like that when talking about Pharisees, because it is a little bit strange to define the Pharisees as hypocrites. That isn't exactly what they understood themselves to stand for.

Pharisees were a strict religious group within Jews. They more probably than other groups insisted on keeping the Law of God as fully as possible. Their reasoning was pretty clear. God had given this Law to his people, which meant that his people should follow the Law. If the Law was ambiguous, and yet was to be followed, then, people had to come to some decisions about what it meant to follow the Law. For example, if the Law said that you should keep the Sabbath day holy, and should trade like other days, well then, that meant that you should have figured out what you could and could not do on Sabbath to keep the Law, because God had commanded it. Pharisees, then, developed rules to help them understand how to follow these Laws that God had given.

Paul was a Pharisee, somebody who participated in that kind of discussion, which would have made him a very devout and highly religious Jew. We are not sure why Paul persecuted the Christians prior to converting to Christianity. He never tells us why he persecuted them, although there are some possible hints within his writings. Christians, of course, proclaimed that Jesus was the Messiah. The Messiah was the one sent from God for salvation.

This created some problems for Jews like Paul, for a number of reasons, one thing being, as I pointed out, that the Messiah wasn't supposed to be somebody who was going to be crucified. Proclaiming that the crucified one was the Messiah seems a bit odd, because the Messiah is one who should be blessed by God, but Jesus obviously was not blessed by God. He was crucified.

The mode of execution itself was a problem for Paul. According to the book of Deuteronomy, "Cursed is anyone who hangs on a tree."

"Cursed is anyone who hangs on a tree." In other words, Jesus, however great a preacher he was, or however many good deeds he did, was under God's curse, because he was hanged on a tree, had been crucified. That may have been what caused Paul to persecute the Christians. They were claiming something that would have been blasphemous, namely that the person whom God cursed was the one that God held in special favor. Although we aren't sure whether that's exactly why Paul persecuted the Christians, it may have been why. And as a good Pharisaic Jew, he obviously persecuted Christians trying to make them recant of their faith.

However, something happened to convert Paul, to change him from being the persecutor of the Christian faith to being its greatest apostle. Again, he doesn't give us as much information as we would like, but he does indicate on a couple of different occasions that he had some kind of visionary experience of Jesus after his death, which convinced him that Jesus had been raised from the dead. He had been persecuting Christians.

According to the book of Acts, the way it worked was that he was on the road to Damascus, and Jesus appeared to him in a vision. That may be actually what Paul himself would have said. He doesn't actually talk about going on the road to Damascus and having this vision of Jesus, but he does talk in two passages about having a visionary experience of Jesus that converted him. Since he saw that Jesus was alive after he knew that Jesus had died, that convinced him that God had raised Jesus from the dead. You find this spelled out especially in Galatians chapter 1, and in 1 Corinthians chapter 15, where Paul talks about this visionary experience.

Once Paul became convinced that Jesus had been raised from the dead, that changed everything for him. He had thought that Jesus was God's cursed, but it turns out that Jesus was the one God had raised from the dead. Paul, as a Pharisee, would already have been an apocalyptic Jew, thinking that he was living at the end of the age, before the resurrection of the dead that would bring in the good kingdom. If he thought that he was living at the end of the age, and then he came to think that somebody had been raised from the dead, what would his immediate conclusion be? We must be at the very end. Thus, Paul thought he was living at the end of time. The resurrection had started, and Jesus, as Paul puts it was the "first fruits" of the resurrection, meaning that the rest of the resurrection was going to happen very soon, and that the end of the age was imminent.

Moreover, if Jesus was the one who had been blessed by God, then the death of Jesus must have some kind of divine meaning. Therefore, Paul's trying to do what I tried to do in my last lecture. Paul started thinking backwards. From his knowledge that Jesus is no longer dead, he concludes that Jesus has been raised from the dead. From that, he concludes that the death itself must have been important. Since Jesus was the one blessed by God rather than the one cursed by God, he must not have died because of anything he did wrong. He must have died for the sins of others.

It's important to reemphasize that prior to Christianity, there were no Jews who expected the Messiah to die for the sins of others. The Jewish Messiah was to be a great and powerful figure who overthrew the enemies of God, and established God's rule on Earth. He was not to be a weak and defenseless person executed for crimes against the state. Since Christians like Paul, though, transformed the idea of the Messiah into something else, they had to apply this re-understanding of the Messiah to the person that they accepted as the Christ, namely, Jesus. The thinking was that since Jesus was the Messiah, and since he had suffered, therefore, the Messiah was supposed to suffer.

As I pointed out in the previous lecture, Christian converts like Paul found support for their views by looking at the Jewish Scriptures. They could not go to the passages in Jewish Scripture where they talk about the Messiah, because in those passages, there's no reference to a suffering Messiah. Instead, they went to other passages that talked not about the Messiah, but about a righteous man who must suffer, such as Isaiah 53, Psalm 22, and they claimed that those passages were also talking about the Messiah, and that Jesus fulfilled those passages.

Once Paul came to think that Jesus's death and Resurrection were the keys to salvation, that his death had been for the sins of others, it forced Paul to rethink his own understanding of the Jewish religion, for if Christ is the way of salvation, what about the salvation God had already provided his people through the Law? Did Jesus's death nullify Judaism? You see, if you could have salvation by being a good Jew, then why would God have to send Christ to die? Paul knew that God sent Christ to die, because he had raised him from the dead, and he had to believe that because he had this vision. Therefore, he was looking backwards. If Jesus is the way of salvation, what about Judaism? Has that become nullified?

Paul did not think that Judaism had become nullified. Paul was quite insistent that God had not changed the rules. The ground rules were the same. Paul came to think that Jesus was the fulfillment of the Law, but then he still had the question: Why is it that now the Law is not related to salvation? How does it work exactly?

Paul developed an entirely new way of understanding the Jewish Law, in which he came to think that the Jewish Law was misunderstood, if it was taken to be a way to maintain a right relationship with God. The Jewish Law cannot put a person into a relationship with God. The Jewish Law can only be used to maintain a right relationship with God.

For Paul, the Law in some ways was a problem. Even though it was God's gift to his own people, it was a problem. It was a problem because Jewish Law could tell a person how to live, but it did not provide anybody with the power to do what it demanded. The Jewish Law was good in and of itself, but it was not able to bring salvation. It could only bring condemnation. The reason it brought condemnation was not the fault of the Law. The Law was fine. The Law was perfectly good and righteous, as Paul said in Romans 7.

The problem was not the Law, the problem was that people were controlled by a cosmic power of sin, which compelled them to violate the Law. Now, this gets the little bit complicated, but it relates to Paul's apocalyptic understanding of things, even prior to becoming Christian. Paul, like Jesus before him, was apocalypticist who believed that there were powers in the world that were evil forces that were against God, and were trying to enslave people.

For Paul, sin was not simply an act of disobedience against God. The sin wasn't when you just did something against God's rules. Sin was actually a cosmic demonic power in the world that enslaved everybody in the world. Well, how did sin get in the world in the first place? Well, sin got in the world in first place because the first person, Adam, violated God's rule, when Adam and Eve ate the fruit in the Garden of Eden. This was according to Paul. Once they committed this act of transgression against God, the power of sin, an evil force in the cosmos, in the Universe, entered into this world, and enslaved everybody who was related to Adam. Adam brought this power of sin into the world.

Well, what was this power of sin? This power of sin is a cosmic force that enslaves you and forces you to do things contrary to what God wants. How do you know what God wants? Because it is in the Law. You can't keep the Law, though, because you are trapped by sin, because you are a descendant of Adam. The Law is good, perfect, and just, but you can't keep the Law, because you are enslaved to sin. Sin [sic The Law] tells you the right things to do, but it doesn't empower you to do that. Therefore, sin [sic the Law], rather than bringing salvation, brings condemnation. This was Paul's new understanding of things.

What did that have to do with Jesus? Jesus broke the power of sin. How did he break the power of sin? By dying. When Jesus died, God raised him from the dead. Closely connected with the power of sin in Paul's thinking was the power of death. Death, in Paul's understanding, was, again, not something that simply happened to you when you stopped breathing, or your heart stopped beating, or your brain stopped thinking. Death was actually a power that was trying to enslave you. When death got hold of you, it would annihilate you.

The way the sequence worked, then, was that sin was a power that forced you to go against God. Death was a power that annihilated you and separated you eternally from God. These were cosmic powers. Jesus overcame these powers by his death and Resurrection. How did Paul know? Paul knew that Christ broke the powers of sin and death because Jesus was raised from the dead, so that death had no power over him. That was proof that Jesus was more powerful than death, so that his Resurrection defeated death, and his death defeated sin. Those who believed in Jesus's death and Resurrection could be made right with God not by keeping the Jewish Law, which gave commands but not power. A person could be made right with God by having a relationship with Jesus in which he or she overcame the powers of sin and death.

The Law, therefore, was misunderstood if somebody kept it in order to become right with God, or in order to stay right with God. Salvation did not come by the Law, but by the death and Resurrection of Jesus. This notion of salvation, apart from the Law, was a notion that Paul developed, more than anyone else, and without this notion being developed, Christianity would have remained simply a sect of Judaism. It would not have become a separate religion, because Jesus's own preaching wasn't about his death and Resurrection, overcoming sin and death. His preaching was about the coming Kingdom of God. If people had accepted that, there would have been Jews who expected the Kingdom of God to come soon. Paul's teaching was that Jesus's death and Resurrection was the key to a right standing before God, and so, it is that particular message, then, that becomes the heart of the Christian proclamation.

Salvation comes apart from the Law and was available to everyone—and this is the key point—Jew and Gentile. Jews were not the people who had the special tie to God any longer, even though they were historically God's people. They, too, were under the power of sin, so that it was only people who had faith in Christ, baptized in Christ, that had escaped the power of sin. This was true for both Jew and Gentile, which means that the people of God were no longer simply the Jews. The people of God were those who had accepted the Messiah, Jesus, put their faith in him, and then been baptized by him. Christianity was no longer a Jewish sect. It was a religion for Jew and Gentile.

This was the thought process that Paul went through, in which he came to this conclusion that the salvation God had provided was for Gentiles as well as for Jews.

Paul went on missionary journeys after he acquired this understanding, to take this good news to others. He understood himself principally to be an apostle to the Gentiles. He focused on taking this proclamation to the non-Jews. Paul went on numerous missionary expeditions, setting up Christian churches in major urban areas in Silesia, Asia Minor, Macedonia, Achaia (in modern Turkey and Greece). He converted former pagans to the belief in the one God of the Jews and Jesus, his Son, whose death brought salvation.

It appears that the way Paul worked was that he would move into a town and set up some kind of small business. According to the book of Acts, he worked in leather goods, so, he had some kind of leather goods shop that he would set up. When people would come in, he would talk to them about religion, and he would convert a few people, who would then convert a few more, who would then convert a few more, until there would be enough people for a weekly gathering in a church, and as soon as there was a sufficient size of church in the community, Paul would then move on, go to the next town, and do the same thing all over again.

When he would leave a church, though, problems would erupt, because he had not spent that much time in these individual churches, and other Christian missionaries would arrive and create something slightly different from what Paul had said, or else the people would develop certain kinds of doctrinal questions, or maybe there would be ethical issues that would arise. When problems arose in Paul's churches, he wrote letters back to them in order to explain what they needed to believe and how they needed to act.

Some of the churches, as I indicated, were plagued with what Paul would call "false teachers." For example, in his churches in Galatia, Paul writes to the Galatians, to a church founded in the middle region of Asia Minor. Some Christian missionaries had come to teach that it was fine to believe Paul's message about the death and Resurrection of Jesus, but if you really wanted to be right with God, you men had to become circumcised, because every man had to be circumcised to belong to the people of God, according to the Jewish Scriptures.

Paul wrote his letter to the Galatians to indicate that, in fact, that was a mistake. Gentile men did not have to be circumcised—I believe they were quite happy to receive this letter—and that, in fact, if you received Christ, you did not have to receive circumcision; if you did get circumcised, in fact, you probably had misunderstood what the Gospel was all about, which was the salvation that God provided through Christ apart from the Law.

Paul, then, wrote letters to various churches—the Galatians, the Corinthians, the Philippians—as ethical problems had arisen, as moral or doctrinal problems had arisen, and he wrote these letters to resolve the problems. That means that all of Paul's letters we have are occasional letters, meaning that they were written for specific occasions.

We look in vain in these letters for a systematic laying out of Paul's understanding of things, because he was not writing a systematic treatise. He was writing a letter that we happen to be reading, a letter written to other people. The one partial exception to that is Paul's Letter to the Romans. The Letter to the Romans was written to the church of Rome, which Paul had not established. In fact, Paul tells us in this letter that he had never visited the Roman church. Paul wanted, though, to get to know the Roman Christians, because he wanted to go on a westward mission to Spain, and he wrote the Letter to the Romans to explain to these Christians what his gospel message was. The clearest explanation of Paul's gospel message that I've laid out for you in this lecture can be found in Romans, because he was trying to convince these Christians in Rome to support his westward mission, and so he detailed to them what it was that he preached.

To sum it up, Paul was an extremely important person to the spread of early Christianity, and in the development of Christianity into a religion that was more than a sect within Judaism. For Paul, it was not Jesus's teachings, but his death and Resurrection that could bring salvation. Paul's writings, then, formed the core of the New Testament, and they stand at the heart of the beginnings of early Christianity as a major world religion.

Lecture Six
The Beginning of Jewish-Christian Relations

Scope: This is the first of three lectures dealing with the relationship of Jews and Christians in the ancient world. In it, we will consider how Christianity started as a sect within Judaism, yet quickly became a religion separated from Judaism, because most Jews refused to accept the Christian claim that Jesus himself was the Jewish Messiah. In particular, we will consider three of the key figures for Jewish-Christian relations, the historical Jesus himself, who was deeply rooted in the Jewish tradition; the (anonymous) author of the Gospel of Matthew, who stresses the Jewish character of Jesus and the need for his followers to keep the Jewish Law; and the apostle Paul, who insisted that salvation came to all people, Jew or Gentile, apart from the Law. The perspectives of both Matthew and Paul survived into the second century, when some Christian groups held on to their Jewish ethnic identity, whereas other Christians rejected the Jews and all things Jewish.

Outline

I. To this point, we have looked at the social and historical milieu of the birth of Christianity and considered several of the main features of its early years: the historical Jesus, the traditions about him in circulation throughout the Roman Empire, and the life and teachings of Paul. In this lecture, we begin the second part of our course, issues pertaining to the relationship of Christianity to the religion from which it sprang, Judaism.

    A. Judaism and Christianity, of course, are two of the great religions of the West, with a long and well-documented history of both beneficial interaction and mutual antagonism.

    B. The three lectures that follow are all driven by an important but complicated historical question: How is it that early Christianity, a sect within Judaism, became so quickly and decisively a virulently anti-Jewish religion?

    C. In this lecture, we will examine three key figures in this transformation, all of whom considered themselves to be thoroughly Jewish, yet who understood their relationship to historical Judaism in different ways: the historical Jesus himself, the author of the Gospel of Matthew, and the apostle Paul.

II. As we have seen, Jesus of Nazareth cannot be understood apart from his Jewish context.

   A. This has not always been recognized; Christian lay people and scholars alike for centuries understood Jesus to stand over against Judaism. The logic appears to have been that if his followers were anti-Jewish, he must have been, as well.

   B. But one of the emphatic conclusions of modern historical scholarship is that Jesus was thoroughly Jewish and had no idea or intention of being anything else.

   1. Modern scholars have devised a variety of ways of understanding Jesus—as a Jewish rabbi, a Jewish teacher of wisdom, a Jewish holy man, a Jewish proto-Marxist, a Jewish proto-feminist, a Jewish cynic philosopher, a Jewish apocalyptic prophet.

   2. What these various understandings all share, however, is the sense that whatever else we say about Jesus, he was totally Jewish.

   C. This can be seen in all of the earliest surviving reports about Jesus in our ancient sources.

   1. His teachings are all drawn from the Jewish Scriptures and his interpretations of them, including the commandments to love God above all else and to love one's neighbor as oneself.

   2. He followed Jewish customs, including Sabbath observance and keeping of Jewish festivals.

   3. His followers were all Jewish and considered him a great teacher of the Law.

   4. His controversies were all with Jewish opponents and typically concerned how best to interpret the will and Law of the God of the Jews (whether with Pharisees, Sadducees, or anyone else).

   D. If the reconstruction of his message that we laid out in our earlier lecture was correct, then the burden of his message was that the Jewish people needed to repent in light of God's coming judgment, that they might enter into God's Kingdom when it arrived.

    1. This message is comparable to that of prophets of the Hebrew Bible, and it stood completely within the confines of Judaism in Jesus's day.

    2. His disciples followed him precisely because they, as faithful Jews, adhered to this message.

  E. How is it, then, that Christianity, the religion founded on Jesus, became so virulently anti-Jewish?

III. The key to answering that question involves what happened after Jesus's death.

  A. As we saw in the last lecture, some of Jesus's followers came to think that Jesus was raised from the dead. This changed everything for them.

    1. His followers began to understand that the Resurrection of Jesus demonstrated that he was the Messiah.

    2. Most Jews, of course, did not expect anything like Jesus as a Messiah, because he was a relatively unknown itinerant preacher from Galilee who was arrested, tried, and executed as a common criminal for crimes against the state. How could *he* be the powerful Messiah? He appeared to most Jews to be anything *but* the Messiah.

    3. Jews who believed in Jesus, though, insisted that that's precisely what he was. This naturally led to serious conflict between traditional Jews and those who re-understood Judaism in light of their belief in Jesus.

  B. Jews who believed in Jesus were opposed by the vast majority of Jews, who found their message absurd and even blasphemous.

  C. In response, the Jewish believers in Jesus argued that those who did not accept him were blind to the truth and, because they had rejected the Messiah sent by their own God, they had rejected God himself. Further, because they rejected God, he rejected them.

  D. Thus began a long history of antagonism between Christians and non-Christian Jews.

  E. As we will see in this and the following lectures, different Christian authors reacted to this situation and dealt with it in a variety of ways.

IV. The anonymous author of the Gospel of Matthew has an ambivalent relationship to historical Judaism.

    A. On the one hand, he stresses more than our other Gospel writers that Jesus himself was Jewish, the Jewish Messiah sent from the Jewish God to the Jewish people to fulfill the Jewish Law.

        1. This can be seen in the opening passages of his Gospel (the birth narratives).

        2. And it is a theme that recurs throughout, for example, at the beginning of the Sermon on the Mount (Matt. 5:17–20).

    B. On the other hand, he blames the Jews who refused to acknowledge Jesus for his death and portrays them as blind, hypocritical, and opposed to the will of God.

        1. The Jewish leaders are condemned in vitriolic terms in this Gospel (chapter 23).

        2. The Jewish people are portrayed as complicit in their blind rejection of Jesus (for example, 27:25).

    C. Even so, this understanding of the Jewishness of Jesus was significant for some later groups of Christians, who saw themselves as the "true" Jews and who kept the Jewish Law and customs on the understanding that Jesus himself was thoroughly Jewish.

V. The apostle Paul took a different tack and maintained a different perspective, one that became yet more important historically for the development of Christianity

    A. Paul, too, accepted Jesus's Jewishness and saw himself as thoroughly Jewish, a worshiper of the Jewish God and a believer in his promises.

    B. As we saw in the previous lecture, however, Paul came to believe that Jesus's death and Resurrection were the only way of salvation and concluded that the Law of the Jews, although itself embodying God's righteous demands, had no role to play in salvation.

        1. As a result, he insisted that Christians are made right with God apart from the Law.

        2. For him, this meant that Gentiles, who were quickly becoming the majority in the church by the middle to late first century, did not need to keep the provisions of the Law (such as circumcision, Sabbath observance, and kosher food laws).

3. Paul understood this as being the goal of the Law itself—the salvation to be brought by Christ apart from the Law.
4. The result was that faith in Christ was not just a Jewish option but was available to all.

C. This marks the beginning of Christianity as a *non-Jewish* religion, which stood over against Judaism and could portray the Jews themselves as outsiders to the promises that God had made to the Jewish ancestors— promises now seen, by the Christians, as being fulfilled not for the Jews but for the followers of Christ, whether Jew or Gentile.

D. This is probably why Paul is commonly understood as anti-Jewish. But it is important to realize that he saw himself as thoroughly Jewish and representing the views of the Jewish God as set forth in the Jewish Bible.

E. Even so, once Paul's doctrine was established that a person's relationship to God is independent of the Jewish Law and Jewish culture, something new had obviously begun, leading to the developments of Christianity as an anti-Jewish religion.

Essential Reading:

Bart Ehrman, *After the New Testament*, chapter 5.

———, *New Testament: A Historical Introduction*, chapter 25.

Supplementary Reading:

John Gager, *The Origins of Anti-Semitism*.

Rosemary Ruether, *Faith and Fratricide: The Theological Roots of Anti-Semitism*.

Samuel Sandmel, *Anti-Semitism in the New Testament?*

Questions to Consider:

1. Compare Matthew's claims that a person must keep the Law to be right with God (Matt. 5:17–20) with Paul's claims that the Law can have no bearing on one's relationship with God (for example, Gal. 2:15–16). Do you think these views can be reconciled, or are they hopelessly at odds with each other?

2. If Matthew's understanding of the importance of the Jewish Law for the followers of Jesus were still adhered to by Christian churches, what might be different about Christianity today?

Lecture Six—Transcript
The Beginning of Jewish-Christian Relations

To this point of our course, we have looked at the social and historical milieu of the birth of Christianity and considered several of the main features of its early years: the historical Jesus, the traditions about him and their circulation throughout the Roman Empire, and the life and teachings of Paul.

In this lecture, we began the second part of our course, which involves issues pertaining to the relationship of Christianity to the religion from which it sprang, Judaism. Judaism and Christianity, of course, are two of the great religions of the West, with a long and well-documented history of both beneficial interaction and mutual antagonism. The three lectures that follow are all driven by an important but complicated historical question: How is it that early Christianity, a sect within Judaism, became so quickly and decisively a virulently anti-Jewish religion?

In this lecture, we will consider three key figures in this transformation, all of whom considered themselves to be Jewish, yet who understood their relationship to historical Judaism in different ways. First, the historical Jesus himself; second, the author of the Gospel of Matthew; and third, the apostle Paul.

First, the historical Jesus. As we seem, Jesus of Nazareth cannot be understood apart from his Jewish context. This has not always been recognized, as Christian laypeople and scholars alike for centuries have understood Jesus to stand over against Judaism. The logic of this older way of thinking appears to have been that if Jesus's followers were anti-Jewish, he must have been so, as well. One of the emphatic conclusions of modern historical scholarship, though, especially during the second half of the 20th century—one of the decisive conclusions of modern historical scholarship is that Jesus was thoroughly Jewish, and that he had no idea or intention of being anything else.

Modern scholars have devised a variety of ways of understanding Jesus. Some have portrayed Jesus as a Jewish rabbi, someone who, like other rabbis, gathered followers around him and taught them his understanding of the Jewish Law. Thus, he was principally understood as a rabbi.

Others have understood Jesus as a Jewish holy man who, like other Jewish holy men, had a particularly close relationship with God, so he could call God his father, and thought of himself as God's son, and had special powers because of his special relationship with God. Thus, Jesus was a Jewish holy man.

Other modern scholars have portrayed Jesus as a Jewish proto-Marxist, one who was against the ancient systems of economic systems, just as Marxists today might be opposed to the current economic systems that Jesus supported, not the expenditure of capital, but, in fact, taught everybody to give away all of their possessions and to live communally together, a kind of proto-Marxist, Jewish proto-Marxist.

Other modern scholars have portrayed Jesus as a kind of Jewish proto-feminist. Of course, Jesus's closest disciples were all men, but Jesus associated with women in public. He touched women in public, healed women in public, had dialogues with women in public, and raise the status of women above where they were in the oppressive society of the first century, as this line of teaching goes, so that Jesus is best understood as a proto-feminist, but a Jewish proto-feminist.

Others have insisted that Jesus was a kind of Jewish cynic philosopher, somebody who taught that people should not be connected to the things of this world, to the material goods of this life, but to give away everything they have, to consider the birds of the air. They don't have to reap and sow, but they nonetheless are clothed in beautiful raiment. "Consider the lilies of the valleys," Jesus said. "You should be like them. Don't worry about what you eat, what you drink. Don't be concerned about what you wear. Be concerned, instead, about spiritual things." Well, that sounds like a Jewish cynic philosophy.

Other scholars have portrayed Jesus as a Jewish apocalyptic prophet. That's a portrayal that I have laid out for you in an earlier lecture, a portrayal of Jesus as one who was anticipating that the God of Israel was going to intervene in the course of affairs and overthrow the forces of evil to bring in a good kingdom here on Earth. Jesus as a Jewish apocalyptic prophet.

Even though these portrayals of Jesus are quite diverse, the one thing that they all share is the sense that whatever else we may say about Jesus, we have to say that he was totally Jewish. There is, in fact, good evidence for the Jewishness of Jesus that has been so compelling that now it is virtually commonplace among all scholars working in these materials.

First, it is worth pointing out that Jesus's teachings are all drawn from the Jewish Scriptures and his interpretations of them from, including the commandments to love God with all of one's heart, soul, and strength, and to love one's neighbor as oneself. These are sayings found in the Torah, the Law of Moses, Deuteronomy chapter 6, Leviticus chapter 19. Jesus thought that these two Laws fulfilled all of the law and the prophets. These were the laws that were to be given centrality and focus when trying to consider what God wanted for people. But, as I am pointing out, these were Jewish laws, they were not laws that Jesus just came up with himself. So first, Jesus is to be understood as an interpreter of Jewish Scriptures.

Second, Jesus followed Jewish customs, including the custom of Sabbath observance and the keeping of Jewish festivals. These customs themselves are, of course, written in the Law of God found in the Torah, and indicates that one must observe the Sabbath day to keep it holy, and is to keep annual Jewish festivals. I should point out in this connection that Jesus is sometimes understood to be one who violated the Law, one who went against Jewish Law in order to set up a new religion. When you look carefully at the Gospel traditions, though, it is very difficult indeed to find instances in which Jesus actually broke any of the Jewish laws.

He acquired a reputation at one point for violating the Sabbath, and many people think that Jesus would commonly violate the Sabbath, but I think that's probably a misreading of our early traditions about Jesus. It's absolutely true that Jesus was accused of violating the Sabbath, principally by the Pharisees, whom you recall from a previous lecture were a sect of Jews who were intent on keeping the Law as fully as possible, and so devised rules and regulations that would assist them in keeping the Law. So that if the Law said that one had to keep the Sabbath day holy and distinct from what happened on the other days, then, one should not have worked on the Sabbath. "If that's the case, then," the Pharisees reasoned, "we have to know what it means to work on the Sabbath."

Well, is it work on the Sabbath to harvest your crops? Well, yes, that's what you do on the other days, so you shouldn't harvest your crops on the Sabbath. Well, what if you are going through a field, and you are not actually harvesting your crops, but you're just pulling off some grain to eat yourself? Is that a violation of the Sabbath?

Well, Pharisees had debates about whether that was a violation of the Sabbath or not. Some would say, "Well, no, that's not a violation of the Sabbath, because you aren't harvesting." Others would say, "Well, yes, that is, because you are doing the same thing as harvesting, even if you aren't doing it in a big way. You are doing a harvest, so you shouldn't walk through a grain field, pull up grain, and eat it on the Sabbath."

Well, what if you walk through the grain field and don't pull up the grain to eat it on the Sabbath, but you walk through the grain field, and you accidentally knock off the grain? Is that harvesting? Well, some would say, "No, that's not really harvesting. You're just accidentally knocking off the grain." Other people would say, "Well, in fact, it is kind of like harvesting, and so you probably shouldn't walk through a grain field on the Sabbath, because if you do that, you'll be knocking off grain."

Pharisees would have debates among themselves about what would constitute work with respect to walking through a grain field on the Sabbath. Some Pharisees said one thing, some said another thing. They had arguments with Jesus about the same thing. Jesus evidently did not think it was a violation of the Law to walk through a grain field and eat the grain during the Sabbath. That was fine to do. Other Pharisees probably agreed with him, but some Pharisees disagreed with him, and so there were these disputes. The way the disputes got recorded in the New Testament was in such a way that it was as if you'd had the Pharisees (who all were of one mind) against Jesus, who was the only one in trouble. You then had these arguments with Jesus and the Pharisees, but that is probably a skewed vision of how, in fact, it really worked.

Jesus doesn't, in fact, do anything in the Gospels that directly violates the Laws of Torah. As far as we know, Jesus, in fact, kept the Jewish customs that are rooted in Jewish Law, including Sabbath observance, and observance of Jewish festivals. Thus, Jesus appears to be Jewish.

The third point in support of his Jewishness is that his followers were all Jewish, and they considered him a great teacher of the Law. One of his titles that you find in early traditions is rabbi, "teacher."

Fourth, Jesus's controversies all had to do with Jewish opponents. They typically were concerned with how best to interpret the will and Law of the God of the Jews; whether he was having a controversy with Pharisees, Sadducees, or with anyone else, these controversies were all about the Jewish Law. I should point out, by the way, that there have been scholars that have argued that Jesus himself was a Pharisee. Now, that might strike one as odd, since it seems like his enemies were always Pharisees. They were the ones he was always arguing with.

With whom do you argue the most, though? You argue the most with the people you are closest to. If people don't have anything in common with you, you don't have anything to argue about. Therefore, some people have argued that maybe Jesus himself was a Pharisee. I personally don't think so, but you can see why it's an interesting case to be made.

If the reconstruction of Jesus's message, that we laid out in an earlier lecture, was correct, then the burden of his message was that the Kingdom of God was soon coming, and people needed to repent in preparation for it, so that they might enter the kingdom when it arrived. If that was the heart of his message, that's comparable to the message you can find in the prophets of the Hebrew Bible. The Hebrew prophets—Isaiah, Jeremiah, Amos, Hosea, Joel—all emphasized that people needed to repent from the way they had lived, because God was soon going to enter into judgment with them. They needed to prepare for this judgment by repenting and returning to God. If that was Jesus's message, then he stands perfectly aligned with the other Jewish prophets of Hebrew Scripture, and prophets that we know about from Jesus's own day, other Jews also predicting an imminent judgment of God.

My point in all of this is that Jesus is best understood as thoroughly Jewish. He was an interpreter of the Jewish Scriptures, he kept Jewish custom, and he had Jewish followers. The burden of his message was a Jewish, prophetic message. His followers, of course, were his followers because they agreed with that message, which meant that his disciples on Earth were faithful Jews themselves, who understood Jesus to provide an accurate and authoritative interpretation of Judaism, and they, then, themselves, maintained their Jewish identity.

Given that circumstance, that both Jesus and his followers were thoroughly Jewish, how is it that Christianity, the religion founded on Jesus, became so virulently anti-Jewish? That's the key question we're dealing with over course of these three lectures.

The key to the answer, I think, involves what happened after Jesus's death. The key is not so much what happened during his life as what happened after his death. As we saw in the last lecture, some of Jesus's followers came to think that Jesus was raised from the dead after he was crucified, and we saw that this changed everything for them. Jesus's followers began to understand that the Resurrection of Jesus meant that he was the Messiah. Most Jews, of course, did not expect anything like Jesus as a Messiah, as he was a relatively unknown itinerant preacher from Galilee who was arrested, and tried, and executed as a common criminal for crimes against the state. How could he be the powerful Messiah? Jesus is the Messiah?

To give my students some sense of the emotional reaction that would come to somebody who was told for the first time that Jesus, the crucified man, was the Messiah, I give an analogy. I get in trouble for this every time I do this, so I want to stress that this is just an analogy. If somebody came up to you and told you that David Koresh was the Lord of the Earth, and the savior of the human race, well, you would laugh and say, "That's ridiculous. David Koresh? The guy at Waco? You've got to be kidding me." "No, no, he's the savior of the human race."

That would strike all of us as completely absurd. Why? "Well, because he got killed in a fire at the FBI standoff, in the compound at Waco." Well, what if somebody said, "Jesus is the Messiah? The guy that got crucified by the Romans? You've got to be kidding me." "No, he, in fact, is the Lord of the Universe."

That kind of the emotional reaction is what most Jews had when they heard Christians say that Jesus was the Messiah, so of course most Jews didn't buy it for second. They didn't believe it, they didn't accept it, they thought it was outrageous, they thought it was blasphemous. This view of Jesus as the Messiah was opposed by the vast majority of Jews.

In response, then, the Jews who had come to believe that Jesus was the Messiah set themselves up over against Jews who did not believe in Jesus as the Messiah. Those who did accept the Messiahship of Jesus claimed that the others, the ones who rejected it, were blind to the truth, and that since they had rejected their own Messiah, sent by their own God, they had rejected God himself, and, maintained these Christians, since these Jews had rejected their own God, he rejected them. So began a long history of antagonism between Christians and non-Christian Jews.

As we will see in this and the following lectures, different Christian authors reacted to the situation and dealt with it in a variety of ways.

For the rest of this lecture, I will deal with two of these authors, the author of the Gospel of Matthew, and the apostle Paul. The anonymous author of the Gospel of Matthew (whom I will continue to call Matthew because I don't know what his name was, and so there's no point in calling him something else) has an ambivalent relationship to historical Judaism. On the one hand, he stresses, more than our other Gospel writers, that Jesus himself was Jewish, the Jewish Messiah sent from the Jewish God to the Jewish people to fulfill the Jewish law. Therefore, he is thoroughly Jewish on the one hand. On the other hand, we're going to see—this is the other side of the ambivalence—this author thought that the current day Jewish leadership had rejected God, and he had rejected them. Is he for or against Judaism? Well, he's for Jewish religion, but he's against the Jewish leaders.

He's for the Jewish religion, and he wants to portray Jesus in a thoroughly Jewish light. This can be seen in the opening passages of the Gospel of Matthew. The Gospel of Matthew, the first Gospel in the New Testament, opens up in a way that my students tend to dislike. He opens up with a genealogy of Jesus; who begat whom, who begat whom, who begat whom. It is not as full as some of the genealogies one gets in the Hebrew Bible. I tell my students, "Look, this genealogy in Matthew is only 16 verses. If you want a real genealogy, go to 1 Chronicles, and you get nine chapters of this stuff. You can live for 16 verses," and, in fact, it's a pretty interesting genealogy, because the genealogy traces Jesus all the way back to the father of the Jews, Abraham. It begins: "An account of the genealogy of Jesus the Messiah, the son of David, the son of Abraham."

"Why does it say, 'the son of David, the son of Abraham'? I thought he was the son of Joseph." Yes, but his ancestors were David and Abraham. Why would he emphasize that? Because David was the greatest king of the Jews, whose descendent was to be the Messiah, and Abraham was the father of the Jews.

Why stop with Abraham, though? Why not go back to Abraham's father in this genealogy? Because the point of this genealogy is to show Jesus's Jewish lineage, back through the greatest king, back all the way through the father of the Jews, and so it starts: "Abraham was the father of Isaac, Isaac was the father of Jacob, Jacob was the father of Judah and his brothers," and so forth, and it goes on listing father to son, until it gets down to, "Jesse was the son [sic father] of King David, David was the father of Salomon, Salomon the father of Rehoboam." It keeps on going to, "Josiah was the father of Jeconiah and his brothers at the time of the deportation to Babylon." After the deportation to Babylon, "Jeconiah was the father of Shealtiel," etc. When you get down to near Jesus's time, "Jacob was the father of Joseph, the husband of Mary, of whom Jesus was born, who was called the Messiah."

This is a very strange genealogy, because, in fact, Jesus doesn't belong in this line. It is traced to Joseph, who is not Jesus's father. Joseph was married to Mary, of whom Jesus was born, whom was called the Messiah.

Then, it gets stranger still. Verse 17: "All the generations from Abraham to David are fourteen generations, from David to the deportation to Babylon, fourteen generations. From the deportation to Babylon to the Messiah, fourteen generations." Fourteen generations, fourteen generations, fourteen generations. Fourteen, fourteen, and fourteen. It's like, this is a miraculous thing. Every fourteen generations in the history of Israel, something big happens.

You start with the father of Jesus, go fourteen generations, the greatest king of the Jews. You go to the next fourteen generations, something big happens, the Babylonian empire overthrows Judaism, destroys the Temple, the biggest calamity of the Jews. You go another fourteen generations, there's Jesus, the Messiah of the Jews. This must be a miracle. It's divinely planned to work this way, until you start looking closely at the genealogy.

As it turns out, the last bit of fourteen have only 13 names. Even worse, in the first part of the genealogy, the author has left out three generations. As you know, when you go back to read this thing in 1 Chronicles, this long genealogy, this author has made a father and son combination out of what was, in fact, a father and a great-great-grandfather combination. He skipped three generations. Well, why would he do that? Because he wanted fourteen generations. Why did he want fourteen generations? Well, there are several theories about that. Of course, the perfect number is "7." What is fourteen? It's twice 7, so it's a really perfect genealogy.

Another theory is that if you take the name "David," the king of the Jews, in ancient Hebrew, every letter had a numerical value, so the first letter is "1," the second letter is "2," and add up David's name. You know what you come up with? Fourteen. Maybe this is showing that this is the Messiah, son of David, the genealogy of Jesus.

Well, it is a very interesting genealogy, and it is trying to emphasize the Jewishness of Jesus. You find the emphasis on the Jewishness of Jesus throughout this entire account. Throughout Matthew's Gospel, things happen, one after the other, that are said to fulfill what was predicted in the prophets. Why was Jesus born in Bethlehem? Because Micah chapter 5, verse 2, said the Messiah had to come from Bethlehem, according to Matthew. Why is his mother a virgin? Because Isaiah chapter 7, verse 14, said that: "A virgin shall conceive and bear a son," and so it is a fulfillment of Scripture. Why do Joseph and Mary flee to Egypt, and then come back out of Egypt to resettle in Nazareth? Because the prophet said so, Hosea, chapter 11, verse 1: "Out of Egypt have I called my son."

All of these things are said to be fulfillments of prophecy. The point is Jesus is a fulfillment of the Jewish Scripture. This author drives the point home time and time again, not only in the birth narrative, but actually in the text of the Gospel dealing with Jesus's life, we find repeated affirmations of the Jewishness of Jesus. Only in Matthew do you find any of these passages that I am talking about, by the way. They are not found in Mark, Luke, or John.

Jesus begins at the early part of his very famous Sermon on the Mount, which is a sermon found only in Matthew's Gospel. Jesus states his own standing in relationship to the Jewish Law:

> Don't think, [says Jesus in Matthew 5, verse 17] that I have come to abolish the Law or the Prophets; I have come not to abolish, but to fulfill. For truly I tell you, until heaven and earth pass away, not one letter, not one stroke of the letter, will pass away from the Law until all is accomplished. Therefore, whoever breaks one of the least of these commandments and teaches others to do the same will be called least in the kingdom of heaven, but whoever does them and teaches them will be called great in the kingdom of heaven.

Jesus's followers, like Jesus himself are to keep the Law. Jesus fulfills, he accomplishes, the entire Law, and his followers cannot break one of the least of the commandments. You find that in Matthew, but not in other Gospels. Why? Because Matthew is trying to emphasize the Jewishness of Jesus.

At the same time, Matthew wants to show that the Jewish leadership who have refused to acknowledge Jesus, and are responsible for his death, are blind and hypocritical, and are opposed to the will of God. Matthew makes a special point of stressing that the Jewish leaders of Jesus's day, in fact, were opposed to God. For example, in chapter 23, there are a series of condemnations of the scribes and Pharisees, in which Jesus condemns them using vivid imagery. He says they are like "whitewashed sepulchers," so that on the outside, they have the nice paint job for these tombs, but on the inside, they are filled with rotting flesh. That's what his enemies, the Jewish leaders, are like; or they are hypocrites; or they are "people who strain out a gnat" when they are drinking their tea, but they swallow a camel, so that they are just interested in picky little things, not the big things, unlike Jesus, who is interested in this gospel on the big things, loving God with all your heart, soul, and strength, and your neighbor as yourself.

This understanding of the Jewishness of Jesus found in Matthew's Gospel, that the Jewish religion needs to be embraced even if Jews themselves have not gotten it, becomes very important for some later groups of Christians who understood themselves to be true Jews. These later Jewish Christians kept the Jewish Law and customs on the understanding that Jesus himself was Jewish.

The view eventually died out. We will see later on in this course that there were Christians in the second century who still maintained their Jewishness, largely because of their acceptance of this message of Matthew's Gospel. By and large though, this view died out even though Matthew became part of the New Testament canon. But when it was put into the canon, it was put into the canon with other books. That ended the sharp edges of any one of them, since you read all these books together now, the sharp edges were taken away in relationship to the others. That's a view of Matthew. Jesus is thoroughly Jewish. Jewish leaders, however, are problematic.

The third character I want to look at briefly, since I have just devoted a lecture to him, is the apostle Paul. Paul took a different tack altogether from that of Jesus and Matthew, maintaining a different perspective. In some ways, Paul's perspective became more important historically for the development of Christianity.

Paul, like Matthew, accepted Jesus's Jewishness, and he saw himself as thoroughly Jewish. Paul continued to see that he was the worshipper of the Jewish God and a believer in God's promises. As we saw in the previous lecture, however, Paul came to believe that Jesus's death and Resurrection were the only way of salvation, and he concluded that the Jewish Law, even though it embodied God's righteous demands, had no role to play in salvation. As a result, Paul insisted that Christians were made right with God apart from the Law. For Paul, this meant that Gentiles, who by his day in the 50s and 60s of the first century, were becoming the majority in the church, did not have to keep the provisions of the Law, such as circumcision, Sabbath observance, and kosher food laws.

Paul understood that Christ himself was the goal of the Law. The Law was looking forward to Christ to fulfill the Law. So Christ was the goal of the Law, but that now his followers did not have to keep the Law, because the salvation Jesus brought, he brought to all people, whether Jewish or Gentile. The irony of this is that Paul thought the Jewish Law itself taught that salvation comes apart from the Law. Paul thought that the Jewish Law itself taught that the Law had no bearing on salvation.

He pointed especially to the father of the Jews, Abraham, who was the first patriarch, and was told by God that he had a right standing with God. God promised Abraham a son, even though Abraham was a very old man, and

Abraham believed God. It was counted to him as righteousness (Genesis chapter 15, verse 6). Abraham was put into a right standing before God because he trusted God. He believed in God, and that was hundreds of years before the Law was given to Moses. That means that a person could have a right standing with God by believing God without the Law. That particular passage is found in the Torah, in the Law, and so Paul uses that in an ironic way to show that the Law itself teaches that salvation comes by faith, not by keeping the Law.

This understanding of Paul's marks the beginning of Christianity as a non-Jewish religion that stood over against Judaism, because the Law had no relevance for salvation anymore, and a person was made right with God by believing in Jesus rather than keeping the Law. That is probably why Paul is typically understood as anti-Jewish, because he promoted an understanding of Christianity apart from the Jewish law, but it is important to realize that he saw himself as thoroughly Jewish, and is representing the views of the Jewish God set forth in the Jewish Bible. Paul did not think he was anti-Jewish at all.

Even so, once Paul's doctrine that a person's relationship to God was independent of the Jewish Law and Jewish culture happened, something new had clearly begun, leading to the development of Christianity as an anti-Jewish religion.

Thus, we have three perspectives: Jesus, who was thoroughly Jewish from beginning to end; Matthew, who understood Jesus as the fulfillment of all that was Jewish, yet in opposition to Jewish leaders; and, third, Paul, who saw Jesus as the savior of all people, including Gentiles, who did not have to become Jewish in order to be right with the Jewish God.

Lecture Seven
The Anti-Jewish Use of the Old Testament

Scope: Most early Christians, even those who rejected the ways of Judaism, held on to the Jewish Scriptures as the revelation from God. But how could they claim these Scriptures for their own when they did not follow many of the laws set forth in them?

Disputes arose among Christians and Jews over who were the legitimate heirs to the promises made to the Jewish ancestors. In this lecture, we will consider two key figures in the early Christian-Jewish debates: Justin of Rome, who engaged in harsh arguments with Jews over the interpretation of Scripture in an effort to show that Christianity, rather than Judaism, was the way to worship the Jewish God, and Barnabas of Alexandria, who insisted that the Old Testament was a Christian, not a Jewish book.

Outline

I. In the previous lecture, we began to ask the key historical question about the relationship of Christianity and Judaism.

   A. If Christianity started out as a sect within Judaism, beginning with Jesus himself, how and why did it become such a virulently anti-Jewish religion, within just a century or so of its inception?

   B. We saw that, even among the New Testament writers, there were radically different understandings of the relationship of this new faith in Christ to the Jewish Law.
      1. Matthew, for example, stressed the ongoing importance of observing the Law as given by God, so that followers of Jesus were, like him, to do all the Law commanded.
      2. The apostle Paul, on the other hand, stressed that salvation comes to all people, Jew and Gentile, only in the death and Resurrection of Jesus, not in doing what the Law commands. For Paul, it is an affront to God and his Christ for non-Jews to keep the Jewish Law.

II. Because the Law was so intimately connected with Jewish identity, the developing understanding of the importance of the Law for Christians became a central issue in the relations of Jews and Christians.

A. Some Christians, after Paul and Matthew, took extreme positions on the importance of the Jewish Law (extreme from the perspective of most other Christians).
   1. Some Christians of the second century, known as the *Ebionites*, took the position of Matthew to a logical conclusion: Anyone who wants to be a follower of Jesus needs first to become Jewish and follow all the dictates of the Jewish Law.
   2. Other Christians of the second century, known as the *Marcionites*, took the position of Paul to a logical conclusion: Because salvation comes only by believing in Jesus, the Law has no role in salvation. In fact, the God of the Law is not the same as the God of Jesus.
B. Most Christians accepted neither of these two options. Instead, they understood the Jewish Scriptures as a revelation from the Jewish God, on the one hand, but as the Scripture of Christians, who were principally Gentiles and did not follow the scriptural laws, on the other. This led to some serious and difficult issues:
   1. Why would and how could Christians hold onto the Jewish Scriptures, the Old Testament, and claim it as their own, if in fact, they did not follow its laws?
   2. How could they explain that the Scripture was theirs—these people who didn't follow its laws—when Jewish communities continued to exist and thrive, communities of historical Jews who did keep its laws?
   3. These issues became instrumental in the antagonisms between Jews and Christians in the early centuries, as both claimed to be heirs of the same religious traditions yet stood at odds with each other.
   4. Two mainline positions were taken on these issues by various Christians in the second and third centuries.
III. The first position maintained that the Jewish Scriptures, called now the Old Testament, foreshadowed and predicted the New Testament and Jesus. The New, therefore, supersedes the Old, so that the Old can be done away with, except insofar as it is used to show the prognostication and prophecy of the fulfillment of God's promises. But it has no ongoing validity of its own on its own terms.

A. As a representative of this view, we can consider the writings of the second-century *apologist* (that is, "defender of the faith") Justin of Rome, known to history as Justin Martyr.

    1. Justin was one of the first serious intellectuals to convert to Christianity in its early years.

    2. Born and raised in Samaria, he converted to Christianity, then moved to Rome, where he set up a kind of school of instruction in the Christian philosophy.

    3. He was eventually turned over to the authorities as a Christian believer during one of the persecutions and was martyred then for his faith.

    4. He wrote numerous works, of which three survive: two defenses of the faith (*apologies*) and one attack on Jewish understandings of their own Law from a Christian perspective, in which he argues that the Law predicts Christ and has been misunderstood by the Jews themselves.

B. This book is called the *Dialogue with Trypho*. It is set up as an actual debate that Justin allegedly had with a Jewish philosopher and teacher, Trypho, probably some time around the year 135 (and written about 20 years later).

C. In it, we see Justin's Christian understanding of the Old Testament and Judaism.

    1. In arguing against his Jewish opponent about circumcision, the sign of the covenant God had given Jews to make them his special people, Justin argues that circumcision cannot really be needed for righteousness, because the Old Testament tells of men who were righteous before the law of circumcision was given to Moses (such as Enoch and Noah).

    2. Therefore, God must have given Jews the sign of circumcision to separate them from all others, for punishment.

    3. The same is true of the other laws of Moses. These cannot be necessary for a right standing before God, because the Jewish forefathers living before Moses had such standing without the Law. These laws were, therefore, given to Jews because they are a recalcitrant people who needed to be kept in line until the savior, Christ, came.

    4. According to Justin, Christ is already revealed in the Old Testament, but Jews are blinded to his presence. In fact, he is there in the very beginning, at the Creation, when God says, "Let *us* make man." God, in Genesis, is speaking to Christ.

IV. An even stronger line was taken in an anonymous work known today as the Epistle of Barnabas, which argues that the Old Testament is not and never was a Jewish book. It was a Christian book, which the Jews have misunderstood from the beginning.

   A. This anonymous book was attributed to "Barnabas," writing around 130 A.D. in Alexandria, Egypt

   B. His book is designed to show Christians that they should not be tempted to join up with the Jewish community, because their Scriptures are in fact Christian, not Jewish.

   1. He maintains that from the beginning, Jews broke their covenant with God (literally: when Moses smashed the tablets of the Ten Commandments when he saw the children of Israel committing idolatry with the Golden Calf).

   2. They were then misled into interpreting their laws literally, when in fact, they were meant to be taken figuratively.

   3. Barnabas then goes through the key laws of Scripture—laws for kosher foods, Sabbath observance, Temple worship, circumcision—and shows that when interpreted figuratively, they point to Christ.

   4. The Jews, with their literal interpretations, have missed the point all along and are not and have never been the people of God. It is the Christians who are God's people, and the Old Testament is their book.

V. To later historians, it may seem strange that Christians would want to take over the book containing the laws of another religion, claim that book for their own, while self-consciously deciding not to follow its laws. Why would they want to keep this book if they did not want to keep its laws? And how did that affect their relations with Jews who were not Christians? We will address those questions in the lecture that follows.

Essential Reading:
John Carroll, *Constantine's Sword.*
Bart Ehrman, *After the New Testament*, chapter 5.

John Gager, *The Origins of Anti-Semitism.*

Rosemary Ruether, *Faith and Fratricide: The Theological Roots of Anti-Semitism.*

Supplementary Reading:

Claudia Sezter, *Jewish Responses to Early Christians.*

Jeffrey Siker, *Disinheriting the Jews.*

Questions to Consider:

1. How do you imagine a second-century Jew might have responded to Justin's claim that the entire point of the Old Testament was to anticipate the coming of Christ?

2. In your judgment, is it possible to claim that the Old Testament is a book for Christians rather than for Jews without being anti-Semitic?

Lecture Seven—Transcript
The Anti-Jewish Use of the Old Testament

In the previous lecture, we began to ask the key historical question about the relationship of Christianity and Judaism. If Christianity started out as a sect within Judaism, beginning with Jesus himself, how and why did it become such a virulently anti-Jewish religion within just a century or so of its inception? We saw that even among the New Testament writers, there were radically different understandings of the relationship of this new faith in Christ to the Jewish Law.

At this point, I want to make sure that we're on the same page when I'm talking about the Jewish Law. The Jewish Law is the law given to Moses by God on Mount Sinai as reported in the pages of the Hebrew Bible, the Old Testament. The term "law" itself sometimes refers specifically to these laws God gave Moses, which include the Ten Commandments, but also a large number of other commandments about how the Jews were to live in community with one another, and how they were to worship God. The term "law" can also refer to the books in which those laws are recorded. Those would be the books of the Pentateuch, the first five books of the Hebrew Bible—Genesis, Exodus, Leviticus, Numbers, and Deuteronomy—sometimes simply called "the Law," sometimes called the Torah, which is the Hebrew term for "law."

When we talk about the Jewish Law in relationship to Jews, or in relationship to Christians, then, we can be using it in any of these senses. Specifically, when we're referring to the "Testament" view of the Law, we are referring to how the New Testament writers related to the laws themselves given to Moses on Mount Sinai. We saw that there were radically different views of the Jewish Law within the pages of the New Testament itself.

The Gospel of Matthew, for example, stressed the importance of the ongoing observance of the Law, as given by God, so that the followers of Jesus, like Jesus himself, were to do all that the Law commanded. Not just the Ten Commandments, but the entire Law, according to Matthew. "Not one letter, not one small part of a letter, will pass away from the law until all is fulfilled," said Jesus.

Moreover, the one who kept these laws down to their smallest detail would be the ones who would be called "great" in the kingdom of heaven. Those who didn't keep the laws would be called "least" in the kingdom of heaven.

Matthew insisted that Jesus's followers keep the Jewish Law. That stands in some contrast with the apostle Paul, who stressed that salvation came to all people, Jew and Gentile, based on the death and Resurrection of Jesus Christ, not based on doing what the Law commanded. Paul, in fact, maintained in his letter to the Galatians that "it is an affront to God and his Christ for non-Jews to keep the Jewish Laws."

Once again, I want to make sure that we're on the same page. When Paul said that Gentile Christians were not to keep the Law, he did not mean that Gentiles should be lawless. He didn't urge them, for example, to break the Ten Commandments. If the Commandment said, "Do not murder," Paul didn't say, "You can't keep that law; therefore, you should murder."

Paul does indicate, though, that Christians should not follow some of the laws found in the Jewish Scriptures. Well, how did Paul differentiate between which laws should be kept and which laws should not be kept? Unfortunately, Paul did not tell us exactly how he differentiated among the laws, but it does appear that Paul seemed to think that there were some laws that were universal for everybody. For example: Do not murder, do not commit adultery, do not bear false witness.

There were other laws, though, that were not for everybody, Jew and Gentile. There were other laws that were just for Jews, laws that make Jews Jewish. What kind of laws would those be?

Well, Paul didn't spell it out, but it does appear that he meant such laws as the laws of circumcision, where Jews would circumcise their baby boys on the eighth day, to show that they had become members of the covenant of God. There were laws of Sabbath observance: "Keep the Sabbath day holy." Laws of kosher: You were not to eat shellfish, pork, or certain other kinds of foods. These were laws that Jewish people understood, and were given in order to make them Jewish, as part of their covenant with God. Paul was insistent that Gentile Christians who came to believe in Christ were not to keep these laws. Laws of circumcision, and Sabbath, and kosher foods.

That isn't the same thing as saying, by the way, that Paul thought that Christians should only keep the Ten Commandments and nothing else, because one of the Ten Commandments is, in fact, Sabbath observance. Paul therefore did not differentiate the Ten Commandments from the other

Jewish laws. He thought the Christians should not be observing the Sabbath the way the Jews should, or probably, that's what he thought. He certainly thought that Christians should not be circumcised unless they were Jewish, since the law was so intimately connected with Jewish identity in the ancient world.

The developing understanding of the importance of the Law for Christians became a central issue in the relationships of Jews and Christians in antiquity. Some Christians after Paul and after Matthew took extreme positions on the importance of the Jewish Law, extreme, at least, from the perspective of most other Christians.

Some Christians in the second century known as the *Ebionites* (this is a group of Christians that we will be talking about a later lecture) took a position that was closely related to Matthew's. In fact, they took Matthew's position that everybody should keep the Law to a logical conclusion. These Ebionites, who were Jewish Christians, Christians who maintained their own Jewish identity, argued that if anyone wanted to be a follower of Jesus, they needed first to become Jewish, and to follow all the dictates of the Jewish Law. For these Ebionite Christians, being Christian meant being Jewish, and they had a certain logic behind their view.

Their logic was that Jesus was the Jewish Messiah, who was sent from the Jewish God in fulfillment of the Jewish Law to the Jewish people. If one was to accept the Jewish Messiah, one had to become Jewish. Therefore, Christians were to keep the Law. This was taking Matthew's logic to an extreme.

On the other end of the spectrum, there was another group of Christians in the second century who were known as *Marcionites*. These Marcionites, or followers of a man named Marcion, took the position of Paul to a logical conclusion. They argued that since salvation came only by believing in Jesus, and not by keeping the Law, the Law had no role in salvation at all. In fact, according to them, the Law was not related either to salvation, to Christ, or to the God who sent Christ.

Well, how could the God of Jesus have no relationship to the Jewish Law? These Marcionites maintained that there was a distinction between the Law of the Jews and the gospel of Christ. There was a distinction there because there was a distinction between the God of the Jews and the God of Jesus Christ. Marcionites maintained that there were two different Gods: A God of the Old Testament, and a God of Jesus. Christians were those who followed the God of Jesus, and rejected the God of the Old Testament. Therefore, they rejected the Old Testament Law.

These were two extremes in the understanding of Christians' relationships to the Law. On the one hand, the Ebionites said that Christians had to become Jewish and keep all the laws, and on the other hand, the Marcionites said the Christians were to reject the Law, and the God who gave the Law.

Most Christians in the second and third centuries accepted neither of these two options. Instead, most Christians understood the Jewish Scriptures as a revelation from the Jewish God on the one hand—these laws did come from the Jewish God—but also as the Scripture of the Christians who were principally Gentiles, and therefore did not need to follow the scriptural laws, especially the laws that made Jews Jewish.

This understanding that God had given the Law, and yet Christians did not have to keep all of the laws, naturally led to several serious and difficult issues. For example, why would and how could Christians hold onto the Jewish Scriptures, the Old Testament, claim it as their own Scripture, if, in fact, they didn't follow its laws? What where they thinking? How could they claim, "These are our Scriptures, these are our sacred books," and yet not follow the laws in them? It's a difficult question that we will need to explore. How could these Christians explain that the Scriptures were theirs—we're talking about people who didn't follow the laws—when there were Jewish communities still in existence and thriving, communities of historical Jews who did keep the laws? In other words, these Jews had Scripture, and they kept the laws. Christians claimed the same Scripture, but didn't keep the laws. How did Christians explain that?

These issues became instrumental in the antagonisms between Jews and Christians in the early centuries, as both groups claimed to be heirs to the same religious traditions, yet stood at odds with one another.

Two mainline positions were taken on these various issues by various Christians in the second century. I've already laid out what the two extremes were: the Ebionites and the Marcionites. There were two mainstream positions, two mainline positions that were taken by Christians that we will look at in the rest of this lecture.

The first position maintained that the Jewish Scriptures—which Christians were now calling the Old Testament—foreshadowed and predicted the New Testament and Jesus. Again, this first position was that the Old Testament foreshadowed the New Testament and Jesus. The New Testament, therefore, superseded the Old, so that the Old could be done away with, except insofar as it was used to show the prophecy of God's promises. The

Old Testament was useful because it prophesied what actually happened with Christ, but had no ongoing validity on its own terms, because its value was being shadowed to represent the reality that was to come, a prophecy that was to show the fulfillment that was to come. Therefore, the Old Testament was superseded by the New, and therefore, had no independent worth.

As representative of this particular view, we can consider the writings of the second century author, a very famous second century author, known as Justin of Rome, more commonly known to history as Justin Martyr. In this case, "Martyr" was not his last name. "Martyr" was his fate. After he was martyred for his Christian beliefs, he became know to history as "Justin Martyr."

Justin was one of the first serious intellectuals to convert to Christianity in its early years. We don't know when he was born. He was thriving in Rome in the middle of the second century, around the year 150. He had been born and raised in Samaria, in ancient Palestine. He wasn't born to a Christian family. He converted as an adult, and then moved to Rome, where he set up a kind of school of instruction in the Christian philosophy, and so Justin was one of the very first Christian philosophers, an intellectual who converted to the faith. Eventually, Justin was turned over to the authorities as a Christian believer during one of the persecutions, and he was martyred, then, for his faith, hence his nickname.

Justin wrote numerous works, of which three now survive. Two of the three that survive are books that are called *apologies*. We will be talking about Christian apologies later on in this course. I should say now that the term *apology* in this context doesn't mean saying, "I'm sorry." These were not Christians who were apologizing, saying that they were sorry they were Christian, and they would try to do better next time. The word "apology" comes from the Greek word *apologia*, which means "defense." Apologies are defenses of Christianity, intellectually reasoned defenses of faith against their cultured despisers. Two of Justin's apologies survive that are still available now, and you can read them in English translation; very interesting books. We will be looking at some of what he says later during this course.

Of greater relevance for us in this lecture is his third book. This third book is an attack on Jewish understandings of their own law from a Christian perspective, in which Justin argues that the law predicts Christ, and has been misunderstood by the Jews themselves. This third book is called *Dialogue with Trypho*. The book is set up as an actual debate that Justin allegedly had with a Jewish philosopher or teacher whose name was

Trypho. He records this as an actual debate that transpired probably some 20 years before the book itself was written, so that this may have been an actual conversation that he had with Trypho around the year 135. The book itself was written in 155.

The book proceeds autobiographically. Justin begins by saying that he was out for a walk, and as he was walking, somebody observed him, and came up to talk to him. It was a man who had several other people with him, and the man introduced himself as a philosopher who was living in Corinth, whose name was Trypho, and he was Jewish. This started a conversation between Justin and Trypho on the validity of Judaism and the Jewish Law.

The account, of course, was written by Justin, and so even though there is a back and forth in this book, where Trypho will say something and develop a case, and Justin will say something and develop a case, you're hearing Trypho's side, but you're only hearing it from Justin's point of view, so as it ends up, of course, Justin looks like he gets the upper hand, but he was the one who did the writing. This is a typical form of reporting a philosophical debate in the ancient world that you are probably familiar with, Plato's *Dialogue*, in which Socrates has a confrontation with somebody, and they have a long debate about the meaning of a term or concept, and Socrates always looks better than the other guy, but it's because he was writing it. The other guy was not writing it. Well, that is the kind of thing you get here in the *Dialogue with Trypho*.

In this book, whether or not we can see the historical Trypho's position about what Judaism is all about, we can certainly see Justin's understanding of the Old Testament and Judaism. Here, I will simply talk about some of the main points that are germane to the topic of this lecture.

In arguing against his Jewish opponent about the Jewish Law, Justin focused at one point on the law of circumcision. Circumcision was given to the people of Israel, according to the Hebrew Bible, in order to show that they were the people of the covenant. How you know that a Jew is a member of the covenant of God? Well, circumcision is a sign of the covenant, and so Jews have kept circumcision to show that they stand in a special covenantal relationship with God. Justin wanted to argue that, in fact, circumcision was not necessary for a right standing before God, and that Jews are wrong for thinking that it is. Justin mounted several arguments for this. One argument that probably has occurred to you already is that if circumcision is the sign somebody is in a right relationship with God, doesn't that leave out half the human race? Women aren't circumcised. Surely, then, circumcision isn't an indication of a right standing before God.

Moreover, Justin pointed out that there are people recorded in the Hebrew Bible as being right before God who were not circumcised. The laws of circumcision were given under Moses. What about people living before Moses? The Law of Moses is found in the second of the five books of the Torah, Exodus. Exodus tells the story of Moses saving the children of Israel from slavery in Egypt, and then being given the Law on Mount Sinai. In the second part of Exodus, Leviticus, Numbers, and Deuteronomy, you have records of these laws being given.

Well, what about the first book of the Torah, Genesis? There were plenty of people in Genesis who were right before God: Abel, the son of Adam; Enoch, who was so righteous that God took him up into heaven without ever dying; Abraham, the father of the Jews, who made right with God because he believed in God, and it was recounted to him as righteousness. These people were made right with God without circumcision. Therefore, circumcision could not a requirement for being right with God. Well, why then was circumcision given?

Justin had an answer, an answer that was no doubt not very pleasing to Trypho or to other Jews of his day. According to Justin, circumcision was given in order to mark Jews off separately from all other peoples, but they were marked off not to show that they were members of God's special community, but were marked off to show who the people who were deserving of punishment. You can see that this was a point of view that was quite anti-Jewish, and that could eventually lead to serious anti-Semitic views.

Justin said, (I'm quoting from the *Dialogue with Trypho*, chapter 16):

> Indeed, the custom of circumcising the flesh, handed down from Abraham, was given to you as a distinguishing mark, to set you off from other nations, and from us Christians. The purpose of this was that you and only you might suffer the afflictions that are now justly yours.

When he says "the afflictions that are justly yours," this thing was written in the year 135. That's a significant moment in Jewish history, because it was the end of the second uprising against Rome. Jews in Palestine rebelled against the Roman Empire, wanting to set up their own sovereign state, and the Roman legions marched against the Jewish armies, and devastated them, destroyed them, kicked the Jews out of Jerusalem, and did not allow the

Jews to return to Jerusalem. Justin was saying that the circumcision was to set Jews apart for this punishment. "Therefore, the above-mentioned tribulations are justly imposed upon you. Why? Because you murdered the just one."

Meaning that these Jews murdered Jesus, and God now had imposed punishment on them. Jews were being portrayed as Christ-killers, an accusation against Jews that continued, of course, on down through the Middle Ages, and have led to very ugly acts of anti-Semitism ever since.

Circumcision, then, was not given to show that these were the special people of God, but was given or to show which people God had set apart for punishment.

According to Justin, Christ was the one who was revealed in the Old Testament, and the point of the Old Testament was to prophesy Christ. He shows that throughout the Old Testament you can, in fact, find instances of Christ appearing, even though Jesus had not been born yet. Christ was there as the pre-existent being who was with God in the past.

In the account of the book of Genesis, when God is creating the world, he decides to create humans. What does he say? "Let us make man, and make him in our own image." Who is God talking to, exactly? Well, he's talking to Christ, the pre-existent Christ who was with God at the beginning of the creation.

Throughout the Old Testament, according to Justin, one finds passages in which Christ is referred to. The Old Testament, then, is not simply a book for Jews. It is book for Christians because it is prophesying, pointing ahead, to the coming of Christ into the world.

That's Justin's *Dialogue with Trypho*. Now, that sounds like a fairly strong line to take on the Hebrew Bible, the Old Testament, but in fact, the second position I want to talk about is even stronger. The second position doesn't only indicate that the Old Testament is valid in that it points forward to Christ. The second position argues that the Old Testament never was, and still is not a Jewish book at all. The Hebrew Scriptures, or the Old Testament, in fact, from this point of view, is a Christian book. This stronger line is taken by an anonymous work known today as the Epistle of Barnabas. The Epistle of Barnabas argues that the Old Testament is not and never was a Jewish book. It was a Christian book that the Jews have misunderstood from the beginning.

The Epistle of Barnabas was allegedly written by Barnabas, who was a companion of the apostle Paul. In fact, the book is anonymous. We don't know who really wrote it. It certainly was not written by Barnabas, because it wasn't written until about 130 or 135, again, around the time that Justin had his *Dialogue with Trypho*.

The book is designed to show Christians that they should not be tempted to join up with a Jewish community, because the Scriptures, in fact, don't belong to the Jewish community. They belong to the Christian community. The anonymous author maintains that from the beginning, Jews broke their covenant with God, and in fact, they broke it in quite a literal way. He points out that in the Hebrew Bible, when Moses went up on Mount Sinai, and received the Ten Commandments on the two tablets, he was up on the mountain for a long time, but then God said that he needed to go down, because the people were committing idolatry.

He went down the mountain, and saw the children of Israel worshipping a golden calf. What did he do with the two tablets with the Law on them? He threw them down and smashed them to smithereens. For Barnabas, this was something that actually happened, and it showed that the covenant that God had made with Moses on Mount Sinai was immediately broken and smashed, and in fact, was never reinstated. Jews then took the laws that were subsequently given to Moses in an incorrect way, not knowing any better, because they were not members of the true covenant, since they had broken the covenant.

How did they take laws incorrectly? They were misled by an evil angel into thinking that the laws God gave were to be taken literally rather than figuratively, but in fact, according to Barnabas, these laws were not to be taken literally. They were figurative representations of how one ought to behave.

Thus, what Barnabas did through most of the letter was to go through the laws that God gave the children of Israel, and showed that, in fact, they are misunderstood if taken literally. He took the laws that made Jews Jewish. For example: The kosher food laws, Sabbath, circumcision, etc.

I will give you a couple of examples. From chapter 10 of the Epistle Barnabas, there are some very interesting interpretations of the kosher food law. Moses commands in the law that the people of Israel were not to eat pork. Well, why not in fact eat pork? It's not a literal command that you're not to have a pork chop or ham sandwich. Barnabas explains: "Accordingly, Moses mentioned that you are not to eat swine, for this reason. You must not associate," he says, "with such people, people who are like swine. That is, when they are well-off, they forget the Lord, but when they are in need, they acknowledge the Lord, just as the swine ignores its owner when it is feeding, but when it is hungry, it starts to squeal, and fall silent only after being fed again."

You know how pigs and hogs behave. They make a lot of noise, and they get fed. When they get fed, then, they are silent. Don't be like that. "Don't eat pig" means "don't behave that way, as a pig," where you come to God only when you are in need of something. It is a figurative interpretation. Moses commands, "You shall not eat the hyena." Well, why not eat the hyena? Moses is commanding that you should not become an adulterer, or seducer, or even resemble such people. Why? "Because this animal, the hyena," Barnabas says, "changes its nature from year to year, and it becomes male one time and female another time." One year, the hyena is male, and the next year, it's female, so you should not be like that and be a seducer or an adulterer. That's what he means.

He also hated the weasel, Barnabas tells us. Why not eat the weasel? Well, in fact, the Old Testament doesn't say, "don't eat the weasel," but Barnabas is on a roll here, and he wants to indicate why you don't want to behave like a weasel. "Moses also hated the weasel with good reason. Do not become," he says, "like those people whom we hear, with immoral intent, do things with the mouth that are forbidden, nor associate with those immoral women who do things with the mouth that are forbidden, for this animal conceives through its mouth." In other words, the commandment not to eat the weasel is a commandment not to engage in oral sex.

Well, he goes on, and has lots of other laws that he gives explanations for. Let me just take one other example, getting away from kosher food, the big law on circumcision. What is circumcision all about? Once again, Barnabas wants to insist that this is not a literal law to be taken literally. God is not commanding Jews to circumcise their baby boys on the eighth day. Instead, it is something else altogether.

Barnabas points out that the first instance of circumcision in the Hebrew Bible is with the father of the Jews, Abraham, who was going out to rescue his nephew Lot, in the book of Genesis. He had been taken captive by some foreign kings, and before he went out to recapture Lot, Abraham circumcised 318 servants of his household. It's a very strange story, in Genesis 14 and Genesis 17. Why, in this first instance of circumcision, does he circumcise 318 people? Barnabas thinks that this is a symbolic number. In Greek, the language Barnabas is writing in, "318" is made with the letters

Iota, Eta, Tau. That's how you write out "318" in Greek. Each of these letters has a numerical value. The letter Iota (I) is 10, the letter Eta (H) is 8, that is 18, and the letter Tau (T) is 300. Well, what is that all about?

Barnabas points out that Iota-Eta (IH), 18, are the first two letters in the name "Jesus," "IHSOYS." The letter Tau looks like our letter "T"—in other words, it's in the form of a cross. Circumcision is really the cross of Jesus. It's not a literal cutting of the flesh. It is a foreshadowing of what is to come when Jesus is the one who brings true salvation. Well, Barnabas concludes this little lesson on circumcision by saying, "No one has ever learned from me a more reliable lesson, but I know that you are worthy," so he's rather pleased with this little interpretation of the numerical value of circumcision.

Well, these, then, are two different views. One, that the Old Testament foreshadowed the new, and is no longer of any independent importance, and the other that the Old Testament was, and is, in fact, a Christian, not a Jewish book, to be interpreted figuratively as a revelation of Christ.

To later historians, it may seem strange that Christians would want to take over this Jewish book containing the laws of another religion, and claim that the book was their own, while at the same time self-consciously deciding not to follow its laws. Why would they want to take over this book if they did not want to keep its laws, and how did that affect their relationship with Jews who were not Christians? These are the kinds of questions we'll be addressing in the lecture that follows.

Lecture Eight
The Rise of Christian Anti-Judaism

Scope: This lecture explores the social and historical situation that led to the rejection of Judaism by many Christians of the early centuries. Most Jews could not accept the Christian belief that a crucified criminal was, in fact, the powerful Messiah of God and rejected the Christian claim that Jesus's death was in accordance with the Scriptures. This led to a split between the two religions. Yet Christians claimed the Jewish Scriptures as their own—even as they refused to follow many of its laws—in part because in the ancient world, no religion would be taken seriously if it could not claim for itself ancient roots, and without the Jewish Scriptures, Christianity would be perceived as an "innovation" rather than a serious religion.

The polemical stakes were quite high, as evident in the writings of Melito of Sardis, a Christian bishop from the end of the second century who preached a sermon that proclaimed, for the first time on record, that Jews were guilty of "murdering God."

Outline

I.   To this point of our lectures, we have seen some of the views of Judaism in evidence among several key figures in the development of early Christianity: the historical Jesus, the apostle Paul, the author of Matthew, Justin Martyr, and Barnabas.

   A.   One of the important issues in the rise of an anti-Jewish attitude among Christians was the claim to the Jewish Scriptures: To whom do they belong, Jews or Christians? What does it mean for Christians to accept the Scriptures if they refuse to adhere to its laws?

   B.   We have not yet considered at any length why Christians wanted to hold on to these sacred books of the Jews and to consider them their own. That question is part of what we will address in this lecture.

   C.   In particular, we will build on the literary views of Christians, found in such texts as Justin's *Dialogue with Trypho* and the letter of Barnabas, in order to reconstruct something of the *historical* relations between Christians and Jews in the early centuries. What can we say about the actual social interactions between these two groups?

II. Our earliest records indicate that there were harsh and bitter conflicts among social groups of Christians and non-Christian Jews from the outset.

    A. Even in the New Testament, both the Book of Acts and the apostle Paul indicate that Jews rejected the Christian message and persecuted the Christians who proclaimed it.

        1. Paul is a particularly important witness in this development, because he indicates that before his conversion to become a follower of Jesus, he himself was a Jewish persecutor of Christians.

        2. Later, as a Christian, his letters indicate that he suffered violence at the hands of non-Christian Jews.

        3. This coincides well with what we read in the Book of Acts about early Christian persecution—it always came at the hands of Jews.

        4. It is not difficult to understand why: Christians were seen as a troublesome, rabble-rousing, and outspoken minority with completely unacceptable views.

    B. At the same time, we must acknowledge that in the middle of the first century, before the books of the New Testament were written, Christianity was still recognized as a Jewish sect.

        1. The Roman authorities, in any event, did not differentiate between Christian Jews and non-Christian Jews

        2. This is evident in an event during the reign of Emperor Claudius (c. 49 A.D.), in which he cast the Jews, both Christian and non-Christian, from Rome (without differentiating between them).

    C. Some years later, however, Roman authorities did differentiate between the two groups, as is evident in the first persecution of Christians at the hands of an emperor, Nero's punishment of Christians for arson in Rome—where he singled out Christians, not Jews, for torture.

D. Further indications of a separation of Christians from Jews came soon thereafter in the Jewish uprising against the Romans in Palestine, leading to a three-year war and the ultimate destruction of Jerusalem and the Temple in the year 70 C.E. Old traditions indicate that Christian Jews refused to participate in the struggle.

E. By the end of the first century, Christianity had moved from being a persecuted sect within Judaism to being a separate religion from Judaism.

III. The separate existence of Christianity as a distinct religion led to heightened hostilities between the two groups, because in the face of a predominantly pagan world, both groups had to claim legitimacy or face opposition.

A. Jews were, by and large, tolerated throughout the Greco-Roman world and, in fact, had been extended special privileges by imperial authorities, who respected the fact that they represented such an ancient and venerable religion.

B. Once Christianity separated from its mother religion, it no longer enjoyed such protection. It was subject to problems of legitimation of its own.

    1. If religious legitimation came on the basis of ancient tradition, and Christianity was a religion that had begun just recently, then it was easily subject to the charge of being a troublesome innovation.

    2. Christians were compelled to argue that their religion was ancient, in fact, that it was older than any of the pagan religions, even older than Judaism.

    3. How could Christians make such a claim, when Jesus had lived and died so recently? They argued that their religion was the true fulfillment of the Jewish Scriptures; that Moses and the prophets had predicted Christ; that from the foundations of the Earth, it was the Christians and the Christians alone who had the truth.

    4. This naturally led to heightened antagonisms with Jews, who maintained their own laws and customs based on these Scriptures, and who could point out that Christians refused to do so. To protect themselves, Christians attacked the Jews as representing a false religion. The result was some of the comments we have already seen in Justin and Barnabas.

IV. A further result was the even more exaggerated and vitriolic polemic we find in the writings of a later figure significant for the conflict between Jews and Christians, Melito of Sardis.

    A. Melito was a Christian bishop in Asia Minor in the late second century.

    B. For years, we had none of his major writings, but in the 1940s, a sermon was discovered that he had written and delivered.

    C. It is a sermon that was preached on Easter during the Jewish feast of the Passover, which uses the Passover (Exodus) story of the Old Testament to show that the entire account prefigured none other than Jesus.

    D. Melito then uses the occasion to bemoan the fact that this one who had been predicted in the Jewish Scriptures had come to be rejected by the Jewish people. The Jews, in fact, rejected their own Messiah. More than that, for Melito, because Jesus is God, the Jews have rejected God.

    E. In fact, because they were responsible for executing Jesus, the Jews are guilty of killing God. This is the first instance we have of the charge of deicide in the conflicts of Christians against Jews.

V. At this point of the history of Jewish-Christian relations (late second century), such polemic was little more than a defensive posturing by a tiny minority splinter group with no real power. Christians were scattered and politically innocuous.

    A. That was to change over time, as numbers of pagans began to join the fold, and eventually, Christians began to assume positions of authority. I will give a fuller account of how that happened in a later lecture. For now, I can simply give some figures.

        1. Christians made up maybe two to three percent of the empire near the end of the second century; by the beginning of the fourth century, maybe five to seven percent.

        2. But then the Roman emperor Constantine converted (as we will see more fully later), and that changed everything. Massive conversions transpired, including of the elite classes in the empire; thus, by the end of the fourth century, nearly half the empire was Christian.

3. Constantine made Christianity a legal, even favored religion. One of his later successors, Theodosius, made it the official state religion at the end of the fourth century.

B. With the success of Christians came the persecution of the Jews, as later Christians in power took the rhetoric of their weak predecessors seriously and treated Jews as those who were opposed to God and his Messiah.
   1. During Constantine's day, there were no officially sanctioned acts of violence against Jews.
   2. There were, however, plenty of instances in which officials looked the other way when synagogues were burned or properties were confiscated.

VI. With the victory of Christianity came a serious heightening of anti-Jewish polemic, with Judaism being seen as a false religion; further, this polemic was backed by imperial power. Thus, Jews moved from being a highly respected religious community to being an economically handicapped, socially ostracized, and persecuted minority in the empire—the ignominious situation Jews found themselves in throughout the Middle Ages and down to modern times.

Essential Reading:

John Carroll, *Constantine's Sword*.

Bart Ehrman, *After the New Testament*, chapter 5.

John Gager, *The Origins of Anti-Semitism*.

Rosemary Ruether, *Faith and Fratricide: The Theological Roots of Anti-Semitism*.

Supplementary Reading:

Claudia Sezter, *Jewish Responses to Early Christians*.

Questions to Consider:

1. Is there a difference, in your opinion, between harsh polemic produced by a weak and defenseless outcast group and the same polemic invoked by a socially and politically powerful group? Or is it all the same?

2. In your judgment, would we have had the modern history of anti-Semitism apart from the rise and conquest of Christianity?

Lecture Eight—Transcript
The Rise of Christian Anti-Judaism

To this point in our lectures, we have seen some of the views of Judaism in evidence among several key figures in the development of early Christianity: the historical Jesus, the apostle Paul, the author of Matthew, Justin Martyr, and Barnabas. One of the important issues in the rise of an anti-Jewish attitude among Christians, as we have seen, was the claim to the Jewish Scriptures. To whom do they belong, Jews or Christians? What does it mean for Christians to accept the Scriptures as their own if they refuse to adhere to its laws?

We have not yet considered at any length why Christians wanted to hold onto these sacred books of the Jews and to consider them their own. That is part of what will be doing in the present lecture. We will be setting this question, however, into a broader context. Up until now, we have been considering the literary Christians, in other words, the views spelled out in their books, literary perspectives. These books indicate what Christians thought about non-Christian Jews. Now though, we want to consider how Christians actually interacted with Jews in their social lives. We want to move away, in other words, from literary portrayals of Jews and Christians in order to reconstruct something of the actual social historical relations between Christians and Jews in the early centuries. The key question we will be asking in this lecture, then, is: What can we say about the real-life social interactions between these two groups, Jews and Christians?

Our earliest records indicate that there were harsh and bitter among social groups of Christians and non-Christian Jews from the outset. I am trying to differentiate between non-Christian Jews and Christians, because, of course, there are some Jews who became Christians, so you have Jewish Christians, Gentile Christians, but you can also have non-Christian Jews.

Our earliest records indicate that there was conflict between non-Christian Jews and Christians. The earliest records happen to come from the New Testament. Even within the New Testament, both the Book of Acts (the Acts of the Apostles) and the writings of the apostle Paul indicate that Jews rejected the Christian message about Jesus and persecuted the Christians who proclaimed it. The earliest Christian persecutions, in fact, were at the hands of Jews. Paul is a particularly important witness in this development.

As he indicates, prior to his own conversion to become a follower of Jesus, he himself was a persecutor of Christians, while he was still Jewish. We get this indicated from Paul's own hand in the letter that he wrote to the Galatians. Galatians is one of those few letters in which Paul actually gives some autobiographical background to his life. He says in chapter 1, writing to the Galatians: "You have heard, no doubt, of my earlier life in Judaism," he says. "I advanced in Judaism among many of my people of my same age, for I was far more zealous for the traditions of my ancestors, and I was violently persecuting the church of God, and trying to destroy it."

This portrayal of Paul as a persecutor of the Christian church coincides with what we find in the Book of Acts. The Book of Acts is an account of the lives of the apostles after the ascension of Jesus. Its basic theme is that Christianity spread throughout the Roman world rapidly as the apostles took the message abroad. This spread of Christianity faced certain kinds of hardships along the way, one of which was persecution. We saw that in an earlier lecture, that in some respects, Acts is not a perfectly reliable historical source for us, but nonetheless, it does have historical accounts that do appear to be trustworthy. In this particular case, we have confirmation from what Paul himself said about his being a persecutor of Christians. Paul, by the way, uses two different names. "Paul" is the Greek name; "Saul" is his Hebrew name. In this account, in Acts, chapter 9, he's going under the name "Saul."

> Meanwhile, Saul [chapter 9, verse 1] still breathing threats and murder against the disciples of the Lord, went to the high priest of Jerusalem, and asked him for letters to the synagogues at Damascus, so that if he found anyone who belonged to the way [That's the ancient term for Christianity], men or women, he might bring them bound to Jerusalem.

Paul was going off to Damascus in order to find Christians, in order to bring them back to Jerusalem and have them stand trial. Both Paul himself in his letters, then, and the Book of Acts, concede while he was a non-Christian Jew, Paul was persecuting the Christians.

Later, after Paul converted to Christianity, he gave an indication that he himself suffered violence at the hands of non-Christian Jews. This is a very interesting passage in Paul's writing. It is found in 2 Corinthians, chapter 11, in which Paul is talking about how it is that he is a chief apostle. He is trying to show that he is a better apostle than others, and the way he tries to show that he is a better apostle than others is by showing that he suffered more than others. The idea is that a real apostle will be like Jesus. Well, what happened to Jesus? He got crucified. Well, if you're going to be his follower, you too are going to suffer, and if you're not suffering, then you are obviously not really imitating Christ. Paul wants to show that he imitates Christ better than anyone.

> Are they [These are Christian opponents of his] ministers of Christ? I'm talking like a madman, [he says]. I am a better one, with far greater labors, far more imprisonments, with countless floggings, and often near death. Five times I have received from the Jews the forty lashes minus one.

What's that? Well, there was a law adopted in some circles that 40 lashes were excessive as a punishment, and therefore, if you wanted to get the full extent, you had 39 lashes. Paul said that he received this from the hands of the Jews, which must indicate that within the synagogues Paul preached in, he was sometimes taken out and fogged for his blasphemous views, views considered blasphemous. The point is, that is a synagogue form of punishment, according to Paul, so that Jews are actively trying to stamp out these people, these Jews who were saying that Jesus was the Messiah. This is an internal Jewish conflict at this point. It's Jews who believe in Jesus, and Jews who don't believe in Jesus. Those who do believe in Jesus are the small minority, being persecuted by the majority, who find the claims of these Christian Jews to be ludicrous.

In any event, this statement of Paul's in 2 Corinthians coincides well with the view found throughout the Book of Acts about early Christian persecution. The earliest persecutions always happened at the hands of Jews. It's not difficult to understand why this happened. Christianity started off as a Jewish sect, with Judaism, which saw Jesus as the Jewish Messiah, sent from the Jewish God, to the Jewish people, in fulfillment of the Jewish Law. These Christians remained within the Jewish synagogues for their worship, because they considered themselves still to be... They were, as they would call themselves, the "true" Jews, and they would try to convince others that they, too, should accept Jesus as the Messiah. But these views about Jesus were rejected by the vast majority of Jews. Those who were propounding these views of the Messiahship of Jesus were often seen as a troublesome and rabble-rousing group, an outspoken minority with completely unacceptable views.

Up until about the middle of the first century, before the books of the New Testament themselves had been written, Christianity was still viewed as a

Jewish sect, not just by Jews. This is something many people don't understand. They tend to think that once Christianity started, it was immediately separate from Judaism. In fact, it started out as Jewish, and continued as a Jewish sect up through a good part of the first century.

We have evidence for this outside of the New Testament itself, evidence from people who were not directly involved in the conflict. Roman authorities indicate that when they paid any attention at all to Christians, which was not often, because Christians were a very small group at the time—when Roman authorities did pay attention to Christians, they treated them as a sect of Judaism through the first part of the first century, not differentiating between Christian Jews and non-Christian Jews. The evidence comes from an episode referred to both by the Book of Acts, and by the Roman historian Suetonius, who had nothing to do with Christianity, and may not even have known much of anything at all about Christianity.

Suetonius was a historian writing in the early century, who wrote a number of biographies of the Roman emperors. In one of his biographies, on the Roman emperor Claudius, he described an event during Claudius's reign in the year 49 A.D. of the common era, in which he indicates that Claudius expelled the Jews from Rome at the instigation of riots caused by a man named "Chrestus." Well, that sounds an awful lot like "Christos," and so some scholars have thought that in fact this was referring to an episode referred to in the Book of Acts, in which Claudius kicked Jews out of Rome because there were conflicts between Jews and Christians over who Jesus was that had led to some disturbances, and to quell the disturbances, he simply kicked the whole lot of them out.

That would mean, though, that instead of just kicking the Christians out, he kicked all of the Jews out, so that he was not differentiating one kind of Jew from another kind of Jew, a messianic Jew from a non-messianic Jew. Around the year 50, then, 49-50, there was not a differentiation between Christians and Jews. Soon thereafter, though, there was a differentiation among the Roman officials between Christians and Jews. We have evidence of this from the writings of another Roman historian, a friend of Suetonius whose name was Tacitus.

Tacitus, also writing in the early second century, produced a history of Rome called the *Annals of Rome*, in which he describes historical events of some significance in the history of the city and the empire.

Tacitus, at one point, was discussing the Emperor Nero and the famous event that happened in the year 64 (15 years after this event I mentioned about Claudius). In the year 64, Rome burned. There were questions about why Rome burned. There were massive fires that destroyed a good part of the city. Tacitus, writing about 55 years after the event, claimed that, in fact, Nero was the one responsible for the fires in Rome. Evidently, according to Tacitus, Nero had some plans for the city of Rome, but he couldn't implement these architectural plans because the city of Rome was still standing, and so, in order to allow him to implement these plans, he had to have the city torched. A good part of the city was burned, and then, he could rebuild it the way he wanted to.

According to Tacitus, people suspected that it had been Nero himself responsible for these massive fires that had destroyed their businesses and their homes, and in order to get the blame taken off of himself, Nero needed to find a scapegoat, somebody he could blame for the fires, and as it turns out, he picked on the Christians as a group who were, as Tacitus says, "the hatred of the human race." Nobody liked the Christians, for reasons we will see in a later lecture.

They were therefore a likely scapegoat, and Nero blamed the Christians for starting the fire. He had them rounded up, and then he put them to awful public torment and torture, and killed these Christians as a way of blaming them for the arson that he himself had committed.

My point for this lecture is that Nero did not round up Jews. He rounded up Christians, which must mean that he knew enough to differentiate between the two. My conclusion is that Christians came to be seen as a separate social group sometime in the early second half of the first century, separate from Jews.

Further indications of a separation of Christians from Jews came soon thereafter in the Jewish uprising against the Romans in the year 66. There was an uprising in which Jews tried to drive out the Roman occupiers and set up their own independent state in Israel. It led to a three-and-a-half-year war that culminated with the destruction of Jerusalem, and the Temple in Jerusalem, in the year 70. There are old traditions that indicate that Christians who were living in Jerusalem at the time refused to fight with the Jews. They escaped and went elsewhere in order not to have to side with Jews. This would be a further indication that Christians were not understanding themselves as Jews supporting Jewish causes in the second half of the first century.

In any event, by the end of the first century, Christianity had moved from being a persecuted sect within Judaism to considering itself as something like a separate religion over against Judaism. There was a separation that was occurring in the second half of the first century. This separation, this separate existence of Christianity as a distinct religion, actually led to heighten hostilities between the two groups.

The reason it led to heightened hostility was because in the face of a predominantly pagan world, both groups, the non-Christian Jews and the Christians, whether Jewish or Gentile, had to claim legitimacy over against the rest of the world, or face opposition. Jews were by and large tolerated throughout the Greco-Roman world. In fact, Jews by and large had been extended special privileges by imperial authorities of Rome, who respected the fact that they represented such an ancient and venerable religion. Therefore, Jews were by and large exempted from certain obligations that were imposed on everybody else in the Roman Empire. For example, Jews were not forced to serve in the military. This was probably to the Romans' advantage as well, because if Jews took every seventh day off, and refused to participate in daily activities on the seventh day, they didn't make very good soldiers, and so, out of respect for the ancient Jewish traditions, they were exempt.

Then, however, Christianity came along, and claimed that it represented true Judaism, but most of the people in Christianity were not Jews. How were they going to have legitimacy in the face of the Roman Empire and in the face of their pagan neighbors? Once Christianity separated from its mother religion, Judaism, it no longer enjoyed the protection extended to Jews, and it was subject to problems of legitimation of its own. If religious legitimation came on the basis of ancient tradition in the world of antiquity—as it did, by the way; ancient people did not have our understanding of legitimacy. In the modern world, people are for things that are new, that are creative, that are inventive, that are imaginative. It was not that way in the ancient world. The ancient world valued antiquity. If something was true, it had to be old. If something was new, how could it be true? You mean everybody else got it wrong? That didn't make sense to people in antiquity. The way to establish the validity of a religion or philosophy, then, was to show that it was very old. Jews could do that. Even if you didn't agree with the Jews, or even if you didn't like the Jews, you would at least admit, "You've got a really old religion here." So that it was fine, it was protected.

Christianity came along, though, and it obviously was not ancient. Christianity worshipped Jesus, who was just around 100 years ago. It was a recent thing. How could Christians claim any kind of legitimation based on anything like ancient tradition if it was a recent innovation? Well, Christians were compelled to argue that, in fact, the religion was ancient. In fact, that it was older than any of the pagan religions, and that it was older, even, than Judaism. How can they possibly claim, though, that Christianity was older than anything in paganism, and older than anything in Judaism, if it had just started?

Well, Christians had an argument, and they pushed it quite hard. Christians argued that their religion, in fact, was the true fulfillment of the Jewish Scriptures, that Moses and the prophets had predicted Christ; that from the foundations of the Earth, it was the Christians, and the Christians alone who had the truth. We asked earlier: Why would the Christians want to claim the Jewish Bible as their own if they didn't keep its laws? Because by claiming that they were the true fulfillment of the Jewish Bible, they, in fact, had traditions supporting their religion to go back all way to Moses. Moses, by the way, lived 400 years before Homer, the author of the *Iliad* and the *Odyssey*. He lived 800 years before Plato, the great Greek philosopher. If you want to claim antiquity for your religion, and you can claim hold of Moses, then, in fact, you have antiquity. That's one of the reasons why Christians held onto the Jewish Scriptures, because it provided them with a means of legitimation in the face of opposition.

At the same time, this stance toward the Old Testament, the stance that we saw, for example, in both Justin Martyr and the Epistle of Barnabas, in which Christianity claims it as its own, naturally led to heightened antagonisms with Jews, who were still around, and who still claimed the Scriptures as their own, and who actually kept the laws and customs outlined in the Scriptures. They could also point out that the Christians, in fact, did not do so. In order to protect themselves from these attacks from Jews, who would say, "You don't even keep the Laws, so how can you claim these are your Scriptures?", Christians went on the counterattack and portrayed Jews as advocating a false religion. Therefore, we have seen some of the comments already in Justin and in Barnabas.

The kinds of comments we saw in Justin and Barnabas were obviously inflammatory toward Jews. We find it even more exaggerated in vitriolic polemic, when we come to the writings of a later figure in the conflict between Jews and Christians, a Christian bishop whose name was Melito. He was the bishop of a town in Asia Minor called Sardis, and so this person is commonly known as Melito of Sardis.

We don't know very much about Melito of Sardis, just a few references in ancient histories about him. In the 1940s, though, one of his writings was uncovered. It was a very important writing, and a strongly anti-Jewish writing. In fact, it is a sermon that Melito evidently preached at Easter (we're talking sometime near the end of the second century) during the Jewish festival of Passover. If you recall, Passover was and still is an annual Jewish feast in which Jews recall their deliverance from slavery in Egypt. The Jews had been captive in Egypt for hundreds of years until God raised up Moses. Moses brought them out of the land of Egypt, they escaped from the wrath of the Pharaoh, and they got away. Every year, Passover celebrates the Exodus from Egypt.

Christians, in some parts of the world, in the second century, celebrated their Easter festival during the Jewish Passover, because if you recall, in the Gospels, it is during Passover that Jesus was killed, and then he was raised from the dead three days later. This Easter sermon, then, that Melito preached is sometimes called his "Passover homily."

In the sermon, Melito used the Passover Exodus story of the Old Testament in order to show that the entire account of Passover prefigured none other than Jesus. The Passover feast is a meal still celebrated in which symbolic foods are eaten in order to commemorate this Exodus from Egypt. In the event itself, in the book of Exodus, Moses was told by God to perform these ten plagues against the Egyptians, so that they would be convinced to let the people of Israel go. Therefore, there were these ten plagues. The tenth plague was the death of the firstborn child. In the tenth plague that happened, Moses was instructed that all children of Israel were to slay a lamb, take the blood of the land, spread it on the door post of the houses they were in, because the angel of death was going to come at night and kill every firstborn child in Egypt. The angel, though, would see the blood on the door posts, on the lintel of the doors of the Israelites, and pass over those doors, and go to the next door neighbors', who didn't have the blood on the door, and kill the firstborn child there.

Moses did that, and so every year after that, they have this meal commemorating the event, which includes eating the Passover lamb; unleavened bread (because they didn't have time to let the bread rise, since they had had to escape that night); they ate bitter herbs (to remind them of the bitterness of slavery in Egypt). There were several symbolic foods.

Melito used the story in order to show that, in fact, it was Christ who was the one who was the true Passover lamb. Salvation came to the children of

Israel not simply because of killing a lamb, but this was foreshadowing Christ, who as a lamb was going to be sacrificed for the salvation of the world. Melito took the occasion of the sermon to bemoan the fact that this one, Christ, who had been predicted in the Scriptures, ended up becoming rejected by the Jewish people, even though their own Scriptures predicted him. The Jews, in fact, had rejected their own Messiah for Melito. More than that, since for Melito Jesus himself is God, by killing him, Jews have rejected God, and in fact, they have killed God.

This is a very powerful sermon, rhetorically very effective. Let me read some of the key passages:

> This is the lamb that was slain [He is referring to the lamb slain in the Passover account in the book of Exodus]; this is the lamb that was silent. This is the one who was born of Mary, the beautiful ewe lamb, the one taken from the flock, was dragged to sacrifice, killed in the evening, buried at night. This one was murdered, and where was he murdered? In the very center of Jerusalem. Why? Well, because he healed the lame and cleansed their lepers. He guided their blind with light. He raised up their dead. For this reason, he suffered.

He's asking, "Why did Jews do this? Because he did such good things for them, they killed him?"

> Why, oh Israel, did you do this strange injustice? You dishonored the one who had honored you. You held in contempt the one who had held you in esteem. You denied the one who publicly acknowledged you. You renounced the one who proclaimed you his own. You killed the one who made you to live. Why did you do this, oh Israel?

Well, these are very powerful rhetorical questions. He continues:

> Pay attention, oh families of the earth, and observe. An extraordinary murder has taken place in the center of Jerusalem, in the city devoted to God's Law, in the city of the Hebrews, in the city of the Prophets, in the city thought of as just. And who has been murdered? And who is the murderer? I am ashamed to give the answer, but give it I must. The one who hung the earth in space is himself hanged. The one who fixed the heavens in place is himself impaled. The one who firmly fixed all things is himself firmly fixed to the tree. The Lord is insulted. God has been

murdered. The king of Israel has been destroyed by the right hand of Israel.

To my knowledge, this is this is the first time that any Christian charges Jews not just with the death of Jesus, but with the death of God. Jews here are accused of committing deicide, the murder of God. At this point in Jewish-Christian relations, polemic such as this has to be seen, I think, as little more than defensive posturing by a tiny minority splinter group with no power. Melito had no power. He was an unknown bishop of a tiny little church in a remote part of the empire with no power to do anything about his ranting about Jews killing Christ. Christians, at his time, were scattered, and they were politically innocuous. They were being persecuted, and they had this kind of rhetoric as a way of defending themselves. That was to change over time as numbers of pagans began to join Christians, and eventually, Christians began to assume positions of authority. I am going to give an account of how that all happened in a later lecture. For now, let me just give you a couple of figures.

Probably about the time Melito is writing, at the end of the second century, Christianity comprised 2 or maybe 3 percent of the Roman Empire's population, by the end of the fourth century, maybe 5 to 7 percent. Later, though the Emperor Constantine converted, as we have seen already, and I will talk more about that later. Once Constantine converted, massive conversions followed, including conversions of the elite, authoritative classes in the empire, so that by the end of the fourth century, nearly half of the empire was Christian. In the fourth century, there were huge conversions, until half the empire was Christian. Constantine made Christianity a legal religion, even a favorite religion. One of his successors, the Emperor Theodosius, at the end of the fourth century, made Christianity the official state religion.

When Christianity took over the empire, the Christians who were in charge then were people who had power and authority, and they started taking this rhetoric, of people like Barnabas, Justin, and Melito quite seriously. At first, they didn't pass any legislation against Jews. Constantine passed some laws, but not very many. His successors started passing laws, but they did start turning an eye when Christians who were inflamed by this kind of rhetoric started taking it out on Jewish neighbors. The logic was, "If these Jews have rejected God, God has rejected them. What we do to people who have rejected God? God is going to punish them, and therefore, we should start punishing them."

That couldn't happen when Christians were a small, persecuted minority, but when they became powerful, and acquired authority—legal, military, and economic—then, they started to use the rhetoric of their predecessors and take it seriously, and began to persecute Jews.

I can conclude by pointing out that with the victory of Christianity, there came a serious heightening of this kind of anti-Jewish polemic. Judaism was being seen as a false religion, but even more in this later period, the polemic was backed by imperial power, so that Jews moved from being a highly respected religious community to being an economically handicapped, socially ostracized minority. The ignominious situation the Jews found themselves in throughout the Middle Ages was a result of this that has come down for us to modern times.

Lecture Nine
The Early Christian Mission

Scope: This is the first of two lectures that deal explicitly with the spread of Christianity throughout the Roman Empire. Within 300 years, the religion moved from being a small group of Jesus's lower-class Jewish followers in Jerusalem to being a world religion that commanded the attention and, eventually, the respect of the highest echelons of Roman society and government. How did that happen?

This lecture considers the earliest phases of the Christian mission by exploring the missionary strategy and message as reflected in the writings of one our most well known Christian missionaries, the apostle Paul, and in the New Testament Book of Acts. Here, we will consider what Christian evangelists told people to convince them to abandon their pagan religions and to accept the God of Jesus and the death and Resurrection of Jesus for salvation. In particular, we will examine the early Christians' claim that miracles demonstrated the truth of their message.

Outline

I. To this point in the course, we have seen how Christianity began as a sect within Judaism, starting with the historical Jesus, then with the proclamation of his death and Resurrection by his followers. We have also considered how Christianity separated off from its Jewish roots to become an anti-Jewish religion over the first few centuries of its existence.

II. Related to the separation of Christianity from its Jewish roots was its attraction to those of non-Jewish extraction. In this lecture, we will begin to consider Christianity's relationship with the Greco-Roman world at large.

   A. In particular, for the next two lectures, we will consider the spread of Christianity throughout the Roman world.

   B. Our consideration will be driven by an overarching question: How did a small band of Jesus's lower-class Jewish followers in Jerusalem manage to create a world religion that commanded the respect of the highest echelons of Roman society and government, within 300 years?

III. We can begin by discounting the view commonly propounded, still today, that Christianity just happened to emerge in a world that was suffering spiritual malaise, that the time was ripe for a new religion to pick up where all the others had failed.

A. Recent scholarship has shown that the period of Christianity's spread, the second and third centuries, represented a time of religious fervor and excitement, a revival of religious interests, rather than a widespread spiritual malaise.

B. Moreover, it would be wrong to consider only what was unique about Christianity to see why it succeeded when so many other religions failed. For Christianity to succeed, it obviously had to relate to people and their views; it had to make sense to people; it had to speak in the common religious idiom, not in a completely foreign tongue.

C. In our reflections of what made Christianity so attractive to people that they would be willing to give up their old religions to embrace it, we will need to consider both what about Christianity was like and what about it was unlike other religious traditions in the Roman world.

IV. We will begin our reflections in this lecture by looking at the two earliest sources we have for the Christian mission, the apostle Paul and the Book of Acts.

A. In Paul's own letters, he indicates that he worked in major urban areas through Asia Minor, Macedonia, and Achaia (modern-day Turkey and Greece) to establish communities of Christians.

1. He does not ever say that he engaged in open-air evangelism or tent revivals.

2. Instead, it appears that he met people to preach to them by going into a new city, opening up a business (possibly a leather goods shop), and using it as a point of contact to meet people (1 Thes. 2:9–12).

B. Throughout his letters, Paul gives several hints concerning what he said to potential converts.

1. His audience consisted of pagans; thus, he first had to convince them that their worship was pointless, because the pagan gods didn't really exist (1 Thes. 1:9–10).
2. Moreover, the one true God had sent his Son into the world to die for the wrongdoing of which everyone was guilty. For people to have a right standing before God, therefore, and to be saved when the imminent day of judgment arrived, they needed to believe in the one true God and trust in the death of his Son.
3. In other words, Paul preached a message of coming judgment and salvation through Christ. This was an apocalyptic message (1 Cor. 15:3–4).
4. The truth of Paul's message was proved by the Resurrection of Jesus from the dead. Moreover, there are indications in other letters of Paul that the people he converted believed that his message was authenticated by miraculous deeds he performed (2 Cor. 12:12).

C. Much of this is consistent with the accounts of the missionary activities of the apostles found in the Book of Acts.
   1. This account was written decades after the events that it narrates. It appears to contain some legendary exaggerations about the effect of the Christian mission (for example, when many, many thousands convert in Jerusalem in the first months of the Christian mission).
   2. In its essentials, however, it agrees in many respects with Paul's accounts: The apostles proclaim their faith to unbelievers; they are said to do miracles that validate their message; and people convert as a result (cf. Acts. 2:31; 4:4).
   3. Moreover, the mission is said to be more successful among Gentiles than Jews, who, therefore, had to give up their worship of pagan gods and accept the God of Jesus to become his follower.

D. One gets a similar message from later accounts of the Christian mission in the legendary Acts of the Apostles of the second and third centuries, for example, the so-called Acts of John, where many people convert to follow Jesus when they see the powerful miracles of his followers.

V. In sum, the earliest Christian missionaries spread their religion by proclaiming Christ as the Son of the one and only true God who had brought salvation to the world and would bring salvation from the coming judgment

   A. Their words were persuasive, in part, because they were believed to be able to perform divinely inspired miracles as verification of what they said.

   B. It is impossible for historians to say, as historians, that Jesus's apostles really did such things, but it is possible to say that they were *believed* to have done such things. In the next lecture, we will explore further why belief in such miraculous doings was so central to the advance of the Christian mission.

Essential Reading:

Bart Ehrman, *After the New Testament*, chapter 2.

————, *The New Testament: A Historical Introduction*, chapter 19.

Supplementary Reading:

Robin Lane Fox, *Pagans and Christians*.

Ramsey Macmullen, *Christianizing the Roman Empire*.

Rodney Stark, *The Rise of Christianity*.

Questions to Consider:

1. Why would the accounts of miraculous deeds prove a successful missionary tool for Christians working among pagan worshippers of many gods?

2. Can you explain why Christianity might overtake pagan religions at a time when they were flourishing (rather than when they were in decline)?

Lecture Nine—Transcript
The Early Christian Mission

To this point in the course, have seen how Christianity began as a sect within Judaism, starting with the historical Jesus, and then with the proclamation of his death and Resurrection by his followers. We have also considered how Christianity separated off from its Jewish roots to become an anti-Jewish religion over the first few centuries of its existence. Related to the separation of Christianity from its Jewish roots was its attraction to those of non-Jewish extraction, Gentiles.

In this lecture, we will begin to consider Christianity's relationship with the Greco-Roman world at large. In particular, for the next two lectures, we will consider the spread of Christianity throughout the Roman world. Our consideration will be driven by an overarching question: How did a small band of Jesus's lower-class Jewish followers in Jerusalem manage to create a worldwide religion that commanded the respect at the highest echelons of Roman society and government, all within 300 years? How did it happen? How do we go from Jesus's small band of followers to the very capital of the empire, to the upper echelons of its government within 300 years?

I want to begin our reflections on this issue by discounting the view that is commonly propounded still today. A common view that you still hear and read about is that Christianity just happened to emerge in a world that was suffering from spiritual malaise, that the time had become ripe for a new religion, to become where all the others had failed. The theory behind this view that I am discounting was, and is, that the empire grew increasingly wealthy, and people had more resources available to them and more education. They began to doubt the old myths and the old religions that presupposed them. With this widespread skepticism came a spiritual malaise. Temples were being abandoned. People were simply going through the motions of religion for the sake of tradition, not out of conviction. Then, according to this theory, Christianity came along, to fill the void that had been left with the bankrupt religions being deserted by their followers. Christianity came along with something completely new and other than the old bankrupt pagan religions.

This theory, which one still hears today, makes a lot of sense. The main problem with it, though, is that there's scarcely any evidence at all to support it. Recent scholarship has shown that the time of Christianity's spread, the second and third Christian centuries, the second and third centuries A.D., represented a time of religious fervor and excitement among pagans. This was a time of revival of religious interests, rather than a widespread spiritual malaise. Temples were being rebuilt in this period, and being repopulated. Sacrifices were becoming increasingly popular. Cities were sponsoring more and more religious festivals. Paganism was enjoying real success. So this older theory really doesn't work, because when you look at the record, it was not decline of paganism during this period. In fact, paganism, which had earlier suffered a kind of decline, was on the increase, as people were getting more religious and more interested in their pagan religious traditions.

Moreover, it would probably be wrong for us to consider just what was unique about Christianity to see why it succeeded. In other words, this whole theory maintained that Christianity gave something to the world that it didn't have. It was unique and different from anything else, and that's why people started going for it, because everything else that they had in front of them was spiritually bankrupt.

In fact, though, it is probably wrong to consider what was only unique about Christianity to see why it succeeded, when so many other religions failed, because for Christianity to succeed, it obviously had to relate to people and their views on their own terms. Christianity had to make sense to people. It had to speak in the common religious idiom rather than in a completely foreign tongue if it was going to be attractive to people. And so, in our reflections of what made Christianity attractive, we have to consider not only what was different about Christianity, but also what was similar to the other religions in the Greco-Roman world. That is the task before us, to see what it was about Christianity that made it attractive to people, so that people would give up their pagan traditions in order to follow the worship of the one true God.

We will begin our reflections in this lecture by looking at the two earliest sources we have for the Christian mission. The two earliest sources, again, are in the New Testament. They are the writings of the apostle Paul and the book of the Acts of the Apostles.

Starting with Paul, our earliest author, as we have seen, Paul wrote a number of letters that have been incorporated into the New Testament. We don't have letters by Paul outside of the New Testament that are authentic. We have some forged letters by Paul outside of the New Testament, but within the New Testament, we have 13 letters that claim to be written by

Paul, and as we saw in an earlier lecture, seven of these indubitably were written by Paul. These letters of Paul's are the earliest Christian writings we have of any kind.

This is confusing to some people who read the New Testament, because the Gospels are given first: Matthew, Mark, Luke, and John. You don't get to Paul until later, but Paul's letters themselves were actually written before the Gospels. They are the earliest writings. His very earliest writing is the book of 1 Thessalonians, written around the year 49 A.D. It is the first of Paul's letters to survive that he wrote. He undoubtedly wrote letters before this, but we don't have them any longer. They have been lost. 1 Thessalonians is probably the first that he wrote that we have, written in the year 49. This makes 1 Thessalonians the first piece of Christian literature from the ancient world.

As it turns out, 1 Thessalonians will be important for our task in this lecture as we try to see what Paul said in order to convert people, how he converted people, what his modus operandi was. After Paul came to believe in Jesus, after he had been persecuting the church, and then he had become a believer, he understood himself to have been called by God to engage in missionary activity throughout the urban Mediterranean. He worked in areas throughout Asia Minor, Macedonia and Achaia, particularly. These would be areas in modern-day Turkey and Greece. He worked in these areas in order to establish communities of Christians.

Paul was not a paid missionary. There was not some church back home that was paying him. Paul had to work, and it was in the process of his working that he converted communities, going from one community to the next as he established churches there. One of our questions is how he went about doing so, how he managed to set up these churches in the various areas that he visited.

Paul himself never said that he ever engaged in anything like an open-air evangelism or tent revival. We might have the idea that what he did was to go into town, or go to the marketplace maybe, where lots of people were, and start making his proclamations, and people would listen to him and convert. He may have done something like that, but he gives no indication that that is what he did. Nor does Paul indicate that the way he proceeded was the way the Book of Acts says he proceeded.

According to the Book of Acts, the way Paul proceeded was to go into a town, and go to the local Jewish synagogue, the place of worship for the Jews, where prayers were said, Scripture was read, and a sermon would be preached, and that Paul, as a Jew from out-of-town, would naturally go to the synagogue. In the synagogue, then, he would be a stranger from out-of-town. The group, they would ask him to get up and give a little speech, and he would get up, but instead of doing what they would expect, which would be to talk about the Hebrew Bible, he would talk about Jesus as the Messiah. According to the Book of Acts, then, that's how he made his contacts with people, because he was naturally welcomed into the synagogue. But in every case in the Book of Acts, once he did this, the people would become incensed that he was talking about Jesus as the Messiah and would kick him out of the synagogue.

Having been kicked out of the synagogue, Paul would then at least have made a few contacts with people, and maybe some of them would convert, although the majority would reject his message, and he would use these contacts to build up a kind of support base, from which he would then take his message to the non-Jews, the Gentiles. According to Acts, then, he would first go to the synagogue. When he got kicked out of the synagogue, then he would start talking to the Gentiles.

That may also be the way he proceeded, but it's not at all what he himself says about his modus operandi. What he does tell us is that when he would go into these urban areas to set up the churches—he never, ever mentions the synagogue, by the way, in this context—what he does say in some places is that he went in with several companions who were fellow Christians. In particular, he names people like Timothy and Sylvanus, and he indicates that when they would go into town, they would open up some kind of business.

As I pointed out earlier, the Book of Acts says that he worked with leather goods, and so, it might have been some kind of Christian leather goods shop. The tradition, of course, is that Paul was a tent-maker, that he made tents for a living. This is based on one verse in the Book of Acts, which is translated in some Bibles as the fact that he made tents, but the word used in Greek in the Book of Acts does not indicate that he made tents. It indicates that he worked with leather. Now, he may have been making tents, because tents were made from leather, but he might have been making belts, sandals, and other kinds of leather goods. We don't really know.

What he indicates is that he would go into a new city, open up a new business, and use that as a point of contact in order to meet people. And as he met people within the context of his business, then, he would talk to them in order to try to convert them to faith in Christ. Let me read you one of the key passages from this earliest of his letters, 1 Thessalonians, when he's reminding the Thessalonians how he had met them and converted them: "You remember," says Paul; this is chapter 2, verse 9, "our labor and toil, brothers and sisters. We worked night and day so that we might not burden any of you while we proclaimed to you the gospel of God."

It doesn't tell you everything there, but if you read it carefully enough and look closely enough, it looks like in fact, he's saying that they were engaged in manual labor so that they didn't have to get money from these people who had converted to Christianity. They worked "day and night." Scholars take this, now, as a reference to their actual manual labor, working, probably in some kind of shop that they had set up.

"While we proclaimed to you the gospel of God," so that the situation is they are busy during the workday talking to people, "work day and night," talking to people in order to convince them of the gospel, and then once people convert to the faith, they continue to come into the shop in their free time, and they talk things over while Paul and his companions engage in their work.

That appears to be the way Paul proceeded, then, setting up a business in town as a way of contacting people, meeting people, and then sharing the gospel with them. What is it, though, that he said to these people when he was trying to convert them? Paul considered himself a missionary to the Gentiles, so that presumably, that's principally the ones he was talking to, but what did he say to these people? Recall that these were Gentiles and even pagans who worshipped many gods. Before Paul could convert them to believe that Jesus was the Son of God, he had to convince them that the God of the Jews was the one true God. There must, then, have been something like that going on in his proclamation.

Fortunately, he again gives us at hint of what it is he told people that he met in his business day. Chapter 1 of 1 Thessalonians, verses 9 and 10:

> For the people of these other regions report about us that kind of welcome we had among you, and how you turned to God from idols, to serve a living and true God, and to wait for his Son from heaven, whom he raised from the dead—Jesus, the one who rescues us from the wrath that is coming.

People from around the world have heard about how the Thessalonians have converted from serving idols to serve the living and true God. That may give us a hint about what it was Paul was preaching to these people. These people were pagans; they had many gods, gods of many functions, gods of many places. These gods were represented by idols in the pagan temples. Paul was apparently convincing these potential converts that their gods were dead and false, because he convinced them to move from worshipping the "idols" to serve the "living and true God," so that it's a contrast between the "living God" (the God of the Jews) versus these "dead idols." Moreover, this God is true, whereas these gods are false.

This may indicate that as part of strategy, Paul may have used Jewish polemic against paganism, in which Jews would look at the idols in the temples, and point out that these idols, made out of wood and stone, in fact were dead. How could they represent a divine being? These were something that somebody simply had carved, or fashioned in some way. Those were dead. Only God was alive and true, a God who was not represented by an idol.

Evidently, then, Paul would teach these people coming into his shop that the true God was not to be found in an idol, but was living in heaven. He was alive, and he was true, and moreover, that Jesus was his Son, and that they needed to await Jesus, because Jesus was coming to save them from the wrath that was coming. Paul was a Jewish apocalypticist, who maintained that he was living at the end of the age. The Resurrection of Jesus showed that the end of the age was imminent, and people needed to prepare for the coming end of the age. Paul, in other words, was converting people to an apocalyptic understanding of the faith. For people to have a right standing before God and be saved, when the imminent Day of Judgment arrived, they needed to believe in the one true God and trust in the death of his Son, Jesus. That appears to have been the message that Paul preached.

We get an indication that this apocalyptic message was Paul's major form of proclamation. In one other passage that we will look at quickly, 1 Corinthians, chapter 15, written to a different community, this one Corinth, a group of former pagans had converted to believe in Christ. Paul had converted them, apparently by setting up a shop in Corinth, and having them come in to talk to him. He indicates in chapter 15 what it is he had preached to these people to convert them. 1 Corinthians, chapter 15, verses 3 and 4:

I handed on to you as a first importance what I, in turn, had received [okay, he handed these people his message, namely], that Christ died for our sins in accordance with the Scriptures, and that he was buried, and that he was raised from the dead on the third day, in accordance with the Scriptures, and that he appeared, then, to Cephas and to the Twelve.

Paul appears to have had a very basic message: You have to worship the one true God, you have to accept that Jesus died for our sins, according to the Scriptures, and that he was raised from the dead, according to the Scriptures. Moreover, one needs to be aware of the fact that Jesus is returning in judgment, and so if the people are not ready for this, they themselves will be destroyed at the second coming of Jesus.

This is an apocalyptic message. Why would people be convinced by it? What was Paul saying or doing to convince people? It's important to recognize that Paul's message included a reference to the Resurrection of Jesus—that Jesus was raised from the dead. The Resurrection of Jesus would be important as a demonstration of the truth of Paul's message that Jesus's death was a death for sin, because if Jesus was raised from the dead, that is a miraculous verification of the message about his death.

It is interesting that when you read the accounts of Paul in his own writings, and in the Book of Acts, and in the proclamation of the other apostles in the Acts of the Apostles, and then when you read the other accounts elsewhere in early Christian literature, miracles are always talked about as providing the verification of the Christian message. The message is validated by the miracles that the apostles were able to perform.

I asked earlier what it was that would have been convincing to pagans about the Christian message, and I pointed out at the beginning of the lecture that there must have been some kind of tie between what the apostles were saying in spreading the message, and what pagans themselves already believed. This, in fact, is probably a tie-in. Pagans, as we saw in an early lecture, were engaged in religion precisely because of what it could give them for their present-day lives. Most pagans were not concerned about what would happen to them in the afterlife. There are debates among scholars today about whether most pagans even believed in an afterlife.

Of course, when you read ancient Greek and Roman literature, you come across references to the afterlife, the Elysian Fields in the writings of Homer, for example. Plato talks in places about a place of blessing and a place of damnation after death. Consequently, some people think, "Well, maybe most pagans did believe in an afterlife." Scholars point out, though, that in the inscriptions found on tombstones throughout the pagan world, there are very strong indications that most pagans thought that when you died, that was the end of the story, period. You are dead and gone; that's it.

In any event, it is pretty clear that religion, for most pagans, was not a matter of how to secure the afterlife, it was a matter of how to secure the present life. People were living very near the edge. There were no such things as modern medicine, modern methods of irrigation, no way to control the weather, no way to distribute goods through mass transit, so people were living near the edge and needed help in order to survive in the present.

Well, who could help? Not humans, because humans were in the same bind everyone was. Only the gods could help. How did the gods help? Well, the gods provided miracles. If your child was sick, there was a god who could heal your child. If there was no rain, the gods could send rain. If another village attacked yours, the gods could protect you. The gods were more powerful than we were and could do the miracles necessary to bring about what we needed to thrive and prosper.

When the Christians proclaimed their message of Jesus, they always proclaimed it in the context of the miracles that Jesus performed, and in the miracles that God was performing through the apostles. This is true of Paul, and of all the others. I point this out in this context, because the message of Paul is about a miracle: God raised Jesus from the dead. What could be more miraculous than a resurrection from the dead? If one became convinced that God had done that for Jesus, one would be convinced that this was a powerful God. This was a God who could provide us with what we needed. It is therefore no accident that throughout the accounts of the apostles preaching, in all of our sources, we have accounts both of Jesus's miracles and of the miracles of the apostles.

We get a hint of this in Paul's writings themselves, that Paul himself evidently was reputed to have done miracles as a way of validating his proclamation of Jesus. We find this in the letter of 2 Corinthians. It is a very interesting passage, because Paul, in 2 Corinthians, did not want to emphasize that he was a glorious figure himself. Paul's view was that if you really wanted to be a follower of Jesus, you were going to experience his fate, which was to be crucified. Paul therefore emphasized throughout 2 Corinthians that, in fact, he was a lowly person who was weak and frail, and always being persecuted, flogged, imprisoned, and stoned, etc.

At one point, though, they wanted to emphasize that when he preached the gospel to these people, he gave the verification that was needed by doing some kind of miracle. He didn't tell us what they were: "The signs of a true apostle were performed among you," he says in 2 Corinthians 12:12. "The signs of a true apostle were performed among you, with utmost patience, signs, and wonders, and mighty works."

Paul was claiming that he was empowered by God to do signs, wonders, and mighty works as a verification of his proclamation. This view that miracles accompanied the missionary proclamation of the apostles is found throughout the Book of Acts. The Book of Acts, of course, was written decades after the events that it narrates, and it does, I think, fairly clearly contain some legendary exaggerations about the effect of the Christian mission. In its essentials, though, it agrees in most respects with Paul's own accounts. The apostles in the Book of Acts proclaim their faith to believers and are said to have done miracles in order to validate their message, and as a result of people seeing these miracles, they convert to faith in Jesus.

You see this early in the Book of Acts, in its early chapters. For example Acts, chapter 2, narrates an event that happened 50 days after Jesus's death, during the day of Pentecost. There are group of followers of Jesus's who believe that Jesus was raised from the dead; they're gathered together at one place. We are told there are 120 of these people, and suddenly, something miraculous happens on the day of Pentecost. The spirit comes upon these people. They hear a mighty wind going through where they are, and flames come down from heaven, tons of flames that go up over their heads, and they start speaking languages that they don't know. All around them are people who are gathered together for this festival of Pentecost, Jews from around the world from different countries, and these people who are the followers of Jesus start speaking to people of different areas, different countries, in their own languages, even though they don't know these languages. This is a miraculous event, and when people had realized what had happened, they convert to faith in Jesus, because Jesus is the one who has caused this, as the apostle Peter tells them.

In chapter 3 of the Book of Acts, Peter and John are going to the Temple of Jerusalem for a time of prayer, and there's a man there who has been lame for 40 years, since he was born. Peter heals the man of his lameness, and the man leaps up and starts running, jumping, and praising God. People see this, and thousands of people convert when they see this miracle happen. So it goes throughout the Book of Acts. It gets to a point were Peter is so powerful that as he passes by people who are sick, if just his shadow falls on them, they become well.

The apostle Paul, who converts later, has miraculous powers, and can raise the dead. At one point, Paul's handkerchiefs are able to heal anybody who is sick, and anybody who sees this naturally converts.

Pagans were interested in the power of the gods that could see them through their daily lives. The apostles allegedly had this power. Therefore, their message about Jesus, which they tied to the power that they had, was confirmed by that power, and that's what proves convincing to people. This idea of the power of God being manifest to the apostles continues on after the New Testament period, into a group of legendary tales of the apostles, called the Apocryphal Acts. One example I will give you here is from an apocryphal story about John, the son of Zebedee, who was one of Jesus's closest followers. According to a book that now survives, called the Acts of John, which is a second century legendary account of the missionary endeavors of John, the son of Zebedee, John used his miracles in order to convince people to stop worshipping the pagan gods and start worshipping the God of Jesus.

He happens to be in the city of Ephesus, in Asia Minor, at the time when there's going to be a big festival at the local temple of the goddess Artemis. Everybody comes to the temple, including John, who is dressed completely in black. He appears, and gives a little sermon to people who are gathered there. John tells these people:

> How many miraculous deeds have you see me perform? How many cures? [The answer is supposed to be, 'We have seen you do a lot.'] Still, you are harder than hard, and cannot see clearly. [He wants to know: Why are you here worshipping this idol, when, in fact, I am the one who has got the power?] What, now, men of Ephesus? I have come up to this idol's temple to convince you that you are wholly without God, and dead to human reason. Go ahead, pray to her that I alone will die, or if you cannot accomplish this, I alone will call upon my God to kill you, all because of your unbelief.

Thus, we are going to have a miracle contest. You pray to your idol, I will pray to my God, and we will see who wins. Well, they pray to the idol, and nothing happens. John, then, prays to God, and the temple starts shaking. The idols all fall over and break apart. The roof of the temple falls down and kills the temple priest, and then everybody realizes which god has the power. It's the God of John, so they all convert, and cry out in one stroke, saying: "There is only one God, that of John. Only one God has compassion for us. You alone are God. Now we have been converted, since we have seen your miraculous deeds."

Well, this is a legendary account, and I don't want to say that the apostles actually could do these miracles that they were reputed to have done, but it is clear that the preaching of the miracles goes hand-in-hand with the preaching of Christ, and that one of the reasons people converted to faith in Christ is because they believed the miracles.

In sum, the earliest Christian missionaries spread their religion by proclaiming Christ as the Son of the one and only true God, who brought about the salvation of the world, and would bring salvation from the coming judgment. Their words were persuasive, in part, because they were believed to be able to perform divinely inspired miracles as verification of what they said. As I just pointed out, I think it's impossible for historians to say as historians that the apostles of Jesus really did such things, but it is possible to say that they were believed to have done such things.

In the next lecture, we will explore further why belief in such miraculous doings was so central to the advance of the Christian mission.

Lecture Ten
The Christianization of the Roman Empire

Scope: In this lecture, we will move into the periods of the Christian mission after Paul to see how far and quickly the religion spread, the reasons for its success, and its ultimate reach to the upper echelons of the Roman government, before becoming, finally, the official religion of the empire by the late fourth century. We will see the role played by the claims for the miraculous in the Christian mission and, in particular, the unique aspect of Christianity as an *exclusivistic* religion that claimed it was right and, as a consequence, all other religions were wrong. The lecture will end by considering the conversion of the Roman emperor Constantine in the beginning of the fourth century and the enormous implications this conversion had for the future of the Christian religion.

Outline

I. In the previous lecture, we began to see how the earliest Christians spread their religion throughout the Roman Empire.

    A. It was largely spread by word of mouth, as Christians tried to convince their pagan friends, family, neighbors, and acquaintances in the essence of the Christian message.

    B. This message was believed to be validated by the miraculous deeds performed by Jesus's apostles.

    C. In this lecture, we will consider further aspects of the Christian mission: how far and quickly the religion spread, the reasons for its success, and its ultimate reach to the upper echelons of the Roman government, before becoming, finally, the official religion of the empire by the late fourth century.

II. The Christian religion appears to have spread by fits and starts but steadily over the first three centuries.

    A. The statistics are hard to come by, because we lack adequate sources for firm numbers.

B. Clearly, Christianity started off simply as a small band of lower-class peasants in Jerusalem, possibly 20 to 100 people, who had been followers of Jesus during his life and continued to believe in him after his death.

C. It is difficult to know how many people this small band of followers converted in the early years, but we do know that small Christian communities were started throughout the entire Mediterranean over the decades that followed.

D. Over the course of 300 years, the religion had grown to be about five percent of the population of the empire, or some three million adherents.

E. That rate of growth does not require massive conversions but simply a steady stream of converts. It represents a growth of about 40 percent every 10 years (which happens to be the growth rate of the Mormon Church over the course of the 20th century; see Rodney Stark).

F. This growth was not achieved by massive evangelistic campaigns but by social networking, as one person who converted would then convert his spouse and (some of his) children, neighbors, and friends; over time, each of the converts would do the same.

G. The enormous change came with the conversion of Emperor Constantine in the early fourth century. Then, the church took off by leaps and bounds so that by the end of the century, fully half of the empire called itself Christian.

H. It was Theodosius I (emperor, 374–395 C.E.) who made Christianity the "official" state religion at the end of the fourth century, outlawing pagan religious practices.

III. Why, though, was Christianity so successful in the earlier years and throughout the second and third centuries, before Constantine?

    A. It is important to recall that Christianity's success must have involved the way it related its message to the pagans that it converted.

        1. As earlier indicated, there is nothing to suggest a widespread spiritual malaise throughout the empire in this period. On the contrary, religious cults and practices appear to have experienced a serious resurgence. Why, then, would

Christianity succeed in displacing so many religions over time?

2. To answer that question, we must remember that pagan religions were principally concerned with life in the present world, acquiring what is needed and wanted in life through powerful deities who can provide what humans are unable to provide for themselves: rain for the crops, personal health, healing from sickness, power over evil, victory over enemies.

3. This can explain why the reports of the apostolic miracles (and those of Jesus) played such a major role in the Christian mission: These showed that the Christian God was more powerful than all others; those who came to believe that, in order to receive the benefits of that power for themselves, needed to abandon their old gods to worship this one.

B. This intimates another aspect of the Christian message that contributed to its success: its exclusivity.

1. None of the other religions in the empire was exclusivistic, not even Judaism.

2. Christianity, though, proclaimed an exclusive attachment to the one God, who was jealous and would brook no rivals. Following him meant abandoning all others.

3. For this reason, Christianity destroyed all the other religions while promoting its own. In this, it was unique among the religions of antiquity, which explains a good deal of its success.

C. The exclusive claims of the religion were matched by the fierce devotion of some of its followers. This, too, may have accounted for Christianity's success.

1. Little of such exclusive devotion could be found in pagan religions.

2. But some Christians were willing to stay true to their religious commitments even when faced with torture and death. According to early Christian authors, such as Justin and Tertullian, this made an impression on bystanders. In Tertullian's words, "The blood of the martyrs is seed."

IV. Christianity grew at a steady pace over the decades, up to the early fourth century, when Constantine converted and changed everything.

A. The details of Constantine's conversion are sketchy, and the surviving accounts are legendary.

B. The most well known account—allegedly described by Constantine himself—involves his dream the night before his significant battle with his rival for power, Maxentius, in 312 C.E., in which he saw the sign of the cross and was told, "by this, conquer."

V. The steady growth of Christianity over the decades of the second and third centuries was largely based on a message of exclusivistic devotion to the Christian God, backed by reports of acts of miraculous power demonstrating the religion's superiority to all others. When the Roman emperor finally converted to this once-persecuted faith, it was on its way to becoming the religion of the empire and, from there, the most significant religion in the history of Western civilization and culture.

Essential Reading:

Robin Lane Fox, *Pagans and Christians*.

Ramsey Macmullen, *Christianizing the Roman Empire*.

Rodney Stark, *The Rise of Christianity*.

Supplementary Reading:

John Carroll, *Constantine's Sword*.

Bart Ehrman, *After the New Testament*, chapter 2.

Questions to Consider:

1. What would the world be like today if the vast majority of religions were inclusivistic—as they were in the Roman world—rather than exclusivistic? Would this have any effect on social and political conflicts?

2. Try to mount arguments for Constantine's conversion being (a) a good thing and (b) a bad thing for the future of Christianity.

Lecture Ten—Transcript
The Christianization of the Roman Empire

In the previous lecture, we began to see how the earliest Christians spread their religion throughout the Roman Empire. It was largely spread by word of mouth, as Christians tried to convince their pagan friends, family, neighbors and acquaintances of the essence of the Christian message. This message was believed to be validated by the miraculous deeds performed by Jesus's apostles.

In this lecture, we will consider further aspects of the Christian mission, how far and quickly the religion spread, the reasons for its success, and its ultimate reach to the upper echelons of the Roman government before becoming, finally, the official religion of the empire by the late fourth century.

The Christian religion appears to have spread by fits and starts, but steadily, over the first three centuries. Before considering the reasons for its success, I'd like to give a thumbnail sketch of the success of the Christian mission.

Statistics for the ancient world are notoriously difficult to come by, since we lack adequate sources to give us the firm numbers we might need. Clearly, though, Christianity started off as a very small of band of lower-class peasants in Jerusalem, who had been followers of Jesus during his life, and continued to believe in him after his death. According to the Gospel accounts, Jesus spent almost his entire ministry in the northern part of Israel, in the area of Galilee, and it wasn't until the last week of his life that he went down to Jerusalem with his 12 disciples.

After his death, his disciples appear to have remained in Jerusalem. By this time, there would have been 11 of them, with Judas Escariat having killed himself, but there were also women who had accompanied Jesus from Galilee, including the women who discovered his empty tomb.

It is therefore difficult to say from the Gospels how many people were left after Jesus's death who were still believers, but I guess it would be around 12 or 15 people. The Book of Acts, though, indicates that there were more believers in Jesus right after his death, who were together with everybody else who were also believers in Jerusalem. Acts indicates that there were perhaps 120 people who had been followers of Jesus. This may be an exaggerated number. As we will see in this lecture in a minute, the Book of

Acts does tend to exaggerate its numbers when it comes to determining how many people were actually following Jesus.

In any event, we're talking about a handful of people, perhaps 15 or 20, possibly up to 100. These were the original followers of Jesus, who would have started the Christian mission. Over the course of 300 years, the religion had grown to something like 5 to 7 percent of the population of the entire empire, so that over 300 years, there are three or four million adherents of Christianity, rather than, say, 15 or 20, or up to 100.

This means that the small group of Jesus's followers—15 or 20, maybe up to 100—must have spread rather quickly, and in a far-reaching way throughout the empire, so that conversions were going on regularly through the period. It's a question of how these conversions happened. In fact, we have very few records of mass conversions to Christianity (in other words, there are masses that convert at once), although we do have some accounts of that happening, especially in the Book of Acts. There is some question of the accuracy of these reports; we get these reports especially early on in the Book of Acts.

In the previous lecture, I talked about the day of Pentecost, where the Holy Spirit came upon the followers of Jesus, and they spoke in other languages, in tongues, preaching the gospel to people, Jews, from different nations, who happened to be in town for the festival of Pentecost. We are told that after they gave these speeches to these people, preaching the gospel in these various languages, other people were looking on, wondering what was going on. These people were speaking in strange tongues. They suspected that perhaps these people were drunk, and Peter got up and gave a sermon. He says, "People of Jerusalem, these people are not drunk. It is only nine o'clock in the morning. In fact, what has happened is that the Spirit has come upon them to proclaim the good news," and then Peter gives a speech, a sermon, the first long missionary sermon in the Book of Acts, chapter 2. In it, he says that Jesus has been killed unjustly, but that God will forgive those at fault, and that everybody needs to repent of their sins so that they can be saved. We are told at the end of this sermon, chapter 2, verse 41, that on that day, about 3,000 people were converted to the church.

A couple of days later, we have the incident that I referred to in the previous lecture, where Peter and John go into the temple, and heal a man who was lame from birth. People saw them healing this person. They recognized the person as the lame beggar who had been there every day for a very long time, but then, he was walking, jumping, leaping, and they credited this to the miracle abilities of Peter and John. Peter and John tell them that, in fact, it was nothing they had done. This was the power of God, "showing the truth of our message." We are told, then, in chapter 4, verse 4 that many of those who heard the word believed, and they numbered about 5,000.

Thus, on one day, we have 3,000 converting, and a few days later, 5,000 converting. These numbers appear to be exaggerated. At this rate, Jerusalem would almost be exclusively a Christian city, with this many thousands of people converting. In fact, though, the numbers seem to be exaggerated. The author of Acts liked to play up the importance of the preaching successes of his apostles.

Outside of books like that, we don't have records of massive conversions. What we have are records of individual conversions, as Christians probably spread the word by word-of-mouth, and managed to convert people on a steady basis.

Sociologists who have crunched the numbers have pointed out that if you start with a fairly significant, small group of people in the year 30, and end up with a very large group of people, say, three or four million people by the year 320, you don't actually need to have massive conversions. All you need is steady increase, and in fact, one scholar, Rodney Stark, who is a sociologist of religion, has pointed out that if Christianity simply grew at a steady rate of a 40 percent increase every decade, you could get from the small numbers of Jesus's followers in Jerusalem, to the three or four million followers by the year 300 or so; a 40 percent increase every decade will do that.

Stark points out that there's nothing particularly miraculous about that rate of growth. As it turns out, that happens to be the rate of growth of the Mormon Church throughout the 20th century. It grew, on average, 40 percent every decade. Well, early Christianity may have grown at a comparable rate up to the time that Constantine converted, and we will talk about Constantine's conversion at the end of this lecture.

It appears that these conversions were not effected principally by evangelistic campaigns, but by a kind of social networking, as one person who converted would then convert his spouse, who would then convert the woman next door, who would then convert her husband, who would then convert a co-worker, who would convert his spouse, and it went on like that, one person converting the other over time.

Conversion, of course, meant more than having somebody simply say, "Okay, I believe in Jesus." These people were principally pagans.

Converting to faith in Christ meant abandoning one's own traditional religion, accepting the God of the Jews as the one true God, accepting Jesus as his Son who died for the sins of the world and was raised from the dead, and expecting also that Jesus would soon come back in judgment on the Earth. These were basic things people would have to believe—giving up the old and accepting the new.

Once someone converted, of course, they would also need to be taught about the message of the faith, and so you had people talking about stories of Jesus in order to convert people, and telling what Jesus himself did, why he died, how he died, telling the stories that ended up in the Gospels, but then also instructing in the rudiments of Christian doctrine and Christian ethics for those who had already converted.

My point is that you don't need massive evangelistic campaigns for this to happen. It can happen through simple social networking. The enormous change that led to Christianity becoming the religion of the empire was when the emperor, Constantine, himself converted in the early fourth century. Once that happened, the church took off by leaps and bounds, so that by the end of the fourth century, fully half of the empire called itself Christian. Something like 50 percent of the empire identified with Christianity, because once the emperor converted, it just changed everything. The Emperor Constantine bestowed certain favors on the churches, which previously had been persecuted, as we will see in a future lecture.

Now, instead of being persecuted, the churches were favored. Constantine gave lands to the churches. He constructed churches. He gave authority to bishops. By the end of the fourth century, one of Constantine's successors, an emperor called Theodosius, usually identified as Theodosius I, who was emperor from 374 to 395, at the very end of the fourth century, made Christianity the official state religion, and he outlawed pagan religious practices. This meant that Christianity, a very tiny group in the year 30, had become half of the empire by the end of the fourth century.

One of the overriding questions one has to ask is why Christianity was so successful in those earlier years. It might make sense as to why Christianity was successful after Constantine, because it became a popular thing to be a Christian. It had become a financially advantageous thing to be a Christian, and it could be a politically advantageous thing to be a Christian. Therefore, after Constantine's conversion, it made sense. Once Constantine converted, by the way, all the subsequent emperors of Rome were Christian with one exception. The exception was an emperor called Julian, who, in the 360s, had a very short rule on the emperor's throne.

Julian was a nephew of Constantine, and had been raised a Christian, but once he came emperor, he renounced his Christianity, and tried to force the empire back into its pagan ways, but he died several years after becoming the emperor, and it reverted once again to having Christian emperors from there on out.

What about those earlier years, though? Why was Christianity succeeding in converting people to its faith? It's important to recall what we saw in the last lecture, that the success of Christianity had to involve the way it related its message to the pagans that it converted.

Pagans, as we have seen, were not experiencing any kind of particular malaise during this period, so it's isn't that Christianity was filling some kind of a void. In fact, it's probably because religion was on the uprise that Christianity was helped, because people were increasingly religious, and were looking for valid religious expression. It is therefore not that there was a malaise. In fact, there was some kind of spiritual excitement that may have helped Christianity.

Moreover, we have seen that Christianity was able to build on one thing that pagans expected of religion. Probably the main thing that pagans expected of religion was help for life in the present. Christians, by claiming convincingly that their God was the one true God, who had power over nature, who could do the miracles that were needed for life to be sustained, were able to convert people who, of course, wanted rain for their crops, and personal health (healing from sickness), power over evil, and victory over enemies. That's what people wanted. Christians could claim that their God was more powerful than the other gods, and if they won that particular debate—"Whose god is more powerful? Ours or yours?"—then, they would get converts.

That's why reports of the apostolic miracles, as well as the miracles of Jesus, played such a major role in the Christian mission. The miracles that were reported showed that the Christian God was more powerful than all others. Anyone who came to believe that in order to receive the benefits of that power for him- or herself, needed to abandon the old gods in order to worship this one, because of this God was more powerful than all others, then this was the one that needed to be worshipped exclusively. I want to give another example of an account that we have from an early source. It indicates that in fact, this is part of what was converting people, the belief that the God of the Christians was the most powerful god there was.

In the previous lecture, I mentioned an important apocryphal act, called the Apocryphal Acts of John. These are the accounts of the missionary exploits of John, the son of Zebedee, after Jesus's Resurrection. This Book of Acts, along with all the other apocryphal acts, was an attempt to show what Jesus's followers were doing after his death, Resurrection, and ascension. These apostles have had legendary tales told about them, in which their exploits are portrayed. They are shown to be powerful representatives of the one true God. They convert many people, principally by doing miracles.

I want to look, now, not at the Acts of John, but another legendary account of acts that we have, the Acts of Thomas. The Acts of Thomas is a very famous book from antiquity, best known for being the first account of a legend that you have undoubtedly heard of. That is that Thomas was the missionary to India, and this is the account of his mission to India, and his adventures, of on the way there and while he is there in India.

I should say that this Acts of Thomas is interesting for a lot of reasons, one of them being that this particular Thomas is thought not just to be one of Jesus's followers. This Thomas is thought to be Jesus's brother, and he is not only Jesus's brother. As it turns out, he is Jesus's twin brother. The word "Thomas" is an Aramaic word that means "twin." This person's full name in some of our other records is Didymus Judas Thomas. *Didymus* is a Greek word that means "twin." "Judas" is the person's name, even though he typically goes by "Thomas" in this account. This is Jesus's brother Jude. If you know from the New Testament, Jesus had several brothers, James, Jude, and others. Jude is thought by some Christians in the ancient world to have been not just Jesus's brother, but his twin brother.

That gets played out here in this particular book, the Acts of Thomas, in a rather amusing way at one point. The book is largely about what Thomas preaches in order to convert people, and one of the things he preaches to people who have converted is that they need to lead lives of chastity, so that he's constantly telling people not to engage in sex even if they're married. One of the very strange passages—one of the very strange stories in this account of the Acts of Thomas is that Thomas goes to a town where the king's daughter is being married, and Thomas is invited to the ceremony, and to the celebration afterwards. He doesn't approve of marriage, and he certainly doesn't approve of sex, even sex after marriage, but he has to go, so he goes. When the marriage ceremony is over, and the party is nearly over, the bride and bridegroom are to go into the bridal chamber to consummate the marriage. Thomas tells them that they would be better off not doing so, but they aren't going to pay attention to his advice, so he leaves with everybody else. The bridegroom then opens the door of the bridal chamber to go into his beloved, but he sees her there talking to somebody who looks just like Thomas, and he doesn't understand, because he just saw Thomas leave.

Well, in fact, this was not Thomas. She was now talking to Jesus, the twin brother, who turned out to be much more effective in proclaiming the need for chastity. He convinced both the bride and bridegroom that there was really no point in consummating the act: "You don't want to beget children, because if you do, they will end up being good-for-nothing, lazy. Kids are more of a pain than you could possibly imagine, not only that, but they might end up being non-believers, which means that you will be bringing people into the world that will have to pay the eternal price of punishment. You don't want to do that." Jesus is very effective rhetorically, and he convinces them, so they don't. The end up not having sex, according to the account, and they live happily ever after.

The whole scene is played out on fact that Thomas and Jesus are look-alikes, you see, so Thomas is the twin. I don't know how they imagined that Jesus could have a twin brother. If Mary was a virgin, and Jesus was the unique son of God, born to the virgin, how she has another child, I don't know, except that there are Greek and Roman myths in which you've got instances of a woman bearing both an immortal and a mortal son. The Greek god Heracles (Roman Hercules) had a twin brother, Iphicles. His mother was made pregnant both by her husband and by Zeus, and so, she gave birth to twins, one a mortal, one immortal. I don't know if that's what these people who were passing along the Acts of Thomas were thinking, but maybe they were thinking that Joseph got Mary pregnant, and God got Mary pregnant, so that there were twins. It's a possibility.

In any event, one of the accounts of the Acts of Thomas is a very interesting story of how it was that Thomas could convert people to faith in Jesus. It is an account of a miracle that he performed, and is a rather long, involved story, but really quite interesting. Thomas was in India, and there was a religious ceremony there, where he was actually giving out communion. A young man comes to take the communion, but as soon as he takes the communion bread, his hands wither up. So they know something is going wrong here. He had apparently has taken communion while he was still living in sin.

The young man fell at the apostle's feet and confessed what had happened. What had happened, he said, was that he was in love with a woman, and she with him, but he had become convinced by the apostle's preaching the people should not engage in sex. He tried to persuade her to live in a chaste and pure environment with him, but she refused, and so, to solve the problem, he took a sword, and he killed her. He had now come to communion with blood on his hands, because he had killed this woman.

The apostle says, "Take me to the inn where this happened," since it had apparently just happened. They went to the inn, and they found the dead young woman, and the apostle raised her from the dead. He asked her to tell them what she had been seeing, where she has been, while she has been dead. Well, she had had a very short journey to hell, and had seen what it was like. Verse 55 of the Acts of Thomas:

> He said to her: Tell us where you have been. And she commenced by saying: There was an ugly-looking man who received me, and his clothing was exceedingly filthy. He took me into a place where there were many chasms, and a great stench, and a most hateful vapor were given forth thence. He made me look into each chasm, and in the first, there was a blazing fire, and fiery wheels running, souls were hung up on those wheels dashing each other; and there was crying and great lamentation, and no savior was there.

She saw the torments of hell. Chapter 56:

> He brought me to another chasm, and as I looked into it, I saw mud and worms spouting forth, and souls swallowing there. I heard a great gnashing of teeth coming from them. That man said to me: These are the souls of women who left their husbands, and committed adultery with others. They have been brought to this torment. He brought her to another chasm, and there, she saw souls hung up, some of them by their tongues, some by their hair, some by their hands, and some by their feet, dangling over reeking smoke and sulfur. The ones being hanged by their tongues were slanderers, had spent their lives slandering people; those hung by their hair were shameless, who go around making themselves pretty for the sake of adultery. Those who were hung up by their hands were thieves, and those who had been hanged by their feet were those who lightly and eagerly walked in wicked ways.

It goes on detailing all of the torments of the damned, here, that this woman had seen. After she went through her account, the apostle said, "Well, you heard what the woman has recounted, and those are not the only punishments. There are even others worse than these." So he says: "Therefore, believe in Christ Jesus. Let everyone of you put off the old man, and put on the new," and people then realized that they had better convert, or this was what they were going to have facing them, and so, everybody converted. The apostle goes about, then, doing more miracles, and his miracles convince still other people that they need to convert and believe in Christ.

That's a very interesting account that stresses that the afterlife is being preached as a way of convincing people, so that we have the powers of the apostles convincing people, and belief in the afterlife convincing people.

There's a third aspect of the proclamation that I think is very important in explaining why it succeeded in converting people. The third aspect is tied up in this Acts of Thomas I was just reading. One of the things that makes Christianity both unique in the ancient world and compelling to people is its exclusivity. Only by believing in Christ will somebody be able to escape these terrors of hell. There's no other religion that will help. This religion is right, and all others are wrong.

Throughout the Roman world, there were no other exclusivistic religions that that claimed if they were right, everyone else was wrong. This is especially true, of course, of pagan religions. Pagans were polytheists. Pagans did not insist that if you worshipped Zeus, you could not also worship Aphrodite. The local gods did not say that you could only worship them, not the great gods. In fact, pagan religions were, by and large, tolerant of one another. Judaism was tolerant to the extent that Jews would worshipped just their own God, but they had no qualms about you worshipping your God, and Jews never maintained that unless you converted to Judaism, you were going to roast in hell forever.

Christians, though, proclaimed an exclusive attachment to the one God, and maintained that this one God was jealous, and would brook no rivals. Following this God meant abandoning all others. This means that when Christians converted people to their faith, they necessarily led people away from their former religions. That was unusual, virtually unheard of in the ancient world.

To imagine the situation, it worked like this. Suppose there are two of us who are equally compelling proclaimers of our gods, I'm a pagan and this other fellow is a Christian, and we are equally good at convincing people that our God is a true God. We are preaching to a crowd of 100 people. We are equally good, and equally successful. These 100 people are pagans. I convince half of these pagans to start worshiping my God, my pagan deity they had not worshipped before. The Christian convinces half the people to worship his God. I have gained no pagans, but lost 50. He has lost no Christians, but has gained 50 pagans, so that the pagans have lost half and gained none. The Christians have gained half, and lost none, because the Christian is exclusivist, and the pagan is not.

In other words, Christian missionaries are destroying other religions in their wake, because they and they alone are exclusivistic. Christians were not only exclusivistic, but they were firmly committed. They had fierce devotion to their faith, so much so that, as we will see in future lectures, many were willing to die for their faith, to undergo public torment, humiliation, and death.

This is a part of their exclusivity: "We are so right, we're not willing to give it up. If I'm right about my beliefs, but you are right, too, and you are right too, it doesn't matter; if you are all right, I will change my beliefs, but as I am the only one who is right, I'm not willing to change." Christians were willing to die for their faith, and that may have had some impact on people, they saw that this was an exclusivistic religion that people were willing to hold onto to their deaths. That's why Tertullian, in the second century, when talking about Christian conversions and persecution could say, "You can mow us down all you want, kill us all you want. The blood of the martyrs is seed," meaning that as people saw that Christians were willing to stand up for their faith, they would convert to the faith. We therefore have an exclusive religion that people are fiercely devoted to.

Thus, Christianity goes on year after year, converting people to its ways. So that Christianity then succeeds by word-of-mouth, increasing at a steady state, until Constantine. It's hard to know why Constantine converted. His own account is given in the works of Eusebius, a fourth century church father who wrote *A Life of Constantine*, and claimed that Constantine had a vision, in which he was going to battle against an enemy. Constantine, who was a Roman general, was going to battle with an enemy and was scared before the battle. He had a dream in which he saw a cross in the sky that had the words: "By this, conqueror" on it. "By this, conqueror." Constantine took this as a vision coming from Christ, that if he would be devoted to the cross, he would win his battle.

He had the emblem of the cross with Christ's two initials placed on trophies set up around his army, and in fact, he won the battle he was undertaking.

It's hard to know if Constantine was a firm convert to Christianity, or if he converted for religious or political reasons, but he certainly did convert. He wasn't baptized until he was on his deathbed, but nonetheless, many people think he was sincere in his conversion, and he certainly started pouring out favors upon the Christian church. As I have indicated, once that happened, Christianity took off like gangbusters, until, several decades later, it had become the majority religion within the Roman Empire.

Lecture Eleven
The Early Persecutions of the State

Scope: This lecture is the first of four dealing with persecution and martyrdom in the early church. As Christianity spread, it was widely opposed, first, on the local level by antagonistic mobs and, later, officially by Roman imperial authorities. Why were Christians seen as problematic and singled out for punishment?

In this lecture, we will examine a graphic account of Christian persecution from the mid-second century (the martyrdom of Christians in Lyons and Vienne) and move from there to consider both why Christians were persecuted and what their reactions to opposition were. En route, we will unravel several "myths" about early Christian persecution (for example, that Christianity was "illegal" and that Christians were always in hiding). The lecture will conclude by considering the scattered evidence for the emperors' involvement in early persecution (under Nero, Trajan, and Marcus Aurelius).

Outline

I. In the previous two lectures, we saw how Christianity spread throughout the Roman world.

   A. In those lectures, I argued that the religion spread by word of mouth and proved attractive to some pagans because the Christian God appeared to be so powerful, that is, capable of doing great miracles for his people.

   B. Moreover, the exclusive claim of the Christians—that their God alone was true and all other gods were false, that their views alone were right and all others, wrong—was unique in that world and facilitated the spread of Christianity, because it necessarily destroyed the other religions when pagans converted.

   C. It would be a mistake to think that the conversion of the empire happened quickly and unproblematically. In fact, there were major obstacles, seen in the circumstance that most pagans rejected the Christian message, finding it offensive and worthy of violent opposition.

D. In this lecture and the three that follow, we will consider the persecution of Christians throughout the empire during the first three centuries.

E. We have numerous accounts of Christian persecution, some by Christian authors who celebrated the torture and martyrdom of the faithful as signs of divine favor, others by Roman authors who considered the Christians' refusal to give up their religion in the face of torture and death to be reprehensible and idiotic.

II. We can begin our reflections by considering one of the most graphic and significant firsthand reports of a significant persecution against Christians, which occurred in the towns of Vienne and Lyons in Gaul (modern-day France) in the middle of the second century.

A. The account is preserved for us in a letter written by the Christians who survived the persecution to Christians in Asia Minor and preserved for us in the writings of the fourth-century church historian Eusebius.

B. The account indicates that the driving force behind the persecution was the devil, who inspired the mobs to oppose Christians and deprive them of public privileges and civil rights.

C. The anger of the mobs against the Christians increased, and they physically assaulted the Christians and finally urged the authorities to have those professing faith in Christ to be arrested.

D. The general unacceptability of the Christians was heightened by the claims of some of their slaves that Christians engaged in highly immoral and illegal activities, including cannibalistic practices and incestuous orgies.

E. We then have an account of the arrest, trials, torture, and martyrdom of several Christians, including a church leader named Sanctus and a woman named Blandina.

   1. The narrative provides graphic details of the public torments that these Christians endured (beatings, floggings, the rack, the iron seat).

   2. It also stresses their absolute refusal to abandon their Christian faith, despite such horrible suffering.

   3. Eventually, these Christians were put to death by being thrown to wild beasts; their bodies were left on display as an act of further humiliation, until they were burned and their ashes cast into the river.

III. This account raises a number of disturbing questions about the early persecution of the Christians.

    A. What motivated the pagan opponents to treat Christians in this way?

    B. How involved were the civil authorities? Why did they go along with the mob mentality? Was the religion seen as illegal? If so, for what reasons?

    C. What were the actual charges against the Christians, and could any of them have been true?

    D. How often did this sort of thing happen? Was it going on all the time, all over the empire?

    E. How did Christians react? Did they all willingly face torture and martyrdom for their faith? Or did some recant to save their skins?

    F. What drove those Christians who willingly underwent such public humiliation, torment, and death? Why were they so willing to die for their faith?

    G. These and similar questions go on and on. I will try to address them in what remains of this lecture and the ones to follow.

IV. To begin our reflections, I would like to dispel some common myths about early Christian persecution.

    A. Myth 1: Christianity was an illegal religion in the empire, constantly opposed by the Roman emperors. In point of fact, it was never declared illegal by an emperor until the middle of the third century. The emperors almost never were involved with Christian persecution.

    B. Myth 2: During the first three centuries, Christians were everywhere hunted down and martyred for their faith. In fact, in most times and places, Christianity was tolerated, just as other religions were.

    C. Myth 3: Christians had to go into hiding in the Roman catacombs to avoid detection. In fact, Christians did not have to go into hiding, and they certainly did not set up camp in the Roman catacombs.

D. Myth 4: Many, many thousands of Christians died in the early persecutions. In fact, the number was probably in the hundreds.

E. Myth 5: Christians were opposed because they worshipped Jesus as God, which was seen as a threat to the Roman belief that the emperor was god. In fact, there was no difficulty in worshipping Jesus as God. The problem was not whom the Christians worshipped, but whom they refused to worship: the Roman gods.

V. It is useful to consider some factual information about the course of "official" persecution of the early Christians.

A. The first emperor to be involved with persecutions was Nero (c. 64 A.D.), who used Christians as scapegoats for the fire in Rome that he evidently started himself.

    1. It is important to note, however, that in this case, Christians were condemned for arson, not for being Christian.

    2. Moreover, this persecution was localized to Rome. It may, however, have set a precedent for later civil authorities.

B. The next emperor known to be involved with persecutions was Trajan (c. 112 A.D.), who authorized a persecution of Christians in the province of Bythinia when Pliny was governor.

    1. In this case, Christians were persecuted simply because they claimed to be Christian.

    2. But anyone who recanted was excused. This shows that having been a Christian was not a crime; refusing to stop being one was.

C. Persecutions occurred sporadically from then onward (for example, under Marcus Aurelius—thus, the letter of Lyons and Vienne).

D. It was not until Christianity had grown into a sizable minority in the empire in the middle of the third century that any emperor made an empire-wide attempt to eliminate the religion.

    1. This was the emperor Decius in 249 C.E.

    2. But even this declaration of the religion as illegal lasted only a little more than two years (Decius died in 251).

E. The most significant attempt to wipe out Christianity came at the beginning of the fourth century with the emperor Diocletian, whose "Great Persecution" lasted several years, until Constantine became emperor, converted to the faith, and brought an end to imperial opposition to Christianity.

VI. In sum, Christianity was a minority religion throughout these years and faced sporadic, local, and occasionally violent opposition, with occasional "official" backing. In the lectures to follow, we will consider more fully the questions of why pagans opposed this new religion and how Christians reacted to this opposition.

Essential Reading:

Bart Ehrman, *After the New Testament*, chapter 3.

Everett Ferguson, *Church and State in the Early Church* (especially the articles by de Ste. Crois and Sherwin-White).

Robert Wilken, *The Christians as the Romans Saw Them*.

Supplementary Reading:

H. Musurillo, *The Acts of the Christian Martyrs*.

Judith Perkins, *The Suffering Self*.

Questions to Consider:

1. Why do you imagine that a set of religions that was otherwise so tolerant (paganism) would be so intolerant of the Christian religion?

2. Why do you suppose that the Christian persecutions appear to have sprung from the ground up (that is, from the pagan mobs), rather than from the top down (that is, from the imperial authorities)?

Lecture Eleven—Transcript
The Early Persecutions of the State

In the previous two lectures, we saw how Christianity spread throughout the Roman world. There, I argued that the religion spread by word of mouth, and proved attractive to some pagans because the Christian God appeared to be so powerful, capable of doing great miracles for his people. Moreover, the exclusive claims of the Christians—that their God alone was the true God and all others were false, that their views alone were right and that all others were wrong—were unique in that world and facilitated the spread of Christianity, in that it necessarily destroyed the other religions when pagans converted to Christianity. This made Christianity unique; it destroyed the other religions in its wake.

It would be a mistake, though, to think that the conversion of the empire happened quickly and unproblematically, for, in fact, there were major obstacles, seen in the circumstance that most pagans (as most Jews before them) rejected the Christian message, found it offensive and worthy of violent opposition.

In this lecture, and the three that follow, we will consider the persecution of Christians throughout the empire during the first three centuries. We have numerous accounts of Christian persecution, some of them by Christian authors who celebrate the torture and martyrdom of the faithful as signs of divine favor, others of them by Roman authors, who considered the Christians' refusal to give up their religion in the face of torture and death to be reprehensible and idiotic.

We will begin our reflections by considering one of the most graphic and significant first-hand reports of a significant persecution against Christians, which happened in the towns of Vienne and Lyons in ancient Gaul, which would be modern-day France. This persecution took place in the middle of the second century, during the reign of the Roman emperor, Marcus Aurelius. We happen to have an account of the persecution of Christians from a first-hand source. There was a letter that was written by Christians who survived the persecution. The letter was addressed to other Christians who lived in Asia Minor. It has been preserved for us in the writings of the fourth-century church historian Eusebius.

Eusebius is an important source for most of our information about the first three centuries. He was writing soon after the conversion of Constantine to Christianity, and Eusebius gives an account of Christianity up to his own day. One of the things most valuable about Eusebius is that he would sometimes quote documents, letters, and reports in his history of early Christianity. He wrote a ten-volume history of the early church. This letter, then, the letter from the churches of Lyons and Vienne is incorporated into his account totally, so that we can extract it, and see what these second-century Christians were saying, even though the writing, now, is preserved in a fourth-century source.

The account of the persecution of the Christians in Lyons and Vienne begins by indicating that the driving force behind the persecution was none other than the devil, who inspired the mobs to oppose Christians, and to deprive them of their public privileges and civil rights. Let me read just the very beginning of this letter, so you get a bit of a sense of how it works. It begins by saying: "The servants of Christ at Vienne and Lyons in Gaul, to our brothers in Asia and Phrygia. The severity of our trials here, the unbridled fury of the heathen against God's people, the untold sufferings of the blessed martyrs, we are incapable of describing in detail. Indeed, no pen could do them justice," they say. "The adversary swooped upon us with all his might, giving us, now, foretaste of his advent, which, undoubtedly is imminent." This is referring to the devil, who has started this persecution against the Christians, and according to these authors, this is showing that they are living at the end of time. Remember, in apocalyptic thought, Jews and Christians who were apocalypticists maintained that the world had been given over to evil forces who were going to increase in power until the end of this age, when literally, all hell would break out, before God would intervene to overthrow the forces of evil. These Christians living in Lyons and Vienne were sensing that this persecution that had happened was a sign that the end was near, so that the devil was pulling out all stops now, and that was an indication that his own demise was imminent.

They went on to indicate the devil had left no stone unturned in his efforts to gain adherents, and to equip them to attack the servants of God. Then, they went on to tell exactly what happened in the cities against the Christians: "We were debarred from houses, baths, and the forum. They actually forbade any of us to be seen in any place whatsoever," meaning that the local pagan townspeople forbade Christians to appear in public.

"These charged into the fight, standing up to every kind of abuse [They are referring now to the Christians who were being persecuted] and punishment, and they made light of their heavy load as they hastened to Christ, proving without a doubt that the sufferings of the present are not to be compared with the glory that is in store for them." It went on to indicate that the crowd surged against them, heaping blows upon them. They were marched into the forum, and were interrogated by the tribune, and by city authorities, and they ended up being arrested, then, for being Christian.

The cost, the persecution began by forbidding Christians to appear in public places, and then, it turned out that there was a hunt for the Christians authorized by the authorities, and they ended up, then, being arrested.

The general unacceptability of the Christians was to the populace at large. It was heightened by the claims of some of the slaves of the Christians, who were taken, and accused the Christians of engaging in highly immoral and illegal activities. Some of those who were arrested, we're told in the letter, "are heathen domestics." Christians, like other well-to-do people in the ancient world had slaves, domestics who took care of their household affairs, and in this case, these Christians had slaves who were pagan.

These pagan slaves who were arrested were afraid of being tortured under interrogation. In the ancient world, the idea was that if you wanted to get the truth out of somebody under interrogation, you would torture him or her. This is a very different point of view from our point of view, where we think that if you torture somebody, they'll simply say anything they can to get off the hook. In the ancient world, the idea was that pain took somebody so close to the edge that it forced them to tell the truth, and so these domestics, these slaves who were arrested, were afraid of being tortured, and so before the torture began, they actually told the people what they wanted to hear, which is not at all what their Christian owners would have wanted them to hear. "These pagan slaves falsely accused us of Thyestean banquets and Oedipean incest, and things we ought never to think or speak about, or even believe that such things ever happened among human beings."

What does this mean, that they were accused of "Oedipean incest" and "Thyestean banquets"? As we will see in the next lecture, two of the common charges against Christians were that they engaged in incestuous orgies and that they performed acts of cannibalism. Christians met secretly so that outsiders couldn't actually see what was happening in their midst, and rumors floated around that these were the kinds of activities that Christians were engaging in, because why keep meetings secret? Why weren't they open? What are you doing in there that we don't know about?

These charges of cannibalism and incest were quite common against Christians, as was the charge, as we will see later, and as I mentioned before, that they were atheists. This isn't exactly what people today think about in regard to Christians and their worship services, but these were the kinds of rumors floating around about Christians, which then stirred up mobs even more to attack them. In fact, the attack was quite forceful.

> The whole fury of crowd, governor, and soldiers fell with crushing force on some of our members. Sanctus was the name of one fellow who was the deacon from Vienne. On Maturus, very recently baptized but heroic in facing his ordeal; on Attalus, who had always been a pillar and support of the church in his native Pergamum; and on Blandina [a woman] through whom Christ proved that things which men regard as mean, unlovely, and contemptible are by God deemed worthy of great glory.

These people were going to be publicly tortured for their faith, in an attempt to get them to recant, to give up their Christianity. We're given some details. I will read you a little bit of some of these gory details:

> Blandina was filled with such power that those who took it in turns to subject her to every kind of torture, from morning to night, were exhausted by their efforts, and confessed themselves beaten. They could think of nothing else to do to her. [They were torturing her, and she would not recant no matter what they did.] They were amazed that she was still breathing, for her whole body was mangled, and a net her wounds gaped; they declared that torment of any one kind was enough to part soul and body, let alone a succession of torments of such extreme severity. But the blessed woman, wrestling magnificently, grew in strength as she proclaimed her faith, and found refreshment, rest, and insensibility to her sufferings when she uttered the words, 'I am a Christian; we do nothing to be ashamed of.'

She was unwilling to admit that they had done anything immoral or illegal. On the contrary, she insisted that being a Christian was a moral act, and she strengthened in her sufferings, according to this.

Now, as you remember, in our last lecture, you saw that Christians could claim that the miracles that were performed by the followers of Christ were a vindication of the Christian message. Well, that's part of the ideology behind this text. They can't make these people recant, no matter what tortures are against them.

Then, it goes on to describe some of the tortures applied to Sanctus:

> Sanctus was another, who with magnificent, superhuman courage nobly withstood the entire range of human cruelty. Wicked people hoped that the persistence and severity of his tortures would force him to utter something improper, but with such determination did he stand up to their onslaughts that he would not tell them his own name, race, and birthplace, or whether he was slave or free; to every question he replied in Latin, 'I am a Christian.' Consequently, the governor and his torturers strained every nerve against him, so that when they could think of nothing else to do to him, they ended by pressing red-hot copper plates against the most sensitive parts of his body. These were burning, but Sanctus remained unbending and unyielding, firm in his confession of faith.

Well, the story goes on and on for a number of pages, describing the tortures that these people underwent, and their refusal to recant in the face of such awful torments.

Eventually, these Christians were put to death by being thrown to the wild beasts. Their bodies were then left on display as a further act of humiliation, until they were burned, and their ashes cast into the sea. In these persecution narratives in which Christians were martyred, often, the bodies were dismembered and burned, and Christians were not allowed access to the bodies, for fear that the Christians would use the relics of the martyrs as objects of worship.

Moreover, by burning the bodies and throwing the ashes into the sea, the pagans were mocking the doctrine of the resurrection. Christians proclaimed that their flesh would be raised on the last day. Therefore, pagans, to mock that belief, burned the bodies and scattered the ashes, and said, "What body are you going to live in? You don't have a body anymore; you're just ashes."

This account of the persecution of the Christians in Lyons and Vienne raises a number of disturbing questions about the early persecution of the Christians. What motivated the pagan opponents to treat Christians in this way? I thought these pagans were, by and large, tolerant of religion. How could they be tolerant if they were treating Christians this way?

How involved were the civil authorities? Did they start the persecution? In this account, it's a mob that starts the persecution, and then the civil authorities come in and go along with the mob mentality. Why did they do that? Was this religion seen as illegal, against actual laws? If so, what was the illegality of it? If not, why were they being persecuted?

What were the actual charges against the Christians, and could any of these charges have been true? How often did this sort of thing happen? Was it going on all the time? All over the empire? Or was it sporadic and local?

How did Christians react? Did they all willingly face torture and martyrdom for their faith, or did some recant in order to save their skins? For those Christians who did willingly undergo such public humiliation and torment and death, what drove them to do so? Why were they so willing to be tortured and killed for their faith?

These and similar questions go on and on. I will try to address them in what remains of this lecture, and in the ones that follow. To start, I would like to dispel some common myths about early Christian persecution, five common myths that I will try to dispel.

Myth One: The myth that Christianity was an illegal religion in the empire and was constantly opposed by Roman emperors.

That, in fact, is a myth. Christianity, for most of the first two centuries, in fact, was not illegal per se. It is difficult to have a discussion about the legality of Christianity, because law in the Roman world was so different from law in our world. Romans did have a very substantial body of civil law, but they had very little by way of criminal law.

Most of the empire, of course, consisted of provinces outside of Rome, provinces that were ruled by people who had been appointed as governors. The appointees were either Roman aristocrats who were trying to rise up in the echelon of Roman aristocracy, or they were local client kings, local aristocrats, who were made client kings to Rome. There was not such a thing as federal law throughout the Roman Empire that was to govern criminal activity. The governors were given local responsibility to deal with local affairs, following local custom, and doing whatever was required in order to achieve their two overarching tasks, which were to keep the peace and to raise the taxes. Governors, then, ruled the provinces not on the basis of some kind of federal law but on the basis of what was required in the local situation.

Christianity was not declared illegal throughout the empire until the middle of the third century, and then only briefly, as we will see. The emperors themselves, in fact, were almost never directly involved with Christian persecution. We will see how they were involved momentarily. That was Myth One.

Myth Two: During the first three centuries, Christians everywhere were hunted down and martyred for their faith.

That's a myth. In fact, it is not true. In most times and in most places, Christians were tolerated just as the devotees of other religions were. I have indicated before that Roman religion tended to be highly tolerant. Christians were largely tolerated unless something happened that started a persecution. By and large, though, Christians were not being hunted down and martyred.

Myth Three: The Christians, therefore, had to go into hiding in the Roman catacombs to avoid detection.

That's a complete myth, even though you might see it occasionally on bad late-night movies about the early Christians being in hiding in the catacombs. The catacombs were burial places for the Roman dead. You could go visit the Roman catacombs today and see parts of them, these underground burial places that are amazing, huge, fantastic places where there were burials performed, for pagans principally, but Christians eventually came to be buried in the catacombs as well. But they certainly didn't hide out in the catacombs in order to avoid detection. Christians didn't need to go into hiding because for the most part, Christians were not being hunted down throughout these centuries.

Myth Four: Many, many thousands of Christians died in the early persecutions.

That is probably false. In fact, we don't know the exact number, but when you read the ancient sources, you get an impression that some hundreds were possibly martyred for their faith, but certainly not many, many thousands.

Myth Five: The Christians were opposed because they worshipped Jesus as God, and this was seen as a threat to the Roman belief that the emperor was god.

That's a complete myth. It is not a myth that Christians worshipped Jesus as God; in fact, they did so, but there was no problem with worshipping Jesus as God. Remember, pagans worshipped many gods. They thought that some human beings were divine and could be worshipped. Pagans had no difficulty with Christians saying that Jesus was a divine being. That, in itself, would not preclude them from saying additionally that the emperor was a divine being, because the people who thought that the emperor was a divine being also had many gods. It was not against the law for Christians to consider Jesus as God. The problem was not their worship of Jesus. The problem was their failure to worship the Roman gods. Failing to worship the Roman gods was one of the chief reasons for the persecutions, as we will see, principally, in the next lecture.

At this point, it might be useful to consider some factual information, as opposed to these myths, about the course of official persecution of the early Christians. Let me give you some factual information, some things we know about the early persecutions, from an imperial point of view.

The first emperor to be involved with the persecutions of Christians was not the emperor who was around when Jesus died. When Jesus died, the emperor was Tiberius, who was the second Roman emperor, the first being Caesar Augustus. Jesus was born during the reign of Caesar Augustus, and we have no indication from any source at all that is reliable, at least, that Caesar Augustus had ever heard of Jesus. Undoubtedly, he had not. Caesar Augustus died in the year 14 A.D., when Jesus would have been a late teenager.

His successor was Tiberius, under whom Jesus was killed. During the reign of Tiberius, Pontius Pilate was the governor of Palestine. Even though Jesus was executed under Pontius Pilate, we have no secure information to suggest that Tiberius was aware of Jesus's crucifixion or of Jesus's existence.

The first indication we have of an emperor who knew anything about the Christians was much later, in the year 64, the Emperor Nero. You will recall from my earlier lecture that Nero was the first to persecute the Christians in Rome because of the fire that had started in Rome. Our Roman source, Tacitus, indicates that it was Nero himself who started the fire, but because people in Rome were suspicious that he had started the fire, he isolated the Christians and picked on them as scapegoats, and chose to punish them for starting the fire, in order to take suspicion off of himself. Therefore, Tacitus indicates that since the Christians were the hated of the human race, Nero could use them as his scapegoats, and he did some horrific things to the Christians in Rome, blaming them for the arson. We're told the Christians were rounded up, that Nero had some of these individuals rolled in pitch, and then set afire while still living, to function as human torches to light his gardens at night.

Tacitus indicated that he had other Christians wrapped in animal skins, and set ravenous dogs upon them to kill them. There were a variety of public tortures and executions designed to penalize these Christians for what they had done. Of course, they had not done it, even according to Tacitus. Nero had done it, but it is important to note that in this particular case, the

Christians being persecuted were not being persecuted for being Christians. They were being persecuted for arson. There's a big difference. Christians were not named as being illegal because there were Christians. There were being persecuted because they had allegedly committed arson.

Moreover, it is important to note that this particular persecution was localized to Rome. There was no empire-wide persecution of Christians under Nero. It was a local situation in Rome. This may have set a precedent for later civil authorities. It may be that later emperors or governors remembered, "Oh, yes, didn't Nero persecute the Christians? Maybe they're worth persecuting," but there were no laws set against the Christians even after Nero had done this thing that he did to the Christians in the year 64.

The next emperor known to have been involved with persecutions at all was the emperor Trajan, in the year 112, so some 60 years later. The emperor Trajan authorized a persecution of Christians in the province of Bythinia, when Pliny the Younger was governor there. Pliny the Younger was a Roman aristocrat who was made the governor of Bythinia. I mentioned this Pliny the Younger in an earlier lecture, and a bit about his persecution. Pliny's province had this rule against groups gathering together. It was illegal for groups to gather together, because they were afraid of political insurgency resulting.

Christians, though, gathered together, and Pliny found out about it. When he found out about it, he wasn't quite sure how to proceed, because he didn't know what the rules were about these Christians gathering together. He had some arrested, and he interrogated them, and he found that, in fact, they would meet together before the sun came up, and they would celebrate a religious service together, in which they would worship Christ as a God, and then they would take oaths not to hurt anybody, they would have a meal together of innocent food, and there didn't seem to be a problem with them.

However, Pliny did note that they refused to worship the Roman gods, and so Pliny designed a kind of procedure to decide whether Christians ought to be punished or not. He would bring out a bust of the emperor, and tell the Christians to perform an act of sacrifice to the emperor by throwing some incense on an altar. If they refused to do it, then he had them executed. If they would do it, then he let them off the hook.

Pliny wrote a letter to the Roman emperor, Trajan, in which he told him that this was his procedure, and Trajan wrote a letter back indicating that in fact, that was acceptable procedure: "Christians should not be hunted down," said Trajan, "but if they refuse to perform an act of sacrifice, then, they are to be executed."

Well, why executed? For the reasons I've pointed out earlier. If one refused to worship the state gods, or to acknowledge that a god was working in the emperor, then, that was a political act of treason against the state. If Christians refused to do that, then they deserved to be taken out of the way to be executed.

In any event, in this case, Christians were being persecuted simply because they were Christians. If anyone recanted, they were not punished. That's a very interesting phenomenon. It meant that being a Christian was not a crime, or having been a Christian was not a crime, unlike other crimes. If you committed murder, and then agreed not to do it anymore, you will still get punished for having committed murder. Having been a Christian, though, you didn't get punished for it if you recanted. Having been a Christian, then, was not a crime. Continuing to be a Christian was the crime that ended up being penalized.

After the days of Trajan, persecutions continued to occur sporadically onwards, for example, under Marcus Aurelius, as in the letter of Lyons and Vienne that I read at the beginning of this lecture. It was not until Christianity had grown into a sizable minority in the empire sometime in the middle of the third century that any emperor made an empire-wide attempt to eliminate the religion.

The first emperor to try to eliminate the religion throughout the entire empire was the emperor Decius, in the year 249, who made a requirement that every citizen of Rome needed to perform a sacrifice to the Roman gods. Those who refused to do so were executed. Moreover, everybody who performed the sacrifice had to get a little acknowledgment that they had performed the sacrifice, a *libellus* saying that they had performed the sacrifice.

Christians had to perform the sacrifice, then, or be executed. We do know that a number of Christians bribed other people to get one of the *libelli*, so that they could show they had sacrificed even though they had not, to save their skins. This became a huge controversy in Christianity: What about those who bribed to get this little *libellus*? What about those who sacrificed and then later recanted? What do you do about such people?

This persecution did not last long, because Decius didn't last long. The rule went into effect in the year 249. He died two years later, in the year 251. Christianity continued to be persecuted sporadically afterward, but there was no real systematic attempt to get rid of Christianity until the beginning of the fourth century, when the emperor Diocletian instigated the "Great Persecution," which lasted for nearly ten years, until Constantine became emperor.

Diocletian passed laws starting in the year 303 that required Christians to give up their sacred books, which were then burned. These laws required the demolition of Christian churches, and they removed class privileges from the Christians. High-ranking Christian officials were imprisoned. In the year 304, a law was passed that all Roman subjects had to perform sacrifices to the Roman gods.

This persecution, designed to break down Christianity by imprisoning its leaders, burning its books, and forcing everybody to perform sacrifices, was enforced to different degrees in different parts of the empire. The persecution lasted for about ten years, until Constantine became emperor, and he himself converted to Christianity.

To sum it up, Christianity was a minority religion throughout these years of the second and third centuries, and it faced sporadic local, although occasionally violent, opposition, sometimes with official backing. In the lectures that follow, we will consider more fully the questions of why pagans opposed this new religion and see how Christians reacted to this opposition.

Lecture Twelve
The Causes of Christian Persecution

Scope: This lecture provides a historical sketch of the course of persecution from the first to the third centuries, asking what motivated the two major kinds of violence against Christians: (a) grassroots, mob uprisings, which sometimes compelled official involvement, and (b) top-down persecutions ordered by the state. The earliest Christian *martyrology* ("account of a martyr"), the Martyrdom of Polycarp, will guide our reflections. Among other things, we will see that state-sanctioned persecutions did not appear until the middle of the third century. In particular, the lecture will consider several key reasons for pagan opposition to the religion, including the sense that Christians were stirring up the wrath of the gods and that they were engaged in antisocial and licentious activities.

Outline

I. In the previous lecture, we began to discuss the persecution of the early Christians and tried to dispel some of the myths surrounding their opposition in the early centuries of the church.

    A. There, we saw that the early persecutions tended to be local, occasional, and sporadic, rather than empire-wide, constant, and systematic.

    B. Moreover, we saw that by and large, persecutions began at the grassroots level, as non-Christians opposed the Christians, sometimes violently, and sometimes took their complaints to officials, who then took matters into their own hands.

    C. But why were Christians seen as offensive in that world, which otherwise seemed to be so tolerant of a vast array of religious beliefs and sensitivities? That is the question we will explore in this lecture.

II. We can begin by examining another martyrological account from the period—this one, in fact, is the earliest written account outside of the New Testament—of a Christian martyr, the famous bishop of Smyrna (Asia Minor), Polycarp, who was executed around 156 A.D.

A. The Martyrdom of Polycarp comes to us, again, in the form of a letter, this time from the Christians of Smyrna to those of another town, Philomelium.

B. The author of the letter indicates that he wants to show how Polycarp's martyrdom was "in conformity with the Gospel."

    1. Even though this is an eyewitness account, it is difficult to separate historical fact from theological fiction here.

    2. This is principally because the story is told in a way to emphasize the similarities of Polycarp's death to the death of Jesus in many of its details. For example, Polycarp predicts his death, he is betrayed by one of his own, the officer opposed to him is named Herod, he rides into town on a donkey, and so on.

C. Still, there is a historical kernel to this intriguing account, and it can be used to help us understand a bit more about why and how non-Christians opposed the followers of Christ in the early centuries of the church.

    1. The account stresses that others were tortured to death before Polycarp.

    2. It then goes on to detail the burning desire of the pagan crowds to have the leader of the Christians arrested and put on trial.

    3. The arresting officials try to persuade Polycarp to acknowledge the divinity of the Roman gods, but he refuses.

    4. When brought into the arena before the Roman proconsul, Polycarp is again urged to acknowledge the divinity of the emperor and to reject the "atheists" (that is, the Christians, who are "atheists" in that they do not accept the worship of the gods).

    5. When Polycarp steadfastly refuses, the proconsul urges him to persuade the masses.

    6. But Polycarp remains firm, despite threats of torture, because, as he says, the brief sufferings awaiting him pale in comparison with the eternal torments reserved for those who reject Christ.

    7. The crowds are incensed and urge his death. Polycarp is then burned at the stake. The narrator indicates that before his death, God worked miracles to demonstrate the truth of the gospel and to validate Polycarp as a true witness to it.

III. This account helps to illustrate several important historical facts about why the early Christians were persecuted.

    A. The religion was not understood to be illegal per se. Polycarp could have been spared had he simply recanted (unlike other crimes, for which expressing regret does not relieve one from punishment).

    B. Persecutions occurred because the pagan mobs opposed the Christians.

        1. Their opposition appears to be rooted in a fear of what the gods would do to communities that harbored their opponents (see 12:2).

        2. This coincides with other evidence from early sources, including the famous lines from the Christian apologist ("defender of the faith") Tertullian: "They [the pagans] think the Christians the cause of every public disaster, of every affliction with which the people are visited. If the Tiber rises as high as the city walls, if the Nile does not send its waters up over the fields, if the heavens give no rain, if there is an earthquake, if there is famine or pestilence, straightway the cry is, 'Away with the Christians to the lion!'" (*Apology* 40).

        3. This position makes considerable sense when one remembers that pagans saw the gods as their helpers and defenders against disaster; in exchange for their protection, the gods were to be worshipped in proper ways.

        4. This is also why Pliny could use a "litmus test" to see if someone were a Christian worthy of death or not: If the accused would sacrifice to the emperor, he was released as not deserving punishment.

        5. The problem, then, was not that Christians worshipped the Christian God or Christ; it was, instead, that they refused to worship the pagan gods.

        6. This problem can be seen with particular clarity in the account of the acts of the Scillitan martyrs.

    C. Support for the dangerous aspects of Christianity was found in the charges commonly labeled against Christians that they engaged in immoral religious ceremonies that included incestuous orgies and cannibalism.

1. These charges were already seen in the account of the martyrs of Lyons and Vienne.

2. They can be seen even more clearly in the charges leveled against Christians by a mid-second–century philosopher named Fronto, the tutor of Marcus Aurelius, who details the Christians' nefarious practices in graphic detail.

3. The charges may seem odd to people today, but they make sense given what we know about early Christians, who met in secret (outsiders weren't allowed in) and often at night (because most of them were lower class and had to work all day every day); who called one another "brother" and "sister" and exchanged kisses as greetings (incest?!); and who then ate and drank the body and blood of the Son of God (cannibalism?!).

IV. There were numerous motivating factors behind the persecution of the early Christians. Principally, the persecutions were driven by the sense that Christians had offended the gods and were an immoral presence in society. Occasionally, the mob reaction against Christians was taken to the authorities, who acted in what they saw as the best interest of their people and tried to make Christians recant their beliefs or pay the horrific consequences.

Essential Reading:

Bart Ehrman, *After the New Testament*, chapter 3.

Everett Ferguson, *Church and State in the Early Church* (especially the articles by de Ste. Crois and Sherwin-White).

Robert Wilken, *The Christians as the Romans Saw Them.*

Supplementary Reading:

W. H. C. Frend, *Martyrdom and Persecution in the Early Church.*

H. Musurillo, *The Acts of the Christian Martyrs.*

Questions to Consider:

1. In considering the accounts of early Christian persecutions, why do you suppose the state officials usually seemed less eager than the mobs to subject the Christians to torture and death?

2. Consider the charges leveled against Christians. Can you think of other instances throughout history, or even today, in which "opponents" of a group have been tarnished with claims of crass and flagrant immorality? What is one to make of such claims?

Lecture Twelve
The Causes of Christian Persecution

In the previous lecture, we began to discuss the persecutions of the early Christians and tried to dispel some of the myths surrounding their opposition in the early centuries of the church. There, we saw that the early Christian persecutions tended to be local, occasional, and sporadic, rather than empire-wide, constant, and systematic.

Moreover, we saw that the persecutions, by and large, began at the grass-roots level, as non-Christians opposed the Christians, sometimes violently, and sometimes took their complaints to officials, who then took matters into their own hands. Why were Christians seen as offensive though, in that world, which otherwise seemed to be so tolerant of a vast array of religious beliefs and sensitivities?

That's the question we will be exploring in the present lecture: Why were Christians seen as offensive? We can begin by examining another martyrological account from the period. This one, in fact, is the earliest written account outside of the New Testament of a Christian martyr. This is the martyrdom of the famous bishop of Smyrna, in Asia Minor, a man named Polycarp, who was executed around 156 A.D.

By way of background, I should point out that we know a lot about this Polycarp. He may be the best-known Christian from the early second century, because we have not only this account of his death, written by people who saw it happen, but we also have a letter written to Polycarp some 45 years earlier by another Christian martyr, Ignatius of Antioch, and we have a letter written by Polycarp to Christians who lived in the city of Philippi. Thus, we have a book about Polycarp, a letter written to him, and a letter written by him, so we're fairly well-informed of Polycarp, a very famous bishop of this town of Smyrna in Asia Minor.

The Martyrdom of Polycarp, as it is called, comes to us again in the form of a letter, just as the letter of the churches of Lyons and Vienne was written by the Christians to describe what had happened in the persecution of martyred Christians there. In this case, we have Christians of the town of Smyrna, who write to the Christians of another town, Philomelium, in order to tell them about the martyrdom of their revered bishop.

We will be looking at this account in some detail, because it is so interesting and can enlighten so clearly for us circumstances surrounding martyrdom in the mid-second Christian century. We're told by the authors of this letter that Polycarp's martyrdom was particularly significant, because it was a martyrdom that was in accord with the Gospel. A martyrdom that was in accord with the Gospel. What does the author mean?

Well, in part what the author of this letter means is that Polycarp's martyrdom had a lot in common with the death of Jesus in the New Testament Gospels. This author, his community, of course knew the Gospels of the New Testament, and portrayed the martyrdom of Polycarp in such a way as to show that he was imitating Christ in his own death. In fact, even though this is an eyewitness account of Polycarp's death, it's sometimes difficult to separate out the historical facts from the theological fictions here. This is principally because the story that is told in this letter is told in such a way as to emphasize the similarities of Polycarp's death to the death of Jesus in many of its details.

For example, we're told in this letter that Polycarp predicted his own death, just as Jesus in the Gospels told his disciples that he had to go to Jerusalem, be rejected by the scribes and elders, and then be executed before he would be raised from the dead. So, too, in this letter, Polycarp predicted that he would have to die, and he knew the manner of his death. Just as Jesus knew the manner of his death by crucifixion, Polycarp knew that he was going to be executed by being burned at the stake, and he predicted it in advance.

Just as Jesus was betrayed by one of his close disciples, Judas Iscariot, according to the Gospels, Polycarp was betrayed by a member of his own household in this account. Just as Jesus was put on trial before the Jewish king Herod in the Gospels, so, too, here, the officer who was opposed to Polycarp, who took him off to his execution, happened to be named Herod. Just as Jesus is portrayed in the Gospels as riding into town on a donkey before his arrest, so too, here, Polycarp was portrayed as riding into town on a donkey.

There are incidents throughout this account, in other words, that appear to be attempts by the author to show that Polycarp imitated Christ not only in the fact that he was killed, but in some of the details surrounding this martyrdom.

At the same time, there is a historical kernel to this intriguing account, and this historical kernel can help us understand a bit more about why and how non-Christians opposed the followers of Christ in the early centuries of the church, so that this just isn't a fictitious account. In fact, there is a historical nugget here that we can look at and examine, for trying to understand how martyrdoms happened, and why they happened.

Therefore, I will be reading parts of this account to show the historical kernel. This account stresses that Polycarp was not the only one who was being persecuted at the time. In fact, there were others who were tortured to death before Polycarp. In chapter 2, verses 1 and following, the author says:

> Blessed and noble, therefore, are all the martyrdoms that have taken place in accordance with the will of God, for who could fail to admire the nobility and patient endurance, and loyalty of the master of those who are martyred? For even when they were so torn by whips that the internal structure of their flesh was visible, as far as the inner veins and arteries, they endured so patiently that even the bystanders had wept with pity. But they themselves reached such a level of bravery that not one out of them uttered a cry, or a groan, thus showing to us all at the very hour when they were being tortured, the martyrs of Christ were absent from the flesh, or rather, the Lord was standing by and conversing with them. [So there was a miraculous ability to withstand pain by these martyrs.] These martyrs turned their thoughts to the grace of Christ, and they despised the tortures of this world, purchasing at the cost of one hour an exemption from eternal punishment.

This is a theme we're going to see recurring throughout these martyrdoms. These martyrs believed that if they could withstand this momentary, temporary torture, that they would escape eternal torment, whereas the ones who were torturing them may have been able to torture in the present for a short time, but they were the ones who were going to pay an eternal price: "The fire of their inhuman tortures felt cold to them, for they set before their eyes the escape from that eternal fire which is never extinguished," and so forth.

The account then goes on to talk about the pagan crowd's burning desire to have the leader of the Christians arrested and put on trial. Once they killed these others, they decided that they really wanted to go after the leader of these Christians, namely, Polycarp himself.

Polycarp, we're told, did not try to get arrested. He didn't try to get martyred for Christ. In fact, he initially went into hiding, but eventually, he decided there was no point in trying to hide out, because they were going to get him anyway, and so he eventually allowed himself to be caught. It says that he wanted, in fact, originally to remain in town so he would be captured right away, but some of his parishioners urged him to withdraw, and so, he went out into a country manor, where he stayed.

We're told that he fell into a trance three days before his arrest, and he saw his pillow being consumed by fire. He had this dream that his pillow was on fire, and he turned to those around him and said, "It's necessary that I be burned alive."

Well, they ended up searching for him, and arrested a couple of slave boys, one of whom confessed under torture where Polycarp was. They sent out a mounted guard, and they arrested him. When they came, they were surprised that there was such an urgency to arrest him, because he was an old man. What was the urgency to capture an old man? Polycarp asked them for time to have a chance to pray before he was put under arrest, and they did. They gave him a chance to pray, not knowing that when Polycarp prayed, he prayed at long time. He actually stood for two hours, unable to stop, and they had to wait, but at least he had arranged for them to have some food and drink in the interim.

Anyway, they decided to bring Polycarp into town. They brought him into town and had him sit in the carriage between two officials. These officials were trying to get him to repent of being Christian, so that he would not have to be executed, but it was to no avail. He refused. They said, "Well, what harm is there in saying, 'Caesar is lord,' and offering some incense?" Polycarp, though, insisted, saying, "I'm not about to do what you are encouraging me to do."

Polycarp entered into the arena, then, where crowds were gathered around for some of the Roman games that were going on. It appears that what was going on was that this was something like a gladiatorial contest. There were humans fighting, there was an animal hunt going on, where they set loose animals on prisoners, who then were to fight them. Of course, the prisoners always lost.

They were going to treat Polycarp as a criminal in this way, and kill him in some public spectacle. He had not been tried, yet, though, and the trial actually happened within the arena itself. He was brought by those who arrested him before the proconsul, the governor, who tried to get him to recant, saying such things to Polycarp as: "Have some respect for your age," or "Swear by the genius of Caesar, the divine being that inspires the Caesar," and "Say, 'Away with the atheists,'" (meaning, "I have nothing to do with these Christians").

Well, Polycarp did a little play on words, ironically. He looked at the crowds surrounding him, who were urging his death, and he groaned and sighed, and said, "Away with the atheists," meaning, "These are the people who are atheists. We are the ones who have God on our side."

The magistrate persisted, saying, "Swear the oath, and I will release you. Revile Christ."

Polycarp replied, "For 86 years, I have been his servant, and he has done me no wrong. How can I blaspheme my king, who saved me?"

Well, Polycarp, then, steadfastly refused to perform the sacrifices necessary to get off the hook. The proconsul urged him to persuade the masses, but Polycarp remained firm, despite threats of torture, because, as he said, the brief sufferings awaiting him paled in comparison to the eternal torment reserved for those who refused to accept Christ.

As Polycarp said: "You threaten with fire that burns only briefly, and after just a little while, is extinguished, but you are ignorant of the fire of the coming judgment and eternal punishment, which is reserved for the ungodly. Well, why do you delay? Come, do as you wish."

Well, the crowds were incensed, and they urged his death. Polycarp was then burned at the stake. The narrator indicates, though, that prior to his death, God worked miracles to demonstrate the truth of the gospel, and to validate Polycarp as a true witness to it.

They built a pyre, and put a stake in the middle of it that they were going to nail him to. He said, "I don't need to be nailed to this. If Christ has made me strong to this point, he will allow me to stand firm," so, they did not secure him.

They lit the fire, but then a miracle happened. The flames, rather than attacking his body, formed a kind of envelope around him, like a sheet around him, and instead of the reek of burning flesh, they smelled a perfume coming out of it, kind of like baked bread, coming out of this sheet of fire that was surrounding him.

They decided that if they could not kill him by fire, they would order an executioner to come up and kill him with a dagger. The executioner came up, and stuck in the dagger, and a dove flew from Polycarp's side. This must be a fictional account of the holy spirit returning to heaven, his holy spirit. Then, there they out so much blood that it put out the fire, which is a nice little touch, but he was dead by now anyway, because of the dagger wound.

They ended up taking his body, and refusing to let the worshipers, the Christians, have the body, because they were afraid they would use it as a holy relic, and disposed of the body, so that the Christians could not have access to it. That, then, is the end of the story of the martyrdom of Polycarp.

It's a graphic account, a very interesting account. As I pointed out, it's an account apparently written by eyewitnesses, even though they fabricated parts of it order to show the theological truths that they wanted to affirm.

The account is also helpful, though, in illustrating several important historical facts about why the Christians were persecuted, and so I would like to go through what some of these historical facts are that are worth our knowing.

First, the religion of Christianity was not understood to be illegal per se. Polycarp would have been spared if he had simply recanted. As I pointed out in my last lecture, this was different from other crimes. Being of the Christian religion was not exactly illegal, because you could stop being a Christian, and were not punished. The first thing to notice, then, is that the religion was not being treated as something that was illegal.

Second, the persecutions occurred because the pagan mobs opposed the Christians. The arrest of Polycarp was instigated by the pagan mobs who cried out, "Go for Polycarp now." The governor was not the one who started it.

The opposition of the pagans appeared to be rooted in a fear of what the gods would do to communities that harbored their opponents. You can see this in a part of this that I didn't read. When the crowds were urging for the arrest and execution of Polycarp, they cried out: "This man, Polycarp, is the teacher of Asia, the father of the Christians, the destroyer of our gods, who teaches many not to sacrifice, or worship."

They were therefore urging the proconsul to kill Polycarp because he was a sacrilegious person. He had destroyed the gods, and taught others not to sacrifice during worship. Well, what are they afraid of?

They appeared to be afraid of what the gods would do to a community that harbored people in their midst who did not worship the gods. Remember how we saw that pagan religion was largely driven by the desire to keep peace among the gods, and driven by a fear of the gods. These people seemed to be afraid that if they harbored people such as Polycarp, the gods would penalize them.

This understanding of why pagans were opposed to Christians, for religious reasons—this may not be how we normally think of it, but pagans were actually opposed to Christians for their own religious reasons, for fear that the gods were going to penalize the community—that understanding coincides with other evidence we have from early sources, including the famous line from the second and third century church writer named Tertullian.

Tertullian was a very famous Christian author who wrote a number of defenses of Christianity (apologies). He appeared to have had some kind of legal training and had a very sharp, rapier wit. He indicated in several places that pagans were afraid of Christians in their midst, because of what the gods would do to their cities, and so, there is his famous line he had. In one of his books, *The Apology*, in chapter 40, he said:

> They [meaning the pagans] think that the Christians are the cause of every public disaster, of every affliction with which the people are visited. If the Tiber River rises as high as the city walls, if the Nile River does not send its waters up and over the fields, if the heavens give no rain, if there is an earthquake, if there is famine or pestilence, straightaway the cry is, 'Away with the Christians to the lion!'" (Tertullian's *Apology* 40.)

In other words, whenever there was a disaster that hit—not enough rain, too much rain, flood, drought, pestilence, famine—if there was a disaster that hit, the pagans said, "It's because of these Christians. The gods are punishing us because of them, and so, away to the lion." In other words, "Kill the Christians, and that will take care of the problem."

This position makes considerable sense when we recall that the pagans saw the gods as helpers and defenders against disaster; in exchange for their protection, the gods were to be worshiped in the proper ways. That's why, if you recall, the Governor Pliny of Bythinia had a kind of litmus test in order to see whether somebody was worshiping the gods or not, he would bring out a bust or statue of the emperor, and the person had to offer some incense to this statue of the emperor. If he or she didn't offer this incense, then he or she was taken off to be executed.

Why? Because this would show that the person was not worshiping the state god, and someone who was not worshiping the state god was seen to not only be committing a political act, but a dangerous religious act, because the gods were the ones who had made the state great, which meant that you needed to worship these gods, or else they would harm the state.

The problem the Christians had, then, was not that they worshipped the Christian God, or that they worshipped Christ. It was, as we have seen, that they refused to worship the pagan gods.

It appears that the Roman governors who were in charge of these persecutions were not all that enthusiastic about persecuting the Christians. We have seen this in the case of Polycarp, where the proconsul was, in fact, trying to get Polycarp to recant, and was doing everything he could, because he didn't want to kill him, even though that's what the mob wanted. "Just perform the sacrifice. Just say the word." Well, these Christians refused to do so, however.

There's a very interesting account that we have that is earlier than the account of Tertullian, from the same place Tertullian lived, North Africa. It's an account of early martyrs that is called the Acts of the Scillitan Martyrs. It's a very brief text, but it's useful because it shows how a local governor was not at all eager to persecute Christians, but in fact was eager to let the Christians off the hook, if the Christians would just cooperate with him a little bit. The Acts of the Scillitan Martyrs is the oldest Christian document we have from North Africa. It's document that is written in Latin, and it's an account of an actual trial of Christians before a governor, a proconsul, who was putting them on trial because they were Christian.

It's a short text, and so I will read parts of it to you, because it gives you a sense of how these governors were reacting to the Christians:

"In the consulship of Praesens and Claudianus, on the seventeenth day of July, there were arrayed at Carthage in the governors chamber's..." Then, it gives a list of names: Speratus, Nartzalus, Cittinus, etc., a list of names. These were people who were Christians.

The proconsul, whose name was Saturninus, he said, "If you return to your senses, you can obtain pardon of our lord the emperor." In other words, "Just change your mind, and you'll be forgiven."

"Speratus [who was a Christian] 'We've never done wrong. We've never lent ourselves to wickedness. Never have we uttered a curse, but when abused, we have given thanks. We hold our own emperor in honor." We haven't done anything wrong at all.

Saturninus, the proconsul, then says: "We, too, are religious people, and our religion is a simple one." (This is the pagan governor talking.) "We, too, are religious people, and our religion is a simple one. We swear by the genius of our lord the emperor, and we offer prayers for his health, as you ought also to do." He is saying: Don't tell us that you are religious, and we are not. We are religious. All you need to do is offer prayers for the emperor.

Speratus, the Christian, said: "If you will give me a calm hearing, I shall tell you the mystery of simplicity." In other words: I will tell you the real religion, if you will just give us a chance, the Christian said.

Saturninus replied: "If you begin to malign our sacred rites, I will not listen to you, but swear rather by the genius of our lord the emperor." In other words: I don't want to have a religious day, here. This is very simple. Just swear by the genius of the emperor. (Genius, by the way, as I pointed out earlier, doesn't mean that he's really brilliant. The genius is the guiding spirit of the imperial house, and so you are swearing by the divine element in the emperor.)

Speratus, the Christian, said: "I don't recognize the empire of this world. Rather, I serve that God whom no one has seen, nor can see with these eyes. I have not stolen, and on any purchase, I pay the tax, where I acknowledge my lord is the emperor of the kings and all nations."

Then, the proconsul Saturninus says to the others (he's getting nowhere with Speratus): "Cease to be of this persuasion." They refuse. Saturninus, the proconsul says: "Have no part in this folly," and they refuse. The proconsul, Saturninus, says again to Speratus: "Do you persist in remaining a Christian?" Speratus says: "I am a Christian," and everyone else agreed with him.

Saturninus, the proconsul, was starting to be exasperated, here. He said, "You wish no time for consideration?" In other words: I will give you some time to think about it." "In so just a matter, there's no need for consideration," said Speratus.

The proconsul, Saturninus, said, "Okay, you're granted a reprieve of thirty days. Think it over." Once again, Speratus said, "I am a Christian," and with him, all the others agreed.

Thus, not only could Saturninus not get them to perform the sacrifice to the emperor—just throw some incense on the altar; just say the oath and get out of here— they refused; they insisted on it.

Saturninus's hand is forced: "Whereas Speratus, Nartzalus, Cittinus, Donata, and these others have confessed that they have been living in accordance with the rites of the Christians, whereas, though given the opportunity to return to the usage of the Romans, they persevered in their obstinacy. They are hereby condemned to be executed by the sword."

Speratus said: "We thank God." And so it happened. They took them out, and beheaded them. End of story.

Well, it's a very interesting account, because it shows that these persecutors of the Christians were not anti-religious at all. They were religious, and they were trying to persecute Christians for religious reasons, and they were not eager to do so. These governors, in fact, were doing so reluctantly, because they didn't see what the point was in this obstinacy that these Christians had.

One other aspect that we need to look at and that we've touched on briefly, but I want to end with has to do with one other reason for persecuting the Christians, involving the alleged immoral religious ceremonies that they were engaged in. I mentioned earlier the incestuous orgies and cannibalism that the Christians were charged with, charges that we saw in the account of the martyrdoms of Lyons and Vienne.

Christians, in fact, were widely suspected of engaging in these kinds of wild activities. One of the best references to this comes from a Christian apology written by a Christian named Octavius, who also lived in North Africa. Octavius gives an account of the charges leveled against Christians, a very interesting set of charges, which show that many pagans thought that Christians were engaged in wild, profligate activities. This is the charge that he's recording: "The notoriety of the stories told of the initiations of new Christian recruits is matched by their ghastly horror." This is what they're told to do with their new recruits: "A young baby is covered with flour, the object being to deceive the unwary. It is then served before the person to be admitted into their rites. The recruit is urged to inflict blows upon it. They appear to be harmless, because of the covering of flour. Thus, the baby is killed with wounds that remain unseen and concealed. It is the blood of this infant, it is this blood, that they lick with thirsty lips. These are the limbs they distribute eagerly. This is the victim by which they seal their covenant. It is by complicity in this crime that they are pledged to mutual silence. These are their rites, more foul that all sacrileges combined."

He goes on to describe orgies that Christians engage in at night, people who are related to each other engaged in sexual activities together at night.

What is this all about? Christians were widely charged with having incestuous orgies, with killing babies, and eating them. Where did these charges come from? Well, these charges may seem odd to people today, but they make sense given what we know about early Christians otherwise. Remember that Christians were meeting in secret. They often had to meet at dark, because they were of the lower classes. These were people who had to work during the day. They called each other "brother" and "sister," and they were known to great one another with a kiss.

Brothers and sisters kissing? In the dark? What's that all about? Rumors of incest flew.

Moreover, they were known to eat the body and drink the blood of the Son of God. They are eating the body and drinking the blood of the Son? They are killing babies and eating them. The charges, then, were of incestuous orgies, infanticide, and cannibalism. These charges are found not just in the writings of Octavius, but in a number of ancient sources. These were the sorts of rumors that flew concerning the Christians. These were the sorts of things that the masses may well have been persuaded by. We have seen that the governors were not all that eager to persecute the Christians. These governors would have been more highly educated. It may be that the masses were driving the governors to do this, forcing their hands, based on this kind of libelous accusation against the Christians.

To sum it up, there were numerous motivating factors behind the persecution of the early Christians. Principally, the persecutions were being driven by the sense that Christians had offended the gods, and that they were a more immoral presence in society. Occasionally, the mob reaction against Christians was taken to the authorities, who acted in what they saw to be the best interests of their people, their society, and tried to make Christians recant their beliefs, or pay the horrific consequences.

In our next lecture, we will consider how Christians themselves reacted to their hostile reception, persecution, and martyrdoms.

Lecture Thirteen
Christian Reactions to Persecution

Scope: In this lecture, we try to understand how Christians reacted to their persecution at the hands of pagan mobs and local authorities. We will see that many Christians recanted their faith in the face of persecution, but many others stayed faithful to what they believed to be the truth. We will use the moving tale of the passion of Perpetua and Felicitas and the letters of Ignatius of Antioch to guide our reflections. From these texts, we will see that many Christians were willing to face torture and death because they believed that doing so would ensure them an afterlife of eternal bliss, whereas those who refused to accept the faith would face eternal torment. Moreover, some Christians believed that in suffering martyrdom, they were imitating the example set for them by Christ, their Lord.

Outline

I. In the previous lecture, we saw some of the reasons for the violent opposition to Christians throughout the empire.

    A. Christians were seen as a threat to society because they refused to worship the state gods. Disasters that struck could be seen by pagans, then, as divine retribution for cities that harbored such "atheists."

    B. Moreover, Christians were thought to be morally reprehensible and, therefore, socially dangerous.

    C. Christians, of course, denied that they were dangerous, and many of them refused to recant their beliefs even in the face of violent opposition and concerted official efforts.

    D. In this lecture, we will shift from considering the persecution from the pagan perspective (why did pagans act this way?) to the Christian perspective (how did Christians react to their opposition?).

II. We have already seen that some Christians recanted of their faith in the face of violent opposition.

A. This is clearly stated in the letter of the Christians of Vienne and Lyons.

B. It can also be seen in the Martyrdom of Polycarp in the story of Quintus, a Christian who voluntarily offered himself as a martyr, until he became terrified of the consequences and recanted.

C. We know of some Christian groups who opposed martyrdom on theological grounds—that Christ died precisely so that his followers would not have to do so. These Christians maintained that it was God's will to do (in bad faith) what the authorities insisted on and, thus, live.

D. It is difficult to know how many Christians recanted or pretended to recant in the face of physical torment.

E. Most of the surviving accounts are written by Christians who celebrate martyrdom and want to show the supernatural strength given the martyrs in the face of their death, as seen in the accounts of the martyrs of Vienne and Lyons and of the martyrdom of Polycarp.

III. A similar message of a Christian stalwart bearing up in the face of death can be seen in the powerful account of the martyrdom of Perpetua.

A. Perpetua was a 22-year-old recent mother and new convert to Christianity, living in North Africa around 203 A.D.

B. The story of her martyrdom for the faith is based in part on a firsthand account—her own diary kept while in prison—in which she records what happened to her and her fellow Christian martyrs, her reactions, her fears, and a series of visions she had while awaiting her death.

C. One of the most gripping elements of the story is her reaction to her poor father, a pagan who does not understand why she is insisting on dying for the faith and who tries in vain to get her to see reason—for his sake, the sake of her child, and for her own sake.

D. She spurns his pleas, however, relinquishes her child, and goes to her death willingly, even eagerly.

E. The account of her death in the arena is then narrated by an editor who took her diary and incorporated it into a longer martyrology, popular down through the ages until today.

IV. Why were such Christians as Blandina in Lyons, Polycarp in Smyrna, and Perpetua in North Africa so firm in refusing to recant, so stalwart in the face of death?

A. We can never know their personal reasons. But we do have some indications from the writings about them (by the Christians left behind) concerning why Christians preferred public torture, humiliation, and death to release and long life.

B. It appears that many Christians were convinced that as bad as the torments of the present were, they were not nearly so bad as the torments awaiting those who rejected Christ in the world to come (as explicitly stated in the Martyrdom of Polycarp and the letter of the churches of Lyons and Vienne).

1. This view is rooted in a theodicy that maintained that God would reward the righteous but punish the unrighteous.
2. This message became one of the central features of Christian preaching and related closely to its exclusivistic claims. Not only were Christians right in what they believed, but those who chose not to agree would be punished with horrific torments eternally.

C. Moreover, some Christians saw that a violent death at the hands of the authorities was a way to imitate Christ, who had died a similar death.

1. This view can be seen most clearly in the writings of one of the first Christians known to be martyred after the New Testament period, Ignatius of Antioch.
2. Ignatius was the bishop of Antioch, arrested for Christian activities, and sent to Rome to be thrown to the wild beasts.
3. En route, he wrote six letters to various churches that had sent representatives to greet him on the way. He wrote one other letter to the Christians in Rome, urging them not to interfere with the proceedings against him once he arrived, because it was by a violent death that he would be united with Christ and, thus, "attain to God."
4. The longing of Ignatius for violent death may seem pathological to modern ears, but it was only logical for him:

This world was of no importance to him; what mattered was the other world of God, which he could attain by imitating the martyrdom of Christ.

V. It is difficult to know how many Christians actually had to face death in this way (because the writings about the martyrs presuppose so many survivors, we can assume that not many were actually killed).

    A. Some evidently recanted of their Christian faith—or at least pretended to do so—when put to the test.

    B. Others, though, submitted themselves to public torment and death, because in doing so they were escaping the real and eternal suffering that would come to non-believers in the afterlife and because in dying this way, they could imitate their Lord and master, Christ.

Essential Reading:

Bart Ehrman, *After the New Testament*, chapter 3.

Everett Ferguson, *Church and State in the Early Church* (especially the articles by de Ste. Crois and Sherwin-White).

Judith Perkins, *The Suffering Self*.

Supplementary Reading:

H. Musurillo, *The Acts of the Christian Martyrs*.

Robert Wilken, *The Christians as the Romans Saw Them*.

Questions to Consider:

1. Can you imagine ways in which the persecution and martyrdom of Christians may have actually helped the Christian mission?

2. Why do you suppose that such people as Perpetua or Ignatius—who presumably had so much to offer people in this world and who could have no doubt led happy lives here—were so eager to sacrifice their bodies and leave this world?

Lecture Thirteen—Transcript
Christian Reactions to Persecution

In the previous lecture, we saw some of the reasons for the violent opposition to Christians throughout the Roman Empire. Christians were seen as a threat to society because they refused to worship the state gods. Disasters that struck could be seen by pagans, then, as divine retribution for cities that harbored such atheists. Christians were called "atheists" because they didn't worship the gods of the state. Although today, we would think of an atheist as someone who did not believe in God, in the ancient world, an atheist was someone who did not believe in sacrifice to the gods.

Christians were also thought, sometimes, to be morally reprehensible, in that they were thought to perform acts of incest, infanticide, and cannibalism during their worship services on a weekly basis. Remember, they would meet early before the sun came up, they would call one another "brother" and "sister," and they would greet one another with a kiss, so that outsiders who didn't understand the ritual would assume that there were some acts of incest going on. Moreover, they were known to "eat the flesh" and "drink the blood" of the Son of God, and so people assumed that they were performing acts of infanticide and cannibalism.

Christians were thought, then, to be socially dangerous. Christians, of course, denied that they were dangerous, and many of them refused to recant their beliefs, even in the face of violent opposition, and concerted official efforts.

In this lecture, we will shift from considering persecution from the pagan perspective; that is, we won't now be asking: Why did pagans act this way? We will now look at the Christian perspective: How did Christians react to their opposition by pagans? How did they react to the persecutions and threats? First, as you might expect, we do have record of some Christians recanting of their faith in Christ in the face of violent opposition. This can be seen in some of the literature that we've looked at already.

In the previous lecture, we considered the case of the Christians of Vienne and Lyons, in a letter written by the survivors of the persecution that happened around the year 177. Christians in Vienne and Lyons were persecuted first by the mobs, then by officials, and underwent horrible torments and tortures, with some of them actually martyred. We find in this letter written by the survivors, though, recorded for us by the church historian Eusebius, that not everybody who was a Christian decided to go through with persecution. Some, in fact, apparently recanting of their belief so as to avoid persecution. Thus, the authors tell us:

> The rest of the Christians fell into two groups. It was clear [says the author] that some were ready to be the first Gaelic martyrs [In other words, the first martyrs in Gaul, ancient France]. These people, these Christians, made a full confession of the testimony with the greatest eagerness, but it was equally clear that others were not ready, that they had not been trained, and were still flabby [This is a reference to the Christians who were willing to be persecuted as great warriors, and were in good shape, and trained, but that these others who were not willing to be martyrs were not trained, and were still flabby.]; in no fit condition to face the strain of a struggle to the death. Of these, some ten proved stillborn, causing us great distress, and inexpressible grief, and dampening the enthusiasm of those who were not yet arrested.

Thus, this author notes that there were ten individuals who had been Christian, or who had at least claimed to be Christian. When the heat was turned up, however, they recanted of their faith. Therefore, they were not "born again," but were "stillborn." These were people, then, who recanted of their faith in the face of violent opposition.

The same theme can be found in another book that we've looked at, the Martyrdom of Polycarp. One passage we did not consider in the Martyrdom of Polycarp concerns a person who recanted of his faith when being faced with persecution. This is in chapter 4 of the Martyrdom of Polycarp. Remember, Polycarp was the bishop of Smyrna, who was arrested and put on trial in the arena, and refused to recant of his faith, and then was burned at the stake. There was a miracle surrounding his death, but eventually he did die by the executioner's sword.

Early on in the account, we find reference to another person who was tested as well, and who had a completely different fate. This was a person named Quintus, and we are told that Quintus was from the region of Phrygia, who, "when he saw the wild beasts being leashed upon him, turned coward. This was the man," says the author of this letter, "who had forced himself and some others to come forward voluntarily." In other words, this was somebody who turned himself in as a Christian so that he could face martyrdom, but when the beasts came out, he chickened out, and said, "No, I recant."

"The proconsul, after many appeals, finally persuaded Quintus to swear the oath to the emperor, and to offer the sacrifice." Then, the author adds a little note: "For this reason, therefore, brothers, we do not praise those who hand themselves over, since the Gospel does not so teach." This author does not think that Christians should have voluntarily undergone martyrdom, but that if they were sought out and arrested because they were Christian, they should, of course, have gone through with it. They should not, however, have put themselves forward, because here was an instance of somebody who put himself forward, and yet, recanted afterward. They didn't want that.

We know of some Christian groups who actively opposed martyrdom, Christians who advocated recanting, or pretending to recant, so as to avoid being tortured and killed for the faith. In particular, we know of one group of Christians who maintained it was better to recant, and not be killed, precisely on theological grounds. These were people who insisted that because Christ died for others, others should not die. If Christ paid the price for sin, then others should not have had to pay the price, and therefore, Christ (God) did not want people to be martyred. Christ (God) wanted people to live, and therefore, it was better to do whatever the authorities said to escape martyrdom. You would just have had to do it in bad faith, and just crossed your fingers behind your back when you made the sacrifice, swore the oath, and that, in fact, is what God wanted. There were therefore groups of people who did precisely that, maintaining that it was God's will to do in bad faith whatever the authorities insisted upon, and so, live.

It's difficult to know how many Christians recanted or pretended to recant in the face of physical torment. One of the reasons it is difficult to know is because most of our surviving accounts are written by Christians who celebrate martyrdom, who want to show the supernatural strength given the martyrs in the face of their deaths, as seen in the lengthy accounts of the martyrs of Vienne and Lyons, and in the Martyrdom of Polycarp. Since the people who were actually doing the writing had survived and were in support of martyrdom, you won't find too many instances of people recanting in them, and therefore, historically, it's hard to know how many recanted. These authors of the surviving works wanted to celebrate martyrdom as a Christian virtue to show that, in fact, these Christians were strong and supported by God in the face of death.

A similar message of a Christian who was stalwart in the face of death can be seen in the powerful account of the martyrdom of a woman named Perpetua. This account, the Martyrdom of Perpetua, is a very famous document from the early third century. Perpetua was a 22-year-old matron, a mother who was a recent convert to Christianity, and who lived in North Africa. Her martyrdom took place in the year 203 A.D.

The story of her martyrdom is remarkable in several respects, most particularly because a good deal of the account that we have of her arrest and imprisonment is written in her own hand. She actually kept a diary, and we have the diary. It is quite unusual, from the ancient world, to have a firsthand account of this sort, and it is especially unusual to have it from a woman.

Perpetua was a highly educated woman who was able to compose in Latin, and she had kept this diary. Somebody, a Christian, later discovered the diary. It was bequeathed to Christians who survived this particular martyrdom in early third century North Africa. Somebody took the diary that Perpetua had prepared and added a short preface to it. Then, he or she added an ending to it that actually describes her martyrdom. The diary records the events transpiring while she was in prison awaiting her martyrdom. It is therefore quite a remarkable and unique piece of literature that we have the Martyrdom of Perpetua.

Included in this diary is a record of what happened to her and her fellow Christian martyrs while they were awaiting their executions. It records accounts of her trials, her reactions, her fears, and it also includes a series of visions that she had while awaiting her death, where she described dreams that she had had, which were symbolic of what she expected to have happen to her.

One of the most gripping elements of the story was the reaction that Perpetua herself records toward her poor father, not economically poor, but as a poor fellow whose daughter was facing death and refused to recant in the face of her approaching execution. Her father was a pagan who didn't understand why she was insisting on dying for the faith. He tried in vain to get her to see reason for his sake, and for the sake of her own child. She had a young infant who was still nursing, and he was trying to get her to recant, because this baby was hers, and if she died, what was to happen to the child? He's also, of course, trying to get her to recant for her own sake.

Let me read several passages from this diary of Perpetua's about her reaction towards her father:

While we were still under arrest [she says in her diary] my father, out of love for me, was trying to persuade me, and to shake my resolution. 'Father,' said I, 'do you see this vase here, for example, or water pot, or whatever?' 'Yes, I do,' he said, and I told him, 'Could it be called by any other name than what it is?' He said, 'No.' 'Well, so, too, I, cannot be called anything other than what I am, a Christian.' At this, my father was so angered by the word 'Christian' that he moved towards me as though he would pluck my eyes out, but he left it at that, and departed, vanquished, along with his diabolical arguments.

She therefore considers his arguments to be diabolical, so she was rejecting her father, who after all, was just concerned for her own well-being. A little later, we have another account:

My father arrived in the city again, worn with worry, and he came, again, to see me with the idea of persuading me. 'Daughter,' he said, 'have pity on my gray head. Have pity on me, your father, if I deserve to be called your father, if I have favored you above all your brothers, if I have raised you to reach the prime of your life. Do not abandon me to the reproach of others. Think of your brothers. Think of your mother and your aunt. Think of your child, who will not able to live once you are gone. Give up your pride. You will destroy all of us.'

Again, it was to no avail. She did not yield. She went on trial before the proconsul. They were trying, one by one, these Christians. When her turn came:

My father appeared with my son, dragging me from the step, and saying, 'Perform a sacrifice. Have pity on your child.' But Hilarianus, the governor, who had received his judicial powers, said to me, 'Have pity on your father's gray head. Have pity on your infant child.'

Thus, again, you have a case of the governor trying to get these people to recant. He did not want to kill these people. He just wanted them simply to recant so that they didn't have to go through with this.

'Offer the sacrifice for the welfare of the emperors.' 'I will not,' I retorted. 'Are you a Christian?' said Hilarianus, and I said, 'Yes, I am.' When my father persisted in trying to persuade me, Hilarianus ordered him to be thrown to the ground, and beaten with a rod. I felt sorry for my father, just as if I myself had been beaten. I fell sorry for his pathetic old age.

She didn't feel sorry enough to recant, however. She spurned her father's pleas, ended up relinquishing her child to others, and went to her death eagerly.

I mentioned that she had several visions. I want to talk about one of these visions, because it is quite interesting. She had several dreams that she recorded while she was there in the prison, one of which was described in what is now chapter 10. It was a vision of her approaching death. It was the day before they were to fight the wild beasts, and she had this dream in which one of the deacons of her church came and opened the door, and led her into the arena.

They came into the amphitheater, and he led her to the center of the arena: "He told me, 'Do not be afraid. I am here struggling with you.' Then, he left." This was all in a dream she was having the day before the event itself. "Then, there came out an Egyptian against me, of vicious appearance, together with his seconds to fight with me."

It was going to be gladiatorial combat. She, this 22-year-old woman, was going to fight this very vicious Egyptian. "My clothes were stripped off, and suddenly, I was a man." She had become a man in this vision. "My seconds began to rub me down with oil, as they are wont to do before a contest, and I saw the Egyptian, on the other side, rolling in the dust." I guess those were two different ways to make your body slippery for your opponent.

"Next, there came forth a man of marvelous stature." There was a huge giant who came into the arena with a wand, and a green branch, and this apparently was a vision of Christ coming to the arena, and he said that if the Egyptian defeated her, he would slay her with the sword, but she defeated him, she would receive the branch. Then, he withdrew.

"We drew close to one another, and began to let our fists fly," so that she was fighting this Egyptian. "My opponent tried to get hold of my feet, but I kept striking him in the face with the heels of my feet. Then, I was raised up into the air, and I began to pummel him without, as it were, touching the ground." I can't read this anymore without thinking of *The Matrix*. This is exactly like those scenes in *The Matrix*, exactly what was going on here in this dream.

"Then when I noticed there was a lull, I put my two hands together, linking the fingers of one hand those of the other, and I got hold of his head. He fell flat on his face, and I stepped on his head." She ended up defeating him.

Then, Christ came back, and gave her the branch of peace. "Then, I awoke. I realized that it was not with wild animals that would fight, with the devil, and I knew that I would win the victory."

Egyptians are always portrayed in biblical narratives as, of course, the enemy of the people of God, and so, this was an Egyptian, the enemy, who, in fact, was the devil, and she saw that she was going to overcome this Egyptian.

She became a man. That was a theme in many these of these early martyrdoms, that to be a real man meant to be courageous. The word in Greek for "courageous," in fact, is the translation for "being a man," and so, she took on male characteristics, so that she could fight this Egyptian, progress to victory, and then onto God.

The account of Perpetua's death in the arena was then narrated by the editor, who took her diary and incorporated the diary into the longer martyrology. It has been popular through the ages down until today. You can obviously still buy this and read it. It is quite interesting.

The death itself was narrated by the editor. What happened was that they took her and a female slave who was a Christian, a woman named Felicitas, who had just given birth and was still lactating. They stripped them naked, put them in nets, and took them into the arena, but the people saw that there was a young matron, and a slave woman whose breasts were still lactating, and the crowd got upset about this. They wanted them to be dressed. Apparently, the crowds didn't mind if they were fully dressed and getting mauled by the beasts; they just didn't want to see them naked and being mauled by the beasts. They dressed them, and let a wild heifer loose onto them, thinking that it would be interesting to have a female beast destroy these females, these women, these female humans.

The heifer attacked them, knocked them over, and mauled them, but didn't kill them. The crowds thought that was enough for one day, and sent them back to jail to bring them out the next day. The next day, they sent out gladiators to kill them. One by one, the gladiators struck them with the sword and killed them, but when the gladiator came up to Perpetua, he apparently tried to stab her, but the sword hit a bone, stopped, and didn't get to her heart. We're told that Perpetua herself took the gladiator's hand—it isn't quite clear whether it was a short sword or a dagger—forced it up to her own throat, and killed herself by thrusting it through her throat, showing that she was in control of her own death, even to the very end.

Well, it's a disturbing account. This was a young woman who had everything ahead of her: Educated, a young mother. Why were Christians like this so willing to die? We have seen other instances: The woman Blandina in the letter of Lyons and Vienne; Polycarp, the aged bishop in Smyrna; now Perpetua in North Africa. They were so firm in refusing to recant, so stalwart in the face of death, so eager to die. What was it that was driving these people to want to escape this world?

We can never know, of course, their personal reasons. Even though we have Perpetua's diary, we don't really know what was going on inside their minds, but we do have some indications from the writings about them by the Christians who were left behind, concerning why Christians might have preferred public torture and humiliation, and death, to a long life, why they would prefer one to the other.

The first thing is something we've noticed already. It appears that many Christians were convinced that as bad as the torments of the present were, they were not nearly so bad as the torments awaiting those who rejected Christ in the world to come. This is explicitly stated in the Martyrdom of Polycarp, and in the letter of the churches of Lyons and Vienne, namely that as bad as the torment was being experienced in the present, it was nothing compared to the torment that awaited, if, in fact, you weren't on the side of God.

Thus, for example, in the Martyrdom of Polycarp, we find this statement, that not Polycarp itself, but these other martyrs:

> turned their thoughts to the grace of Christ, so that they despised the tortures of this world, purchasing at the cost of one hour an exemption from eternal punishment, and fire of their inhuman tortures felt cold to them, for they set before their eyes the escape from that eternal fire, which is never extinguished.

This was rooted in a kind of "theodicy." Theodicy is an important word for many of these texts. The word theodicy refers to the righteousness of God. How is God righteous when so much suffering is in this world? Early Christians maintained that this world was controlled by forces of evil. Some Christians maintained that God had relinquished control of this world to these evil forces, but they insisted that ultimately, God was going to triumph, if not in this life, then in the afterlife. God was going to have the final say. "Those who are torturing us now are going to have their full reward later. God is going to have the last say, and so it is better to side with God and pay the ultimate price now, because then, you'll have eternal reward. Refusing to pay the price now means that you'll pay the price later."

This message, then, became one of the central features of Christian preaching. It's relates, as you can notice, to the exclusivistic claims of these Christians. These Christians were saying that not only were they right in what they believed, but they were saying that those who chose not to agree with them would be punished with horrific torments eternally. "There is one set of truths. These truths have to be adhered to. If you don't adhere to these truths, then you'll pay the price forever."

One reason, then, that Christians may have been willing to undergo this was because of their belief in the afterlife. Secondly, some Christians saw that a violent death at the hands of the authorities was a way to imitate Christ in this world, who had himself died a public, humiliating, painful death, and so some Christians insisted that the way to be a real imitator of Christ, their savior, was to suffer similarly.

This view can be seen most clearly in the writings of one of the first Christians known to be martyred after the New Testament period, an author whose name was Ignatius of Antioch. Ignatius was the bishop of the major city, Antioch, in the early second century. Around the year 110, roughly 90 years before Perpetua, Ignatius was arrested in Antioch, apparently for Christian activities, and he was sent off to Rome to be thrown to the wild beasts.

While en route to Rome to face his own martyrdom, Ignatius wrote a number of letters, and we still have these letters. This is another, quite remarkable corpus of writings that we have, letters written by a Christian who is about to be martyred, en route to Rome, where he is to be thrown to the wild beasts. Six of these letters, he wrote to various churches, representatives of which he had met on the way. Thus, we have six letters written to various churches, in which he tells the churches how to deal with their particular problems, how to be unified, that they ought to follow their bishops, that they ought to be submissive to what their bishops say. He tried to get rid of heresy in these various churches. He was concerned about their welfare.

However, one of the letters was not written to a church that had sent representatives to meet him along the way, one of the letters was written to the Christians in the city of Rome, where he was going. He wrote the Christians in Rome in order to urge them not to interfere with the proceedings against him once he arrived. He didn't want them to stop his execution, since, in his view, it was by dying a violent death that he would be united with Christ, and therefore, as he said, he would "attain to God."

We have these seven letters. These seven letters have survived through the Middle Ages, down to today, and they make for very interesting reading, especially this letter to the Romans. Let me read several parts of this letter. This may sound rather pathological to you, but one person's pathology is another person's common sense. This was common sense for Ignatius:

> Let me be fodder for the wild beasts [said Ignatius to the Roman Christians]. That is how I can get to God. I am God's wheat, and I am being ground by the teeth of wild beasts to be made a pure loaf of bread for Christ. I would rather that you fawn the beasts, so that they may be my tomb, and no scrap of my body be left. Thus, when I have fallen asleep, I shall be a burden to no one. Then, I shall be a real disciple of Christ. Then, the world will see my body no more. What a thrill I shall have from the wild beasts that are ready for me. I hope they will make short work of me. I shall coax them on to eat me up, all at once, and not hold off, as sometimes happens. Now is the moment I am beginning to be a disciple. May nothing seen or unseen begrudge me making my way to Jesus Christ. Come, fire, cross, battling with wild beasts, wrenching of bones, mangling of limbs, crushing of my whole body, cruel tortures of the devil. Only let me get to Jesus Christ.

Thus, he went on, talking about how he wanted to imitate the passion of Christ, the death of Christ, so that he would be worthy of meeting Christ in the afterlife.

As I pointed out—well, I didn't need to point it out—this longing for violent death may sound pathological to our ears, but for him, it was only logical. This world was of no importance to Ignatius. What mattered was the other world, the world of God, which he could attain by imitating the martyrdom of Christ himself. This appears to have been a view of many of the early Christian martyrs. Not only were they thinking that the afterlife would be much better for them if they suffered this torment, but if they refused to suffer, they themselves would go through the torment. They were also thinking about imitating Christ's own martyrdom.

To sum up, it is difficult to actually know how many Christians went to face their deaths in this way. We don't know what the numbers are because nobody recorded the numbers. The church father Eusebius, who recorded some of these incidents, sometimes said that six people were killed here, ten people killed there. By and large, though, we don't know how many people actually died, and I should point out that the people writing the accounts of the martyrdoms were always Christians who survived, so that these persecutions were not going after every Christian; a lot of people were left to witness the event, and wrote about it. It is difficult to know, then, how many Christians had to face death this way.

Some of these people facing their deaths by martyrdom evidently recanted of their Christian faith, or at least, they pretend to recant of their faith when they were put to the test, so that they would not have to go through with it. Others, though, submitted themselves to public torment and death, both because in doing so they understood that they were escaping the real and eternal suffering that would come to nonbelievers in the afterlife, and because they thought that by dying in this way, they could imitate their Lord and master, Christ. "If Christ got flogged and then crucified for the sins of the world, and we want to be his followers, we are going to experience his fate, which means we, too, will suffer and die at the hands of the enemies."

There were other Christians who decided to try to defend themselves against the charges leveled against them. The Greek word for "defense," as I pointed out earlier, is *apologia*, our English word "apology."

In our next lecture, we will be examining the writings of the Christian apologists, the defenders of the faith against its cultured despisers, those who tried to make an intellectual defense to show why it was that Christians should not be persecuted and martyred.

Lecture Fourteen
The Early Christian Apologists

Scope: In the middle of the second century, an elite group of Christian intellectuals emerged who decided to take on their cultured despisers from among the pagans and to defend Christianity against the charges of atheism and rank immorality commonly leveled against it. These Christian *apologists* ("defenders of the faith") wrote open letters, often to the emperor, explaining the true nature of the religion, showing that the charges against it were groundless, and urging that Christians be allowed to worship their God in their own (socially innocuous) ways.

In this lecture, we will consider these strategies by looking at one of the most interesting apologists of the late second century, Athenagoras, whose writing has survived till today and can show us the ways Christians defended themselves against the attacks of those in power.

Outline

I. In the three previous lectures, we have discussed the persecution and martyrdom of Christians in the Roman Empire.

   A. We have seen some of the reasons that Christians were persecuted.
      1. Because they failed to worship the state gods, they were sometimes seen as the cause of disasters that occasionally struck.
      2. They were suspected of engaging in antisocial and flagrantly immoral behavior.

   B. We have also seen how Christians reacted to their persecution, with some Christians recanting their faith to avoid prosecution and others remaining committed to the point of torture and death, thinking that the pains they suffered in the present were nothing in comparison to the joys that would be theirs after death.

   C. In this lecture, we will move on to consider how Christians defended themselves against the charges of atheism and immorality commonly leveled against them. In particular, we will look at the "reasoned defenses" made by Christian intellectuals to their cultured despisers among the pagans.

II. The treatises written by these Christians are usually called *apologies*, the Greek term for "defense." Christian apologies began to appear as a literary genre in the middle of the second century, but there were precedents for them already in the New Testament period.

   A. The book of 1 Peter is often thought of as an early piece of Christian apology.
      1. The book was written near the end of the first century to a group of Christians experiencing severe persecution (4:12).
      2. It appears that the persecution started at the grassroots level, among friends and neighbors opposed to those who converted to Christianity (4:3).
      3. The readers are urged to give their persecutors no grounds for opposition (4:14–15) and to be ready to give a reasoned "defense" (*apologia*) for their beliefs (3:14–16).

   B. The Book of Acts is also thought by some to be an apology; it was written to a Roman official (Theophilus) to explain that Christians had never done anything contrary to Roman law or custom requiring punishment.

III. It was not until the mid-second century, however, that intellectuals began converting to the faith and writing reasoned defenses of their religion to try to prevent persecutions.

   A. These were often "open letters" written to the emperor or other leading Roman officials (although there is considerable question whether anyone high in the administration would have bothered reading them).

   B. We have already met several of these authors, such as Justin Martyr in Rome and Tertullian in Carthage, North Africa.

IV. One particularly interesting apology came from an otherwise virtually unknown author, Athenagoras, living and writing in Athens around 177 A.D.

   A. Athenagoras addressed his apology to the joint emperors, Marcus Aurelius and Commodus, just at the time of the persecution at Lyons and Viennes that we have already considered.

B. He takes on the arguments against the Christians one by one, using his considerable rhetorical skills to show their absurdity.

C. He argues that Christians cannot be "atheists," because in fact, they believe in the God who created all things. In other words, they are not *materialists*, as were some Greek philosophers who really did not believe in any super-mundane beings.

    1. Moreover, this God is in three persons, Father, Son, and Holy Spirit, so that Christians do acknowledge the "true" Gods.

    2. In addition, they affirm the existence of other divine beings (angels and the like).

D. The objection that Christians do not worship certain state gods is likewise absurd, because different gods are worshipped by different peoples in different states, which meant that Christians should not be singled out for persecution.

E. In addition, the charges of immorality—especially cannibalism and infanticide—are ridiculous for anyone who knows about the Christian faith.

    1. In fact, not only do Christians believe in not committing adultery but also in not thinking lustful thoughts.

    2. They are committed to the principle of not killing, as well as not observing violence (such as in the gladiator games) and not exposing infants.

    3. In a nice rhetorical twist, Athenagoras claims that pagans charge Christians with doing what the pagans' own gods are said to do in their myths (commit murders, adultery, and the like).

F. Athenagoras's conclusion is that it is senseless to persecute the Christians simply for taking the name Christian, when they have done nothing illegal or wrong but, in fact, are both theologically right and morally upright.

V. These arguments are repeated throughout the various apologists, along with several others that became standard fare.

    A. Christians are not a threat to society; instead, because they alone are holy and close to God, it is their prayers that preserve society. They are, in fact, the salt of the Earth.

    B. For that matter, Christianity alone is true religion.

        1. It is proved true by its miracle-working leaders.

2. Its truth claims are demonstrated by "proof from prophecy," in that the predictions of the ancient Hebrew prophets came to be fulfilled by the life of Jesus.

3. Thus, Christianity is far more ancient than anything found among the pagan religions; it is rooted in the teachings of Moses, who lived 800 years before Plato and 400 years before Homer—key figures for pagan notions about the gods.

C. Therefore, the state should leave Christians in peace to worship as they choose. In fact, the apologists argued—in anticipation of ideas promulgated many centuries later under a completely different set of conditions—that there should be a separation of religion and politics, church and state. This argument never caught on in antiquity, especially once the empire converted and the government took up the Christian cause against the pagans and Jews.

VI. As we said, starting in the mid-second century, some intellectuals converted to the Christian faith and wrote apologies in its defense, proclaiming its theological superiority, its moral virtue, and its social value in an attempt to bring the persecutions to an end.

A. These intellectual defenses were not themselves effective in averting persecution.

B. As the writings of the first serious Christian intellectuals, however, the apologies became important for later Christian theological and ethical reflection, as the religion continued to spread its appeal throughout the Roman world.

Essential Reading:

————, *After the New Testament*, chapter 4.

Bart Ehrman, *The New Testament: A Historical Introduction*, chapter 26.

Supplementary Reading:

Arthur Droge, *Moses or Homer*.

Robert M. Grant, *Greek Apologists of the Second Century*.

Questions to Consider:

1. Suppose you were a Roman pagan of the mid-second century who considered the Christian faith socially dangerous. How might you

respond to the views and arguments of the Christian apologists? Why would you not find them convincing?

2. Why do the apologists' arguments sound so commonsensical to many people today?

Lecture Fourteen—Transcript
The Early Christian Apologists

In the three previous lectures, we have discussed the persecution and martyrdom of Christians in the Roman Empire. We have seen some of the reasons why Christians were persecuted; they failed to worship the state gods, and so were called "atheists" (those who were without the gods). Sometimes they were seen by people as the causes of disasters that occasionally struck the cities, the logic being that the gods were the ones to protect the cities, and therefore, if one failed to worship the gods properly, then the gods would go on the attack. If disasters hit a city, then who was at fault? Those who didn't worship the gods, namely, the Christians. Secondly, sometimes the Christians were suspected of engaging in antisocial and flagrantly immoral behavior, including infanticide and cannibalism.

We have also seen how Christians reacted to their persecutions. Some Christians recanted their faith in order to avoid prosecution. Others remained committed to the point of torture and death, thinking that the pains they suffered in the present were nothing in comparison to the joys that would be theirs after death.

In this lecture, we will move on to consider how Christians defended themselves against the charges of atheism and immorality commonly leveled against them. In particular, we will look at the reasoned defenses made by Christian intellectuals to their cultured despisers among the pagans. The treatises written by these Christians are usually called *apologies*, the Greek term for "defense."

Christian apologies began to appear as a literary genre in the middle of the second Christian century, but there were precedents for apologies already in the New Testament period. Again, I need to emphasize that "apology," in this sense, does not mean saying that you are sorry. These people were not apologizing for being Christian in that sense. They were defending their Christian beliefs, coming from this notion of an apology being a reasoned defense.

The book of 1 Peter, within the New Testament, is sometimes understood to have been a kind of apology, written by a Christian to defend the faith. 1 Peter is an interesting book for a number of reasons. There are two books called "Peter" in the New Testament, 1 and 2 Peter. Most scholars think that

2 Peter is pseudonymous, that it wasn't written by Simon Peter, the disciple of Jesus, even though it claims to have been written by Simon Peter. It's fairly clear that whoever wrote 2 Peter is not the same author as the one who wrote 1 Peter. That's hard to demonstrate to people unless they can read it in the Greek, but the Greek writing style, in fact, is quite different between 1 and 2 Peter. 2 Peter is usually thought to be a pseudonymous writing from the early second century.

There is considerable debate about 1 Peter, whether Simon Peter actually wrote the book or not. We know about Simon Peter from the Gospels of the New Testament, where he appears as a lower-class, illiterate peasant who lived in Galilee, and whose native tongue would have been Aramaic.

1 Peter, as it's called, is a letter allegedly written by Peter, written in good Greek. Evidently, whoever penned this letter was well-trained and well-educated. It doesn't appear that it was actually composed by a lower-class, uneducated peasant whose primary language was Aramaic. Therefore, some scholars suspect that even 1 Peter is pseudonymous, or may actually have been a work that was written by Peter, or possibly dictated by Peter to somebody who was proficient in Greek, who then modified the style accordingly, to make it more acceptable.

In any event, whoever wrote the book of 1 Peter was writing to Christians in the context of intense suffering. The term "suffering" occurs more frequently in this little five-chapter book than in any other book of the entire New Testament. Therefore, I wanted to look at some aspects of 1 Peter as an apology.

The book was written near the end of the first century—whoever wrote it— to a group of Christians who were experiencing some kind of severe persecution. We can get this from the pages of the book itself. In chapter 4, verses 12 and following, the author says:

> Beloved, do not be surprised at the fiery ordeal that is taking place among you to test you, as though something strange were happening to you, but rejoice insofar as you are sharing Christ's sufferings, so that you may also be glad and shout for joy when his glory is revealed. [This is somebody expecting that Jesus will soon return from heaven, in judgment on the earth.] People are suffering now, but it's only for a short time, until he comes back. People should rejoice at the suffering, because it's the same suffering that Christ himself experienced. [Verse 15:] But let none of you suffer as a murderer, a thief, a criminal, or even as a mischief maker. Yet

> if any of you suffers as a Christian, do not consider it a disgrace, but glorify God because you bear this name.

Clearly, people are suffering some kind of Christian persecution, and the author is urging them not to suffer for doing anything wrong, but if you suffer from being a Christian then, well and good. You should bear with the suffering, because it will end soon, and by suffering, you are imitating Christ.

Well, what was the suffering that they were experiencing, and who was causing it? It appears that the persecution being discussed in this book started out at the grass-roots level, among friends and neighbors opposed to those who converted to Christianity. This is a phenomenon that we have seen earlier, where it appears that most persecutions were not started by imperial authorities but by the masses.

Why would the masses be upset about Christians being Christian? We get some indication here in this book, chapter 4, verses 3 and following:

> You have already spent enough time in doing what the Gentiles like to do [says the author], living in licentiousness, passions, drunkenness, revels, carousings, and lawless idolatry. They are surprised that you no longer join them in the same excesses of dissipation, and so they blaspheme, but they will have to give an accounting to him who stands ready to judge the living and the dead.

Why were these people being persecuted? Because they used to carouse with their friends and neighbors, and they weren't doing so any more. Their friends and neighbors were upset about this. They wondered why these people had "gotten religion," you might say. They were upset about that, and that was starting the ball rolling toward some kind of persecution.

The readers were urged to give their persecutors no grounds for opposition. They were, instead, to be ready to give a reasoned defense, an apologia, for their beliefs, and so, chapter 3, verses 14 and following:

> Even if you do suffer for doing what is right, you are blessed. Do not fear what they fear, and do not be intimidated, but in your hearts, sanctify Christ as word. Always be ready to make your defense, your apologia. Make your defense to anyone who demands from you an accounting for the hope that is in you, yet do it with gentleness, and with reverence. Keep your conscience clear, so that when you are maligned, those who abuse you for your good conduct in Christ shall be put to shame.

People were, then, to defend themselves, to give reasoned defense as to why they believed what they believed. If they suffered, well and good. That was in imitation of Christ, and that would not last long, because Christ was soon to return to vindicate himself and his people.

It is therefore possible that the book of 1 Peter could be understood as an early Christian apology, one of the earliest that we have, written sometime during the first century, possibly by Peter, or possibly in his name by somebody who revered Peter's stature within the Christian community.

A second example from within the New Testament is the Book of Acts, the Acts of the Apostles, which is thought by some scholars to be a kind of apology for Christianity in the face of opposition by imperial opponents. The Book of Acts is an interesting book for a number of reasons. It is the sketch of early Christianity after the death of Jesus, that shows the spread of Christianity throughout the Roman world, and shows how Christianity moved from being a purely Jewish religion, to being a religion largely adopted by Gentiles.

It is an account of the missionary adventures and exploits of the apostles of Jesus, particularly the apostle Peter in the first 12 chapters, and then, the apostle Paul, who starts off as an opponent of Christianity, but who then converts to be a follower of Jesus in chapter 9. And then in chapters 12 through 28, the bulk of the book, we have an account of Paul's missionary endeavors as he tries to convert Gentiles to the faith.

This book, the Book of Acts, is the second volume of a two-volume work, as I pointed out in an earlier lecture, the first volume of which is the Gospel of Luke. Luke and Acts, then, are two volumes: Luke covering the life and death of Jesus; the Book of Acts doing the life and missionary endeavors of his apostles. Together, they are actually one book in two volumes. The two volumes are both dedicated to a person named Theophilus. Theophilus is the person to whom the author, whom we will call Luke, is writing.

Who was Theophilus? There have been various explanations for who Theophilus was. Theophilus, in fact, was a common name in the ancient world. It literally means "lover of God," or it could mean "beloved of God." When Luke dedicated these books to Theophilus, he dedicated them to "Most Excellent Theophilus." "Most Excellent" is a title reserved in the Book of Acts for Roman officials. Some people, then, think that the books of Luke and Acts are therefore written to a Roman official, to be read by him, to explain about Christianity.

Why would a Christian write books to a Roman official to explain what Christianity was all about? One explanation is that these books were written in order to exonerate the Christians of any wrongdoing, that these books were meant, in fact, to show that Christians were not to be blamed for what they were being persecuted for, that they had not broken any laws and were completely innocent in the face of their persecutors. The reason for doing that, of course, would have been to get the official to relent, in terms of the persecution.

It is interesting, then, in the book of Luke, which is a portrayal of the life and death of Jesus that one of the overarching emphases throughout is that Jesus did nothing wrong to deserve his fate. In the trial narrative, when Jesus is put on trial before the Roman governor Pilate, in Luke's Gospel, Pilate declares Jesus innocent three separate times, and only has him executed because he's forced by the crowds to do so.

When Jesus was being crucified in Luke's Gospel, the Roman centurion, who crucified him, looked upon him, and when he died, the centurion proclaimed: "Truly, this man was innocent." Jesus's innocence is proclaimed repeatedly throughout Luke. Jesus did nothing wrong.

Then, in the Book of Acts, the Christians are said to have done nothing wrong. Whenever they were persecuted, it was because of willful people, who, in fact, got the story wrong, and throughout Acts, in fact, the Jewish leaders were the ones who persecuted the Christians. This was meant to, perhaps, explain to the Roman official, that, "Yes, in fact, we have gotten in trouble, but it is not our fault. The Jews are at fault." In other words, this may have been the beginning of a kind of anti-Jewish strain in some of the early Christian literature.

It is possible, then, that the book of Acts is written in order to show the innocence of Christians before the empire as a kind of apology, to explain why it was Christians were persecuted. It wasn't because of any wrong that they themselves had done, but because of their wrongful opposition by Jews.

These, then, are two instances of apologetic literature within the New Testament, 1 Peter and the Book of Acts. It was not until the mid-second century, after the books of the New Testament had been written, though, that real intellectuals began converting to the Christian faith and began to write reasoned defenses of their religion, to try to prevent the persecutions. Often, these apologies were written as "open letters" to the emperor or to some other Roman official.

A Christian intellectual would write an open letter addressed to the emperor, or addressed to some other high-ranking official, but it would be an open letter, really, for everybody. It's a little bit hard to believe that, in fact, these letters were sent through the ancient equivalent of the postal service to the emperor's palace, where the emperor would be thought to read these things. The emperor had plenty of things on his hands to do besides read letters written to him by Christians. They were written, probably, as open letters, and there are number of scholars who think that these apologies were probably insider literature, addressed to the emperor, but really written for Christians, so that Christians would know how to defend themselves against the charges brought against them.

We have already met a couple of authors who were apologists, including Justin Martyr of Rome, and Tertullian, who lived in Carthage, North Africa. Both of them wrote apologies that still survive and that you can read translated into English. Justin Martyr, writing in Greek, wrote a couple of apologies, and Tertullian wrote in Latin. He also had a couple of apologies—one in particular that is well known and that I have quoted in an earlier context.

One other particularly interesting apology comes from an otherwise virtually unknown author, whose name was Athenagoras. He lived and wrote in Athens—hence his name, Athenagoras—sometime around 177 A.D. We still have this letter, this book, by Athenagoras, his apology. It's a very interesting apology, because he dealt with the charges against the Christians head-on and tried to show why they were invalid.

He began the book by saying to the emperors, Marcus Aurelius Antoninus and to Lucius Aurelius Commodus, conquerors of Armenia and Sarmatia, and what is more important, philosophers. He is therefore writing to the two emperors, Marcus Aurelius and Commodus. If you have seen the movie *Gladiator*, these are the two emperors involved in that particular narrative.

When was this book being written? Around 177, exactly the time when the letter of the churches of Lyons and Vienne was written, a persecution that the Roman emperor Marcus Aurelius authorized. Here was somebody living in Athens who may or may not have known about the persecution going on in Gaulle, and who was trying to write a letter for the emperors, so that they would relent of any persecution going on.

After an introductory statement, Athenagoras addressed the charges brought out against the Christians. He said: "Three charges are brought against us: atheism, Thyestean feasts, and Oedipean intercourse." " Thyestean feasts" refers to urges of cannibalism, and "Oedipean intercourse" refers to incestuous orgies.

"If these are true," he says, "then spare no class. Proceed against our crimes. Destroy us utterly with our wives and children. But if these charges are inventions and unfounded slanders, they arise from the fact that it is natural for vice to oppose virtue."

It's a very clever line: If, in fact, the charges against us are false, then the reason for them is that people who are characterized by vice, are attacking those who are virtuous. He was to maintain that, of course, the Christians were virtuous, so that in explanation for that, those attacking them were the problem, not the Christians.

He then proceeds through the three charges, arguing first that: Christians cannot be atheists, because they, in fact, believe in the God who created all things. He emphasizes the business of "God created all things," because there were people in the ancient Greek and Roman world who would rightly have been called atheists, people who thought that there were no gods, who thought that the entire world they lived in was made up of matter, that there was no supernatural realm, where there were no other gods, and that the whole business was matter.

This was a point of view that is similar to what many people believe today, but according to Athenagoras, that, of course, was not what Christians thought: "Is it not mad to charge us with atheism, when we distinguish God from matter, and show that matter is one thing, and God another, and that there is a vast difference between them? Our teaching affirms one God who made the Universe, being himself uncreated."

In other words, he wanted to show that the Christians couldn't be atheists, because they worshipped God, so of course they were not atheists. Even more than that, though, the pagans had charged Christians with not worshipping "the gods." If you had only one God, you didn't really have "the gods." In that sense, you were an atheist, yes? Well, for Athenagoras, the answer was "no," because the God worshipped by the Christians was one God, but in fact, he was Triune, with Father, Son, and Holy Spirit. In one sense, that is like having three gods. "By whom the Universe was created through his word, it was set in order, and is held together, for we also think that God has a Son. The Son of God is his Word, in idea and in actuality, for by him and through him, all things were made, the Father and the Son being one."

Thus, there's one God, but there are actually two, Father and Son. More than that, he goes on to maintain:

> We say that the Holy Spirit himself, who inspires those who utter prophecies, is an effluence from God, one that flows forth from God. Who, then, would not be astonished to hear those called atheists, who admit God the Father, God the Son, and the Holy Spirit, and who teach their unity in power and distinction in rank. We affirm, too, a crowd of angels and ministers.

What he's doing is pointing out that "we've got God the Father, God the Son, God the Holy Spirit. There are also angels, other kinds of principalities and powers. We know that there are divine beings out there. In fact, we worship the one God, so in fact, it is completely illegitimate to consider us as atheists."

In addition, then, he wanted to go on to point out that Christians are not only not to have been charged with being atheists, but they can't really have been accused of not worshipping the right gods, because all people throughout the empire worshipped a different set of gods. Therefore, now that he had shown that they worshipped divine beings, somebody could not respond, "Yes, the worship those beings, but you don't worship our gods," his point having been that different people in different parts of the world, in fact, worshipped different gods, therefore, the charge did not hold, because those people were not being persecuted.

"Their other charge," he says, in chapter 14, "that we neither accept nor venerate the same gods as the cities do is quite senseless. The very ones who accuse us of atheism for not acknowledging the same gods they believe in are not agreed among themselves about the gods." He points out that in Athens, they worshipped one set of gods; in Troy, they worshipped a different set of gods; in Samia, they worshipped a different set of gods; in Silicia, a different set of gods. He goes through a whole bunch of these and then concludes: "The day is too short to enumerate the rest. When, then, they fail to agree among themselves about their gods, why do they charge us with disagreeing with them?" Therefore, Christians were not unusual in having their own gods to worship.

He goes on, then, to talk about the charges of immorality leveled against Christians, especially the charges of cannibalism and infanticide, and points out that these are ridiculous charges for anyone who knows anything about the Christian faith. The Christians commit cannibalism? They kill babies, and then eat them? That's absurd. He pointed out that Christians, in fact, had a much higher standard of morality than the rest of the world.

The rest of the world agreed that you should not kill somebody. Christians, even more than that, not only didn't kill people, they didn't expose infants. This was a common phenomenon in the Roman world, as it is in some parts of our world today, that if an unwanted baby was born, it was left outside, hoping somebody would pick it up. If it was not picked up, the baby died. Christians refused to do that. Other apologists pointed out that Christians did not support abortion at all, and they would use the arguments to show, "We are not only not killing people, but we don't expose infants, we don't believe in abortion. In fact, we are more ethical, more moral than the rest of you."

In fact, Athenagoras went on to say, "We don't even go to the gladiatorial contests. You have gladiators that you see killing each other. We refuse even to look upon somebody who kills another. Therefore, to charge us with infanticide and cannibalism is absurd."

Moreover, Christians were being charged with engaging in these wild, licentious orgies. In point of fact, said Athenagoras, "if you knew anything about our religion, you would know that not only do Christians commit themselves not to engage in adultery (taking somebody else's spouse), but our teachers taught us not even to look upon a woman with lust in our hearts, so that we go beyond the morality that most people do, and so, there are no incestuous orgies happening among the Christians." In fact, Christians don't commit adultery. Even more than that, Christians are trained not even to think lustful thoughts. This was, then, a kind of one-upmanship in the moral realm, which was being used to show that the charges against Christians were absolutely false.

In a nice rhetorical twist, Athenagoras goes on to claim that the pagans charging the Christians with engaging in this wild, licentious activity must have gotten things confused. They must be thinking about their own gods, who, in fact, according to the Greek and Roman mythology, do all sorts of crazy things. In chapter 32, he says: "It is nothing surprising that our accusers should invent the same tales about us that they tell of their own gods. They present their sufferings as mysteries," referring to the mystery, secret religions that worship these gods in pagan cults, "and had they wanted to judge shameless and indiscriminate intercourse as a frightful thing, they should have hated Zeus, for he had children from his own mother, Rhea, and his daughter, Kore, and he married his own sister." If you want to see immorality, read your own myths. You are blaming us for things that you found in your stories about your own gods. This is just a nice little twist that he's throwing out, but there's a nice irony to show how silly these arguments are.

Athenagoras, then, was an important apologist, living in the second century, who went point by point through the charges leveled against Christians to show that they were absurd, ridiculous, and should be no grounds of our persecution. The arguments that Athenagoras raised would be seen throughout the various apologists, along with several other arguments that he didn't get around to making, but that eventually became standard fare. Let me give several of these other arguments found throughout the Christian apologists in the second and third centuries.

First, Christians are not a threat to society at all. The apologists insisted that since Christians alone were holy and close to God, it was their prayers that preserved society. They were, literally, the salt of the Earth, a reference to salt being a preservative of meat. The way you preserved meat was to use salt. Christians were the salt of the Earth. They were not a threat at all. In fact, they were the ones responsible for society surviving.

Second, for that matter, Christianity, in their opinion, alone, was the true religion. Thus, these apologists actually went on the attack. They attacked paganism for worshipping dead and false idols, so there was this kind of standard polemic against idol worship. "If you worship these idols, they are just stone or wood. They are dead. They are nothing. You can knock them over with your hand. These are your gods? If you have a temple, and your god is in there, and you temple burns down, is your god destroyed? We believe in a God who is not material at all, the one true God."

In fact, they go on, then, and give reasons for thinking that Christianity is the true religion. It is proved to be true by the fact that its followers can do miracles. Throughout these accounts, then, you have references to the apostles of Jesus performing miraculous deeds, as we saw earlier.

It is also proven to be true because of "proof from prophecy." These apologists point out that hundreds and hundreds of years before Jesus, there were Jewish prophets who predicted what would happen to Jesus, and what Jesus would do. The prophet Isaiah predicted that the savior would be born of a virgin, and Jesus was. The prophet Micah predicted that the savior would come from Bethlehem, and Jesus did. Isaiah, chapter 53, Psalm 22, predicted that the savior would be crucified, and so he was.

Even as far back as the book of Genesis, we have evidence of Christ. God, in the beginning, when he creates humans, says, "Let us make man in our own image." Who is he talking to? He's talking to Christ. Christ is found in the book of Genesis. Genesis was written by Moses. This religion is much older than anything the pagans have. Pagan religions might trace themselves back to hundreds of years earlier. You could possibly trace them back to Homer, writing the *Iliad* and the *Odyssey*, but Moses lived 400 years before Homer did, 800 years before Plato, so that these key figures, for the pagan religions, in fact, are much later than the key figures for the Christian religion, Moses and the prophets.

The conclusion that the apologists drew was that Christianity alone was the true religion. Christianity was not a threat to society, and for these reasons, the society, the state, should have left Christians in peace, to worship as they chose. "Even if you don't want to convert to this one true religion, you should at least leave it alone." The apologists, in fact, argued in anticipation of the ideas that were promulgated many centuries later under a completely different set of circumstances. The apologists argued that there should be a separation of religion and politics, a separation of church and state. "Let us alone to worship as we want. Don't interfere." This argument for separation of church and state, which had never been seen in the world before this, never actually caught on, because, of course, the empire converted to Christianity, and the government took up the Christian cause against pagans and Jews. Then, nobody wanted to argue separation of church and state anymore.

To sum up, starting in the second century, there were some intellectuals who converted to the Christian faith and wrote apologies in its defense, proclaiming the theological superiority, the moral virtue, and social value of Christians, in an attempt to bring the persecutions to an end. These intellectual defenses, these apologies, were not themselves effective in averting persecution, as it turns out, but as the writings of the first serious Christian intellectuals, the apologies became important for later Christian theological and ethical reflection as the religion continued to spread its appeal throughout the Roman world.

Lecture Fifteen
The Diversity of Early Christian Communities

Scope: This is the first of four lectures that will consider the wide-ranging
theological diversity of early Christianity and the internal conflicts
that emerged as Christians tried to determine once and for all the
"right" beliefs and practices. Contrary to what one might think,
early believers in Jesus held an enormous variety of beliefs: Some
claimed there were two or more gods, some insisted that the world
was created by an evil deity, some argued that Jesus was not really
human or not really divine, some maintained that Jesus's death had
nothing to do with salvation, and others claimed that he never
actually died.

In this lecture, we will begin to consider early Christian diversity
by examining the views of the opponents of the apostle Paul (for
example, in Galatia and Corinth), people who claimed to represent
the true faith as proclaimed by Jesus. We will then move to look at
forms of Christianity outside the New Testament, such as those
found in the opponents of Ignatius of Antioch and non-canonical
books, including the Gospel of Thomas, discovered in modern
times.

Outline

I. In our course to this point, we have considered a number of significant
external features of early Christianity: its relationship to the Jewish
religion from which it emerged, its spread throughout the Roman
world, its persecution, and the defenses that it made to local and
official opposition.

II. In this lecture, we shift our focus to internal developments in the
religion. This will be the first of four lectures dealing with key aspects
of the diverse character of early Christianity.

III. Christianity in the modern world is extremely diverse (cf. the Greek
Orthodox, Pentecostals, Anglicans, Southern Baptists, Seventh Day
Adventists, and Roman Catholics!). But it was even more diverse in the
first three centuries of the church.

A. People who called themselves Christians were identified by others as Christians and were persecuted as Christians; they held an incredibly wide range of beliefs about God, the material world, Christ, Scripture, and nearly everything else.

B. In some senses, the religion was so diverse that it may make more sense to speak of early *Christianities* rather than early *Christianity*.

IV. We do not need to wait until the second century to see these developments emerge, however. They are evident already in the New Testament period, the first century.

A. This can be seen in the range of views represented among the opponents (who were themselves Christian) of the apostle Paul, our earliest Christian author.

1. He wrote his letter to the Galatians to oppose Christian missionaries who believed that to be full members of the people of God, Gentiles needed to become Jewish and adopt the laws God had given his people through Moses, including the requirement of circumcision. (These laws were, after all, presented in the Old Testament as part of an "eternal" covenant, not a temporary one.)

2. Paul wrote his letters to the Corinthians to oppose Christian leaders who thought that believers had already experienced a spiritual resurrection and, thus, were reaping the full benefits of salvation in the here and now—making their physical lives of no importance to God. (In other words, people could behave in any way they chose and use their bodies for any purposes they wished.)

3. These opponents—and all the others Paul and his contemporaries had to face—naturally believed that they were right and Paul was wrong. But they lost these arguments, and no one bothered to preserve their writings.

B. Even among the writings of the New Testament—that is, the books that later came to be regarded as Scripture and were placed within the same canon—there is a remarkable range of belief expressed.

1. The differences among the New Testament books are usually overlooked, because they all occur now within the same canon of Scripture and are treated as one book (with, therefore, one point of view), rather than 27 books, by different authors, writing at different times to different audiences, and embodying different perspectives.

2. But there are important distinctions. What was Jesus's message? The answer depends on whether you read Mark or John. Should the Jewish Law be accepted by Jesus's followers? That depends on whether you read Paul or Matthew.

V. After the books of the New Testament were written, the diversity of Christian beliefs become even more evident.

A. This can be seen, for example, in the letters of Ignatius of Antioch, whom we have met already as one of the first Christian martyrs.

1. In his seven surviving letters, written mainly to churches of Asia Minor that he had come to know en route to his martyrdom, he is particularly concerned with "heretical" forms of belief that were threatening the communities.

2. In particular, he appears to be concerned about *Judaizing* Christians who urged believers to accept the Jewish Law (cf. Paul's enemies in Galatia) and *docetic* Christians who insisted that Christ was not a real flesh-and-blood human being but, as fully divine, only appeared to be human (from the Greek word *doceo*, to "seem" or "appear").

B. The diversity can also be seen in books taken as Scripture by other Christian groups that did not, however, make it into the New Testament. As just one example, we can consider the Gospel of Thomas.

1. This book was discovered in 1945 near the village of Nag Hammadi, Egypt, along with a cache of other "heretical" writings, known collectively as the Nag Hammadi library.

2. The book is significant because it contains 114 sayings of Jesus (and nothing else), many of which are completely unlike what we find in the New Testament (others of them are very similar to the New Testament sayings).

3. Some of the sayings presuppose a view that the world is an inherently bad place in which human spirits are entrapped, imprisoned; that they need to escape this material world to find their salvation; and that this escape can come only by uncovering the secret teachings of Jesus.

4. The opening lines are particularly instructive (sayings 1–2): The way to have eternal life is by correctly interpreting the secrets divulged by Jesus.

5. This obviously stands in sharp contrast with Paul and the Gospels of the New Testament, which maintained that it was by Jesus's death and Resurrection, not his teachings, that one can find eternal life.

6. Yet this book, and others found with it in the Nag Hammadi library, were accepted as sacred truth by the Christians who read and preserved it.

VI. In sum, early Christianity was an extremely diverse phenomenon from the outset, with a wide range of beliefs and practices adhered to by those who claimed to be followers of Jesus. In our next lecture, we will begin to consider some specific Christian groups that we know about from the second century, then move on to discuss how one form of Christianity ended up becoming dominant, deciding what creeds to believe and which books to include in sacred Scripture.

Essential Reading:

Bart Ehrman, *Lost Christianities*.

———, *Lost Scriptures*.

Elaine Pagels, The Gnostic Gospels.

Supplementary Reading:

Walter Bauer, *Orthodoxy and Heresy in Earliest Christianity*.

James Dunn, *Unity and Diversity in the New Testament*.

Questions to Consider:

1. Try to think of as many "varieties" of Christianity as you can in the modern world. What holds all of these forms of belief together (if anything), and in your opinion, how "different" does a belief have to be before it ceases to be "Christian"?

2. Why has Christianity historically placed such a strong emphasis on "correct belief" (unlike most other religions); are there forms of Christianity that do not do so?

Lecture Fifteen—Transcript
The Diversity of Early Christian Communities

In our course to this point, we have been considering a number of significant external features of early Christianity: Its relationship to the Jewish religion from which it emerged, its spread throughout the Roman world, its persecution, and the defenses that it made to local and official opposition. In this lecture, we shift our focus to internal developments in the religion. This lecture will be the first of four dealing with key aspects of the diverse character of early Christianity.

Christianity in the modern world is extremely diverse—the Greek Orthodox Christians, the Pentecostals, the Anglicans, the Southern Baptists, the Seventh Day Adventists, the Roman Catholics—all of them claim to represent legitimate forms of Christianity, and yet, all of these groups have different beliefs, different views of Scripture, different ritual practices, different church organizations.

As diverse as Christianity is in the modern world, though, Christianity in the ancient world, in the first three centuries of the church, was even more diverse. In that period, people who called themselves "Christians," who were identified by others as Christians, who were persecuted as Christians, held an incredibly wide range of beliefs about God, the material world, Christ, Scripture, and nearly everything else. For example, some Christians, during the first three centuries of Christianity, believed in many gods. Some believed that the one true God did not create this world, but that an evil deity had, who was to be escaped rather than adored. For these Christians who thought such a thing, this God to be escaped was, in fact, the God of the Old Testament.

Some Christians did not believe that Jesus was human. Others did not believe that he was divine. Some Christians did not think that Jesus's death mattered for salvation. Some Christians did not think that Jesus ever died. How could such people be Christians? It seems odd to call them "Christians" now, because we tend to mean one thing when we think of Christianity, even if that one thing comes in many guises. But the many forms of Christianity today do have some central unity. For example, the belief in one God, the belief that Jesus is his Son, some kind of belief in the Holy Spirit, etc.

Radically different views from these do not seem to us to be Christian. Still, that's because in ancient Christianity, there was one perspective that won out in the debates. This one perspective decided how many gods there were. There's only one God for Christian beliefs. They decided whether this God created the world. Yes, he did. They decided whether Jesus was divine or human. Well, they decided that he was both. These Christians who won the debates canonized our New Testament. They decided which books would be in the New Testament that we read today, so that, of course, there's only one correct answer to all of these questions. The victory of this one party in antiquity, though, was a later phenomenon, and the New Testament was a collection of books that they made, excluding other books from their canon.

Before their victory, Christianity was remarkably diverse, far more so than it is today. In some sense, this religion in antiquity was so diverse that it may be better to talk about ancient *Christianities*, rather than ancient *Christianity*. We don't need to wait until the second century, though, to see these developments. There are already in the New Testament period itself, many different forms of Christianity. This can be seen in the range of views represented among the opponents of the apostle Paul, our earliest Christian author.

The opponents of Paul, who, in nearly every other instance, considered themselves to represent true Christianity, and who naturally thought that since they were opposed to Paul, Paul was wrong about his views of Christianity. Take, as an example, Paul's letter to the Galatians, a letter that Paul wrote to a group of churches in the central part of Asia Minor, modern-day Turkey, a group of churches that Paul himself had established. After establishing the churches principally among Gentiles, in the region of Galatia, Paul left, and went on to other missionary grounds.

He heard, later, that some other Christian missionaries had come into the region and had advocated within his own churches that the Gentile men who had become Christian needed to be circumcised in order to be full members of the Christian church, and so, these Christian men were being circumcised. These other Christian missionaries maintained that Gentiles had to become Jewish. They had to adopt the laws of God found in the Jewish Scriptures, the laws given through Moses, including the requirement of circumcision, and possibly the observance of Sabbath, and other festivals, possibly the adoption of kosher food laws. People had to take these laws and make them their own if they wanted to be members of the eternal covenant that God had made with his people, Israel, that Christians were now claiming for their own. It made a lot of sense to the people in

Galatia, that to worship the Jewish God one had to become Jewish, but it made no sense to Paul. Paul argued that, in fact, this was completely wrong, and he wrote his letter to the Galatians in white-hot anger that these people were adopting the practices of circumcision for themselves. Galatians is the one letter of Paul that does not begin with thanksgiving toward the congregation. He was really angry in that one.

What I want to emphasize, though, is that the opponents of Paul who thought that they were right, and Paul was wrong, they probably also wrote books. They also wrote letters. All of their writings are lost.

Take another instance, Paul's letters to the Corinthians. Corinth, the city in what is now modern-day Greece, was a large city, a port city, where Paul had visited and established a congregation of Christians in it. He left after he had established the community, and he heard that there were problems that had arisen in the community (numerous problems if we can gauge them from his letter to the Corinthians). We have two letters that he wrote to this congregation. There were all sorts of problems that had arisen.

There was disunity in the church, where people were fighting over what the right way to run the church was. The disunity was evident in lots of ways, one of them being that some people were so much at odds that they were taking each other to secular court over their differences. The church was split, some following one leader, some following another, some following another.

There were instances of crass immorality in the church. There were instances of men visiting prostitutes and then bragging about it in church. One fellow was shacking up with his stepmother. There were instances within the church of all sorts of immorality and disunity. Sometimes these were evident in their congregational meetings together, where chaos would erupt as people would try to take over the worship services in order to show their superior spirituality.

During their communion meals, which were kind of a once-a-week-bring-your-own potluck supper affair, some people were coming early, gorging themselves, and getting drunk. Other people were coming late, and having nothing. This was one messed up church. These problems, though, were rooted in one big problem that Paul saw, which was that there were people in the church supporting the view that they had already experienced a resurrection with Christ, that they had died with Christ by participating in his death, by being baptized, but that they had also already been raised with Christ. Just as Christ had been raised to the heavenly place, so, too, had they. They were apparently thinking that since they had already begun to experience the full benefits of salvation, it didn't really matter how they lived in this world, that they had experienced a salvation, and since the salvation was of the spirit, the body did not matter any more, since salvation is spiritual. If the body did matter any more, then it didn't matter what you did with your body anymore. So, they were doing all sorts of wild things, profligate things, with their bodies.

Paul disagreed with this point of view and wrote two letters to the Corinthians in which he tried to deal with their problems, but especially the problem that they didn't understand: the Resurrection was not a past spiritual event; it was not that your spirit was raised with Christ, in fact, the Resurrection was a future physical event. Your body will be raised. If you have died, your body will be reconstituted and raised from the dead. If you were living, your body would be transformed into an immortal, so that the future resurrection was bodily. God created the material world. God would redeem the material world. God and would redeem your material body, and therefore, it mattered what you did with your body.

My point is that the opponents of Paul and Corinth who advocated this notion of the special resurrection were themselves Christians who had a different point of view from Paul, who probably wrote what their view was in letters to the Corinthian church, and those letters have been destroyed. We don't have them anymore. There were a wide range of differences within the Christian communities in the first century, as evidenced even within the books that made it into the New Testament, and that all of these books either directly or indirectly opposed Christian opponents who had taken a different point of view, and whose points of view had been lost.

Even among the writings that did become the New Testament—that is, books that later became to be regarded as Scripture, and were placed within the same canon—even the books that became canonical have a remarkable range of belief expressed. Normally, we don't see this when we read the New Testament. In part, we don't see it because the New Testament seems to be one book. It is between two covers. There are a number of different books (27 books), but they are all between two covers, so we treat it as one book.

We talk about "the New Testament," as if every author is saying the same thing. That way of reading the New Testament has been handed down to us ever since the day that some people decided these were the books to be included. Therefore, you read Matthew as though it is saying the same thing that John is saying. Why? Well, because it is the same book, the New Testament. But in fact, it is not same book. Matthew wrote a book having no idea that his book was going to be included in a canon of Scripture with 26 other books. John, who didn't know Matthew, wrote his Gospel, and his Gospel disagrees with Matthew's on a number of different points, but you don't see it, because you act as if it's all one book, and therefore, what we do is harmonize any differences, and take off the edges of all of these books, because we are reading them as a unity.

When you read them as they were originally written, as self-standing pieces of literature, there are, in fact, striking differences. Some of these differences actually matter. What is it that Jesus preached? Well, it depends which Gospel you read. In the Gospel of Mark, Jesus preaches about the coming Kingdom of God, he tells parables to illustrate his message. Jesus does not talk about himself in Mark, but he talks about the coming kingdom.

What about the Gospel of John? In John, Jesus teaches about himself, and only about himself. He doesn't ever talk about coming Kingdom of God. And Jesus, in the Gospel of John, never tells a parable.

Well, which did Jesus preach? Did he preach both? The only reason for thinking he preached both was because we have two different books under two different perspectives put into the New Testament, so you say, "Well, he must have said both things."

What about the Jewish Law? Should Jesus's followers keep the Law? If you read the Gospel of Matthew, the answer is quite clearly "yes." You have to keep the Jewish Law. What if you read the apostle Paul? The answer is quite clearly "no." Christian should not follow the Jewish Law. Which way is it? When you put both them into the canon, you come up with some mediating point of view. There are wide-ranging differences among the books of the New Testament themselves, differences that tend to be muted once they are put within the same canon.

After the books of the New Testament were written, the diversity of early Christian belief became increasingly evident. This can be seen in some of the authors we have already looked at, where we find a range of Christian beliefs expressed.

I want to focus our attention back on Ignatius of Antioch, whom we have already met, as being one of the first Christian martyrs. We looked at one of his letters, the letter to the Romans, in which he tries to urge the Romans to not interfere with his coming execution. The letter is unique among the writings of Ignatius, because it's the only letter he wrote to people that he had not met yet. The other six surviving letters of Ignatius were written to churches who sent representatives to support him on his way to martyrdom.

These other letters are all interesting, because each of these other letters are written to churches of Asia Minor, that he had come to know about, that he was concerned about, because he knew of these forms of heresy that were threatening these various communities. He wrote, in part, in order to attack these various forms of heresy. There are two forms of heresy that Ignatius knew about. I need to emphasize that the word "heresy," when I'm using it now, refers to false beliefs, but they are false beliefs from Ignatius's point of view. I'm not saying personally that these are false beliefs. I'm not taking a stand as a historian about who's right or wrong about this, but from Ignatius's point of view, these were heresies, false beliefs. The people who held these beliefs, of course, thought that Ignatius was the heretic; he had the false beliefs, because he didn't agree with them. Therefore, all sides were accusing the other sides of being heretical.

Ignatius dealt with two forms of heresy as he understood them, two forms of false belief. One is a form of false belief that we have seen already. Several of the churches that he had come to know about have Christians in them supporting a *Judaizing* form of Christianity that appears to be comparable to what we have seen already among some groups who thought that, in fact, one had to keep the Jewish Law in order to be Christian. These Judaizing Christians were likely opponents of Paul in Galatia, and who thought that people had to be circumcised, had to keep the Law, had to keep kosher, had to keep the Sabbath, etc.

Ignatius wrote against these Christians, that in fact, it wasn't right, that one was much better off following the teachings of Paul and others, that Gentiles were on equal footing with Jews in the church, and that Christians did not have to accept the Laws of Judaism. It is interesting, by the way, to speculate whether the Christians that Paul opposed in Galatia, and the Christians that Ignatius opposed that had these Judaizing tendencies are related to the communities that produced the Gospel of Matthew, because Matthew's Gospel, in fact, does support keeping the Jewish Law. Is it therefore possible that these groups, in fact, had Matthew's Gospel, or were Christians in support of Matthew's Gospel?

That's one form of Christianity Ignatius opposed, a Judaizing form. The second is a form that we haven't talked about in this course yet. It has to do with a form of Christian belief called "docetism." Docetism is a belief pertaining to Christ. The word *docetism* comes from a Greek word, *doceo*, which means "to seem," or "to appear." A docetic understanding of Christ is one that says that Jesus was not really a human being of flesh and blood. He only seemed to be a human of flesh and blood. He appeared to be human, but he was not really human, so, since he seemed to be human, those who maintain that Christ was only a human in appearance, therefore, are called docetists.

This was an early Christological view among a number of different people. There was some suggestion that some Christians were already starting to think this in the New Testament period itself. It is clearly a problem that Ignatius recognized in some of his churches. One of his letters is written to a group of Christians in the city of Tralles in Asia Minor. This is therefore Ignatius's letter to the Trallians, in which he detailed some of the problems of this heresy and took a stand against it. I will just read a little bit of this so that you can get a sense of it. Ignatius, writing to the Christians of Tralles, said:

> I urge you, therefore, not I, but the love of Jesus Christ urge you, use only Christian food. Keep off of foreign fare, by which I mean heresy, for those people [He was talking about Christian opponents now; he didn't consider them Christian, although they considered themselves Christian] mingle Jesus Christ with their own teachings just to gain your confidence under false pretenses. It's as if they were giving a deadly poison mixed with honey and wine, with the result that the unsuspecting victim gladly accepts it and drinks down death with fatal pleasure.

It's a nice little image. They're giving you poison, but they sweeten it up so that you don't realize it; you therefore have to stay away from these people, because they are dangerous:

> Be death, then, to any talk that ignores Jesus Christ of David's lineage of Mary, who was really born. He really ate. He really drank. [In other words, these people were saying that it was all an appearance, but in fact, it was not all an appearance.] He was really persecuted under Pontius Pilate. He was really crucified and died in the sight of heaven and Earth, and the underworld. He was really raised from the dead, for his Father raised him just as the Father will raise us who believe in him through Christ Jesus, and if, as some atheists say, [Now, he was using the term "atheists."] by which I mean unbelievers [People who were unbelievers were atheists, and now, he was turning this around. It's not that true Christians were atheists; it was any other unbeliever who was an

atheist.] if, as some of them say, Christ's suffering was a sham, [It was really they who were the sham, he said.] why then am I a prisoner? Why do I want to fight with the wild beasts? In that case, I shall die to no purpose.

His point is that if Christ didn't really exist as a flesh and blood human being, but only appeared to, then, his suffering was an appearance. If that's the case, why am I going off to fight the wild beasts? He had something at stake in the answer to these questions. He was opposing Christians who had docetic Christology. Why would they have a docetic Christology? It is actually not so hard to understand. These were people who thought that Jesus was God. If Jesus was God, he couldn't really be a man, any more than a man could be a rock. They are incommensurate entities. If Jesus was divine, then he must not really have been human. Why did he seem to be human? Because he seemed to be human.

Ignatius wanted it both ways. He wanted Jesus to both be divine and fully human. That's the point of view, of course, that ended up winning out, that Christ is both divine and human. That's why Ignatius's writings were preserved and the writings of his opponents were not. Because they were heretical writings, they were destroyed. Ignatius, then, wanted to emphasize that a docetic Christology was wrong, not be accepted, and dangerous, because it kept people away from accepting the true imitation of Christ that comes about by martyrdom.

I'm trying to emphasize that there were a lot of Christian views floating around, and that we may only get one side of the story in surviving literature, but at one time, the views were quite extensive. This diversity of early Christian opinion and doctrine can also be seen in books that were taken to be Scripture by other Christian groups, groups that did not win out. These books did not make it into the New Testament, but some of them have been discovered in modern times. I'm going to talk about one of these books discovered in modern times that some people took to be a scriptural book, but it eventually came to be excluded from anything like a canon of Scripture.

The book I'm going to talk about is called the Gospel of Thomas. We have seen the Acts of Thomas in this course. This book was allegedly written by the same fellow that the Acts was about, Judas Thomas, Didymus Judas Thomas, somebody thought to be Jesus's brother. We've known about a Gospel of Thomas for centuries, because the Gospel of Thomas was mentioned by some of the heresiologists, the "heresy hunters" from early Christianity, including people like Tertullian, Justin, and others.

We knew that the book at one time existed, but we didn't have the book until it was accidentally discovered in 1945, near the village of Nag Hammadi, in Egypt, in a very famous discovery. Several people who were field hands were digging for some fertilizer, and one of these people accidentally hit something hard in the ground. They uncovered it, and it turned out that there was a jar buried in the ground. They were afraid to open the jar, because this was an illiterate group of Bedouins who thought the jar might contain an evil genie. Then, they thought about it a bit more, and realized that it might contain gold. They then smashed it to smithereens. It turned out that there wasn't a genie or gold inside, but a bunch of books, 12 leather-bound volumes, and part of a 13th volume from which the cover had been ripped off, and it was stuck inside of one of the other volumes.

It is a long story I don't need to go into. Eventually, scholars found out about the discovery of these books, tracked them down, and were able to look at them, and read them. These 13 books are anthologies. They have a number of texts within them. The texts within were written on papyrus. The books that were found were buried sometime in the fourth Christian century, and the books themselves were apparently manufactured sometime in the fourth century, but the writings within the books were much older. Just as this book here was manufactured in 1997, but the writings in it were written 1900 years earlier, these books discovered from the fourth century were manufactured hundreds of years earlier. They contained a number of interesting writings, including some Gospels—one Gospel allegedly was written by Jesus's disciple Philip, another allegedly written by Jesus's brother, Didymus Judas Thomas, the author of Gospel of Thomas.

The Gospel of Thomas consists of 114 sayings of Jesus, and nothing else. It is a Gospel, but it doesn't tell any stories about Jesus. Nothing about any of his healings, none of his controversies, none of his exorcisms. It doesn't tell the stories of his death and Resurrection. It is just group of sayings, 114 of them. They are not numbered in the manuscript as 114 sayings, but modern scholars have numbered them in that way.

Some of the sayings are very much like sayings you get within the New Testament. For example, saying 34: "If a blind man leads a blind man, both of them fall into a pit." In fact, it's even a little more terse and pithy than you get in the New Testament. Another, for example, saying 54: "Jesus said, 'Blessed are the poor, for yours is the kingdom of heaven.'" Very much like what you get in the New Testament. The parable of the mustard seed is found here in the Gospel of Thomas.

Some of the sayings, then, are very much what you might find in the New Testament, but some of the sayings are quite different from anything you might find in the New Testament. "Jesus said, 'If the flesh came into being because of spirit, it's a wonder, but if spirit came into being because of the body, it's a wonder of wonders. Indeed, I am amazed at how this great wealth has made its home in this poverty.'" That's kind of an anti-materialistic bent going on there.

Another: "His disciples say to Jesus, 'When will you become revealed to us? When shall we see you?' Jesus said, 'When you disrobe without being ashamed, and take your garments, and place them under your feet like little children, and tread on them, then, you shall see the Son of the living one, and you will not be afraid.'" Take off your clothes, and trample on them without shame, and then...That is not quite what he says in the New Testament. What is that?

"His disciples said to him, 'When will the kingdom come?' Jesus said, 'It will not come by waiting for it. It will not be a matter of saying, 'Here it is,' or 'There it is.' Rather, the kingdom of the Father is spread out upon the Earth, and people do not see it.'" What is he referring to?

These are 114 sayings, some of which presuppose that the world we live in is an inherently bad place, where human spirits have come to be entrapped and imprisoned, and that these spirits need to escape this material world: "Take off your clothes, and trample on them." It's like escaping your body in order to find salvation. This escape can only come by uncovering the secret teachings of Jesus. This is how it begins. It is the key to the whole Gospel of Thomas. These are the secret sayings that the living Jesus spoke, and Didymus Judas Thomas wrote them down. He said, "Whoever finds the interpretation of these sayings will not taste death."

Eternal life for this document comes not by believing in the death and Resurrection of Jesus. It comes by interpreting the secret teachings of Jesus that this Gospel conveys. That stands in sharp contrast with what Paul thought, for example. For him, Christ being crucified was everything. For the Gospel writers of the New Testament, the death of Jesus was what really mattered, and his Resurrection. Not so for the author of the Gospel of Thomas. For this book, the way eternal life comes is to interpret his secret teachings that this book conveys.

This book was accepted as scriptural by some Christians in the early church. Other Christians attacked it, maligned it, saying that its views were wrong, destroyed it, so that it came to be lost until it was accidentally discovered in 1945.

Let me sum up what I've tried to show in this lecture. Early Christianity was extremely diverse from the very outset. It had a range of beliefs and practices that were adhered to by those who claimed to be followers of Jesus: Paul and his enemies, the Gospel of Thomas and its opponents, Ignatius and his enemies.

Our next lecture is going to consider some of these other different groups as social groups, especially social groups of Christians that we know about from the second century. From there, we're going to move on to discuss how one form of Christianity ended up becoming dominant, deciding what creeds to believe, which books to include in sacred scripture for all time.

Lecture Sixteen
Christianities of the Second Century

Scope: In this lecture, we will consider the meaning of the terms *orthodoxy* ("right belief") and *heresy* ("choice," that is, the choice not to believe the right beliefs). We will then examine the beliefs of various groups of Christians of the second century, who all claimed to represent the true understanding of the religion but who disagreed, both among themselves and with the group that emerged as victorious from the conflicts to determine what Christians would believe (for example, by producing the creeds still recited in churches today). In particular, we will look at Jewish Christian Ebionites, who insisted on the ongoing validity of the Jewish Law; the Marcionites, who rejected all things Jewish, including the Jewish God; and Gnostics, who believed the material world was evil and that they had the secret knowledge, revealed by Jesus, necessary to escape it.

Outline

I. In the previous lecture, we began to see the wide internal diversity of the early Christian movement.

    A. We saw this diversity in the earliest period of Christianity, for example, in the arguments raised by Paul against his Christian opponents and in some of the books that came to be canonized into the New Testament.

    B. This diversity continued and intensified with the passing of time, as we saw in the Judaizing and docetic Christians opposed by Ignatius and in such non-canonical works as the Gospel of Thomas.

    C. In this lecture, we will look at several wide-ranging groups of Christians in the second century to compare and contrast the remarkable varieties of belief they evidenced.

II. We can start with a group known to history as the Ebionites, who were Jewish Christians who affirmed the ongoing need of Christians, whether Jew or Gentile, to adhere to the demands of the Jewish Law.

A. We do not know the origin of their name, though it may be rooted in the Hebrew term *Ebyon*, meaning "poor"—possibly because they accepted voluntary poverty, as Jesus did, for the sake of others.

B. We have none of their own writings, but they are described by their opponents as Christians who claimed to follow the leadership of James, the brother of Jesus and leader of the church in Jerusalem, and to have kept Jewish practices of circumcision, kosher food, Sabbath observance, and the like.

C. Their theology may, in fact, have been the oldest form of Christianity, which maintained that this religion was and always had been Jewish. Followers of Jesus who worshipped his God needed to follow the laws his God had given.

D. As strict monotheists, these Christians insisted that Jesus, the Messiah, was the *man* God had chosen for the salvation of the world by dying on the cross. They did not subscribe to the notions of Jesus's divinity or virgin birth.

E. Why did these Christians not simply read the New Testament to see that they were wrong about such things? Because the New Testament did not yet exist. These Ebonite Christians had other sacred books to support their views.

   1. In particular, they accepted something like our Gospel of Matthew, sometimes called the Gospel of the Nazareans (another name for this, or a similar, group).

   2. And they explicitly rejected the teachings of Paul, whom they saw as a heretic who debased the Jewish Law.

III. Prominent at the same time as the Ebionites was a group of anti-Jewish Christians called the Marcionites.

A. In this case, there is no ambiguity concerning their name: They were followers of a famous philosopher/theologian of the second century named Marcion.

B. Quite opposite of the Ebionites, Marcion and his followers looked on the apostle Paul as the apostle of God par excellence.

C. Paul had emphasized that salvation comes to all people, Jew and Gentile, apart from the Jewish Law. Marcion argued that this demonstrated a split between the salvation of Jesus and the Law of the Jews.

1. He further drew out the logic: The God of Jesus could not be the God who gave the Law. Marcion concluded that there were two different gods.
2. The Jewish God had created the world, called Israel to be his people, and given them his Law. But it was a Law that no one could keep, and the penalty for disobedience was harsh.
3. The God of Jesus stood over against this vengeful God of the Jews, known from the Old Testament. This true God of Jesus did not create the world and had nothing to do with the world before Jesus appeared to save people from this other God.
4. Jesus himself was not a material creature of this world (otherwise, he would belong to the creator God) but only "appeared" to be so. Marcionites were, therefore, docetists.
5. By dying on the cross, Jesus satisfied the requirements of the Jewish God and brought salvation from his grasp.

D. The Marcionites had two books that supported their views, both made by Marcion.
1. The first was a collection of sacred texts—the writings of Paul and a form of the Gospel of Luke, both truncated to remove from them any reference to the God of the Jews or his laws. Marcion removed such references, claiming that they had earlier been "inserted" by false believers into these originally pristine writings.
2. The second was a book called the *Antitheses* ("*Contrary Statements*"), in which Marcion spelled out his views of the differences between the Old Testament God of wrath and the God of Jesus.

E. Clearly the Marcionites (with their two Gods and anti-Jewish views) stood in sharp contrast with the Ebionites (with their one God and affirmation of the Jewish Law).

IV. One other group of Christians from the period is commonly called Gnostic, from the Greek word *gnosis*, because these people believed that "knowledge" (*gnosis*) was the key to salvation.

A. There was a wide range of Gnostic religions in the second century.

B. However, they seem to have held several beliefs in common.

1. Gnostics held that the material world was the result of a cosmic disaster and was not the kind and beneficent creation of the one true God.
2. Instead, according to their myths, there were numerous gods in the divine realm. In a catastrophic event in eternity past, one of the divine beings fell from that realm, captured an element of the divine, and created the material world as a place of imprisonment for it.
3. Some humans have this spark of the divine within them. The goal of the religion is to liberate these divine sparks by delivering to them the knowledge of who they really are, where they came from, and how they can return.
4. In Christian Gnostic systems, Jesus is the one who brings this saving knowledge. He is not really a human from here; he comes from above to deliver the secret teachings that can bring salvation to the divine beings who are entrapped.
5. The chosen ones who then receive his teachings know how to return to their heavenly home.

C. This group was seen to be particularly dangerous to Christians that we might call "proto-orthodox," that is, forerunners of the group that eventually determined what Christians would believe in later centuries. Gnostics were dangerous because they could be found in the proto-orthodox churches, seeing themselves as a spiritual elite who understood the real meaning of the religion that everyone else took literally.

D. Numerous Christian authors wrote against the Gnostics, including some of the authors we have already discussed: Justin, Irenaeus, Tertullian, and others.

V. The second century saw a wide range of Christian beliefs, but none of the groups discussed in this lecture established itself as dominant in the religion. It was the proto-orthodox who did so. In a later lecture, we will consider how they managed to become dominant. Before that discussion, however, we will look at some of the surviving writings from various early Christians, many of them forgeries in the names of the apostles, to which believers appealed in support of their views in the face of alternative forms of the religion prominent throughout the Christian world of the time.

Essential Reading:

Bart Ehrman, *Lost Christianities*, chapters 6–8.

——, *The New Testament: A Historical Introduction*, chapter 1.

Supplementary Reading:

Walter Bauer, *Orthodoxy and Heresy*.

E. C. Blackman, *Marcion and His Influence*.

A. F. J. Klijn, *Jewish-Christian Gospel Tradition*.

Elaine Pagels, *The Gnostic Gospels*.

Questions to Consider:

1. Given the enormous range of belief we have seen in this lecture, how could all these groups plausibly consider themselves to be "Christian"?

2. Are there passages in the New Testament to which you could appeal in support of the views of Ebionites, Marcionites, and/or Gnostics?

Lecture Sixteen—Transcript
Christianities of the Second Century

In the previous lecture, we began to see the wide internal diversity of the early Christian movement. We saw this diversity in the earliest period of early Christianity, for example, in the arguments raised by Paul against his Christian opponents, and in some of the books that came to be canonized in the New Testament. This diversity continued and even intensified with the passing of time, as we saw in the Judaizing and docetic Christians opposed by Ignatius, and in some such non-canonical works as the Coptic Gospel of Thomas.

In this lecture, we will consider several wide-ranging groups of Christians in the second century, to compare and contrast the remarkable varieties of belief that they evidenced. We can start this look at social groups of Christians, as opposed to just literature, with a group known to history as the Ebionites.

The Ebionites were Jewish Christians who affirmed the ongoing need of Christians, whether Jew or Gentile, to adhere to the demands of the Jewish Law. To that extent, they sound very much like the opponents of Paul in Galatia. We don't know the origin of the name "Ebionites," although it may be rooted in the Hebrew term *Ebyon*, which means "poor," possibly because these people accepted voluntary poverty like Jesus for the sake of others.

The church fathers who talked about the Ebionites (our main source about the Ebionites), in fact were not sure where the term "Ebionites" came from. Some of them, like Tertullian, said that it came from the fact that they had a leader, the one who started their group, whose name was Ebion. As I have said, though, it probably comes from this term "poor," because they took on voluntary poverty. Some of the church fathers who recognized that it might come from that term made a field day of it. They said that these were people who, by their own name, acknowledged that they were poor in faith, or poor in understanding. Obviously, though, that's not what the Ebionites themselves thought.

In the Book of Acts, early on in chapters 2, 3, and 4, we have evidence that early Christians would sometimes give away all of their possessions because Jesus had said, "Love your neighbor as yourself." If you were rich, and your neighbor had nothing, then you obviously were not loving your neighbor as yourself, and therefore, some of these early Christians would give away everything for the sake of others. It may be, then, that these Ebionites can trace their roots back to these earliest Christians who lived in communes together, giving away all of their possessions. In any event, their name was the Ebionites.

We don't have any of the writings of the Ebionites, so we don't know what they would have said about or for themselves. We do have descriptions of the Ebionites by their enemies, their opponents, Christians who wanted to root out heresy, and considered the Ebionites to be heresy. According to some of their opponents, including people like Tertullian, whom I have mentioned before, and a person named Irenaeus, who was a major heresiologist and heresy hunter at the end of the second century, according to Tertullian and Irenaeus, these Christians, these Ebionites, claimed to follow the leadership of James, the brother of Jesus, and the leader of the church in Jerusalem.

According to the New Testament, Jesus had several brothers. Of course, in later Christian tradition, these brothers came to be thought of as stepbrothers, because they were thought to be the sons of Joseph from a previous marriage, the idea being that Joseph and Mary were married only when Joseph was an old man, and already had a family of his own, so that parts of his family included the sons, James, Jude, and others, so that they would be stepbrothers. Other people in the fourth and fifth centuries said that these brothers, in fact, were not stepbrothers, but cousins of Jesus. The New Testament assumes that, in fact, these were his actual brothers. The assumption there is that Joseph and Mary, after the miraculous birth of Jesus, went ahead and had a family, including brothers and sisters.

In the New Testament, James is described as Jesus's brother, and we know from the writings of Paul that he became the leader of the Christians after Jesus's Resurrection in Jerusalem. These Ebionites claimed that their ideas about Christianity went directly back to James, the brother of Jesus, so that they could claim some serious connections that gave them vindication for their particular points of view.

Their points of view included following Jewish practices as Christians. They maintained that Christians, whether Jew or Gentile, had to follow the laws given by Moses in the Hebrew Bible, including the laws of circumcision, kosher food, Sabbath observance, and the like. This theology of following Jewish practices while believing Jesus was the Messiah may, in fact, have been the oldest form of Christianity. In the earliest of times,

Christians were Jews who understood Jesus as the Jewish Messiah, sent from the Jewish God to the Jewish people in fulfillment of the Jewish Law.

The earliest Christians therefore concluded that, of course, you had to be Jewish in order to be a member of this religion. The Ebionites maintained that tradition. This is an indication, by the way, that heresy was not always some new invention. Within Christian circles, sometimes heresy was a refusal to move on into new directions. These people were staying where the earliest Christians probably were, didn't move on in their theological reflection, and so later were branded as heretics.

What is particularly heretical, though, about saying that Christians have to be Jews in order to be followers of Jesus? That, in itself, was not the major problem that the heresiologists, the heresy hunters, had with the Ebionites. Their major problem was their understanding of Jesus. Since these Ebionites maintained a Jewish understanding of things, they were strict monotheists who insisted that there was only one God: There are not several gods; there are not many gods; there's only one God to be worshipped.

Jesus is obviously somebody separate from God himself. Jesus is a human, which means that Jesus cannot be God, or else you would have two Gods. You can't have two Gods; you can only have one God. The conclusion for these people was that Jesus was a man. He was not God. Jesus was the man whom God had made the Messiah. God chose Jesus to bring about the salvation of the world. Why did he choose Jesus? According to the Ebionites, Jesus was a man who was born to Joseph and Mary, and who was a very righteous man. In fact, he was most righteous man on Earth.

Since he was the most righteous man, God chose him to be his own son, or, in their terms, God adopted Jesus to be his son. Thus, sometimes these Ebionites are known as "adoptionists," because they have an adoptionistic Christology, meaning that they have an understanding of Christ where he is not himself divine, but has been adopted by God to be his son. Jesus, though, is purely human, and not divine. These Ebionites, therefore, denied the doctrine of Jesus's divinity and the doctrine of his virgin birth. For them, Jesus was not born of a virgin. He was born of the sexual intercourse of Joseph and Mary, born just like the rest of us, but he was more righteous than the rest of us.

Well, they denied Jesus's divinity and his virgin birth. How could they? Why didn't they just read the New Testament, and see that they were wrong about this? Well, the short answer is that the New Testament did not yet exist when the Ebionites developed their points of view. These Ebionite Christians, in fact, had other sacred books that did support their views, other books that they thought were the Scriptures, before our canon became formalized.

In particular, the Ebionites accepted something like our Gospel of Matthew. As we have seen in the course already, Matthew is the most Jewish of the Gospels of the New Testament. It advocates Jesus's Jewishness, and advocates the Jewishness of his followers. His followers have to follow all of the Law, down to the jot and tiddle of the Law. The Ebionites, then, were naturally drawn to something like Matthew. It appears that they called their Gospel the "Gospel of the Nazareans." They called it the Gospel of the Nazareans because an alternative name for the Ebionite group is Nazarean.

Their Gospel, then, was called the Gospel of the Nazareans. It is like our Matthew apparently, but it was written in Aramaic, the language of Jesus himself, so it isn't clear whether this was an Aramaic translation of Matthew, or a different book that was somehow related, originally written in Aramaic. Evidently, though, it did not contain chapters 1 and 2 of our Matthew. Why not? Because Matthew chapters 1 and 2 are the chapters that narrate the virgin birth of Jesus, and these people did not accept the virgin birth.

For their scriptures, then, they had something like our Gospel of Matthew, though they called it the Gospel of the Nazareans. The explicitly rejected the teachings and writings of Paul, whom they saw as a heretic, who debased the Jewish Law. Paul advocated salvation based on faith in Christ apart from doing works of the Law, so that Christians didn't have to do the Law. These people, then, naturally saw Paul as the enemy. None of Paul's writings, therefore, were in their Scripture, but they did have the Gospel of the Nazareans.

That's one group, then: The Ebionites, a Jewish Christian sect of believers scattered throughout the Mediterranean, who maintained that Christians had to be Jewish in order to be Christian, and advocated an adoptionistic Christology.

At the same time as the Ebionites, there was another group of anti-Jewish Christians called the Marcionites. In this particular case, there's no ambiguity about where their name came from. The Marcionites were called Marcionites because they were followers of a famous philosopher/theologian of the second century whose name happened to be Marcion. Quite opposite of the Ebionites, Marcion and his followers looked upon the apostle Paul as the apostle of God par excellence.

In Paul's writings, he emphasized that salvation came to all people, Jew and Gentile, apart from keeping the Jewish Law. You find this especially in

Paul's letters to the Galatians and to the Romans, where there is a differentiation between Paul's Gospel of salvation through Christ's death and Resurrection and the Law. Salvation comes apart from the Law.

Marcion was quite taken with Paul's writings. Marcion, living some 80 years after Paul, pushed his writings to a logical conclusion. To him, there was a difference between the Gospel and the Law, and this difference could be pushed very hard indeed by Marcion. Marcion maintained that there was an absolute distinction between the Gospel and the Law, that the Gospel came from Jesus, and the Law from the God of the Old Testament. They were so different, in fact, that they couldn't come from the same God. Marcion's conclusion was that there must be two different Gods, a God of the Old Testament, and the God of Jesus. These were two different Gods.

The God of the Old Testament is the God of the Jews. He's the one who created this world and called Israel to be his people. He's the one who gave Israel his Law. He's the God that people know about here.

The God of Jesus is separate from that God. The God of Jesus sent Jesus into the world to save people from the wrathful God of the Old Testament, for the Old Testament God gave his Law, but nobody can keep his Law. Nobody could possibly keep the Law of the God of the Jews. Included in this Law were such commandments as: "You shall not covet." You cannot covet anything. Well, if you covet something, then you've broken his Law. What's the penalty for breaking God's Law? The penalty is death. Therefore, everybody has to pay the death penalty, but who could possibly go through life without coveting?

This God is not an evil God for Marcion. He's completely fair and just, but he's got a Law, and if you break it, the just sentence is death.

The God of Jesus has nothing to do with this Jewish God. The God of Jesus is an unknown God prior to the coming of Jesus. The Marcionites, in fact, called the God of Jesus "the stranger God." He is a stranger to this world. He's foreign to this world. This God of Jesus did not create the world, and has had nothing to do with the world before Jesus appeared in order to save people from the other God.

Whereas the other God is just and fair, if harsh, the God of Jesus is merciful. He's the God of love. He's the God of grace. The God of Jesus, then, is separate from the Jewish God. The God of Jesus sent Jesus into the world to save people from the Jewish God. That means that Jesus himself cannot belong to the Jewish God, which means he cannot be part of this material world, because the Jewish God created this material world. How do you explain Jesus appearing into this material world?

Well, Jesus himself could not actually have been born, because that's a material process. Jesus cannot actually have flesh and blood as a human being, because that's all being part of the material world. Jesus, therefore, must only have appeared to be a human being. He must've seemed to have flesh and blood. In other words, Marcion and his followers, the Marcionites, were docetists, though some believe that Jesus, himself was, in some sense, divine, but without a real flesh and blood body.

By dying on the cross, Jesus satisfied the requirements of the Jewish God. The penalty for breaking God's Law is death. Jesus suffered death, even though he didn't commit sin worthy of death. His death, then, was accepted as a sacrifice for everyone else, and brought salvation.

Now, it's not quite clear how the Marcionites worked out the niceties of this theological system because a problem immediately arises. It probably has arisen for you. It arises for me. If Jesus didn't have a flesh and blood body, how did he actually die? It would have only been an appearance of death, and if the requirement for sin is actual death rather than the appearance of death, then Jesus's apparent death shouldn't have paid for anybody's sins, because he didn't actually die. I do not know how the Marcionites solved that particular problem, but they did seem to think that the death of Jesus purchased the release of others who owed a debt of death to the creator God.

Well, once again, why didn't the Marcionites simply read the Scriptures to see if this view was not right? They did read the Hebrew Bible quite carefully. They insisted on a literal interpretation of the Hebrew Bible. They did not read our New Testament because our New Testament didn't exist yet.

What did they read to support their views? We know of two books that the Marcionites had that supported their point of view, two kinds of books. The first was actually a collection of sacred texts in one book, a canon of Scripture. As far as we know, Marcion was the first Christian to create a New Testament, to go along with the Old Testament.

Marcion developed his canon of Scripture while he was in the city of Rome, in the 130s or 140s A.D. His time in Rome is usually dated from between 139 and 144 A.D. He didn't start out in Rome. He started out in a city called Sinope, in the north central part of Turkey. The rumor was that his father had been the bishop of a church there in Sinope, and that Marcion had started propounding a heresy; his father, the bishop, had kicked him out of the church. He then went on some travels and ended up in Rome; he spent five years in Rome between the years 139 and 144, developing his point of view and devising his writings that would support his point of view, including a canon of Scripture.

This canon that he came up with consisted of 11 books. First, since Paul was his hero, he had the letters of Paul that he was familiar with. These included ten letters of Paul, the same ten that are within the New Testament minus 1 and 2 Timothy, and Titus. We have 13 books in our New Testament that claim to be written by Paul. Marcion had all those 13, except 1 and 2 Timothy, and Titus, so he had ten letters of Paul. Why Paul? Because Paul was the one upon whose base he built his theological system.

Secondly, Paul talked about his Gospel, talked about proclaiming his Gospel. Which Gospel did Paul have? Marcion took over the Gospel of Luke, and proclaimed that this was the Gospel that Paul had, this was the Gospel that portrayed Jesus. I mentioned that Matthew is the most Jewish of the Gospels. Luke is often thought of as the most Gentile of the Gospels. It has certain anti-Jewish elements to it, as we saw in a previous lecture, and, of course, Marcion was anti-Jewish, because he thought the Jewish God was not the true God, and that the Law of the Jewish God was not be followed by the followers of Jesus. He therefore took over the Gospel of Luke. His canon, then, consisted of 11 books: the Gospel of Luke and ten letters of Paul.

The problem, though, was that even these books, Paul and Luke, seemed to celebrate the creation as having come from God. They quote the Old Testament as an authority. How do you explain all of that? Marcion explained it by saying that these books did not originally have these quotations of the Old Testament, that they did not originally affirm the creation, that, in fact, these books originally supported his point of view, but that later, people who copied these books had falsified them by adding references to creation and quotations of the Old Testament. Therefore, in order to return these books to their original, pristine state, Marcion excised all passages that disagreed with his point of view. As one of his opponents, Tertullian, put it, "Marcion interpreted the Scriptures with a penknife." He cut out the parts he didn't like.

Marcion, then, had a canon of Scripture of 11 books, and he also had a second book, a book that he called, apparently, the *Antitheses*. The word "antithesis" means "a contrary statement," and it was a book in which Marcion spelled out his views of the differences between the Old Testament God of wrath and the God of Jesus, who was the God of love and mercy.

Even today, people often think of the Old Testament God as somewhat different from the God of the New Testament. In this book, the *Antitheses*, Marcion spelled it out, to show how different they are.

For example, in the Old Testament, God tells his people, the children of Israel, to go in and take the Promised Land. Well, the problem was that somebody was already living in the Promised Land. What do you do about that? You get rid of them. God tells them to go into Canaan and kill off the population: "Go into the city of Jericho," says God in the book of Joshua, "and you are to slaughter every man, woman, child, and animal in the city." They do so, because God commanded them to.

Is that the God of Jesus? The God of Jesus says, "Turn the other cheek if someone strikes you." The God of Jesus says to pray for your enemies. Is that the same God that says to go kill everybody that you disagree with? No, those are different Gods. Therefore, he advocated a God of wrath in the Old Testament, which stands over against the God of Jesus in his book, the *Antitheses*.

The Ebionites and the Marcionites stand in clear contrast with one another. It's easy to contrast with the two. The Ebionites were strict monotheists. There was only one God. The Marcionites thought that there were two Gods. The Ebionites maintained that Christians were to follow the Jewish Law, while the Marcionites said the Christians were not to follow the Jewish Law, the Law of the Jews. The Ebionites subscribed to the teachings of the Hebrew Bible, while the Marcionites rejected the Hebrew Bible. The Ebionites accepted the Gospel of Matthew, while the Marcionites accepted the Gospel of Luke.

The Ebionites rejected the teachings of Paul, while the Marcionites accepted the teachings of Paul. These stand very much at odds with one another. The Ebionites understood Jesus to be completely human but not divine, while the Marcionites understood him to be divine, but not at all human. Clearly, in sharp contrast with one another, both groups claiming that they were the original view of Christianity, that they were right, and other views were wrong. They were two sharply contrasting groups.

There were other groups. One another group that will talk about in the remaining part of this lecture was a group of Christians commonly called by modern scholars, Gnostics. There are called Gnostics from the Greek word *gnosis*, which means "knowledge." These people believed that knowledge, rather than faith, was the key to salvation. I should stress that there were a large number of Gnostic religions in the ancient world, but we tend to put them all under the umbrella term of "Gnosticism," because they did appear to hold certain beliefs in common.

For a long time, we knew about Gnostics only from the writings of their enemies, which is also how we know about the Ebionites and the Marcionites, from the writings of their enemies, since their own writings don't survive.

Things changed with the Gnostics in 1945. I mentioned that the Gospel of Thomas was discovered in a collection of books near Nag Hammadi, Egypt. This collection of books, in fact, consisted of 13 different books, and within these books, there were 52 different tractates, most of which, in fact, appear to be books written by Gnostics for Gnostics, promoting Gnostic understandings of the world. We therefore have some first-hand information about what Gnostics held onto within their beliefs. But even within this Nag Hammadi library, as it is called, there's a wide range of views represented. Still, it is possible to synthesize some commonalities among various groups of ancient Gnostics from these books, from what the enemies of Gnostics said, and from what other sources said.

I will try to spell these out to you now, some of the basic beliefs that Gnostics held in common. These are beliefs that stand somewhat at odds with what Marcionites and Ebionites held onto. The Gnostics maintained that the material world we live in wasn't the creation of a good God, and was not actually just the creation of the Jewish God, who was a harsh God, as the Marcionites held. The material world, in fact, was the result of a cosmic disaster that happened, leading to the creation of this world. It was not the kind and beneficent creation of the one true God. Instead, according to the Gnostics, at least in their own myths, there were a number of gods in the divine realm, but in a catastrophic event that took place in an eternity past, one of the divine beings in the divine realm—which is a spiritual realm removed from this material world—fell, was kicked out of, or was removed from this divine realm of the gods.

After this divine being fell, he captured an element of the divine and created the material world as a place of imprisonment for it. Some human beings have this element of the divine within them. This ignorant God, this lower God, sometimes portrayed as an evil God, he captured an element of the divine and trapped it in the world of matter, made the world of matter as a place of imprisonment, and this divine element was inserted into human beings here. That's why we're here. Humans were created as bodies to have the divine element within.

Some people feel that they don't really belong here this world, that they have some kind of alternative existence, that things don't make sense here, and that they don't belong here. It's obvious why anyone who has that sense does. It's because they don't belong here. They have come from another realm. They are entrapped here, and they need to figure out how to escape. The goal of this Gnostic religion, or these Gnostic religions, is to liberate the divine sparks that are within some humans by delivering to them that knowledge they need for deliverance.

Knowledge of what? Well, isn't knowledge just of the world, because the world is the material place of imprisonment. What the divine spark has to learn about is who it is, where it has come from, and how it can return. That's the knowledge that can bring salvation from entrapment here, knowledge of who you really are, how you got here, where you came from, and how you can return.

This isn't knowledge, though, that you can acquire simply by thinking hard. You can't look around the world and figure out how to escape. The knowledge has to come from the divine realm whence you yourself came. Well, how does it come here, then?

In Christian Gnostic systems, the knowledge necessary for salvation comes when there is a divine redeemer from that realm who comes here in the form of human flesh, in the likeness of human flesh, to reveal saving knowledge. This is not a human from here. It is a divine being from here. In Christian Gnostic systems, it's Christ who comes from above to reveal the knowledge necessary for salvation. Those who are chosen, then, the elect who receive his teachings, know how to return to their heavenly home, and so, some people have secret knowledge that will allow them to escape this evil material world.

These groups of Gnostics were particularly dangerous to other Christians, because they did not form their own churches. They were in the regular Christian churches. They claimed to be the spiritual elite within the churches, and so church fathers who were opposed to heresies found these groups to be especially difficult to root out. You see, they would be able to say the same creeds as everyone else, participate in the same worship services like everyone else, read the Scripture like everyone else, but they thought there was a deeper meaning to it all, and they knew the secret meaning and you didn't. If you disagreed with them, you just didn't know, you see, because we are the ones who know—we are the Gnostics.

A number of Christian authors wrote against these Gnostic groups, their enemies, including people I have talked about: Justin Martyr, Tertullian, and the like. Eventually, as with the other groups, they were rooted out, marginalized, and labeled heresies.

Let me sum up. There were a wide range of Christian beliefs in the second century, but none of the groups I have discussed at length in this lecture established itself as dominant in religion. It was a different group that did so, a group that ended up calling itself the orthodox group. In a later lecture, we will figure out how it was that this orthodox group managed to establish itself as orthodox.

Before going there, in the next lecture, we will look at some of the surviving writings from various early groups of Christians, many of which were forgeries in the name of apostles, forgeries that were appealed to in support of their views in the face of alternative forms of religion that were prominent throughout the Christian world of its time.

Lecture Seventeen
The Role of Pseudepigrapha

Scope: All the various groups of early Christians understood themselves
to be "right" and their Christian opponents to be "wrong."
Moreover, each group had sacred texts that supported its views,
books allegedly written by apostles understood to represent
normative understandings of the faith. The vast majority of these
books, however, were forgeries. In this lecture, we will consider
several such *pseudepigraphical* accounts: a gospel of Jesus's death
and Resurrection allegedly by his disciple Simon Peter; a
revelatory vision allegedly recorded by Jesus's disciple John, the
son of Zebeddee; and a letter allegedly written by the apostle Paul
to the Corinthians ("Third" Corinthians).

Outline

I.   We have seen in the preceding two lectures that Christianity was
     remarkably diverse in the centuries between Jesus and Constantine.

   A.   The variety of Christian belief and practice is evident already in
        the earliest writings we have, those associated with the apostle
        Paul, many of which are directed against Christians who take
        alternative views of the faith.

   B.   This diversity becomes yet more evident in the second century,
        when discrete theologies, such as adoptionism and docetism,
        emerge, as well as discrete social groups with distinctive
        understandings of the faith, such as the Ebionites, the Marcionites,
        and the highly variegated groups of Gnostics.

   C.   All these groups, of course, understood themselves to be right and
        thought the others were wrong. What is most striking is that each
        group believed that it had sacred texts written by apostles that
        supported its own point of view. Most of these texts, however,
        were not actually by the apostles, but were forged.

II. The apostles played a significant role in early Christianity.

   A.   Because Jesus left us no writings, the apostles who heard him
        speak, saw him perform his miracles, and witnessed his
        Resurrection were understood to be the direct links back to Jesus.

B. Any writings the apostles left behind were, therefore, treasured.

C. Already by the first century, Christians were forging writings in the names of the apostles, which could then be used to support their own religious perspectives. We will consider several surviving examples in this lecture.

III. We have already seen one example in the Gospel of Thomas, 114 sayings allegedly of Jesus but supporting a Gnostic point of view.

IV. One of the most intriguing early forgeries is a gospel allegedly written by Jesus's closest disciple, Peter.

A. We knew of this book for centuries, from the writings of the fourth-century church historian Eusebius, who tells us that the book was known to the church of Syria but came to be proscribed by church leaders there because it was thought to contain a docetic Christology.

B. Because of its ban, the book eventually went out of circulation.

C. It was discovered in 1887 during an archaeological dig in a cemetery in upper Egypt, which uncovered the tomb of a Christian monk who had been buried with a manuscript that contained a number of important texts, including a fragmentary copy of the Gospel of Peter.

D. This is an account of Jesus's trial, death, and Resurrection, with many similarities to the accounts of the New Testament (especially Matthew), but many key differences, as well.

    1. The account is more heavily anti-Judaic than that in the New Testament Gospels. For example, it stresses the Jews' sense of guilt at what they did.

    2. It is best known, however, for its vivid portrayal of the Resurrection event itself, in which Jesus emerges from the tomb tall as a skyscraper and the cross emerges from the tomb behind him.

    3. There are also passages that may well have been meant to be taken docetically (for example, vv. 10, 24).

E. This book was seen, then, as a heretical gospel and its use was banned.

V. Even more obviously "unorthodox" is a gospel called the Secret Book of John, discovered, along with the Gospel of Thomas, in the Gnostic writings known as the Nag Hammadi library.

  A. This is an account written from a Gnostic point of view of how the divine realm and the material world came into being, as revealed to John, the son of Zebedee, Jesus's close disciple.

  B. The material world here is not said to be the good creation of the one true God. The God who created this world—who is the God of the Bible—is portrayed as an inferior, ignorant deity, far below the one true God.

  C. This inferior God created this world (and made humans) as a place of imprisonment for the element of the divine that he wanted to entrap here.

  D. Christ is understood as a divine emissary sent from the heavenly realm to free the divine sparks entrapped in this material world.

  E. This aspersion of the Creation and of the God who made it fits well into a Gnostic perspective but is completely at odds with the views held by the Christians whose views ultimately became dominant in early Christianity.

VI. Even these proto-orthodox Christians forged documents in support of their perspectives, however, as can be seen in a pseudepigraphical letter written in Paul's name to counter such Gnostic ideas. The letter is called 3 Corinthians.

  A. The letter is preserved in a longer book called the Acts of Paul, a legendary account of Paul's exploits in the missionary field.

  B. According to the Acts of Paul, the Corinthian church wrote a letter to the apostle complaining that false teachers in their midst were casting aspersions on the Jewish Scriptures and saying that the Creation was not good, that Christ was not really a human, and that the flesh would not be raised.

  C. "Paul" responds to these claims one by one, arguing that there is only one God, the creator of all; that Jesus, his Son, really became flesh; and that all people will be raised in the flesh.

  D. This, in other words, is a proto-orthodox forgery designed to counter the forged claims of other Christian groups.

VII. In sum, all sides in the early disputes among Christians could claim apostolic support for their views. They all appear to have had authors who were willing and able to forge documents in the names of the apostles to promote their distinctive perspectives. Only one side ended up winning these disputes. That was the side that decided what Christians should profess as the truth and which books should be accepted as sacred Scripture. Is it possible that the Scriptures they decided on themselves contained forged documents? That is an issue we will address in a later lecture.

Essential Reading:

Bart D. Ehrman, *Lost Christianities*.

————, *Lost Scriptures*.

Supplementary Reading:

Walter Bauer, *Orthodoxy and Heresy in Earliest Christianity*.

J. K. Elliott, *The Apocryphal New Testament*.

James M. Robinson, *The Nag Hammadi Library in English*.

Questions to Consider:

1. The Gospels of the New Testament are written anonymously. Why do you suppose later Christians attributed them to Matthew, Mark, Luke, and John?

2. Try to imagine reasons for forging documents in antiquity (or today). Can you conceive of "legitimate" reasons for trying to perpetuate a literary "falsehood"?

Lecture Seventeen—Transcript
The Role of Pseudepigrapha

We've seen in the previous two lectures that Christianity was remarkably diverse in the centuries between Jesus and Constantine. The variety of belief and practice among Christians was evident already in the earliest writings that we have, those associated with the apostle Paul. Many of them are directed against Christians who took alternative views of the faith.

This diversity became yet more evident in the second century, when there were discrete theologies, such as adoptionism and docetism, as well as discrete social groups with distinctive understandings of the faith. These included the Ebionites, the Marcionites, and the highly variegated groups of Gnostics. All of these groups, of course, understood that each of them were right, and thought that the others were wrong. What's most striking is that each group believed that it had sacred texts written by the apostles that supported its own points of view. Most of these texts, however, were not actually by the apostles but were forged.

In this lecture, we will consider at some length this phenomenon of apostolic forgeries, or the technical term that is often used, *pseudepigrapha*. The term *pseudepigrapha* literally means "false writings." These writings, though, aren't false necessarily in the sense that they are untrue. They are false in the sense that they are attributed to somebody who, in fact, did not write them—so early Christian pseudepigrapha, or the more common term, forgeries.

By way of background, I should say something about the role of the apostles in early Christianity. Jesus of Nazareth, himself, of course left us no writings. We don't know whether Jesus himself could write, but if he did write anything, nothing has survived from his hand. We do have writings, though, that claim to be written by people who were his followers. There continue to be debates about whether the apostles of Jesus, who were reputed to have been lower-class illiterate peasants from Galilee, and who spoke Aramaic, about whether these people actually left us any writings. It is clear, though, that some followers of Jesus from the first century did leave us writings, whether or not there were his disciples, including, for example, the apostle Paul, who was not one of the 12 disciples, but nonetheless, considered himself to be an apostle of Jesus.

The apostles are important in early Christianity because they are the link between later Christians and Jesus himself. The writings of the apostles stood in the place of the apostles themselves; when the apostles themselves were not present, their writings could be read in order to have a direct link back to Jesus. Any writings that the apostles left behind, therefore, are highly treasured. It's an interesting phenomenon to note that already in the first century there were Christians who were forging writings in the names of the apostles. We know this, more or less, as a fact because of certain kinds of evidence that survives.

One very interesting piece of evidence is found in a book allegedly written by the apostle Paul, 2 Thessalonians. In 2 Thessalonians, chapter 2, the author of this letter warns his readers against a letter allegedly in Paul's name, that, in fact, Paul did not write. In the Thessalonians' community, there had been a disturbance that involved the belief in the end of time. Paul himself had preached that there was an imminent end of the age that was coming, that Jesus was soon to return from heaven. The Thessalonians' community had allegedly received a letter in which the end was said to be so imminent that people needed to prepare for it, because it was coming any minute. As a result, evidently, according to 2 Thessalonians, some people had quit their jobs in anticipation of this imminent end, based on this letter that had reputedly come from Paul. The author of 2 Thessalonians, though, said that in fact, he, Paul, did not write it, and that it was a forgery.

This creates a very interesting irony, precisely because many scholars today think that 2 Thessalonians was not written by Paul. 2 Thessalonians is one of the Deutero-Pauline Epistles. Because of some of its theology, it looks unlike what Paul wrote in his other letters. The reason this is an irony, then, is because if 2 Thessalonians was written by Paul, then we know that there's a forgery in Paul's name floating around, a book that Paul did not write. It claims to be written by Paul because of 2 Thessalonians, chapter 2, verse 2.

On the other hand, if Paul did not write 2 Thessalonians, then we also know there's a letter floating around in Paul's name from that time, namely, 2 Thessalonians itself. Thus, whether Paul wrote a letter or not, we know that there are Pauline forgeries from sometime during the first century.

We get similar phenomena in later Christian writings. There's a very interesting case that comes from the fourth century, the book is called the *Apostolic Constitutions*. This is a book written in the name of the twelve apostles, and it did give some directions about how the churches ought to be run. In an interesting passage in the *Apostolic Constitutions*, written in the fourth century, in the name of the twelve apostles, we're told people should not read books that claim to be written by the twelve apostles but are not.

Now, why would somebody say that you shouldn't read forged documents if the document that you're reading, itself, is forged? The reason to write a document like that is to throw people off the scent of your own deceit. It was a common technique, and continues to be a common technique among forgers still today.

We have seen in this course already some examples of forged documents, or pseudepigrapha. For example, we have considered the Gospel of Thomas, sometimes called the Coptic Gospel of Thomas, because it is written in the Coptic language. Coptic is an Egyptian language. The Gospel of Thomas was originally written Greek, but translated into Coptic. This Coptic Gospel of Thomas was discovered near the village of Nag Hammadi, in Egypt. It contains 114 sayings, allegedly of Jesus. Some of the sayings are very much like what's in the Gospels of the New Testament, but other sayings support a Gnostic point of view. The reputed author of this Gospel of Thomas is Didymus Judas Thomas, the brother of Jesus, but, of course, that person did not actually write this Gospel. It was written at a much later date, probably in the early second century, and therefore is a pseudepigrapha, a forged writing.

One of the most intriguing early forgeries that we now have is a Gospel that was allegedly written by Jesus's closest disciple, Peter. I want to spend the bulk of this lecture talking about this Gospel of Peter, because it is a very interesting pseudepigrapha from early Christianity.

For centuries, we knew that there was a Gospel of Peter in existence, because of the passage that is found in the writings of Eusebius, the fourth century author who wrote the first history of the Christian church. Eusebius is often known as the father of church history, because of his ten-volume work describing the course of Christianity from the days of Jesus up to Eusebius's own time in the early fourth century. Eusebius is a valuable source for us in trying to reconstruct what happened during Christianity's first three centuries, because his is the earliest narrative we have of the course of the Christian movement over that period.

Eusebius's work is particularly valuable for us, because in it, he not only tells anecdotes about some of his predecessors in the Christian tradition, but he also quotes writings, sometimes at length. Often, these are writings that have otherwise been destroyed or lost. Eusebius, then, often provides as with our only access to earlier documents; by reading his books, you can find out about other books that had been written in the intervening period between Jesus and Eusebius.

In one of the stories that Eusebius tells in his narrative of the early church, he describes a Gospel of Peter. The story that he tells involves an author who is otherwise not very well known a person named Serapion. Serapion was a bishop in the large city of Antioch, Syria, in the second century. As bishop of Antioch, Serapion had jurisdiction over other churches in his area outside of Antioch. Antioch was the large city, but there are villages and towns around Antioch, and as the bishop of Antioch, Serapion had jurisdiction over the churches in these outlying areas.

In the story that Eusebius tells, Serapion was making the rounds, going to his various churches, checking up on his churches, to make sure that they were conducting themselves properly, not being too influenced by heretical teachers, and what not. One of the towns he visited was a town called Rhossus. In Rhossus, Serapion discovered that the Christians of the church there were using as the Gospel for their worship a Gospel that was allegedly by Peter, the Gospel of Peter. Serapion thought, "Well, if this Gospel was written by Peter, then, it must be fine." Thus, he allowed them to use this in their church.

After Serapion returned home to Antioch, however, some informers came forward and indicated to him that, in fact, this Gospel of Peter was not really written by Peter, and that it contained, in fact, a docetic Christology, a Christology in which it was taught that Jesus was not really a flesh and blood human being, or, at least taught that there was a differentiation between the man, Jesus, and the divine Christ.

There were some Gnostics in the second century from the same time period who taught a kind of docetism that was a little different from the one I've described to you in the course so far. The docetism I have described so far involves the belief that Jesus was not really a flesh and blood human being, but only seemed to be. The reason docetists would have said that was because they believed he was God, and people in antiquity believed that God obviously could not suffer, because if God suffered, he was not God any longer, then he was mortal.

There was another way to describe a docetic Christology, however, that was somewhat different. In this other form of Christology, it's not that Jesus did not have a real flesh and blood body (Jesus was a man who could suffer like everyone else), but that Christ was the divine element that entered into Jesus temporarily, in order to empower him for his ministry, to help him do miracles, to provide for his supernatural teachings. Then, however, this divine element left Jesus before he was crucified, so that the divine element itself did not suffer. For people who held this understanding of Christology, this kind of docetism, it still seemed that the divine element suffered, but it did not, because the divine element had left Jesus.

Support for this particular kind of docetic point of view can be found in the Gospels. In the Gospel of Mark, for example, when Jesus was baptized, we are told that the heavens split open, and the holy spirit descended upon Jesus in the form of a dove. In the Greek text, it actually says that the spirit entered into Jesus. That's when Jesus started doing his miracles.

At the end of Mark's Gospel, when Jesus was hanging on the cross, he cried out, "My God, my God, why have you forsaken me?" Literally, "My God, my God, why have you left me behind?" Gnostics who understood this kind of docetic Christology maintained that the divine element came into Jesus at his baptism, empowered him for his ministry, and then left him immediately before his crucifixion, so that the man, Jesus, died, but the divine Christ did not suffer. That is a second form of docetic Christology.

Serapion, who was informed by some people that this Gospel of Peter, the use of which he had previously allowed, in fact, had a docetic Christology. They didn't specify which form of docetism it had. Serapion then decided to look into matters himself and got a copy of the Gospel of Peter, and he read the Gospel. He realized that even though most of the Gospel of Peter was perfectly legitimate and on the up and up, there were some passages that could be read in a docetic way. Consequently, Serapion wrote a little pamphlet called "On the So-Called Gospel of Peter." He also wrote a letter to the Christians of the church of Rhossus, in which he forbade their use of this Gospel of Peter, and he included the pamphlet that he had written. Eusebius told the story, and he quoted from the letter that Serapion sent to the church of Rhossus. He also quoted from this pamphlet that Serapion had written. Unfortunately, Eusebius did not quote the passages from the Gospel of Peter that Serapion had found to be docetic. That ends up being important for a reason we will see momentarily.

For most of Christian history, the only thing we knew about the Gospel of Peter was this little anecdote that Eusebius told us. That all changed in rather significant way in the year 1887. In 1887, there was an archaeological dig in upper Egypt, sponsored by a French archaeological team working out of Cairo. This archaeological team was digging in a cemetery in the town of Akhmin. This was a cemetery that had been a burial place for several centuries. The portion of the cemetery that they were digging in had graves from the 8th to the 12th centuries. In one of the graves that they excavated, they found a Christian monk buried in a grave who had been buried with a manuscript. The manuscript was an anthology that contained four texts. One of the texts was a fragmentary copy of the Gospel of Peter.

The three other texts included a copy of a book called First Enoch, which is a Jewish apocalypse, and a book called the Apocalypse of Peter, which is a very interesting book in its own right. It's another forged document in Peter's name that is the first instance we have of a guided tour of heaven and hell, the first instance of a Christian account of a guided tour of heaven and hell. The Apocalypse of Peter describes how Jesus takes Peter on a trip through the places of the dammed and blessed, and so, there you have this account, the Apocalypse of Peter, found in this monk's grave. The third tract in this collection is about the life of a medieval saint. Most importantly for this lecture, there was a fragmentary copy of the Gospel of Peter.

The manuscript that we have that was discovered in this monk's grave was actually a complete manuscript, 66 pages long. The first page of the manuscript has a decoration of the cross. The second page has the beginning of this text of the Gospel of Peter, but it begins in the middle of a sentence, which means that this manuscript itself is not a fragment, but the scribe who copied the manuscript in the early Middle Ages only had a fragmentary copy of the Gospel of Peter in front of him that he copied, because, as I said, this begins in mid-sentence, although the text itself is complete. It also ends in the middle of a sentence.

Nonetheless, it looks to be the Gospel of Peter that Eusebius had informed us about. It's a very interesting text, because it is an account of the trial, death, and Resurrection of Jesus, told in a way that is very similar to, and yet quite different from, the account of Jesus's trial, death, and Resurrection found in the New Testament, in Matthew, Mark, Luke, and John. The way the text begins is as follows. It begins in the middle of a sentence, as follows: "None of the Jews washed his hands, neither did Herod, nor any of his judges. As they did not wish to wash, Pilate got up."

Well, it is pretty clear what happened prior to this event in this fragmentary Gospel. Prior to this, evidently, Pilate has washed his hands, proclaiming his innocence of Jesus's blood, because this begins by saying, "None of the Jews washed his hands, nor did Herod, nor any of the judges." Pilate washing his hands is found only in the Gospel of Matthew, of the Gospels of the New Testament, but there's nothing in Matthew saying that none of the Jews washed their hands. Why would this Gospel emphasize that the Jews did not wash their hands as well? It's clearly going to emphasize that the Jews accept the responsibility for Jesus's death. It's not Pilate's fault. It's the Jews' fault, and in fact, throughout this text, we're going to find a heightened responsibility for Jesus's death placed upon the Jews.

The next verse: "Then Herod the king ordered the Lord to be taken away. He said, 'What I ordered you to do to him, do it.'" Here, it is not Pontius Pilate who ordered Jesus's crucifixion; it is the Jewish king, Herod, once again heightening Jewish culpability for the death of Jesus. This is how the story begins. As it goes on through, it contains many of the accounts that we are familiar with from the New Testament Gospels. Joseph of Arimathea wants the body, and is going to perform the burial. They take Jesus off to be crucified. They mock him, they beat him, and then they crucify him. Even though these are the same stories we know from the Gospels, they are told, in most instances, in a somewhat different way. Sometimes these differences are significant. For example, in verse 10 (modern editors have given verse numbers to these passages): "They brought forward two criminals, and they crucified the Lord between them. He was silent, as if he had no pain."

"Silent as if he had no pain." Remember that Serapion thought that some of these passages in the Gospel of Peter could be read docetically. Maybe this is one of those passages. It was "as if he had no pain." Maybe he didn't have any pain. They put an inscription over his head: "This is the king of Israel." They divided his garments among them. "It was noon, and darkness gripped all Judea. The Jews were all worried and anguished." It goes on to say, "Indeed, the Jews fulfilled everything. They brought their sins to full fruition on their own heads." It's making the Jews culpable for the death of Jesus. Jesus is on the cross, and he cries out on the cross. It's like you find in Mark, but somewhat different: "'My power, oh power, you have left me.' He said this, and was taken up."

Is this is the divine Christ leaving the man, Jesus, before his death? It says, "and he was taken up." Jesus, though, is still on the cross there. What was taken up? Maybe the divine element was taken up. "They pulled the spikes out of the Lord's hand. They lay him in the ground," and an earthquake happens, as, again, happened in Matthew's Gospel. We're told the Jews rejoiced, but then later, they became nervous, because they realized they had done something bad. "Then the Jews, the elders and the Jewish priests, knowing what evil they did to themselves, began to beat their breasts, saying, 'Woe to us, for the judgment and the end of Jerusalem are at hand.'" Jews acknowledge their guilt in killing Jesus.

The story goes on. Jesus is buried, and they put a guard at the tomb. Near the end of this text is probably the most spectacular passage that we find in the Gospel of Peter, an actual account of Jesus's coming out of the tomb. You don't find this in any of the Gospels of the New Testament, but here, we have an account of Jesus actually being shown emerging from the tomb. They have the guards standing around the tomb, and they see the heavens open up, and two men descend from heaven. They go into the tomb. The stone has rolled away by itself from the tomb, so they can go in.

They go in, and everybody is watching. Out of the tomb emerge three people, two of whom have their heads reaching up to the sky, supporting a third person whose head reaches up above the sky. Following the three individuals coming out of the tomb (so this is obviously Jesus, the extra tall one, and the two angels) comes the cross: "And they heard a voice speaking from the heavens: 'Have you preached to those who are sleeping?' Obediently, a voice was heard from the cross: 'Yes.'" Here we have a cross that is walking and talking to the voice in the sky, the cross of the Gospel of Peter.

Well, it goes on to say that they then ascend into heaven. The Jewish leaders are disturbed, because everybody now is going to know that Jesus has been raised, and they were at fault for killing him. They devise the lie that the disciples stole the body.

The disciples themselves are grief-stricken, and at the very end, the narrative reverts to first person: "We, the twelve disciples of the Lord, wept and were stricken with grief. Grieving at what happened, we returned to our own homes, but I, Simon Peter, and Andrew, my brother ["I, Simon Peter"—this is somebody writing the Gospel in the name of Peter] took up our nets, and went to the sea, and with us was Levi, the son of Alpheus, whom the Lord..." That's where the text ends. We don't know what happens next, but it sounds like what is going to happen next is an account of Jesus's appearance to the disciples while they fish in the sea, something like is found in John, chapter 21.

Well, this is a very interesting Gospel. It appears that this is the Gospel that Serapion referred to. It is a Gospel allegedly written by Peter that could be taken in a docetic way, even though the bulk of it is similar to the Gospels of the New Testament. It remains debated whether this author knew the Gospels of the New Testament, or rather had simply heard stories like those of the New Testament, and recorded his own account. The book was eventually banned by Serapion and others like him. We therefore have only come to know about it since its discovery in 1887.

Let me talk quickly about a couple of other pseudepigrapha, forged writings. One that is obviously more unorthodox than this Gospel of Peter is one that is called the Secret Book of John, which was discovered along with the Gospel of Thomas in the Gnostic writings that we call the Nag Hammadi library.

This is a very interesting account, this Secret Book of John, because it is allegedly written by John, the son of Zebedee, one of Jesus's disciples, and yet, is a Gnostic treatise that describes how the world we live in came into being, in fact, how the divine realm of the gods came into being. According to this text, the material world here is not said to be the good creation of the one true God. The God who created this world, who is the God of the Bible, is portrayed as an inferior, ignorant deity, far below the one true God. This inferior God created this world, and made humans as a place of imprisonment for the divine element that he wanted to entrap here.

Christ, in this text, the secret book allegedly by John, the son of Zebedee, is understood as a divine emissary, sent from the heavenly realm in order to free the divine sparks that are entrapped in this material world. This aspersion of the creation, and of the God who made it as well, into a Gnostic perspective is completely at odds with the views held by Christians whose views ended up becoming dominant in early Christianity. This, then, is a Gnostic book that recounts the Gnostic myths in fairly full terms. It is not actually written by John, the son of Zebedee, but was simply written in his name by a later Gnostic, probably sometime in the middle of the second century.

Even the Christians who opposed such books as the Gospel of Peter and the Secret Book of John forged their own documents in the name of the apostles. We know this, because we have some of these documents available to us. One example, the only one that I will be able to give in this lecture, is a pseudepigraphal letter written in Paul's name, to counter precisely the Gnostic ideas such as those found in the Secret Book of John. This letter is called 3 Corinthians. It is called 3 Corinthians because 1 and 2 Corinthians are found in the New Testament. This book, of course, was not.

The letter of 3 Corinthians is preserved in a longer account called the Acts of Paul. The Acts of Paul is a legendary account of Paul's exploits in the missionary field. According to the Acts of Paul, the Corinthian church, the church in Corinth, wrote Paul a letter complaining that there were false teachers in their midst. They named two false teachers. These false teachers were casting aspersions on the Jewish Scriptures, and were saying that the Creation was not good, that Christ was not actually a human, and that the flesh would not actually be raised. In this letter, 3 Corinthians, Paul responds to these claims one by one. Paul says, for example, to just quote a couple of passages:

> Paul, the prisoner of Jesus Christ, to the brethren at Corinth, greetings! [He goes on to say that he has delivered to them the matters that are of most importance that he has received from Jesus Christ.] That our Lord Jesus Christ was born of Mary, of the seed of David, that he might come into this world, and save all flesh by his own flesh, that Jesus really did have flesh, that humans will be saved in the flesh, that he might raise us in the flesh from the dead, as he presented himself to us as our example. For the almighty God [there's one "almighty God] maker of heaven and earth, sent the prophets first to the Jews, to deliver them from their sins, and he sent his spirit into Mary, the Galilean, that the evil one might be conquered by the same flesh, by which he held sway, and be convinced that he is not God. For by his own body, Jesus Christ saved all flesh.

There is an emphasis throughout this text of 3 Corinthians that God is the creator of all things, that there is only one God, Jesus is his only son, Jesus really came in the flesh, and all people will be bodily saved in the flesh. This is counter to the kinds of views that you find in the Secret Book of John, which denies that the true God is the creator of this world, denies that Jesus himself was a flesh and blood human being.

Let me sum up this brief discussion of early Christian pseudepigrapha. All sides in the early Christian disputes were claiming apostolic support for their views. Everybody who had a perspective wanted to claim that their perspective was supported by the apostles. How do you demonstrate that your point of view is supported by the apostles? You need to have some writings in the names of the apostles. What if you don't have writings in the names of the apostles? Then you have to forge writings in the names of the apostles, and that is precisely what the early Christians did.

All sides appear to have had authors who were able and willing to forge these documents in the apostolic names, in order to promote their own distinctive perspectives. Of course, only one side ended up winning this dispute, or these sets of disputes, and that was the side that decided what Christians should profess as the truth, and is the side that decided which books should be accepted as sacred Scripture in the canon of the New Testament.

Lecture Eighteen
The Victory of the Proto-Orthodox

Scope: This lecture examines how the conflicts were waged between "heretical" forms of Christianity and the proto-orthodox Christians who eventually established themselves as dominant. First, we consider both the classical understanding of these conflicts, as set forth in the writings of Eusebius, the "father of church history" in the second century, and the dismantling of Eusebius's views by a German scholar, Walter Bauer, in the early part of the twentieth century. We then look at how proto-orthodox writers, such as Irenaeus of Lyons, Hippolytus of Rome, and Tertullian of Carthage, opposed other Christians and labeled them heretical, considering the standard arguments mounted by such *heresiologists* ("opponents of heresy") to show the superiority of their own views and the absurdity and depravity of their opponents'.

Outline

I.   In the past three lectures, we have looked at the wide variety of early Christianity—or, rather, early Christianities—as these can be found in sources surviving in the first three Christian centuries.

   A. From the time of our earliest author, Paul, onward, there were widely discrepant understandings of God, Jesus, the world, and salvation among people claiming to be Jesus's true followers.

   B. All the Christian groups that promoted one form of the faith over another claimed to be right and asserted that the others were wrong.

   C. Moreover, each group had its own separate books—the Gospel of Thomas, the Gospel of Peter, the Secret Book of John, 3 Corinthians, and a host of others—allegedly written by apostles of Jesus and supporting their views over those of others.

   D. How is it that most of these groups disappeared from sight and only one of them endured—that only one emerged as victorious in the internecine disputes for dominance in early Christianity, determining what Christians would believe and which sacred books they would read?

    E. That is what we will consider in this lecture, the victory of the proto-orthodox form of Christianity.

II. The traditional view of the relationship of *orthodoxy* and *heresy* can be found in the writings of Eusebius.

    A. For Eusebius, the terms of the debate correspond closely to their etymologies: *orthodoxy* is "right belief" and *heresy* represents a willful "choice" to adopt a different belief.

    B. The relationship of right and false belief for Eusebius can be seen in his description of the fate of the "father of all heretics," Simon Magus (cf. Acts 8), who created a perversion of the apostolic preaching about Jesus and acquired some pestiferous followers but was eventually defeated by the true power of the Gospel manifest by the apostle Peter.

    C. This represents the "classical" view of orthodoxy and heresy.

        1. Orthodoxy was the original teaching of Jesus as delivered to his disciples, who handed it down to the leaders of the churches that they established. Moreover, it has been the majority view of all the important Christian churches from the beginning.

        2. Heresy is a corruption of this truth by willful individuals inspired by evil demons. By definition, therefore, heresy is derivative, late, and corrupt. Moreover, it is always the minority view, a faulty offshoot of the truth.

        3. Orthodoxy emerges as victorious, then, because it is original, apostolic, true, and superior.

III. The Eusebian understanding of orthodoxy and heresy remained the dominant understanding for some 1,600 years, until the writings of a modern German scholar, Walter Bauer, who completely overturned it based on a careful examination of our earliest surviving sources.

    A. Bauer explored the surviving sources for major regions of early Christendom of which we have some firsthand knowledge (Syria, Egypt, Asia Minor, Rome).

        1. In most of the places for which we have evidence, the *earliest* evidence is of forms of Christianity that were later deemed heretical.

2. It appears that in most places, therefore, heretical forms of Christianity were in evidence before orthodox forms and were the majority view in the earliest stages.

3. Moreover, in many places, there were no hard lines to be drawn between heretical and orthodox views (even in the writings of some of the proto-orthodox fathers later considered forebears of orthodoxy, such as Clement of Alexandria and Origen).

B. Bauer concluded that early Christianity was not composed of a solid and virtually universal majority opinion (orthodoxy) that was occasionally but marginally corrupted by willful heretics.

1. Instead, in the earliest periods, Christianity comprised a wide conglomerate of groups attesting a variety of views.

2. These groups battled for converts, and only one group won out.

3. This was the group that had strongest support in the city of Rome. It was Roman Christianity that began to assert itself over other forms of Christianity in other areas. Eventually, it was Roman Christianity that won out.

4. The Roman church emerged, then, as central, universal in Christianity. Eventually, of course, this became the Roman Catholic church.

C. Bauer maintained that this victory was not predetermined; it was, instead, the result of social and political forces, especially the wealth and administrative "know-how" of Christians in the Roman church.

IV. Scholars today tend to accept major aspects of Bauer's reconstruction, while disputing most of his detailed claims: Earliest Christianity was highly variegated; numerous groups were vying for dominance; and only one of the groups emerged as victorious. Several factors led to this victory.

A. The writings of the proto-orthodox *heresiologists* ("heresy-hunters"), such as Justin, Irenaeus, Hippolytus, and Tertullian, proved remarkably successful.

1. These authors mounted compelling philosophical arguments against their opponents, arguing, for example, against Marcion and the Gnostics that for the divine being to be all-powerful,

he had to be one (because if there was more than one, neither could be "all" powerful).

2. They ridiculed their opponents' views, especially those of the Gnostics, as being fabulous and ridiculous.

3. They maligned their opponents as being morally reprobate.

4. They appealed to apostolic authority in support of their perspectives, both apostolic books and apostolic "leaders" (that is, church leaders who, they claimed, had been appointed by apostles).

B. But the scholars of the other groups could mount comparable arguments for their own positions and against those of the proto-orthodox (even though these scholars' writings were later destroyed, and we no longer have access to them).

C. In some ways, the proto-orthodox ended up victorious because they were well organized and concentrated in their efforts to employ other strategies.

1. They insisted on a set canon of scriptural authorities, a group of apostolic books that could convey the truths necessary for salvation.

2. They constructed set creeds that were to be professed by everyone in their churches.

3. They advocated a group of leaders with apostolic credentials, in that they had been appointed by apostles and their successors, and thus, represented the apostolic perspectives.

V. The history of the internal conflicts of early Christianity was not a neat and tidy affair, as Eusebius would have had us think. There were enormous disputes that lasted for many decades, centuries even. Eventually, these were resolved only when one group managed to win a majority of converts, then rewrote the history of the conflict to make it appear that its view had always been right and in the majority—that it had always been "orthodox."

Essential Reading:

Walter Bauer, *Orthodox and Heresy in Earliest Christianity*.

Bart D. Ehrman, *Lost Christianities*.

———, *The Orthodox Corruption of Scripture*, chapter 1.

Supplementary Reading:

Glenn F. Chesnut, *The First Christian Histories*.

Eusebius, *Ecclesiastical History*.

Robert M. Grant, *Jesus after the Gospels*.

Elaine Pagels, *The Gnostic Gospels*.

Questions to Consider:

1. Based on what we have learned in the lectures so far, detail any of the problems you can see in a Eusebian understanding of orthodoxy and heresy.

2. Does it make sense to use the words *orthodoxy* ("right belief") and *heresy* ("choice" of a wrong belief) as historical terms? Or are they too loaded with theological implications of who was right and who was wrong to be of use to historians of the conflict?

Lecture Eighteen—Transcript
The Victory of the Proto-Orthodox

In the past three lectures, we have looked at the wide variety of early Christianity, or rather, the varieties of early Christianities, as these can be found in sources surviving from the first three Christian centuries. From the time of our earliest surviving author, Paul, onward, there were widely varying understandings of God, Jesus, the world, and salvation among people claiming to be Jesus's true followers.

All of the Christian groups who promoted one form of the faith over others claimed to be right, and insisted that all the others were wrong when they disagreed. Moreover, each group had its own separate books—the Gospel of Thomas, the Gospel of Peter, the Secret Book of John, 3 Corinthians, and a host of others—allegedly written by apostles of Jesus and supporting the views of some over others.

How is it that most of these groups disappeared from sight, and only one of them continued on, that only one of them emerged as victorious in the internal dispute for dominance in early Christianity? Only one of the groups survived, determining what Christians would believe, and which sacred books they would read. That's what we will be considering in the present lecture, the victory of a group I will call the proto-orthodox form of Christianity.

To begin the lecture, I would like to be clear about our terms. The two major terms we have been using up to this point are the terms *orthodoxy* and *heresy*. Both of these terms come from Greek roots, *orthodoxy* from two Greek words that mean "correct belief" or "right opinion." *Heresy* is a term that means "choice," and is used in this context to refer to the choice not to believe the right beliefs.

There are other terms for heresy that you will occasionally find in the literature, for example, the term *heterodoxy*, which means "other opinion." Thus, as opposed to orthodoxy, the right opinion, you can have heterodoxy, the other opinion.

I'm going to using the term "proto-orthodox" in this and following lectures to refer to the point of view that eventually became dominant in early Christianity. Proto-orthodoxy, though, refers to people who subscribed to this point of view prior to its victory. It doesn't make sense to talk about this view as orthodox until it is accepted by the wide range of Christians throughout Christendom, and so, for the second and third centuries, rather than referring to orthodoxy, I will be referring to proto-orthodoxy.

You may already recognize one of the problems with these various terms. Heresy and orthodoxy, the "right" belief, or the "choice" to believe in something else. Of course, nobody believes that they subscribe to a heresy, in the sense that nobody thinks they're wrong. Everybody thinks that they, themselves, are orthodox, that they hold to the "right" belief, because if they didn't think that they held to the right belief, they would change their belief. Nobody believes that what they know is wrong, and so, by definition, everybody thinks that they, themselves, are orthodox.

That makes this term and its related term "heresy," as well as the term "heterodoxy," problematic. How can somebody be orthodox when everybody is orthodox?

Historians have had to wrestle with what these terms really mean, and decide how to use them. The way that scholars have devised used for these terms is in a purely historical way, to refer to "orthodoxy" and "heresy" not in terms of who is actually "right" or "wrong," but to describe social groups. One social group established for all time what it was Christians would believe. We will call that group orthodox, not necessarily saying that they were right, but saying that they were the ones who decided what people would believe.

Heresy, then, pertains to groups that believe something other than what orthodox people believe, and so, in this lecture, I will be using the terms in the historical sense. Orthodoxy was the point of view that ended up winning out. Heresies refer to other perspectives.

The traditional view of the relationship between orthodoxy and heresy can be found in the writings of the father of church history, the fourth century writer Eusebius, whom we have seen on a number of occasions throughout these lectures. Eusebius, in his ten-volume history of the early church, described the theological conflicts between various groups in early Christianity. He talked about Marcion and Marcionites, the Ebionites, and the group I'm calling the proto-orthodox. He also talks about the debates themselves as they went on up to his own day.

For Eusebius, the terms of these debates corresponded closely to their etymologies. For Eusebius, "orthodoxy" really did mean "right belief." Why? because the view of the proto-orthodox, which became triumphant in the fourth century, happened to be the point of view that Eusebius himself shared, and so, he painted his predecessors in this theological tradition as, themselves, orthodox, meaning that they subscribed to the right belief. He also speaks of heresy as a willful choice to adopt a different belief.

The relationship of "right" and "wrong" belief for Eusebius can be seen in his description of the faith of the "father of all heretics," a person known as Simon Magus, "Simon Magus" meaning "Simon Magician."

Simon is a figure that we run across in the New Testament, in the Book of Acts, chapter 8. In Acts, chapter 8, we are told that the disciples of Jesus, now sent out on missions after Jesus's death and Resurrection, have taken the Gospel to the region of Samaria. In Samaria, there was one apostle named Philip, who had converted people to faith in Jesus. Two of the other apostles had come into town, Peter and John, and had laid hands on the converts; these converts had received the Holy Spirit.

Simon was in town. He was not one of the apostles or disciples of Jesus, nor was he originally one of the converts. Simon was a magician who happened to live in Samaria. He was quite impressed with the power that the apostles manifested while in their midst. These apostles could actually do miraculous deeds, while Simon could only do magic. He saw these genuine acts as miracles and was impressed.

He, too, wanted to receive this power, and asked the apostles to give him the power to bestow the Holy Spirit, so that he, like them, could manifest true miracle-working power. They rebuffed him, and sent him on his way.

That's all we hear about Simon Magus in the Book of Acts. Later Christian heresiologists talked about Simon, though, and indicated that this Simon was not just a miracle worker, that he was not satisfied with the rebuff of the apostles, and that he went on to gather followers around him, who became convinced that he, himself, was somebody who was powerful and could do miracles. More than that, that, in fact, he was, himself, in some sense, divine.

The early Christian heresiologists, including Justin Martyr, Irenaeus, Tertullian, and then, eventually, Eusebius, portrayed Simon Magus as the father of all heretics that, in fact, he was the first Gnostic.

If you recall, the Gnostics maintained that in order to have salvation, one needed to receive supernatural knowledge from above. One needed to know where one had come from, who one really was, how one could escape this world to the world above.

According to the heresiologists, Simon Magus proclaimed himself as the person who could deliver that supernatural knowledge, because he maintained that he himself had come from above, here to Earth, in order to convey this knowledge, that he was a divine being.

According to these heresiologists, Simon had a companion he took around with him. This companion was understood to be one of the other divine beings from the divine realm. This companion of his was a woman named Helen. Heresiologists indicate that Simon really did not tell her full story. Simon indicated that this was his divine consort, who had come down from heaven to Earth to reveal her knowledge with him. The heresiologists indicate that, in fact, Helen was a woman that Simon had picked up at a local brothel, that she, in fact, was a prostitute that he had fallen in love with, and was taking around, spreading this lie that he and Helen were both from above, and had come here to reveal the secret knowledge for salvation.

According to these heresiologists, then, Simon acquired certain followers. These followers became famous Gnostic teachers of the second century. These followers of Simon had students, who then became teachers, who then taught others, and then their students became teachers, so that Gnostics go in a direct line all the way back from Simon, as described in Acts, chapter 8.

For Eusebius, Simon was a kind of model of the way to understand the relationship between heresy and orthodoxy. Simon invented a heretical understanding of the faith embodied in himself. He took something that was originally true, and corrupted it. He took the truth that the apostles were espousing, and changed it because of his own desire to be worshipped and adored.

In some ways, this can be called a classical understanding of the relationship between orthodoxy and heresy. This is how the classical view works, as Eusebius spelled it out time and time again throughout his writings. In this understanding of things, orthodoxy was the original teaching of Jesus and his apostles. Jesus taught his followers the truth about himself, about God, about salvation. His apostles then went out and taught this truth to others, and converted others to this faith, establishing churches throughout the Mediterranean, who all, then, subscribed to this faith. Orthodoxy was the original teaching that had always been the majority teaching of most Christians, and most Christian churches from the very beginning.

Heresy, in this understanding of things, is the corruption of this truth by willful individuals inspired by evil demons. Simon was therefore a kind of willful individual inspired by a demon. Moreover, heresy, according to this understanding of things, is always the minority view. It is a faulty offshoot of the truth subscribed to by a small minority of Christians.

According to Eusebius, orthodoxy emerged as victorious because it was the original point of view of Jesus and his followers. It's original, apostolic, true, and superior.

The way to model this, then, is to imagine orthodoxy as one big thing that goes all way back to Jesus, and heresies are just little offshoots that come off at different times by willful individuals trying to corrupt the ultimate truth.

That's one way to understand the relationship of various forms of Christianity in the early centuries. Call it the classical view, call it the Eusebian view.

This Eusebian understanding of the relationship between orthodoxy and heresy remained the dominant understanding for some 1,600 years. This is the view that virtually everyone held, influenced, no doubt, by Eusebius himself, who had written the authoritative account of early Christianity, and who had the only surviving early account of early Christianity, because virtually all the other documents, written by people he labeled heretics, had been destroyed.

Things changed radically in the early part of the 20th century with the writings of a German scholar named Walter Bauer. Walter Bauer completely turned this Eusebian understanding of orthodoxy and heresy on its head by engaging in a careful examination of our earliest surviving sources. Bauer did not believe that orthodoxy was the original teaching of Jesus and that heresies were little offshoots that came off of it over time.

Bauer developed his argument in a book called *Orthodoxy and Heresy in Earliest Christianity*, a book that was published in 1934. Unfortunately, it's was not translated into English for nearly 40 years; the English translation didn't appear until 1971. The way Bauer proceeded in this very important book was by exploring the surviving sources for major regions of early Christendom, of which we have some firsthand knowledge.

He therefore went region by region throughout early Christianity to find the earliest references we have to Christianity, and then, to see what kind of Christianity was talked about in these earliest sources. We know something about the areas of Syria, both Eastern Syria, or Syriac, where the language related to Aramaic was spoken by Jesus, and Western Syria, such as in the city of Antioch. He explored Egypt, Asia Minor, and Rome. These are areas about which we have some ancient sources. Bauer examined these earliest sources for each of these regions, and he found that for most of the places in which we have any evidence, the earliest evidence in most places is of a form of Christianity that was later deemed heretical.

Why is it that the earliest references to Christianity in most of these places entailed references to forms of Christianity that were later branded as heresies? Bauer concluded that in most places, heretical forms of Christianity were, in fact, prior to orthodox forms of Christianity, that what we call "heresy" was, in fact, the majority view in many places, in the earliest stages of Christianity.

Take, for example, Egypt. We have lots of references to Christianity in Egypt in early sources. We don't have references to orthodox Christianity in Egypt, though, until about the beginning of the third century. Prior to that, what kind of Christians do we know about from Egypt? The only Christians we know about were Christians who were Gnostics. Why do the earliest sources refer to Gnostic Christianity, but not to orthodox Christianity?

Bauer concluded that, in fact, Christianity in Egypt at the earliest stages was Gnostic Christianity, so that Gnosticism is not some offshoot of orthodoxy in Egypt. Orthodoxy came in later. The original form, in fact, was Gnostic.

In addition, Bauer argued that in many places there were not hard lines between what we might think of as heretical, and what we might think of as orthodox. Even the writings of some of the proto-orthodox church fathers, that is, the fore-bearers of orthodoxy, we find doctrines that were later condemned as heretical.

I'll give you one example: Clement of Alexandria, writing at the beginning of the third century, was considered to be a proto-orthodox author, the first proto-orthodox author we have from Alexandria. Even so, he had points of view that sound somewhat heretical. We have a number of Clement of Alexandria's writings. In one of them, he described Jesus, wanted to talk about Christology, and the idea of whether Jesus actually had a real body or not. Clement argued that, in fact, Jesus did have a real body, but since he was the Son of God, his body actually did not get hungry and thirsty, because how could God get hungry and thirsty?

Jesus, therefore, ate and drank not because he was hungry and thirsty, but so as to convince people that he really had a body, because otherwise, he would not have had to eat and drink. Nonetheless, Clement thought he really didn't have a body like ours, because it was a body that didn't get hungry and thirsty. It's a paradoxical point of view, then, that Clement has, but it is a point of view that never would have succeeded later in Christianity, because it did presuppose that Jesus didn't have a real flesh and blood body like ours.

Walter Bauer concluded, from the basis of this extensive and detailed study of his, that early Christianity was not comprised of a solid and virtually uniform majority opinion orthodoxy that was occasionally but marginally corrupted by willful heretics. Instead, in the earliest periods, Christianity was comprised of a conglomerate of groups attesting a variety of views. These various Christian groups that believed different things—Gnostics in one place, Ebionites in one place, Marcionites in one place—various groups in different places, each battled for converts, and only one of the groups won out.

The group that won out was one that I have called proto-orthodox. Once they won out, they rewrote the history of the engagement, proclaimed themselves as being orthodox, said that their views had always been the majority view of Christianity, and that it was a view that went back to Jesus and the apostles. Then, all of the other points of view that they had just defeated, in fact, were willful offshoots of a minority of people that were just minor abuses, but in fact, were never a major threat to early Christianity.

Which group won out? There's the group we call the proto-orthodox, but it also was a group that happened to have the strongest support, according to Bauer, in the city of Rome. It was Roman Christianity that began to assert itself. There were forms of Christianity in other areas, but eventually, it was Roman Christianity that won out, and so, there emerged the Roman church as central. The church that was located in the city of Rome managed to assert itself as central, and eventually, of course, this became the Roman church, or the Roman Catholic Church.

Bauer did not think that this victory of the Roman church and its form of Christianity was predetermined. He didn't think that it was inevitable that it would win out. In fact, it won out not necessarily because it was right, or because the Jews happened to go back to Jesus himself, but because of a certain set of political and historical circumstances.

There were social and political forces that helped the Roman Christians to win out in the conflicts among early Christian groups. Who were these forces? Bauer pointed out that the Roman church was a relatively wealthy church. It was a large church. There were more Christians in Rome than in other places. They tended to have a lot of money there. Moreover, the

Roman government, of course, was situated in the city of Rome, and there was a kind of trickle-down effect of administrative know-how from the Roman government administration into the church.

The church in Rome used its political know-how, its wealth, and its administrative skills in order to exert its influence over other churches. Eventually, it got other churches to share its point of view. How did it work, exactly? The Roman church had a lot of money, so suppose that over here, this other place was deciding which person to elect as its bishop. The Roman church then said, "Well, if you will elect so-and-so as your bishop, then, we will be happy to contribute to your alms fund."

"Well, sure, that sounds good to us." They therefore elected the certain person's bishop. Who's the person's bishop? The guy who agreed with the people in Rome about what the major doctrines of Christianity ought to be.

The Romans used their money to set slaves free. Well, what kind of Christianity would these slaves have been attracted to? The kind of Christianity that set them free from their slavery. And so forth, and so on.

So it goes for a long time, until the end of third, beginning of the fourth century, when Christianity becomes more and more prominent, and then, the Roman emperor converted. The Roman emperor converted. What kind of Christianity would a Roman emperor convert to? To a Roman form of Christianity. Is it surprising that it was Roman Christianity that took over the ancient world? No, not at all. Thus, according to this Bauer model of heresy and orthodoxy, orthodoxy is not the original majority view. Orthodoxy was one of the perspectives in the second and third centuries that was fighting it out with other groups for converts. It happened to win out, established itself as the majority view, rewrote the history of the engagement, and called itself "orthodox."

Scholars today tend to accept major aspects of Bauer's reconstruction, which now, after all, is 70 years old, while disputing most of his detailed claims. Scholarship never stands still, and one never allows the claims of an earlier scholar to stand on their own terms. They always have to be nuanced, changed, and disputed, but nonetheless, scholars today still accept many aspects of Bauer's reconstruction, including his claims that Christianity in its earliest period was highly variegated, that numerous groups were vying for dominance, and that one of the groups ended up becoming victorious.

We have had additional evidence to support Bauer's views since his day. I have talked, for example, about the discovery of other writings, for example, those of the Nag Hammadi library. The Nag Hammadi library consists of 52 writings principally by Gnostics and for Gnostics, assuming Gnostic points of view, showing once again that Christianity in Egypt, where these were discovered, was widely variegated, and that Gnosticism was quite prominent there.

Today, most scholars dispute Bauer's view that Roman Christianity was the principal place for what I am calling proto-orthodoxy, and there are various aspects of his reconstruction that have come under detailed consideration since his day. Many scholars, though, still agree that, in fact, the second and third centuries were very messy when it came to these doctrinal disputes. Many scholars also agree that one view did end up establishing itself as orthodox, even though this point of view was not necessarily the point of view of Jesus and his own followers.

How, though, did this group establish itself as victorious? Let me give you several reasons as to why this group emerged as orthodox, according to contemporary scholarship. The writings of the proto-orthodox heresiologists, these heresy hunters such as Justin, Irenaeus, and Tertullian, ended up proving remarkably successful. These writers were very smart, and very well-organized, and they could mount convincing arguments against their opponents, whether Marcionites, Ebionites, or whatever.

These authors mounted compelling philosophical arguments. For example, in the argument concerning whether or not there was only one God or lots of gods. Most pagans, of course, believed in many gods. Christians had a variety of views. The proto-orthodox said that there was one God, the Marcionites said there were two Gods, and some of the Gnostics believed that there were many Gods.

Proto-orthodox authors such as Tertullian made an argument that there must be only one God. It was a philosophical argument. Tertullian argued that the definition of "God" required that there be only one God, because the definition of "God" that he assumed everybody would accept was that God was a supremely powerful being. If God was supremely powerful, then, there could be only one God, because if there were two Gods, then, neither one of them could be supremely powerful, because there would be another God. Since God was supremely powerful, there could only be one God. Marcion could not be right that there were two, and possibly be right that there were many. There were, then, philosophical arguments that the heresiologists built.

The heresiologists also successfully ridiculed their opponents' points of view, especially the Gnostics', as being fabulous and ridiculous. The Gnostics, in order to explain where the world came from, and to explain that the divine realm had a number of divine beings in it, and they told these myths to explain how the divine realm came into being.

These were myths, but anytime you take a myth and pretend that the myth is stating some kind of propositional truth, the myth sounds ridiculous. That's like taking a poem, and trying to figure out how it works if taken as literally true. It is like attacking somebody who says that the sun rose this morning at 6:30. "Well, what an idiot this person is. The sun doesn't rise. Doesn't he understand anything about the modern universe? Suns don't rise. The Earth has been rotating. That's a silly statement." No, it's just how we talk. The Gnostics had myth to describe how the divine realm came into being, and the heresiologists pretended that these myths were propositional statements. They showed how contradictory they were, and so, therefore, the heresiologists argued that these were ridiculous points of view, and that the Gnostics could not possibly be right.

Not only did the heresiologists mount philosophical arguments and ridicule their opponents for their views, they also maligned their opponents for being morally reprobate. The heresiologists took the charges leveled against the Christians of being cannibals, committing infanticide, and engaging in orgies, and said they were true of the heretics. They devoted page after page to maligning the moral probity of their opponents.

Moreover, these heresiologists appealed to apostolic authority in support of their views, claiming that their views were the views of the main churches of the world, that the main churches had bishops who were assigned to be the bishops by the apostles, that the apostles came from Jesus, and Jesus came from God. In other words, the heresiologists developed a doctrine of apostolic succession in which God sent Christ, who picked his apostles, who established the churches, who picked the bishops, and the bishops picked their successors, so that the current ruling bishops of the churches represented the views of all the apostles, back to Jesus himself. This was the doctrine of apostolic succession, which became quite prominent, and was seen to be successful by many people in showing that the views that were now shared widely must have been the views of Jesus and his apostles.

These were the arguments the heresiologists used in order to win the day against their various opponents—the Gnostics, Marcionites, Ebionites, and others. In some ways, the reasons the proto-orthodox were successful, though, is because they were extremely well-organized and concentrated their efforts on several key strategies that we will be looking at in subsequent lectures.

The proto-orthodox insisted that there was a separate canon of Scripture, a group of writings that validated their perspective, and they said what those Scriptures were; they ended up being 27 books of the New Testament. Not only did they have a canon of Scripture, but the proto-orthodox Christians insisted on certain set creeds that spelled out the beliefs to be professed by everybody in the churches. Not only did they have a canon and a set of creeds, they also had a clergy, a group of church leaders with apostolic credentials that supported the points of view that the orthodox themselves wanted to adhere to.

In sum, the history of the internal conflicts of early Christianity was not a neat and tidy affair, as Eusebius would have had us think. There were enormous disputes that lasted for many decades, even centuries, and eventually, were resolved only when one group managed to win a majority of converts, and then rewrote the history of the conflict to make it appear that it was the view that had always been right, that the majority had always been orthodox.

Lecture Nineteen
The New Testament Canon

Scope: This is the first of five lectures devoted to the question of how traditional Christianity—with its canon of Scripture, creeds, liturgy, and church offices—emerged out of the conflicts of the second and third centuries. In this lecture, we will consider the formation of the canon of Scripture. Given the circumstance that numerous books were written in the names of the apostles in the early Christian centuries, how is it that 27 (and only these 27) came to be considered sacred Scripture? Who decided which books should be included in the canon? What criteria did they use? What motivated the decisions? When did the process come to a close?

As we will see, the New Testament did not come into being right after the death of Jesus or even decades later. Even by the end of the fourth Christian century, heated debates continued over which books should be included in the canon.

Outline

I. For the past several lectures, we have been exploring the diversity of early Christianity, with different groups advocating different understandings of the faith, only one of which emerged as victorious. This lecture is the first of five on the form of Christianity that emerged from these conflicts.

    A. I call this *traditional* Christianity, because it is the form of Christianity that began to thrive at the end of the third and beginning of the fourth centuries, when Constantine converted to the faith.

    B. Even though Christianity remained diverse down through the Middle Ages and on into the modern period, there were certain aspects of the religion that were fairly constant throughout much of the church, such as a set canon of Scripture, a set creed to be recited, a set understanding of the church hierarchical structure.

    C. We begin, in this lecture, by looking at a fundamental component of traditional Christianity, the canon of Scripture.

II. Although it may seem commonsensical to us today that a major religion should have a set of authoritative writings understood to be Scripture, this was somewhat anomalous in the Roman world.

    A. The idea of having a collection of sacred books that indicated what one should believe about the divine and how one should live was virtually unheard of in pagan circles, that is, among the vast majority of ancient people.

    B. Judaism was the one exception, in that the Hebrew Scriptures were accepted by Jews throughout the world as providing sacred tales and laws to govern the lives of God's people.

III. Christianity eventually acquired a set of sacred books—a canon of Scripture—because it emerged out of Judaism, which also had a set of sacred books.

    A. There was no set canon of Scripture for Jews in the days of Jesus, but Jesus, like most Jews throughout the Roman world, accepted the Torah as coming from God and taught it to his followers.

    B. The Jewish Scriptures—the Torah, the prophets, some other writings—became a set of sacred authorities for Christians from the very beginning.

    C. Soon, however, Christians started appealing to other, explicitly Christian writings, as being on an equal footing with Scripture. This is the beginning of the formation of a distinctively Christian canon.

        1. Already during the first century, in our earliest author, Paul, Jesus's own words are granted sacred authority (1 Cor. 7; 1 Cor. 9).

        2. By the end of the first century, Jesus's word is considered "Scripture" (1 Tim. 5:18).

        3. Strikingly, so too, are the writings of his apostles (2 Pet. 3:16).

IV. But which apostolic books were to be accepted as Scripture? That was one of the big debates among early Christian churches.

    A. It appears that Marcion was the first to give a definitive canon of Scripture to his followers: the Gospel of Luke and 10 of Paul's writings.

    B. Other Christians, though, accepted different books, including other Gospels (Matthew, Mark, Thomas, Peter, and so on).

C. It may well be that Marcion gave the impetus for proto-orthodox leaders to devise their own canon of Scripture.

D. During Marcion's own day, the proto-orthodox Justin shows no concern for having a fixed set of authorities.

E. Some 30 years later, however, Irenaeus—who stands in the same theological tradition as Justin—insists vehemently that there must be four Gospels (not just one) and that they are Matthew, Mark, Luke, and John. Anyone who chooses just one or the other provides a skewed understanding of the faith.

V. What can we say then about the motivations for establishing a set canon of Scripture among the proto-orthodox?

A. There appear to have been a variety of factors at work, including the need for Christians to distinguish themselves from Jews and the desire to have written (apostolic) authorities to support their points of view.

B. Most significant, however, was the need to decide which of these points of view were right and to have apostolic support for them.

VI. Given the need to have a set collection of sacred texts, how did the proto-orthodox decide on which texts to include? A survey of the early discussions of the canon reveal four major criteria that were applied.

A. A book had to be ancient to be accepted into the canon of Scripture. Any recent production—as valuable as it may be for reading and instruction—could not be considered scriptural.

B. A book had to be connected with an apostle to be considered canonical.

C. A book needed to be widely accepted among the proto-orthodox churches to be seen as canonical.

D. Perhaps most important of all, a book had to evidence a proto-orthodox theology to be acceptable as Scripture. Recall the Gospel of Peter: Because it allegedly contained a docetic Christology, it could not have been apostolic and, therefore, could not be scriptural.

VII. The debates over canon were long and hard.

A. Even though Marcion began the process in the mid-second century, it took centuries for the dispute to be resolved.

B. It does appear that most proto-orthodox Christians accepted a core of texts that eventually became canonical: the four Gospels, Acts, Paul's letters, 1 Peter, and 1 John, for example.

C. But other texts were long debated: The Book of Hebrews, the Apocalypse of John, the Apocalypse of Peter, the Shepherd of Hermas, the Epistle of Barnabas—all were considered by one group or another to be canonical into the third and fourth centuries.

D. It was not until 367 C.E. that anyone listed the 27 books of our New Testament as being the canon (these books and no others).

    1. This was by the famous bishop of Alexandria, Athanasius, in a pastoral letter he sent to his churches in Egypt.

    2. Even after that, however, the matter continued to be disputed for some time.

    3. Eventually, though, there was wide agreement. Today, throughout the Eastern Orthodox, Roman Catholic, and Protestant churches, there is a consensus on what constitutes the canon of New Testament Scripture.

VIII. The debates over which books to consider Scripture were long and drawn out. Eventually, a canon emerged that is accepted by the majority of Christians today. This canon provides the basis of all faith and practice and, to that extent, represents an important and long-reaching aspect of the victory of the proto-orthodox: With the success of this collection of authoritative books, other forms of Christianity were necessarily marginalized and effectively destroyed, while orthodox Christianity could then move on to debates over other issues down into the Middle Ages.

Essential Reading:

Bart D. Ehrman, *After the New Testament*, chapter 9.

———, *Lost Christianities*.

Harry Gamble, *The New Testament Canon*.

Supplementary Reading:

F. F. Bruce, *The Canon of Scripture*.

Bruce Metzger, *The Canon of the New Testament*.

Questions to Consider:

1. Pick one of the non-canonical books we have considered in this course. How might Christianity be different if it had been included among the sacred Scriptures?

2. Why do you imagine it took so long for proto-orthodox Christians to establish a fixed canon of Scripture?

Lecture Nineteen—Transcript
The New Testament Canon

For the past several lectures, we have been exploring the diversity of early Christianity, with different groups advocating different understandings of the faith, only one of which emerged as victorious. This lecture is the first of five on the form of Christianity that emerged from these conflicts. I'm calling this form of Christianity *traditional* Christianity, because it is the form of Christianity that had established itself as dominant from the middle of the third century into the early part of the fourth century, when Constantine, the emperor, converted to the faith.

Even though Christianity remained diverse down through the Middle Ages and on into the modern period, there were certain aspects of the religion that were fairly constant throughout much of the church. Throughout the Middle Ages, for example, a set canon of Scripture—27 books in the New Testament, 39 books in what came to be called the Old Testament—a set canon, a set creed to be recited, a set number of beliefs that had to be adhered to by all believers, and a set understanding of the church hierarchical structure.

We begin this lecture by looking at a fundamental component of this traditional Christianity, namely, it's canon of Scripture. It may seem commonsensical to us that a major world religion would have a set of authoritative writings that it understands to be Scripture. After all, that is true for all of the major Western religions: Judaism, Christianity, and Islam.

It is striking, however, that in the ancient world, the idea of having a collection of sacred books at the heart of a religion was virtually unheard of. It was completely unheard of in most pagan circles in the ancient Roman world, that is, among the vast majority of people living at the time. Contrary to what is sometimes said, the *Iliad* and the *Odyssey* by Homer were not the Bible of Greek and Roman religions. These books were read—read as classics, talked about, and reflected on—but they did not provide any kind of guidelines for faith and practice for those involved in ancient religion. There really was nothing quite like authoritative Scripture for people living in that ancient world.

Judaism was the one exception, of course, in that the Hebrew Scriptures were accepted by Jews throughout the world as providing sacred tales and laws to govern the lives of God's people. Christianity eventually acquired a set of sacred books, a canon of Scripture, because it emerged out of Judaism, which also had a set of sacred books. I should emphasize, though, that there was no canon of Scripture available for Jews in the days of Jesus, in the sense of being a closed canon. Our current English Bibles for the Old Testament have 39 books.

The Hebrew Scriptures accepted by Jews have exactly the same books today, but they are numbered differently. They have 22 books. For example, there are twelve minor prophets in the English Bible. Those are put together in one book in the Hebrew Scriptures, and so, they number the books differently, and arrange and organize the books differently, but they are the same books, 22 books for the Hebrew Bible, 39 for the Christian Old Testament.

My point is that in the days of Jesus, this canon of Scripture had not been finalized yet. It was not a closed canon, although Jews in Jesus's day did, by and large, accept as authoritative the Torah (the first five books of what is now the Hebrew Bible: Genesis, Exodus, Leviticus, Numbers, and Deuteronomy).

Jews throughout the Roman world accepted these books as authoritative texts coming from God. Some Jews accepted other writings, especially writings of the prophets as being scriptural. During Jesus's day, Jesus himself accepted the writings of the prophets and some other books, including the book of Psalms, for example, and some of the other poetic books. Jesus accepted the Torah as an authoritative text, and he taught the Torah to his followers. Since his followers were the first Christians, Christians inherited a canon of Scripture, a collection of sacred books, from the very beginning. The canon of the Christians was then the Torah, the prophets, and some other writings. These were sacred authorities.

Thus, even though other religions throughout the Roman world did not have sacred books, Judaism did have sacred books, and Christianity inherited the books of Judaism.

This remained true even after Christianity became predominantly Gentile. Since it started out as Jewish, with the Jewish Jesus and his Jewish followers, the Gentile Christians who came into the church inherited sacred books as their sacred authorities. It was not long before Christians started to appeal to other authorities as being on a par with their sacred writings, the Old Testament, as they began to call it.

When Christians began to appeal to other explicitly Christian writings as being on an equal footing with their Scriptures, that was the beginning of the formation of a distinctively Christian canon. This began remarkably early in Christianity, when other authorities were being cited as though they were God's own authority. Already during the first century, in our very earliest surviving Christian author, apostle Paul, Jesus's own words were being granted sacred authority.

We don't know how much Paul actually knew about the historical Jesus. Paul rarely says anything about what Jesus said and did during his lifetime. He talked a lot about Jesus's Crucifixion, and a lot about his Resurrection, and about what Jesus was doing in the present, after being raised from the dead, but the Paul said very little about what happened to Jesus during his life. On several occasions, however, he did quote several words of Jesus, and when he did so, he quoted them as if they were authoritative, and for them to be followed as if they were scriptural authority.

We don't know, by the way, why Paul didn't say more about the historical Jesus. Some scholars think that Paul didn't know very much about the historical Jesus. He was, after all, writing before our Gospels were written, and he spent most of his time in the mission field trying to convert people to faith in Christ, and he simply may not have heard very many traditions about what Jesus said during his life. He was principally interested in Jesus's death and Resurrection.

When he did refer to Jesus, though, he referred to him as a sacred authority, as authoritative as the Old Testament Scriptures. Let me give you a couple of examples. The couple of examples I'm going to give you are virtually all the examples there are in Paul, but they are significant for the way that they are phrased.

The first example is 1 Corinthians, chapter 7. Paul was talking to people in the church of Corinth, who had a concern about whether divorce was acceptable or not: "To the married, I give this command," said Paul, "not I, but the Lord" (the Lord is giving the command) "that the wife should not separate from her husband, and the husband should not divorce his wife."

When he said, "The Lord commands this," what was he referring to? He can't have been referring to the Old Testament, because in the Old Testament, it is acceptable for a man to divorce a woman. He instead was referring to the teachings of Jesus, where Jesus said that since God put man and woman together, "the two shall be one flesh, and what God has put together, let no one separate." Paul was referring, then, to a teaching of Jesus, which he considered to be as authoritative, and even more authoritative than the scriptures, because the Old Testament allowed for divorce, and Jesus did not. The apostle Paul accepted Jesus, then, as his authority.

A second example, in 1 Corinthians, chapter 9, verse 14. In this context, he was talking about whether Christian ministers should have been paid for their work: "In the same way," he said, "the Lord commanded that those who proclaimed the Gospel should get their living by the Gospel."

What is he referring to? He must be referring to the saying of Jesus found in our Gospels, that a workman is worthy of his hire, so that one who works on behalf of the Gospel, then, deserves to be paid for it. Paul was quoting the words of Jesus as an authoritative source. By the end of the first century of the Common Era, Jesus's words were being quoted not only as authoritative, but actually were being called Scripture.

They find this in a letter allegedly by Paul, but it is probably pseudonymous, the book of 1 Timothy, a book allegedly by Paul to his younger pastor companion, Timothy, but which most scholars now think is actually a pseudonymous work written near the end of the first century by somebody writing in Paul's name. In this particular context, the author's talking about elders who run the church. The author said, in chapter 5, verses 17 and 8: "The elders who rule well should be considered worthy of a double honor, especially those who labor in preaching and teaching. Why? Because the Scripture says, 'You shall not muzzle an ox while it is treading out the grain, and it says that the labor deserves to be paid.'"

The author was quoting two passages here; the first passage was Deuteronomy, chapter 25 (the Torah), which says, "Don't muzzle an ox that is treading." The second passage, called Scripture though, is not found in the Old Testament. Where is it found? Well, it is found in the Gospels. It is a quotation of Matthew, chapter 10, verse 10. I'm not sure that this author had read Matthew, but he did know that the saying came from Jesus, and was calling the saying "Scripture." This shows that already by the end of the first century, Christians are citing Christian writings, these Christian traditions as scriptural.

We find the same phenomenon in relating not just to Jesus, but also to the writings of his apostles. Interestingly enough, the earliest author of the New Testament, Paul, is cited by the latest writing of the New Testament, by St. Peter, as a scriptural authority. This is found in 2 Peter, probably written around the year 120, so probably the last book to be written. Again, I think it is probably pseudonymous. I don't think Peter actually wrote the book, but whoever did write it in Peter's name considered Paul's writings to be authoritative.

He says, in 2 Peter, chapter 3, verses 15 and 16: "So, also, our beloved brother Paul wrote to you concerning the wisdom given to him, speaking of this adds he does in all of his letters. There are some things in these letters that are hard to understand," (he's got that right) "which the ignorant and unstable twist to their own destruction, as they do the other scriptures."

"The other scriptures." Paul's books were being considered scriptural authority here already by the end of the New Testament period. This is a movement, then, that would continue on through Christianity, as the writings of the Jewish Scriptures are considered canonical texts, and the writings of the early Christians, the words of Jesus, and those of his apostles, are considered canonical.

That is a kind of bipartite canon, in the big sense, and in the smaller sense. In the big sense, the canon the Christians are going to come up with will consist of the Old Testament and the New Testament, two parts. The New Testament itself was also bipartite, because there were the traditions about Jesus (the sayings of Jesus) and the writings of the apostles. Therefore, in the New Testament, in the later period, there'll be the Gospels about Jesus and then the apostolic writings as the two parts of the New Testament.

Christians who began seeing that the writings of the apostles should be considered Scripture, though, had to decide which books to include. This was one of the biggest debates among the early Christian churches. Which books should have been considered for inclusion in the canonical authorities?

As we saw in a previous lecture, it appears that Marcion, the second century philosopher theologian who was later condemned as a heretic, was the first to give a definitive canon of Scripture to his followers. Marcion maintained that something like our Gospel of Luke and 10 of Paul's letters (the 13 in the New Testament, minus 1 and 2 Timothy and Titus) were canonical authorities. He apparently came up with an actual text (put between two covers) of these 11 books that were circulated within the Marcionite churches, and used as sacred authorities for their perspective.

Other Christians, though, accepted other books as canonical. For example, some Christians accepted Matthew, Mark, or John. Some accepted the Gospel of Thomas, or the Gospel of Peter, and so forth. It may well be that Marcion himself provided the impetus for proto-orthodox Christian leaders to devise their own canon of Scripture. There is some evidence to suggest that not only was Marcion the first to come up with a canon, but that he also gave the impetus that led, eventually, to the canonization of the 27 New Testament books.

What is this evidence? The evidence is that proto-orthodox writers of the second and third century, in other words, writers who had the perspective that later became orthodox in the fourth century had certain perspectives on the canon that appeared to develop over time. During Marcion's own day, the proto-orthodox author Justin Martyr, living in Rome, showed no concern at all for having a fixed set of scriptural authorities. As I pointed out earlier, we have three writings from Justin, of which two are fairly lengthy, his *First Apology* and his *Dialogue with Trypho*.

In these lengthy writings, Justin quoted Christian authors, Christian texts, including the Gospels, especially Matthew, Mark, and Luke, but didn't cite those as being part of the closed canon of Scripture. He didn't call those books by their names, nor say how many of them were accepted as authoritative. When he quoted the Gospels, he referred to them as the "memoirs of the apostles." He didn't call them the Gospels of Matthew and Mark, etc.

The reason he called them the memoirs of the apostles was because the authority of these books resided in the fact that they come from apostolic tradition. They were not authoritative because they were part of a canon of Scripture. Justin, therefore, had a fairly loose understanding of Christian authoritative texts. Some 30 years later, though, things had changed rather drastically.

Some 30 years later, there was another proto-orthodox author standing in the tradition of Justin, a heresiologist, heresy hunter, named Irenaeus. Irenaeus stood in the same theological tradition as Justin, but his writing showed that things had changed rather severely by the time we find him having produced his works of heresy, a work that he produced around the year 180, or 185, about 30 years after Justin Martyr.

Irenaeus, unlike Justin, had a set number of authorities he cited as being scriptural. This is in his book, *Against the Heresies*, a five-volume work. The passage I'm looking at it is in the third volume, Book Three of *Against the Heresies*. In it, Irenaeus attacked heretics for not understanding that there were four, and only four, Gospels to be accepted. He pointed out that different heretics used different Gospels as their authorities. "The Ebionites used the Gospel of Matthew, and only Matthew. The Gnostics used the

Gospel of Mark, and only Mark," he said. "Marcion uses Luke, and only Luke. The Valentinian Gnostics use John, and only John."

Irenaeus insisted that all of these groups were wrong, because you couldn't simply take one Gospel as an authority. If you did, you had a skewed vision of who Jesus was. You needed the full picture, provided by the four Gospels, as he said.

Irenaeus, quoting from Book Three:

> It is not possible that the books can be more or fewer in number than they are, for since there are four zones of the world in which we live, and four principal winds, which, while the church is scattered throughout the world, and the pillar and ground of the church is the Gospel and Spirit of life, it is fitting that she should have four pillars.

Get the argument? The four corners of the earth, four winds that drive the Gospel everywhere throughout the earth, and therefore, there also must be four Gospels, not more. You can't have five. You can't have seven. You also can't have fewer. You can't have one or two. There are four, and only four.

Irenaeus had a set number of books that he was considering Gospel authorities. He had a canon, at least, for the Gospels. That kind argument, by the way, seems to be the kind that convinces somebody who already wants to be convinced. It doesn't seem too convincing for anyone else. The point is, though, he appears to have had a set canon of at least the Gospel tradition.

What drove this movement toward having a set number of Gospels? In Justin's day, when Marcion was just starting out, there didn't seem to be any reason to have set authorities. Thirty years later, Irenaeus did have a set number of authorities. What's the difference? The difference was 30 years' worth of Marcionite churches spreading around there canon of Scripture. That appeared to be driving the proto-orthodox to come up with their own canon of Scripture that stood over against the Marcionites' canon.

What can we say further about the motivations proto-orthodox Christians had for establishing a set canon of Scripture? There appear to be several factors that were at work. For one thing, proto-orthodox Christians, as other Christians, felt the need to distinguish themselves from Jews. During the same period the canonization for the Christians is happening with the New Testament, Jews were going through a canonization process for the Hebrew Bible. I pointed out that in Jesus's day, there was no set canonization for

Judaism, but there did come to be a set canon, right about the time we are talking about, in the second century, among Jews.

Christians were trying to differentiate themselves from Jews, and part of the way to do that was to have their own distinctive writings in addition to those of the Hebrew Bible. That was one thing that motivated the formation of the canon of Scripture. A second thing that motivated it was that Christians wanted to have written authorities that could support their points of view. It was important to have some authorization for their point of view, and written texts by apostles provided that authorization.

Related to that, and probably more significant overall, there was the need for proto-orthodox Christians to decide which points of view were right and which ones were wrong. Proto-orthodox Christians wanted to have apostolic support for their points of view, which meant that they needed apostolic writings that they could appeal to. That was part of what was driving the movement toward establishing the canon of Scripture, and I would argue that it was the most important part.

Given the need to have a set collection of sacred texts, how did the proto-orthodox decide which texts to include? Okay, we need some books in our Scripture. How do we decide which ones? Are we going to take the Gospel of Thomas? Are we going to take the Gospel of John? Peter? Matthew? Which books to we include?

When one reads through discussions of the proto-orthodox themselves, it becomes clear what the criteria were that were to be used. Let me refer to the earliest canonical list that we have, a list of books that an author thought belonged to the sacred scriptures, the Christian list for a Christian canon. This earliest list is called the Muratorian Canon. It is called the Muratorian Canon because it's a list of books from probably the second century, that was discovered by an Italian scholar of the 18th century named Muratori. This is, then, called the Muratorian Canon, because the guy who found it was named Muratori.

This is a list of books written in Latin, fairly awful Latin. It is very difficult to read this, because it is ungrammatical. The author, who appears to have been living in the second century somewhere around Rome, listed the books he thought should be included as canonical authorities. The Muratorian Canon is fragmentary. It begins in the middle of a sentence by saying, "But he was present among them, and so, he put the facts down in his Gospel." That's a fragment; the beginning part of this is lost. The next sentence begins by saying, "The third book of the Gospels is that according to Luke." He had obviously given the first two Gospels; the third is Luke.

Then later, he said, "The fourth book of the Gospels is John." It looked pretty obvious that this thing started out by saying Matthew and Mark, and now, we have Luke and John. He gives some details about how Luke and John wrote their Gospels. He continued on to talk about the Acts of the Apostles, the fifth book in our New Testament. Then, he listed the Epistles of Paul, and as it turned out, he had all 13 Epistles of Paul listed as being canonical. He says, then, "There's an Epistle, also, to the Laodiceans by Paul, and another to the Alexandrians which were forged in the name of Paul, according to the heresy of Marcion." Thus, there are two forgeries that he said, "We don't accept, which cannot be received in the general church, for gall cannot be mixed with honey."

He goes on to say that: "the Epistle of Jude, and two letters written by John are accepted in the general church." (We have 1, 2, and 3 John. He had two of the Johns, but I'm not sure which two.) "Also, the Wisdom of Solomon, written by friends in his honor, and we accept only the Apocalypses of John and Peter." (They had the Apocalypse of Peter as part of their canon.) "But Hermas composed the book called The Shepherd, quite recently in our times, in the city of Rome, while his brother Pius, the bishop, occupied the episcopal seat." (Pius was the bishop, and Hermas, his brother, was called "the shepherd.") "Therefore, it should, indeed, be read but it cannot be published for the people in the church." (Thus, it is not a canonical authority.) "We accept nothing whatever from Arsinous or Valentinus and Miltiades, who have also composed a new psalm book for Marcion, together with Basilides of Asia Minor, the founder of the Cataphrygians." (He was listing books that were forged, that he said should not be accepted as Scripture.)

In short, when you read through this Muratorian Canon, it is probably a late second-century Roman document, written in Latin, he ended up with 22 of our 27 books of the New Testament, but he also included the Wisdom of Solomon, and the Apocalypse of Peter, so that he had a 24-book canon.

When you read through what he had to say about why books should have been included or not, you find four criteria that he used that are the same four criteria used in other proto-orthodox of the canon.

How do you know which books should have been included? First, a book had to be ancient. If it was not an ancient book, it could not be a canonical book. That is why The Shepherd, written by Hermas, could not be accepted, because it had been written recently, this guy said. It had been had sometime in the second century, and so was not old enough to be a canonical text.

Second, the book had to be apostolic, written by either an apostle, or a companion of the apostle, so that the Apocalypse of John counted, as long as John was son of Zebedee. The Apocalypse of Peter counted, as long as Peter was the real Simon Peter, himself. If you could show that these people did not, in fact, write these books, then they could not be accepted as canonical. Remember, Serapion rejected the Gospel of Peter because he thought that Peter could not have written it because it had a heretical Christology in it.

Third, a book needed to be widely accepted among the proto-orthodox churches to be seen as canonical. It had to be widely read and accepted.

Fourth, the book had to contain the correct theology, had to be orthodox. The Gospel of Peter allegedly contained a docetic Christology, and therefore, was out, and couldn't be part of the canon.

In addition, as the Muratorian Canon pointed out, there were forgeries written by Marcion, etc. These were Marcionite books, and not orthodox, and therefore, could not be accepted. Those were the four criteria to determine whether a book was canonical or not. A book had to be ancient, apostolic, widely accepted, and orthodox.

The debates over which books to include in the canon were long and hard, even though Marcion began the process already in the mid-second century. In fact, it took centuries for it to be resolved. It does appear that by the end of the second century, proto-orthodox Christianity did accept a core of texts that eventually became canonical. Most proto-orthodox Christians, by the end of the second century, accepted the four Gospels, the Book of Acts, Paul's letters, 1 Peter and 1 John.

There were huge debates about other books, though. For example, the book of Hebrews was accepted by some people, rejected by others. The Apocalypse of John, which was not very widely accepted at first; the Apocalypse of Peter, that some people thought should be included; The Shepherd of Hermas; the Epistle of Barnabas. All of these, at one time or another, were considered to be canonical texts in the third and fourth centuries.

It was not until the year 367 that anyone of record listed our 27 books, and only our 27 books as belonging to the New Testament. I want to emphasize that this is the year 367, 300 years after many or most of these books had been written, so that the canon did not come into place right away, but took centuries of debate.

In the year 367 A.D., the famous bishop of Alexandria, Athanasius, wrote his annual pastoral letter to the churches in Egypt, in which he told them, as part of his pastoral advice, which books were to be considered canonical Scripture, which books were to be accepted as part of the sacred canon, and used in the church. He listed our 27 books, and only our 27 books. This did not end the matter, because, in fact, debates continued in certain parts of the church. In the church in Syria, for example, the Syrian church, even after Athanasius, established its canon in the fifth century, and did not include 2 Peter, 2 and 3 John, Jude, or the book of Revelations. Thus, the Syrian church only had 22 books.

Other parts of the church had more books. But by and large, Athanasius's letter of 367 was used by other orthodox Christians to argue that these 27 books, and only these 27 books, should be accepted, and that has become the canon for most of the churches: Eastern Orthodox, Roman Catholic, and Protestant churches down to today, this 27-book canon of Athanasius.

To sum up, the debates to consider which books were Scripture were long and drawn out. Eventually, a canon emerged that is still accepted by the majority of Christians today. This canon provides the basis of all faith and practice for Christian churches, and to that extent, it represents an important and long-reaching aspect of the victory of the proto-orthodox, and that with the success of this collection of authoritative books, other forms of Christianity were necessarily marginalized, and effectively destroyed, while orthodox Christianity could move into other debates over other issues, down into the Middle Ages.

Lecture Twenty
The Development of Church Offices

Scope: The earliest Christian churches that we know about—those founded by the apostle Paul—were *charismatic* communities, in which there was no single person in charge, but the entire community ministered to one another through the "gifts" (Greek: *charismata*) believed to have been given by the Spirit of God. By the end of the fourth century, however, things were different: Each local church had its leader; every large community had a presiding bishop; and the bishops of major urban areas (such as Antioch, Alexandria, and Rome) were accorded special honor and authority. This lecture considers the movement from one form of church organization to the other, to see how the official church hierarchy developed, with its elders, deacons, priests, and bishops. In particular, we will trace the early stages of this development from Paul to the author of 1 Clement and Ignatius of Antioch and on to the clear church structures set out in the writings of Hippolytus of Rome.

Outline

I.   We began our investigation into the formation of traditional Christianity in the previous lecture by considering the rise and development of the canon of Scripture.

   A.   There, we saw that the establishment of a 27-book canon was largely the result of the internal needs of the church.

   B.   These included the need for self-identity distinct from Judaism and the need to establish ancient and apostolic authorities for "right belief."

II. One other important feature of traditional Christianity was the establishment of a clerical hierarchy to oversee the life, beliefs, liturgy, practices, and ethics of the Christian community.

   A.   Christianity in its early years had nothing like a clerical hierarchy. Our oldest evidence of the organization of the Christian churches comes in our earliest Christian author, Paul.

B. Paul's churches were not *clerical* (run by "clergy") but *charismatic* (run by "gifts of the Spirit").

C. As an apocalypticist, Paul, like most other early Christians, believed that he was living at the very end of the age.

    1. This was the short interim period between the beginning of the end of all things—which started with Jesus's Crucifixion, God's decisive act of redemption for the world—and the climax of all things—to come with the return of Jesus from heaven to bring in a utopian kingdom on Earth.

    2. Given that the end was near, there was no driving need to establish permanent social structures for the churches that had been established.

    3. God had, therefore, made a temporary provision for governance in this brief interim. Each person who came into the church was endowed with the Spirit of God, which provided the person with a "gift" (Greek: *charisma*) that could be used to promote the good of the community in its life together.

    4. These gifts included such things as the power to know God's will (*knowledge*); the ability to speak prophecy directly from God (*prophecy*), sometimes in strange, unknown languages (*tongues*) that could be interpreted by others (*interpretation of tongues*); and the abilities to heal the sick (*healing*), to tend to the needs of the poor (*giving*), and to teach God's truth to members of the congregation (*teaching*).

D. The nature and difficulty of the charismatic organization of Paul's churches can be seen in his First Letter to the Corinthians, which shows that the gifts were being abused and that, without any one person in charge, chaos was erupting.

III. Eventually, this charismatic structure gave way to a more top-down form of organization, with church leaders with established qualifications who were appointed and given charge over church affairs.

    A. A start can be seen already in the New Testament writings, including those associated with Paul, especially the pastoral Epistles.

B. Soon after these writings, the importance of church leaders becomes clear. Especially in a book known as 1 Clement (c. 95 C.E.).

    1. The book of 1 Clement was written by the Christians of Rome to the Christians of Corinth, and it shows that here, some 30 years after Paul's letters to Corinth, the church was being run by a group of "elders" (*presbyters*).

    2. The letter addresses a situation that has occurred in the church: The elders had been deposed and another group had taken over the church.

    3. The letter of 1 Clement works to redress the issue, urging the church to restore the original leaders. One of the arguments it uses is that these original leaders had been appointed by the successors of the apostles and can trace their authority back through their predecessors to the apostles to Christ, who came from God. Anyone who opposes them, therefore, is opposed to God.

    4. This is the earliest instance of the idea of an apostolic succession guaranteeing the validity of the leadership of the church, a useful doctrine in the hands of the proto-orthodox of later times.

C. An even clearer instance of the formation of church offices comes in the writings of Ignatius of Antioch (c. 110 C.E.).

    1. Few themes in his surviving letters are more prominent than his insistence that each church has one solitary leader, a *bishop* (literally, "overseer") who has presbyters and deacons serving under him.

    2. For Ignatius, the church must be completely obedient to the bishop as to God and submissive to the demands of the presbyters.

IV. This movement away from a kind of democratic/charismatic form of church structure to an appointed clerical hierarchy can be seen in later works of the second and third centuries, such as the *Apostolic Tradition* of Hippolytus of Rome.

A. Hippolytus was an important figure in early Christianity—a heresiologist who became convinced that the upper echelons of the leadership of the church of Rome had become heretical; he had himself set up as history's first "anti-pope."

B. Among his writings is the *Apostolic Tradition*, which advances a clear form of church structure.

    1. The means of ordaining church officials are set forth, including major offices, such as bishop, presbyter, and deacon, as well as lower-level offices, such as church widows, readers, virgins, and subdeacons.

    2. Moreover, instructions concerning some of the official duties of these positions are discussed.

V. With the passing of time, the organization of these local churches came to take on more than just local significance.

    A. The leaders of the larger churches had jurisdiction over smaller churches in the vicinity (cf. Serapion of the Gospel of Peter).

    B. Eventually, the bishops of the largest churches had jurisdiction over even major churches.

    C. The bishop of Rome was the bishop of the largest church in Christendom and, by the beginning of the fourth century, was widely seen as the head of the church at large.

    D. When Christianity was made the official religion of the state in the late fourth century by Theodosius I, he ruled that Christianity as interpreted by the bishop of Rome—the eventual pope—was to be the religion of the empire.

VI. Even though Christian churches started out as charismatic communities, it was not long before church structures had local leaders, who soon became leaders of Christians in entire regions. These leaders had to have certain qualifications and were to be ordained in established ways with certain set duties. Eventually, these bishops became extremely powerful, especially the bishop of Rome, who was, ultimately, the bishop over the entire church. This is the church that survived, then, down into the Middle Ages.

Essential Reading:

Bart D. Ehrman, *After the New Testament*, chapter 10.

Hans von Campenhausen, *Ecclesiastical Authority and Spiritual Power*.

Supplementary Reading:

James Burtchaell, *From Synagogue to Church*.

Karen Jo Torjesen, *When Women Were Priests*.

Questions to Consider:

1. In your judgment, was the failure of a charismatic church structure inevitable?

2. What kind of abuses could occur with the development of a more rigidly structured church hierarchy, with power invested in the hands of a few of the elite who had jurisdiction over the faith and practice of others?

Lecture Twenty—Transcript
The Development of Church Offices

We began our investigation into the formation of traditional Christianity by considering the rise and the development of the Christian community. Christianity, in its early years, had nothing like a clerical hierarchy. Our oldest evidence of the organization of the Christian churches comes in our earliest Christian author, Paul.

If you recall, Paul went around the urban Mediterranean establishing churches as part of a larger Christian mission. He would go into a town, set up a shop, meet people, convince them that their worship of idols was false, that they should worship the one true God and Jesus, his Son, who had died for their sins, and was coming back in judgment. When he had converted enough of these people to establish a small community, they would gather together periodically, and in their gatherings together, they would engage in acts of worship. These worship services would probably involve such things as instruction in the rudiments of the faith, reading of the Scriptures, exhortation to one another, and so forth, and so on.

These churches were not organized hierarchically. They did not have a clerical structure in which there were chosen clerics, chosen clergy, who had responsibility over the church. They started off as small communities, and even as they grew, they were not clerical in structure in Paul's own day. As we have learned from his writings, instead of being clerical in structure, Paul's churches were *charismatic* in structure. The word "charismatic" comes from the Greek word for "gift," *charisma*, or *charismata*, the plural of charisma. These churches were charismatic in that they were run not by clergy people, but by the "gifts of the Spirit" given to individuals in the church. This requires a little bit of explanation.

As an apocalypticist, Paul, like most other early Christians, believed that he was living at the very end of the age. If you recall, apocalypticists maintained that history as we knew it was divided into two segments: The age that we were living in at present, which was an evil age, controlled by evil forces; and an age to come, that would be good, when God overthrew the forces of evil, and set up his kingdom on Earth. Jesus believed that his own generation would see the coming of the Son of Man, in which there would be the destruction of this Earth, and the new history begun, bringing in the kingdom of God.

Jesus's follower Paul also thought that he was living at the end of the age. The difference, in this case, was that Paul thought that Jesus was coming back from heaven, and that Jesus would be the judge of the Earth. Like Jesus, Paul thought that this was going to happen very soon. In fact, he thought that he would be alive when it happened. Evidence for this is found in Paul's writings. In 1 Thessalonians, chapter 4, and 1 Corinthians, chapter 15, Paul talked about Jesus's coming and the changes in things. He also talked about people who had died already and would be resurrected in order to enter into the kingdom that Jesus was going to bring.

He also talked about himself, and people that he was writing to, as being alive when it happened. Paul anticipated that there would be a brief interim period between the time that Jesus had died and been raised, and exulted to heaven, and the time that Jesus came back in judgment over the Earth. There was to be a short interim period between the beginning of the end, with Jesus's death and Resurrection, and the end of the end. Paul knew that there would be a short interim, precisely because Jesus had been raised from the dead.

It was at the end of this age that there would be resurrection of dead people, when God would bring in his kingdom, and the resurrection had started with Jesus. That meant that since it had started, the end of all things was very near. That's why Paul called Jesus the "first fruits of the resurrection," because it was like a harvest. The first fruits had been gathered in with Jesus's Resurrection, and then, the rest of the harvest was to be collected very soon. Paul maintained, then, that there was a short interim period between the beginning of the end of all things, and the climax of all things, soon to come with the return of Jesus, to set a utopian kingdom on Earth.

Since the end was near for Paul, he felt no driving need to establish permanent social structures for the churches that he established. He maintained that God had made a temporary provision for governance of these churches in this brief interim moment between Jesus's Resurrection and the end. This temporary provision allowed for the governance of the churches through the Holy Spirit itself, as it gave "gifts" to individual members of the Christian community. Each person in Paul's churches was believed to have been endowed with a "gift of the Spirit" that would enable the functioning of the community together. Each person had been given a gift, given to each person when he or she was baptized. When the person was baptized, he or she would receive the Spirit, and with the Spirit, receive the spiritual gift. This gift could be used to promote the well-being of the community in its life together.

Paul talked about the gifts in several passages: Romans, chapter 12, and especially 1 Corinthians, chapters 12 through 14. The gifts included such things necessary for the governance of the community, as the power to know God's will, which was called the gift of *knowledge*. There was the ability to speak prophecy directly from God, the gift of *prophecy*. Sometimes these prophecies were given in a gift of being able to speak in unknown languages, the gift of *tongues*. One of the gifts was the ability to interpret these foreign or unknown languages. That gift was called the gift of *interpretation of tongues*.

Another gift included the ability to heal the sick, the gift of *healing*. Another gift was for those who were able to meet the needs of the poor, the gift of *giving*. Others received the gift of being able to teach God's truth to members of the congregation, the gift of *teaching*. Every individual in the congregation received one of these gifts, and manifested the gifts as the Spirit led, so that the church could be organized through the Spirit for its well-being in this short interim between the time of the beginning of the end, and the climax of the end.

This kind of church organization makes good sense, if, in fact, the church is not going to be along for the long haul. The nature and difficulty of this charismatic form of organization, however, becomes clear when reading Paul's letters, especially his First Letter to the Corinthians, which shows that the gifts of this community were being abused, and that without any one person in charge of the church, with everybody having an equal "gift of the Spirit," without one person in charge, chaos was erupting, as we see in 1 Corinthians.

We have talked about 1 Corinthians a little in the course already. Let me remind you of some of the difficulties this church was experiencing, because it relates directly to the character of the church as a charismatic community. It turns out that there was chaos in the worship services in Corinth. Paul described this chaos in 1 Corinthians, chapters 12 and 14. Apparently, the people who had been given the gift of speaking in tongues (where they would speak in unknown languages, and somebody else would interpret these languages, and these would be prophecies from God) thought this was to be particularly valued. It showed in a particularly clear way that somebody had been given a special endowment of the Spirit, because it was a much more spectacular gift than the gift of giving, or the gift of teaching. It was somebody who was speaking in a completely unknown language. This showed that the Spirit was really working through the person. That meant, though, that for a person who wanted to show that they had received a special endowment of Spirit, that person would speak in tongues a lot, and chaos was erupting during the worship services. As different people tried to speak in tongues more than anyone else, they were interrupting the services, and chaos was breaking out.

Paul wrote 1 Corinthians, in part, to deal with this problem, and he had pretty clear ways of dealing with it, where he ended up saying, "Only two or three people should speak in tongues at any one time during the worship service, and nobody should speak in tongues unless an interpreter was present. People shouldn't interrupt one another during the service," and etc. He was trying to put some controls on it. This attempt at status spiritual one-upsmanship led to differences within the church. These eventually led to lawsuits that they took to the secular courts. Pretty serious problems emerged precisely because of this charismatic structure. Why did Paul not solve the problems in this church in Corinth by writing to the pastor of the church in charge of the community? It is because there was no pastor in charge of this community.

This community was a community of equals. People had different gifts, but all gifts were important for the well being of the church, so there was nobody in charge of the church who was over the entire affair. A charismatic community may make sense when there is not going to be a long haul. As the end continues to be delayed, however, and Jesus has not come back in judgment, the church hunkers down for a long stay here on earth, and things have to change. Otherwise, chaos is the rule, rather than the exception.

Before long, this charismatic structure of Paul's churches gave way to a more top-down form of organization, with church leaders having set qualifications, who were appointed in set ways so that they could have charge over church affairs. What develops from these charismatic communities, then, were strictly top-down organizations, upon which the churches were being run.

We see the beginnings of this already within the writings of the New Testament itself, including writings associated with the apostle Paul. The Pastoral Epistles are 1 and 2 Timothy and Titus. They are called "Pastoral Epistles" because they are letters being written to pastors of churches allegedly by Paul, in which Paul, probably a pseudonymous Paul, is giving instruction to his younger co-pastors about how to organize affairs in the church.

The Pastoral Epistles, as I've indicated before, were probably pseudonymous, probably written near the end of the first century. One of the reasons for thinking that they are pseudonymous is because the church structure that these books presuppose is quite different from the church structure we know from Paul's own churches. It looks like a later development. These books were concerned about keeping the churches in order. They also presuppose that there's a pastor over each church, and that there are other church offices in the church.

For example, in 1 Timothy, chapter 3, we read a list of qualifications for people who are candidates to be the *bishop*, or the overseer of a church. The author said:

> Now, a bishop must, above all, be above reproach, married only once, temperate, sensible, respectable, hospitable, an apt teacher, not a drunkard, not violent but gentle, not quarrelsome, not a lover of money. He must manage his own household well, keeping his children in submission. Deacons, likewise, must be serious, not double-tongued, not indulging in much wine, not greedy for money.

This book is giving qualifications for the church leaders, and is being written to the person who is the head honcho of the church, this case, Timothy. These pseudonymous books, 1 and 2 Timothy and Titus, then, are presupposing a later situation in which a top-down form of organization has begun to be put into place.

Soon after these books were written, or possibly at about the same time, the importance of having solid church leaders becomes quite clear. We can see this in a book written at about the same time as some of the New Testament books, a book that didn't make it into the New Testament, called 1 Clement. 1 Clement is one of the writings of the collection of writings called the Apostolic Fathers. This collection of the Apostolic Fathers is the collection of proto-orthodox authors writing just after the time of the New Testament, some of these authors writing just at the time of the last books of the New Testament.

1 Clement was probably written around the year 95 A.D. It is a letter written by the Christians of Rome to the Christians of Corinth, the same church we were just talking about. This letter would have been written about 30 or 40 years after 1 Corinthians, and it shows that here, some 40 years after Paul had addressed the church, the church in Corinth was now not being run as a charismatic community, but under the leadership of a group of elders, or *presbyters*. The word "presbyter" is a Greek word that

just means an "older person." As Christianity developed, the leaders were called presbyters, perhaps because originally, they were older and wiser members of the community, but eventually, the term "presbyter" came to be applied to people who held the office of presbyter, whether or not they were an old person.

1 Clement presupposes a specific situation that had occurred in the church in Corinth, namely, that the presbyters who had been running the church had been deposed, taken out of power, and that another group had taken over the church. The letter of 1 Clement is in order to redress the problem. This letter urges the church of Corinth to restore the original leaders. It's not quite clear why the church in Rome felt like it had some say over what happened in the internal workings of the church in Corinth. It has not escaped notice of scholars that it was precisely the Roman church that was trying to call the shots over some other church.

Remember the theory of Walter Bauer, that Roman Christianity tried to extend its influence over other churches, beginning in the late first century, going into the second century, until it became the main form. It may be that, in fact, this is evidence of Roman Christianity trying to establish its dominance over other forms. Walter Bauer's theory was that 1 Clement, which was trying to get the deposed presbyters back into office, wanted them back in office because the deposed presbyters were proto-orthodox, and the people who took over were something else, and that they were trying to straighten this out for theological reasons. There's not a lot of evidence for that, but at least it is an interesting theory. Everyone can agree, though, that this was the Roman church intervening into another situation, or perhaps interfering in another situation, as some people in Corinth may have felt.

One of the arguments that 1 Clement used in trying to get these presbyters reinstated was an argument for what later came to be called an argument for apostolic succession. What this letter argued was that it was an illegitimate move to take the people out of power who had been precisely because they had been duly appointed. Let me read you the passage that I am most interested in. It is in chapter 44 of this rather long letter:

> Now our apostles [the authors wrote], thanks to our Lord Jesus Christ, knew there was going to be strife over the title of bishop [the overseer of the church]. It was for this reason, because they had been given an accurate knowledge of the future, that the apostles appointed the officers we have mentioned. Furthermore,

they later added a codicil to the effect that should these people die, other approved men should succeed to their ministry. In the light of this, we view it as a breach of justice to remove from their ministry those who were appointed either by the apostles, or later on, and with the church's whole consent, by others of the proper standing, and who long enjoy everybody's approval, administered to Christ's flock flawlessly, humbly, quietly, and unassumingly.

The argument worked such that the people who were in charge of the churches at present were appointed by people who had been appointed by the apostles. The apostles had been sent by Christ, and Christ had been sent from God. If you therefore opposed the people who were in charge of the church, you were not just opposing those people, but you were opposing God, because there was a direct line from God, to Christ, to the apostles, to the bishops, to those people at the church. Therefore, by opposing those presbyters, in fact, you hadn't just gotten new leadership, you had actually violated the will of God.

This is a kind of argument of apostolic succession that came to be quite useful in the hands of the proto-orthodox of later times. The argument was that you could not oppose the leaders of the church without opposing God, because their authority comes from a direct lineage, a direct succession back to the apostles and to God. This became a useful argument for theological disputes when there would be a clique within a church that decided to develop some different theological point of view. It could always be argued that was not an authorized perspective, because the authority for theology was to be found in the appointees over the churches. You therefore could not rebel theologically against those appointed, because ultimately, they were appointed by the apostles. That was the doctrine of apostolic succession.

An even clearer instance of this phenomenon, in which you had top-down leadership, where you had leaders that needed to be paid attention to, is found in the writings of Ignatius of Antioch. We have already seen Ignatius of Antioch in reference to martyrdom, because he was one of the first martyrs of Christianity. Even more important, in some ways, for the writings of Ignatius was his understanding of church structure. If you recall, Ignatius wrote seven letters en route to his martyrdom in Rome. One of the letters was to the Romans in order to ask them not to intervene in the proceedings against him, but the others were written to churches whose representatives he had met on his path to martyrdom.

In his letters, he emphasized several things, nothing as strenuously as his insistence that the church follow the bishop who had been set over the church, the presbyters who served the bishop, and the deacons who served the bishop. Ignatius was a major advocate of the monoepiscopacy, *monos*, having a sole bishop over a church, having a group of elders serve under the presbyter, and having the deacons serve under the presbyter. It may be the presbyters had charge over the spiritual well-being of the church, while the deacons had charge over the material well-being of the church. The deacons, then, might have taken alms and distributed them, for example, while the presbyters may have been in charge of the teaching functions of the church, and the bishop was the person who ran the whole show.

Ignatius insisted that everybody within the church be obedient to the bishop, the presbyter, and the deacons. Let me read you a couple of examples from Ignatius's writings. For example, Ignatius's letter to the church in Smyrna, where he said: "Flee from all schism as the source of mischief. You should all follow the bishop as Jesus Christ did the Father." (Just as Jesus followed the Father, you should follow the bishop.) "Follow, too, the presbytery as you would the apostles, and respect the deacons as you would God's law. Nobody must do anything that has to do with the church without the bishop's approval." (You can't do anything without the bishop's approval.) "You should regard that the Eucharist is valid which is celebrated by the bishop, or someone that he authorizes. Where the bishop is present, there let the congregation gather, just as where Jesus Christ is at the Catholic Church. Without the bishop's supervision, no baptisms or love feasts are permitted." (That's referring to baptisms or having Eucharist meals, which were kind of like a potluck that they would have, but they called them Agape meals, love feasts.)

It's striking, by the way, when I have graduate students, and they are learning to read Greek, and they read this passage in Ignatius for the first time, because literally, what this says in the Greek is, "No one should make love without the bishop present." What it means is that you shouldn't have love feasts, Eucharist meals, but my graduate students usually sit up and take notice at that point, and wonder what is really going on with Ignatius.

In any event, Ignatius was very strong on the importance of the bishop and the presbyters. Consider this passage from his letter to the Ephesians: "You should act in accord with the bishop's mind, as you surely do. Your presbyter, which deserves its name, and is a credit to God, is as closely tied to the bishop as the strings are to a harp."

Or, as he said to the Magnesians: "Let the bishops reside in God's place, and the presbyters take the place of the apostolic council, and let the deacons be entrusted with the ministry of Jesus Christ."

The bishop has been equated with God. To disobey the bishop is to disobey God. This is, then, a very strong statement about the need to have this hierarchical structure and to be obedient to the structure.

This movement away from a kind of democratic/charismatic form of church governance that we saw in Paul's writings to more of an appointed clerical hierarchy can be seen in still later works of the second and third centuries, especially in the works of Hippolytus of Rome, who was an important figure Christianity in the second and early third centuries. Hippolytus of Rome lived from 160 to 235 A.D. For our purposes, the most important book that he wrote is one called the *Apostolic Tradition*.

Hippolytus was generally an important figure in early Christianity. He was a heresiologist, a heresy hunter who became convinced that the upper echelons of leadership in the church of Rome had become heretical, and he ended up creating a schism in the church of Rome, in which he had himself set up as the first "anti-pope," which happened a number of times throughout the course of the Middle Ages, but Hippolytus was the first. The church split, and he claimed to have papal authority. He wasn't called the pope in those days, but he claimed to have the bishop's authority of Rome, and people following him.

Among his writings is this book I'm calling the *Apostolic Tradition*, which advances a clear form of church structure. In the *Apostolic Tradition*, the means for ordaining officials is set forth, including major offices, such as the bishop, the presbyter, and the deacon, as well as the lower-level offices such as the church widows, readers, virgins, and subdeacons. When you read through the *Apostolic Tradition*, it tells you how to ordain a bishop, who does the ordination, how to ordain a presbyter. To ordain a presbyter, the bishop lays on hands, and the whole presbytery lays on hands. The other presbyters do, so there's an actual laying on of hands ceremony. What about ordaining deacon? When you ordain a deacon, only the bishop lays on hands, because the deacon is responsible to the bishop, not to the presbytery, so that they don't lay on hands. How do you ordain a widow? A widow is an office in the church during this time period. A widow is a woman in the church whose husband has died, and who devotes herself to prayer for the sake of the church.

There's the office of the reader. The reader is made reader by the bishop actually handing him the book, so there's a little book-handing-off ceremony. This was the person who got up and read the texts during the worship services. There were a number of different kinds of offices, then— bishop, presbyter, deacon, subdeacon, widow, reader, virgin, etc. The *Apostolic Tradition* laid out what the rules were for ordaining these people, and also specified how the daily worship was to have been undertaken. This was, then, getting more rigid in its hierarchical structure.

With the passing of time, the organization of these local churches came to take on more than just local significance. The leaders of large churches ended up having jurisdiction over the small churches in the vicinity. Remember the incident of Serapion and the Gospel of Peter. Serapion was the bishop of Antioch, but he was off visiting the town of Rhossus, because Rhossus was a smaller place, and didn't have its own bishop. They were under the bishop of the larger city nearby.

Eventually, then, the bishops of the largest churches had jurisdiction even over major churches in their area, so that the bishops of the biggest churches, like that in Rome, the church in Jerusalem, and in Antioch, had jurisdiction over other bishops, of places within their regions. Eventually, the bishop of Rome was the bishop of the largest church in Christendom, and by the beginning of the fourth century, the bishop in Rome was seen to be the head of the entire church throughout the world.

When Christianity was made the official religion of the state in the late fourth century—this happened at the end of the fourth century, as we will see later on, of course, Constantine converted at the beginning of the fourth century, and after that, we had Christian emperors—Theodosius I, at the end of the fourth century, more or less made Christianity the official religion of the state, and not only did he specify that it was to be Christianity as the official religion, but Christianity as interpreted by the bishop of Rome was to be the official Christianity.

The Roman bishop, then, of course, became extremely important. He was the head of the church, and the church was the official religion of the empire. It wasn't at this time, but somewhat later, that the bishop of Rome came to be called the pope.

In sum, even though the Christian church started out as charismatic communities, it wasn't long before church structures were in place, where local leaders were put in charge of these churches—bishops, presbyters, deacons—and eventually, these leaders of the local churches became leaders of churches that were also in the wider vicinity. These leaders were to have certain qualifications, and were to be ordained in set ways, with certain set duties. Eventually, these bishops became extremely powerful, especially the bishop of Rome, who was the bishop over the entire church. This, then, is the church structure that survived down into the Middle Ages.

Lecture Twenty-One
The Rise of Christian Liturgy

Scope: This lecture considers how Christian liturgical practices arose, in particular those that became virtually universal throughout the church: baptism and the Eucharist. We will consider the roots of these practices in the ministry of Jesus (and, before him, John the Baptist), and see how they developed in the churches of Paul, as seen, for example, in his letters to the Corinthians and the Romans. We will then move into the second century to see how these practices were defended against outsiders who suspected that they involved acts of immorality (Christians were charged with holding "secret" meetings that included eating flesh and drinking blood!). Finally, we will examine an early attempt to standardize the practices in the writings of an important leader of the church of Rome, Hippolytus.

Outline

I.   To this point in our exploration of traditional Christianity, we have considered the formation of the canon of Scripture and the development of church offices. In this lecture, we will look at an equally important aspect of Christian communal life: the development of the worship services, especially the liturgical practices of baptism and Eucharist.

II.   Because being "Christian" meant, in some sense, being in a special relation with God, from the beginning, Christians understood themselves to be part of a worshipping community.

   A. Much early Christian worship was taken over from Jewish synagogue worship.
   1.   Unlike pagan practices of worship, Christians had no sacred statues, temples, or rituals of sacrifice.
   2.   Like Jews of the second and third centuries, Christians in their services of worship stressed the reading and exposition of Scripture, prayer, confession, exhortation, the singing of psalms and hymns, and the collection of alms.

3. Eventually, Christian practices shared with Jews, such as fasting, came to be differentiated from them.

B. Like many other religions, Christianity developed certain "boundary markers" to indicate what it meant to join the group and, once in, to belong to it.

III. Two of the principal boundary markers from the earliest of times were liturgical, involving the Christian services of worship. These were the practices of baptism and Eucharist.

    A. Both practices came to be seen as rooted in the life and teachings of Jesus: his own baptism and last supper and his commands that his disciples practice these rites.

    B. Both have parallels in Jewish liturgical traditions (special ritualistic washings and periodic celebratory and commemorative meals).

    C. Yet both took on distinctive meaning in the earliest Christian traditions, as evidenced in our earliest source of information for both practices, the apostle Paul.

        1. In Paul's day, baptism was a one-time ritual for adult converts in which they experienced a unification with the dead and risen Christ and a deliverance from the cosmic forces of evil in the world (Rom. 6).

        2. The Eucharist was a common meal that commemorated Jesus's death and Resurrection in anticipation of his return in judgment.

        3. Both practices, therefore, were understood in light of Paul's own apocalyptic views that in Christ, God had begun to overthrow the forces of evil in the world, to be climaxed soon in a cataclysmic act of judgment.

        4. Eventually, these practices took on even more mystical overtones, as evidenced in Ignatius of Antioch's claim that the Eucharist provided the antidote that wards off death (Ign. Eph. 20:2)—a non-apocalyptic image.

    D. Over time, these two rituals came to develop set "forms" and requirements, as seen in the early Christian document known as the *Didache*.

1. Discovered only in 1873 in Constantinople, the *Didache* is an important Christian document that, among other things, discusses the ritual practices of the early church (c. 100 C.E.).
2. In it are explicit directions concerning how to baptize (in cold, running water; in the name of the Father, Son, and Holy Spirit) and how to have the Eucharistic meal (with prayers, first over the cup, then the bread).

IV. Baptism and Eucharist were secret rituals, and rumors about what they involved led to some of the charges we have seen against Christians.

    A. Baptism was in the nude and involved a liturgical kiss of welcome. Eucharist entailed eating the flesh and drinking the blood of the Son of God. Naturally, as word leaked out, Christians were slandered for such "heinous" activities.

    B. To defend Christians against such charges, some of the apologists, such as Justin and Tertullian, went to great lengths to show that the rituals were both innocent and wholesome.
       1. These are some of our most extensive early explanations about what actually happened during these services.
       2. Justin's First Apology, in particular, shows how the practices were followed in Rome in the middle of the second century.

V. Eventually, the practices became more complex and detailed, as can be seen in their description in Hippolytus's work, the *Apostolic Tradition*.

    A. Here, we have a lengthy account of what one must do in preparation for baptism; candidates for baptism undergo a three-year period of learning (a *catechesis*).

    B. There are then complex preparatory rituals of fastings and exorcisms before the baptism (chs. 17–20).

    C. Hippolytus goes on to describe in great detail the actual baptism itself (ch. 21).

    D. After being baptized, the Christian could for the first time partake of the communion meal (the Eucharist), which Hippolytus also describes in detail (ch. 23).

VI. The Christian services of worship continued to involve not just these two rituals, but weekly meetings of prayer, exhortation, Scripture reading, and exposition.

A. Several "homilies" exist from the early church (2 Clement, the Easter homily of Melito).

B. These are expositional treatments that take elements of the scriptural text to instruct, admonish, and edify their Christian listeners.

VII. Christian liturgy developed over time, in ways that paralleled the establishment of the church hierarchy. It became less apocalyptic in its orientation (that is, less concerned with the imminent end of all things) and more highly structured (with long periods of instruction before baptism, for example). Rituals and forms of worship developed that were designed to prepare Christians for their life in community together as a body separate from those around them, emphasizing their distinctiveness from their world and their unique standing before God.

Essential Reading:

Paul F. Bradshaw, *The Search for the Origins of Christian Worship.*

Bart Ehrman, *After the New Testament*, chapter 11.

Supplementary Reading:

Everett Ferguson, *Worship in Early Christianity.*

Questions to Consider:

1. In what ways does Paul's understanding of baptism differ from those you arc familiar with today?

2. Why do you imagine liturgical practices became so much more complex and structured in Christianity with the passing of time?

Lecture Twenty-One—Transcript
The Rise of Christian Liturgy

To this point in our exploration of traditional Christianity we have considered the formation of the Christian canon of Scripture and the development of Christian church offices. In the present lecture, we will look at an equally important aspect of Christian communal life, the development of the worship services, especially looking at the liturgical practices of baptism and Eucharist, two practices still in use throughout the Christian world today.

We want to look at the beginnings of these practices to see what they originally meant, and then see how they developed over time through the second and third centuries. Since being "Christian" meant, in some sense, being in a special relationship with God, from the beginning, Christians understood themselves to be part of a worshiping community. Much early Christian worship was taken over from the Jewish synagogue methods of worship. If you recall, pagan worship was a different item altogether. Pagans, by and large, worshipped through making periodic sacrifices to the gods, especially in their temples.

Unlike pagan practices of worship, Christians had no sacred statues or idols of God, or temples, or rituals of sacrifice, in which an animal or some vegetables would be sacrificed by being offered up to the gods.

The Jewish worship in the ancient world, on the other hand, consisted largely of prayer, the reading of Scripture, the retelling of tradition, exhortation through sermons and such, in the synagogue. The Christian worship, in the second and third centuries, was more like that. It involved the reading and the exposition of Scripture, the saying of prayers, the making of confessions, exhortation from church leaders, the singing of psalms and hymns, and the collection of alms for the poor. Eventually, Christian practices that were shared with Jews, such as fasting, came to be differentiated from Jewish practices. Just to stay with fasting for a second, Christians recognized that Jews celebrated as fast days, Mondays and Thursdays. Christians, then, in order to differentiate their practices from Jews, fasted on Wednesdays and Fridays. Therefore, Christians took over some of the practices, but differentiated themselves from the Jewish religion out of which they emerged.

Like many other religions, Christianity developed certain boundary markers that were meant to indicate what it meant to join with the group of Christians, and once belonging to the group, what it meant to belong to it in perpetuity.

Two of the principal boundary markers from the earliest times for Christians were liturgical in nature, involving the Christian services of worship. These were the practices of baptism and Eucharist. Both of these practices, baptism and Eucharist, were ultimately rooted in the life and teachings of Jesus himself. Jesus, of course, was baptized at the beginning of his ministry, and near the end of his life, he instituted the Lord's Supper. The accounts of the baptism are recorded for us in the Gospels of Matthew, Mark, and Luke in the New Testament. In the Gospel of John, there is an allusion to Jesus being baptized, and John the Baptist appears in the Gospel of John, but there is no actual account of Jesus being baptized. He is said to have been baptized, though, in the other Gospels—Matthew, Mark, and Luke.

The accounts have some differences among them. In the earliest account, we have Mark's, in which Jesus comes as an adult to John the Baptist, who is in the wilderness, baptizing people for the remission of sins. Jesus also comes for baptism, and when he is baptized by John in the Jordan River, we are told that as Jesus came up out of the water, the heavens split apart, the Spirit descended upon Jesus in the form of a dove, and a voice came from heaven that said, "You are my beloved Son, in whom I am well-pleased."

Christians understood that this baptism was the moment at which Jesus's ministry was inaugurated. It's the first thing that happens to Jesus in the Gospel of Mark; and in Matthew and Luke, even though it's not the first thing that happens in those Gospels with Jesus, because in those Gospels we have an account of Jesus's birth and very young life, nonetheless, even in Matthew and Luke, this is the beginning, the inauguration of Jesus's public ministry.

Baptism in early Christianity functioned in a similar way. Baptism was the initiation for the person into the community of God, the inauguration of their life as a Christian, rooted ultimately in Jesus's baptism. So, people would study the baptism accounts in these Gospels to see how Christians themselves were to be baptized in imitation of Jesus.

The Lord's Supper, the Eucharist, goes back to Jesus as well. The word "Eucharist," by the way, comes from a Greek word that means "giving thanks," so this is called a Eucharist meal, because it is a meal of thanksgiving to God in a technical sense, because the bread and the wine consumed at this Eucharist meal are expressing thanks to God for the salvation He's provided in the death and Resurrection of Jesus. This

Eucharist meal, in fact, then, is a commemoration of Jesus's death and Resurrection in early Christianity.

It is commemorating, though, the event that happened in Jesus's life at the end; whereas the baptism was at the beginning, the giving of the Lord's Supper, the last supper in which the Lord's Supper was instituted comes at the very end, the night before Jesus is executed.

According to our oldest account, the Gospel of Mark, they are eating a special Passover meal, Jesus and his disciples, and we are told that while they were eating, Jesus took a loaf of bread, and after blessing it, he broke it, gave it to them, and said, "Take, this is my body." Then, he took a cup, and after giving thanks, he gave it to them, and all of them drank from it. He said to them, "This is my blood of the covenant, which is poured out for many. Truly, I tell you, I will never again drink from the fruit of the vine, until that day when I drink it anew in the Kingdom of God."

This, then, marked a meal in which Jesus indicated that the bread that was broken represented his broken body, which would happen on the next day, and that the cup of wine being drunk as part of the Passover meal, represented his shed blood. Christians eventually, of course, came to think that his broken body and shed blood brought about the salvation of the world, that is why they commemorated this meal that Jesus had on periodic occasions in recollection of Jesus giving his life for them.

Both of these liturgies that end up developing in Christianity have roots in Jewish liturgical traditions. Jews also have had special ritualistic washings, baptisms, if you will. The word "baptism" comes from a Greek word *baptitsa*, meaning "to dip." Usually, you would dip something into water, or you could dip a garment into dye, to submerge something into a liquid. Some Jews practiced ritual washings, although we don't have any indication of Jews having anything like a baptism, which was a once for all sort of occurrence. Jews would have periodic washings to represent ceremonial cleansings, ritual cleansings, from impurities. Christianity developed a baptism, which was a one-time shot, baptism to represent a variety of things, as we will, but that happened only once. Thus, while Christians would only get baptized once, Jews would have periodic washings.

Jews also, of course, had periodic commemorative meals, such as the Passover meal, that we have mentioned on several occasions, an annual celebration of the deliverance of the children of Israel from the slavery in Egypt.

Christians, then, did not make up the idea that you have these liturgical services involving being submerged in water and eating a meal. They took these over from Jewish practices, but instilled new meaning in them, given their understanding of the life of Jesus and these liturgical practices that he began.

Both of these practices, then, took on distinctive meanings, distinctive from what they meant in Jewish contexts, and that was evident already in our earliest source of information about both practices, once again, the apostle Paul, our earliest Christian author. We know about baptism from Paul's writings, because he discussed it on several occasions, most especially in the book of Romans, chapter 6. If you recall, the book of Romans is a letter that Paul wrote to the Christians in the city of Rome, in which he was dealing with a wide range of issues. One of the things he wanted to talk about in Romans was how baptism functions to relieve people from their enslavement to the power of sin.

Paul wrote in Romans, chapter 6, verses 3 and 4: "Do you not know that all of us who have been baptized into Christ Jesus were baptized into his death? Therefore, we have been buried with him by baptism into death, so that just as Christ was raised from the dead by the glory of the Father, so we, too, might walk in newness of life."

In the modern day, there are a number of different interpretations about what baptism is all about. Some churches believe that baptism of an infant is what removes Original Sin from the infant. Others believe that baptizing an infant is what puts the child into a covenantal relationship with God, as a replacement of circumcision as the sign of the covenant. Some churches today maintain that only adults should be baptized, and in those churches, typically, baptism is understood to be an outward sign of an inward reality, so that the inward reality is being born again to a new life. Baptism is like a death, where you are put into the water as if you are put into a grave, and then brought back out, as if you have been raised into a new life, but this is a symbol of an inward reality, an outward show of an inward reality.

There are a range of understandings of baptism in the modern world. None of these understandings of baptism is actually what Paul thought about baptism, even though, of course, these churches would appeal to passages like this in support of their views. Paul, himself, though, didn't agree with any of those perspectives. Paul understood that baptism was not a symbolic act, but it was to be done for adults in them. Of course, in his day, the people who were becoming Christian were actually becoming Christian.

This was early on, before people were born into Christian families. People converted into Christianity.

For Paul, when a person was baptized, something actually happened. The person was united with Christ in the baptism. Just as Christ was buried, so this person was buried in water, but at that point, there was seen to be some kind of unity that took place, a unification of the person with Christ, so that the person experiences the benefits of Christ's death by been baptized, and the person was then made one with Christ. That's why Paul talked about people being "in Christ." There was some kind of mystical union that took place at the baptism. Since Christ died, and thereby killed the power of sin, the person who was in Christ at baptism had overcome the power of sin. That's why the person, then, could have salvation. That's what Paul said. "Those of us were baptized into Christ were baptized into his death."

He went on to say that if we had been united with him in a death like his, we would certainly be reunited with him in a resurrection like his. "Whoever has died," he said, "is freed from sin," and so for Paul, the baptism is a way of being freed from the power of sin by being united with Christ in his death.

This was a onetime occurrence for Paul. It happened to adult converts, and they experienced, then, at that moment, a unification with the dead and risen Christ, and they experienced a deliverance from the cosmic forces and evil in the world. That's baptism for Paul, a liturgical act that happened to every Christian when they converted.

The Eucharist, for Paul, is also discussed in his writings, this time in 1 Corinthians, chapter 11. Paul was upset with abuses of the Lord's Supper in Corinth. There were a lot of problems in the church in Corinth. One of them was an abuse of the Lord's Supper, where apparently some people were engaging in what would be comparable to a potluck supper; some people would come and be gorged on the food, and would drink so much wine they got drunk; while other people, presumably the lower classes who had worked all day, would come late, and have nothing to eat and nothing to drink.

Paul saw this as abuse, because the point of this celebration was to celebrate the unity that is given in Christ and the salvation that comes to all people, so that it is through Christ's death and Resurrection. The point of this was to unify the community, not to break it apart. Paul therefore reminded the Christians in Corinth how they were to celebrate the Lord's Supper, and in so doing, he recalled what happened on the night Jesus instituted this liturgical act:

> For I received from the Lord what I also handed on to you, that the Lord Jesus, on the night he was betrayed, took a loaf of bread. When he had given thanks, he broke it and said, 'This is my body that is for you. Do this in remembrance of me.' In the same way, he took the cup after supper, saying, 'This cup is the new covenant in my blood. Do this as oft as you drink it, in remembrance of me. For as often as you eat this bread and drink this cup, you proclaim the Lord's death until he comes.'

This was to be a commemoration of Jesus's death that brought about salvation in anticipation of his return in judgment. You are to do this until he comes. This is therefore to commemorate Jesus's death at a communal meal.

Both practices, baptism and the Lord's Supper (the Eucharist), were understood by Paul in light of his own apocalyptic views: That in Christ, God had begun to overthrow the forces of evil in the world, and this was going to be climaxed very soon in an act of judgment. For Paul, then, these liturgical moments—baptism and the Eucharist—were apocalyptic in nature, both of them dealing with the forces of evil in the world that were eventually going to be destroyed with Christ's return.

Well, Christ did not return, and people began to instill different meanings in these particular liturgical moments. Eventually, the practices took on more mystical overtones. For example, the Eucharist began to be understood in some circles as a kind of protection against the forces of evil. We find this in the writings of Ignatius of Antioch. In one place, he speaks about the Eucharist in a kind of off-the-cuff way, but it shows something of his understanding of it.

Ignatius, in his letter to the Ephesians, was talking about the meetings that the Christians held under the observance of the bishop and the presbyter, which included a Eucharist meal. "At these meetings," said Ignatius in a letter to the Ephesians, "you should heed the bishop and the presbyter attentively, and you should break one loaf, which is the medicine of immortality, and the antidote, which wards off death, but yields continuous life and union with Jesus Christ."

Taking the communion meal is like taking an antidote to death. It provides immortality, so that this was more, at this point, then simply a commemoration of Jesus's death. This was actually some kind of mystical food that you partook of in order to have eternal life.

Over time, these two rituals of baptism and Eucharist developed into set forms with certain requirements. This can be seen in an early second century document called the *Didache*. The *Didache* is a very important early Christian document that was not discovered until 1873. It was discovered in Constantinople and was published about a decade later; it made a huge splash when it appeared. It was front-page news, not just in religious newspapers, but in regular, old newspapers, because this was a very old document that people realized was probably written near the time of the New Testament itself.

The book is called the *Didache* from the Greek word *didache*, which means "teaching." The title of the book is the teaching of the 12 apostles; thus, the *Didache of the Twelve Apostles*. The book begins by giving a set of ethical instructions, which are called the "two ways." The *Didache* begins with a "two ways" doctrine. The "two ways" are the ways in which people can choose to live. Do they want to choose the way of life, or the way of death? If you choose the way of life, then you need to behave in certain ways. If you choose the way of death, you behave in opposite ways. These are ethical instructions on how you ought to behave, if you want to have salvation.

Included with this "two way" doctrine, though, there's a kind of "church manual" in the *Didache*, the first church manual that we have. The term "church manual" is a technical term that refers to instructions about how to perform church services, including the services of baptism and Eucharist. The *Didache* is our earliest non-canonical reference to these two practices, and it is fairly interesting to see what the anonymous authors of the *Didache* had to say about these practices. In chapter 7 of the *Didache*, he is going to give instructions about how to baptize. "This is how to baptize," he says. "First, give public instruction on all these points," referring to the ethical teachings of the "two ways," "and then you are to baptize in running water, the name of the Father, Son, and Holy Spirit. If you don't have running water, baptize in some other water. If you can't baptize in cold water, then use warm water. If you have neither, then pour water on the head three times in the name of the Father, Son, and Holy Spirit."

You are supposed to use cold running water. "Running water" does not mean from a tap; it means from a river, and so, they are to do it in a river or stream if they can. If not, standing water is okay. If there's no place else to do it, pour water over the head three times. "Before the baptism, moreover, the one who baptizes, and the one being baptized must fast, as well as anyone else who can. You must tell the one being baptized to fast for one or two days beforehand." You are therefore to fast before being baptized, and then he gives these very basic instructions about how the baptism ritual is to go.

He also gives instructions about the Eucharist, the thanksgiving meal, in chapter 9: "Now, about the Eucharist. This is how to give thanks." (Then, he gives a prayer that you are supposed to pray.) "First, in connection with the cup: 'We thank you, our Father, for the holy vine of David, your child, which you have revealed through Jesus your child. To you be glory forever." (That is the prayer you are supposed to say over the cup.) Secondly: "Then, in connection with the piece of bread that is broken: 'We thank you, our Father, for the life and knowledge which you have revealed through Jesus, your child. To you be glory forever.'" (Then, he goes on with a little bit more of a prayer.) It ends by saying: "You must not let anyone eat or drink of your Eucharist except those baptized in the Lord's name, for in reference to this, the Lord said, 'Do not give what is sacred to dogs.'"

A "casting your pearls before the swine" kind of thing. Only somebody who is baptized can take the Eucharist, according to this, and it gives you two prayers, first a prayer over the cup, and then a prayer over the broken bread. This is interesting, by the way, as you may have picked up. According to the *Didache*, the sequence is reversed from the way it ended up developing in Christian circles. Even today, first the bread is given as part of the Eucharist, and then the cup of wine or the cup of grape juice, depending on what your denomination is, but first, it is the bread, and then the cup. In the *Didache*, it is the other way around; it is first the cup, and then the bread.

This is our earliest reference as to how these secret rituals were to be conducted. These are secret rituals. These are rituals for people within the church. Outsiders are not allowed. As the *Didache* says, if someone is not baptized, they are not allowed to participate in the Eucharist.

Since the baptism and Eucharist rituals were secret, rumors floated around about them, rumors that led to some of the charges against the Christians that we have seen. As it turns out, we find out from later church instructions that baptism was given in the nude. Nobody was supposed to take anything with him or her in this new life that he or she was starting as represented by the baptism. The baptism was the death to the old and beginning of the new, and therefore, you didn't take anything with you. The person undergoing the baptism, then, would come dressed in a robe, would disrobe, and be baptized in the nude.

After the baptism, there was a welcome into the community that involved a liturgical kiss. Well, you know, taking a bath in the nude and then kissing sounds a little bit odd to outsiders, if it leaks out that that is what is happening. Moreover, the Eucharist involved "eating the flesh" and "drinking the blood" of the Son of God. There, you get the infanticide and the cannibalism again.

Naturally, as word leaked out about what was going on, Christians were slandered for these kinds of "heinous" activities. In order to defend Christians against these charges, some of the apologists, like Justin Martyr and Tertullian, two people whom we have met already, went to some lengths to show that the rituals were both innocent and wholesome. Therefore, as it turns out, because there were slanders against Christians for these practices, we have some writings that survive that explain in greater detail what actually happened. If they had not been slandered, Justin Martyr and Tertullian would not have spilled the beans, but because they spilled the beans, we do know, and have a better sense of, what exactly was going on during these liturgical practices, because Justin Martyr and Tertullian tried to show that it was all completely innocent.

For example, Justin Martyr, in his *First Apology*, explained to the outsiders why there was nothing untoward in these practices, and he laid out, in what took him about seven chapters, exactly what happened during these practices. He talked about how the baptism took place, how they had to fast in advance before the baptism, and to get baptized in water in the name of the Father, Son, and Holy Spirit. Then, he explained how they went and had this ritual kiss, and then celebrated the Eucharist meal. He described the thanks that was given for this Eucharist meal, and went ahead and gave a full description of it.

Eventually, these practices of Eucharist and baptism became more complex, as church leaders tried to spell out exactly how they were to be performed. Just as the doctrine had to correctly be laid out, and you had to be correct in all the things you said, all the ins and outs of the doctrine, so, too, in your liturgical services. There was a right way to do a liturgical act, and a wrong way. Thus, these church fathers gave indications of both.

One place that is found with particular clarity is in Hippolytus' work, the *Apostolic Tradition*, mentioned in the previous lecture. In the *Apostolic Tradition*, we have a lengthy account of what one must do in preparation for the baptism, and so, he spelled out how many days in advance one needed instruction. There was actually a three-year waiting period before you could be baptized, a period of instruction, in which you learned the rudiments of the faith. Then, there was a complex set of preparatory rituals that involved fastings and exorcisms, where any dealings inside of you were exorcised by the bishop, and this happened on several occasions leading up to the baptism.

Hippolytus went on to provide in great detail what actually happened at the baptismal service itself. After being baptized, the Christian could, for the first time, then, partake of the communion. This was quite important to do, because, as I have indicated, the baptism was necessary to enter into unity with Christ, and therefore, one needed to be baptized. What happened if you died before you were baptized? You could have been in trouble, and so, theologians had to work out what happened to you, even if you believed in Christ, and had not been baptized.

Moreover, taking the Eucharist meal, if the Eucharist was understood as the way of immortality, and you had not taken the Eucharist meal, what happened then? Well, you couldn't take the Eucharist meal until you were baptized; you couldn't be baptized until you were instructed and exorcised; and these were therefore very important events. The Christian, then, who was baptized could, for the first time, partake of the communion meal. And again, Hippolytus explained in some great detail what happened during the Eucharist event.

I should stress that the Christian services of worship involved much more than just these two rituals, of course. The Christian services of worship, in the second and third centuries, also involved weekly meetings of prayer, exhortation, Scripture reading, and exposition. We are quite fortunate that we have several homilies that exist from the early church, and that can give us a sense of what sermons were like. I have already read part of one of these to you, the Passover homily of Melito of Sardis. There's another that survives, probably the earliest to survive, a book called 2 Clement. Earlier, I read from 1 Clement, and it was thought for awhile that both of these books were written by Clement of Rome, one of the early bishops of the Roman church.

2 Clement is actually a homily that uses scriptural interpretation in order to exhort its hearers to be thankful to God for what God has provided. As you read this homily of 2 Clement, you get a sense of what kind of sermons people would have heard in their church's worship services.

To sum up, Christian liturgy developed over time, in ways that paralleled the establishment of the church hierarchy, as we saw in the last lecture. Christian liturgy became less apocalyptic in its orientation. That is, it became less focused on the imminent end of all things, and became more highly structured, with long periods of instruction before baptism, for example, as rituals and forms of worship developed that were designed to prepare Christians for their life and community together, as a body distinct from all those around them, emphasizing the distinctiveness of their Christian world, and their unique standing before God as those who had made right with God by the death and Resurrection of Jesus.

Lecture Twenty-Two
The Beginnings of Normative Theology

Scope: We have already seen a wide range of beliefs in evidence among the earliest Christians. In this lecture, we will consider the development of a normative theology among the proto-orthodox, who insisted that believing the "right" things was essential for salvation and who took care, therefore, to formulate correct doctrine and differentiate it from false doctrine. One of the interesting features of orthodox theology is its paradoxical affirmations (Jesus is human and divine at the same time; God is in three persons, but there is only one God). We will see that these paradoxes emerged as proto-orthodox writers developed their views in opposition to the views of others (who denied, for example, either Jesus's humanity or his divinity). This lecture shows how such doctrines developed from the time of Paul, to Ignatius of Antioch, and on into the early fourth century, when they came to be embodied in the early Christian creeds.

Outline

I. In the past three lectures, we explored some of the important aspects of the development of traditional Christianity: the formation of the New Testament canon of Scripture, the establishment of church offices and an ecclesiastical hierarchy, and the development of Christian liturgy. In every instance, we have seen that the Christianity that had emerged by the fourth century was quite different from the forms of Christianity of the first and second centuries.

II. No aspect of traditional Christianity is more important than the development of a normative set of theological beliefs. Here, too, we can trace a significant change over time, from the early attempts at theological reflection to the more sophisticated and refined doctrinal views advanced by the fourth century.

III. From the very beginning, Christianity was unique in the Roman world for its emphasis on doctrine as an important aspect of religion.

A. Pagan religions were not doctrinal in nature.
    1. Despite their wide-ranging diversity, all pagan/polytheistic
        religion focused on cultic acts, not on beliefs about the gods.
    2. As a result, there was no such thing as heresy and orthodoxy
        in Roman paganism.
B. Not even Judaism stressed belief per se, although belief in the one
    true God was certainly presupposed in the Jewish religion. But the
    religion itself was about worship, life, and practice, not belief.
C. From its beginning, however, Christianity stressed the importance
    of correct belief.
    1. This is due, in part, to the nature of its claims about Jesus: that
        he was, in fact, the Jewish Messiah who was crucified for the
        sins of the world.
    2. This is not at all what any Jews anticipated the messiah would
        be; thus, a major part of the early Christian mission involved
        convincing Jews that the Scriptures predicted a messiah who
        would suffer and die. This view was widely rejected among
        Jews.
    3. But for most Christians, believing in Jesus's death and
        Resurrection is what made a person right with God.
    4. Therefore, knowing the correct things about Jesus (for
        example, that he was the Son of God and the Messiah who
        was crucified for the sins of the world) and having proper
        faith (for example, belief in his death and Resurrection for
        salvation) were determinative, early on, of what it meant to be
        a Christian.
    5. Being a Christian did not mean performing certain sacrifices
        to a certain god in a certain way. It meant having correct
        knowledge and proper beliefs about God and his involvement
        in the world.
D. This doctrinal emphasis can be seen in our earliest Christian
    author, Paul, for example, in his summary of his preaching of
    Christ's death and Resurrection (1 Cor. 15:3–5) or in his vehement
    opposition to Christians who took an opposing theological
    perspective (such as in Galatians).

IV. Because proper belief mattered in early Christianity, a number of the
    major internal disputes involved correct versus incorrect doctrine over

such issues as monotheism (is there only one God?), the nature of Christ (is he human? divine? both?), the character of the material world (is it the creation of the true God? a cosmic mistake?), the way of salvation (does it come through Christ's death? his teachings? his moral example?), and so on.

A. We have already seen that different Christian groups took opposite sides of these debates (cf. the Marcionites and the Ebionites).

B. It was the middle ground of proto-orthodoxy that ended up winning the disputes, but in doing so, it was forced by its opposition to contrasting views to develop a highly paradoxical set of theological affirmations.

1. Against adoptionists, the proto-orthodox stressed that Jesus was divine; against docetists, they stressed that he was human; against Gnostics, they stressed that he was one being, not two. The paradoxical assertion emerged that he was fully human and fully divine, yet only one person.

2. So, too, against the Ebionites, the proto-orthodox stressed that Jesus was God, while against the Marcionites and Gnostics, they stressed that there was only one God. But how could Jesus be God and God be God if there is only one God? That was part of the proto-orthodox paradoxical claim.

3. The resulting paradoxes can be seen at an early stage in the theological claims of Ignatius concerning Jesus (Ign. Eph.7:2).

V. Eventually, proto-Christian authors developed certain set doctrines that were to be subscribed to by all "true" believers.

A. This set of doctrines was often called the "rule of faith" (Latin: *regula fidei*).

B. It is outlined in broadly similar ways by such early proto-orthodox theologians as Irenaeus and Tertullian.

C. Its basic tenets involved belief in one God, the creator of all, and Jesus, his Son, who was both human and divine; belief in Jesus's miraculous life, death, Resurrection, and Ascension; and belief in the Holy Spirit, who is present on Earth until the end, when there would be a final judgment in which the righteous would be rewarded and the unrighteous condemned to eternal torment (thus, for example, Tertullian, *Prescription of Heretics*).

VI. In some ways connected to the *regula fidei* were the early creedal statements that developed.

    A. Originally, these were probably part of the ceremony of Christian baptism, performed in the names of the Father, Son, and Holy Spirit. The creeds tended to be tripartite.

    B. Over time, the statements of the creeds were refined in light of various "false" beliefs that developed; for example, the belief of many Christians in the early fourth century that even though Jesus was divine, he was a subordinate divinity to God the Father.

    C. The orthodox view emerged that Jesus was, in fact, of the same nature as God, though distinct from him in person.

    D. Two of the creeds devised originally in the fourth century have come down to us today and are still recited in many services of worship throughout the world: the Apostles and the Nicene Creeds. These creeds embody many of the paradoxical affirmations that emerged in the conflicts of the second through the fourth centuries.

VII. Christianity was unique in the ancient world for its emphasis on proper belief rather than cultic action. This stress on belief led to a heightened role of doctrine and a correct understanding of the tenets of the religion. These came to be refined over time, especially in opposition to perspectives believed to be aberrant, leading to highly paradoxical affirmations of faith. Nowhere is this development more interesting or historically significant than in the doctrine of the Trinity, which we will examine at greater length in the next lecture.

Essential Reading:

Bart D. Ehrman, *After the New Testament*, chapter 14.

———, *Lost Christianities*, chapter 8.

Jeroslav Pelikan, *The Christian Tradition*, vol. 1.

Supplementary Reading:

Adolf von Harnack, *History of Dogma*, vol. 1.

Richard Norris, *The Christological Controversy*.

William G. Rusch, *The Trinitarian Controversy*.

Questions to Consider:

1. Does it seem strange to you, or natural, that a religion would place an eternal significance on correct propositional statements about the deity and his role in our world?

2. Do you see the paradoxical affirmations of Christianity to be a strength (for example, in acknowledging the "mystery" of God) or a weakness (for example, in simply accommodating various perspectives)? Discuss one of the Christian doctrinal paradoxes, for example, that God is the creator of all there is but not of evil that exists.

Lecture Twenty-Two—Transcript
The Beginnings of Normative Theology

In the past three lectures, we explored some of the important aspects of the development of traditional Christianity: the formation of the New Testament canon of Scripture, the establishment of church offices and an ecclesiastical hierarchy, and the development of Christian liturgy. In every instance, we have seen that the Christianity that emerged by the fourth century, by the time that Constantine had converted to the faith, was quite different from the forms of Christianity of the first and second centuries.

We have been looking at the development of Christianity into what became traditional Christianity at the time of Constantine's conversion. No aspect of traditional Christianity is more important than the development of a normative set of theological beliefs, and here, too, we can trace a significant change over time, from the early attempts at theological reflection, to the more sophisticated and refined doctrinal views that were advanced by the fourth century.

I don't want to claim at all that the events that had transpired by the fourth century were the only developments to ever take place within Christianity. Theology continued to develop and become more nuanced and refined in the fourth, fifth, and following centuries, but major issues had been resolved by the time of the fourth century, so that the later disputes tended to be over smaller, more minor issues, even though combatants at the time saw them as quite major. The extremely large questions of the second and third centuries within Christianity, though, had been resolved by the time of the conversion of Constantine.

From the very beginning, Christianity was unique in the Roman world for its emphasis on doctrine as an important aspect of religion. People today, in our world, tend to think of doctrine as having a central role to play within religion, that it matters what you believe. What you believe is of central importance, far more important than your practices. People therefore they tend to talk about how they are not in support of the organized Christian church, or organized religion; they believe in a kind of private spirituality, which means their own kind of beliefs in what they think is what really matters, but the organized religion itself does not matter.

That way of understanding is a distinctively Christian way of looking at the world, and looking at religion. Prior to Christianity, there were no religions that emphasized one's personal beliefs, personal thoughts, ideas about the divine, over against religion as an organized entity. In the ancient world, religion was the organized, outward, public entity. Personal beliefs played almost no role in religion in the ancient world.

This was especially true with the pagan religions, which were dominant throughout the Roman Empire. Paganism, again, simply refers to the many, many, many polytheistic religions throughout the Roman Empire. They were quite different from one another in a large number of ways, but all had in common certain distinctive features, in particular, the circumstance that they all worshipped different gods, but they did so through periodic acts of sacrifice, and prayer. Paganism took up about 95 percent of the ancient Roman world when Christianity arrived on the scene. Only 5 or maybe 7 percent of the world at the time was Jewish. Everyone else was a member of one or the other of the pagan religions.

Despite their wide-ranging diversity, all of these pagan, polytheistic religions focused on cultic acts, not on beliefs about the gods. I have real trouble convincing my own students of this at Chapel Hill, because my students think of religion as has having to do with doctrines, especially my students who are quite religious themselves. For them, what really matters is what you believe. Do you believe that Jesus is the Son of God? Do you accept Jesus as your Lord and savior? It's a kind of mental exercise of acknowledging certain facts about Jesus and God, and then committing yourself to them that counts as religion for them.

The idea that you could have a religion that does not see belief or personal commitment to an idea or a doctrine, or theology as being important at all doesn't work for many of my students, so that when I tell them that pagan religions, in fact, had nothing to do with doctrine, they have trouble believing me. "Surely they had doctrines in pagan religions. What else is religion but doctrines?" Well, no, in fact; pagan religions did not have doctrines. There was no such thing as heresy and orthodoxy in pagan religions. What you believed about the gods was virtually irrelevant to religion.

Now, what you believed about the gods may have been important to philosophy. Philosophy in the ancient world was concerned about your thoughts, in thinking correctly, and in understanding the world correctly, and even in understanding the world's relationship to God or the gods. That mattered for philosophy, but ancient religion was a matter of going to a temple and performing a sacrifice to a god on, say, the birthday of the idol in the temple, during one of the religious ceremonies for the city or for the town, or involving a family practice of cultic acts that a family might perform before a meal, such as pouring out a little wine on the altar, or saying a little prayer to one of the household gods.

What you believed about these gods was virtually irrelevant. Pagans never persecuted anybody for their beliefs. They might persecute people for not participating in the local cult, but never for what somebody believed.

Not even Judaism stressed belief per se in the ancient world, even though, of course, belief in the one true God was presupposed in the Jewish religion. Jews in the ancient world, though, did not come up with a set of doctrines about God that had to be believed in order to be a good Jew. Being a good Jew meant doing certain things, living in certain ways, and following certain cultural customs. It did not mean having a "correct" set of beliefs or doctrines. The religion of the Jews was not about proper belief. It was about daily life, worship, and ritual and practice. Christianity was unique in the ancient world in stressing not just worship in daily life and practice, but also in stressing the absolute importance of correct belief.

How is it that Christianity came to be so focused on belief, and on doctrine, leading to huge conflicts over heresy and orthodoxy in the time period we have been looking at? How did this come about?

To some extent, the doctrine in Christianity is due to the nature of its original claims about Jesus himself. Jesus talked about the coming Son of Man, who would come in judgment of the Earth, that God, in the coming of the Son of Man, would overthrow the forces of evil, and bring in a good kingdom. After Jesus died, his followers shifted that message away from talking about the coming judgment of God and onto Jesus himself, whose death and Resurrection were taken to be important for the salvation of the world, that in fact, the salvation came from his death and Resurrection.

The earliest Christians were Jews, who tried to convince their Jewish compatriots that Jesus himself was the Messiah that had been predicted by Moses and the prophets. Most other Jews, as we have seen, found these claims about Jesus to be completely ludicrous. No Jews prior to Christianity had anticipated that there would be a Messiah who came, and who was rejected by the Jewish people, by and large, and who was also arrested, put on trial, and executed as a common criminal.

The idea that Jesus was the Messiah was absurd to most Jews, especially Jews who were expecting a messiah, since the Messiah was supposed to be a great and powerful figure that overthrew the enemies of God, and established God's kingdom on Earth, the kingdom in Israel. Jesus was anything but a powerful figure who overthrew his enemies. Jesus was overthrown by his enemies, and was killed by them. How could they claim that he was the Messiah?

Nonetheless, Christians insisted that Jesus was the Messiah, and that his death was the way of salvation. For most Christians, then, Jesus's death and Resurrection were what made a person right with God. Knowing the correct things about Jesus, and accepting certain beliefs about Jesus, was absolutely fundamental to the Christian religion. You had to accept the "facts." These were "facts" that you had to give mental assent to: That Jesus was the Son of God, that he was the Messiah, and his death brought about the salvation of the world.

Moreover, you needed to have proper faith in this death and Resurrection of Jesus, meaning that you had to commit yourself personally to it, and have a trusting acceptance of the death and Resurrection of Jesus in order to be right with God. Doctrine, therefore, necessarily played a part in this religion, because you had to accept and believe the right things about Jesus.

Being a Christian, then, did not mean performing certain sacrifices in a certain way to a certain god. Being a Christian meant having correct knowledge about God, and proper beliefs about him, and his son Jesus, and his involvement in the world.

This doctrinal emphasis of early Christianity can be seen, once more, in our earliest Christian author, the apostle Paul. Paul went about establishing churches by trying to convince people who were pagans of the correctness of his teaching about Jesus. Let me read one of the passages for you that comes from the apostle Paul, and this summarizes what he saw to be central to Christianity. You will notice that what he considered central to Christianity has nothing to do with performing a sacrifice or other practices. It has to do with belief. This is found in the letter 1 Corinthians, where Paul was reminding former pagans who were now Christians in the church in Corinth what it was that he preached to them, and what they believed. 1 Corinthians, chapter 15:

> Now, I would remind you, brothers and sisters, of the good news that I proclaim to you, which you, in turn, received, in which, also, you stand, through which also you are being saved, if you hold

> firmly to the message that I proclaim to you. How do you have salvation? By accepting a message [not by offering a sacrifice, not by saying a prayer, not by engaging in other cultic activities, but by accepting a message; in other words, accepting a doctrinal statement] unless you have come to believe in vain

That is what he said. This is the message:

> For I deliver to you as of first importance what I, in turn, had received, that Christ died for our sins in accordance with the Scriptures, and that he was buried, and that he was raised on the third day, in accordance with the Scriptures, and that he appeared to Cephas, and then, to the twelve.

This is a very interesting statement, because it is modeled very carefully. In fact, the statement is modeled so carefully that scholars have suspected that what Paul was doing here, in 1 Corinthians, chapter 15, verses 3 and 4, was quoting a creed that was floating around in the early church, that this was a pre-existing creed that Paul was quoting. The reason for thinking so is that this is very carefully structured. What is the message? Well, it is divided into two parts. Christ died, and Christ was raised from the dead. Both statements are supported by Scripture. He died in accordance with the Scriptures. He was raised on the third day in accordance with the Scriptures. Moreover, both parts are given physical demonstration, physical proof. He died in accordance with the Scriptures, and he was buried. You see, that is the physical demonstration that he actually died. That he was raised on the third day, in accordance with the Scriptures, and that he appeared to Cephas and to the twelve. His appearances, then, verify that, in fact, he was raised. This is, then, a two-part statement. Each of the two parts has three components: Died, was raised, according to Scriptures; according to Scriptures, he was buried, he was seen, or he appeared.

People accepted this message in Corinth, and that is what made them Christians. They accepted certain historical claims about Jesus. That is what differentiated them from all the pagans who were performing sacrifices to their gods. That's what made them Christian. This was a doctrinal emphasis from the very beginning.

The reason it was a doctrinal emphasis is because the religion was centered not on what humans did—acts of sacrifice and prayer—but on what God had done. He had Christ die, and then raised Christ. The religion, therefore, involved accepting what God had done rather than performing some kind of act. That's why Paul insisted, in his other letters, that a person was made right with God, or was justified by faith, not by doing the works of the Jewish Law. Even though it was the Jewish God, doing the works of the Jewish Law did not put a person in right standing with that God. What put a person in right standing with God was accepting what God had done, by having faith in Jesus, which meant believing certain things about him, and accepting certain facts about what God had done through Christ.

For Paul, anyone who did not see the religion that way was strictly off limits. For example, if you recall, in the letter to the Galatians, Paul was writing the Galatians, to people who insisted that Christians had to follow the Jewish Law in order to be right with God. Paul wrote, in white hot anger, that, in fact, you didn't have to do anything in the Jewish Law. You didn't have to be circumcised, keep kosher, or keep the Sabbath, because doing the Law was not what put a person in right relationship with God, but only the sacrifice of Christ, and accepting the sacrifice, was what put one in right standing with God.

Proper belief mattered in early Christianity, and since it mattered what a person believed, a number of major internal disputes erupted involving correct versus incorrect doctrine. Disputes over monotheism erupted. Christians had disputes: Is there one God, two Gods? Are there lots of Gods? Well, it depended. Were you proto-orthodox Christian? Were you a Marcionite? Were you a Gnostic?

Debates erupted over the nature of Christ. Was he human? That's what the Ebionites said. Was he divine? That's what the Marcionites said. Was he both? That's what the proto-orthodox said.

What about the character of the material world? Was this world the creation of God, or a cosmic mistake? It depended on whether you listened to the proto-orthodox, or the Gnostics. What was the way to salvation? Did it come from Christ's death? That's what Paul said. Does it come through his teachings? That's what the Gospel of Thomas said. Did it come through his moral example, so that if you lived like Christ, you would have the life of Christ, and be saved?

We have seen that different Christian groups took opposite sides of all of these debates. You had Marcionites on one side, and Ebionites on the other. Interestingly, it was the middle ground of proto-orthodoxy that ended up winning the disputes. But in doing so, proto-orthodoxy was forced by its opposition to contrasting views, to develop a highly paradoxical set of theological affirmations. The doctrine that emerged out of proto-orthodoxy was highly paradoxical in its affirmations.

Let me explain how it worked. Against the Jewish Christian adoptionists like the Ebionites, proto-orthodoxy stressed that Jesus was actually divine, and not just human. He was divine. However, against docetists, who said that Jesus was God, therefore, was not really human, the proto-orthodox stressed that Jesus was actually human. Against the Gnostics, they stressed that he was not two different beings, one human and one divine, but only one being. Thus emerged the paradoxical assertion that Christ was fully human and fully divine, but one person, not two.

That's a paradox. How could he be both divine and human? Can a man be both a man and a rock? Can God be both God and man? Yes, and it wasn't that he was half God and half human. He was completely God, and completely human, but he's not two people; he's one person. That is a paradoxical affirmation that the proto-orthodox were forced to make because of who they were opposing, with Ebionites, Marcionites, and Gnostics on all sides.

Let's take another example. Against the Ebionites, the proto-orthodox stressed that Jesus was God. Against the Marcionites and the Gnostics, though, the proto-orthodox stressed that there was only one God. How could Jesus be God and God be God, though, if there were only one God? That was part of the proto-orthodox paradoxical claim. They wanted to claim that Jesus was God, but that he was not the same as God the Father. God the Father was God, but there was only one God, not two gods. How could you have it that way? "That's the way it is."

These paradoxes were therefore forced upon the proto-orthodox Christians. We'll see how that one played out in the next lecture, which will be devoted exclusively to the doctrine of the Trinity, how you get the doctrine of the Trinity out of these paradoxical affirmations.

In any event, the resulting paradoxes forced upon the proto-orthodox by the opponents they had ended up in some theological claims that were paradoxical from the very outset. For example, the church writer Ignatius of Antioch, whom we have encountered on a number of occasions, had a kind of theological statement, a kind of creed that he threw out in the middle of one of his letters that is very interesting, both because it was completely paradoxical in nature, as I have been indicating, but also because it was somewhat unrefined by later standards.

This is his doctrine of Christ, from Ignatius's Letter to the Ephesians, chapter 7, verse 2:

There is only one physician. [He's talking about Christ.] He is both flesh, and of the spirit. He is born, and yet, he is unbegotten. He is God incarnate, genuine life in the midst of death, sprung from Mary as well as God, first subject to suffering, and then beyond suffering, Jesus Christ, our Lord.

He had to affirm two things at once up and down the line, about whether he's flesh or spirit, born or unborn, life versus death, Mary versus God, whether he could suffer or not. It leads to a paradoxical set of affirmations.

Eventually, proto-orthodox Christian authors developed a certain set of doctrines that were to be subscribed to by all true believers. Doctrine became very important, because you had to believe the right thing, and you had heretics out there proclaiming the wrong thing. This set of doctrines, in the second century, came to be known by a Latin phrase, the *regula fidei*, which translates into "rule of faith." I tell my undergraduate students at Chapel Hill that whenever there's a perfectly good English phrase to use, be sure to use the Latin phrase, to show that you are educated, and so, we call this the *regula fidei*, which means, exactly, the "rule of faith."

The *regula fidei* is a set of doctrines that were never actually developed into a set form. It is not that there is a *regula fidei* that is one set of affirmations, the way you get in creeds that we will talk about momentarily. The *regula fidei* is more amorphous, but it is a set of doctrines about God that need to be affirmed by everyone who is a true believer, according to the heresiologists (people like Tertullian and Irenaeus). They therefore talked about this *regula fidei*, and spelled out what is comprised by it.

Tertullian, for example, spelled this out in one of his famous works, called the *Prescription of Heretics*. The *Prescription of Heretics* is a very interesting book. Tertullian had some kind of legal training, and he used legal terminology on occasion. The word "prescription" doesn't mean what we normally mean when we go off to the drugstore for a prescription. This is actually a technical, legal term in Latin law that refers to having a legal case dismissed before it ever comes to trial, on the basis of a technicality, and is therefore a "prescription," meaning, ahead of the trial, writing out a prescription to keep the case from coming up.

In Tertullian's *Prescription of Heretics*, he said that "the heretics have no right to argue with us about correct doctrine." He argued that Christians didn't need to go to trial with heretics over what correct doctrine was, because the only grounds for arguing correct doctrine were the Scriptures. The Scriptures belonged to Christians, not to heretics. Heretics had no right, then, to use the Scriptures to argue with Christians, because the Scriptures were not theirs, but Christians'. Why were they Christians'? Because the Scriptures had been handed down by the apostles, and the apostles appointed the heads of the churches (the heads of the churches were the ones who controlled the interpretation of the texts). Heretics, therefore, could not use these texts, because they didn't own the texts. This was therefore his prescription, so that he did not even have to argue with heretics about what the right thing to believe in was, because the heretics had nothing to argue with.

Of course, he said that, and then wrote these very long treatises against them, arguing against them, so maybe he did not believe it himself. Just with respect to Marcion, for example, Tertullian wrote five volumes, where he argues against Marcion; maybe he didn't believe his own prescription.

At any rate, in this book, the *Prescription of Heretics*, Tertullian laid out the *regula fidei*. Its basic tenets involved believing in only one God, who was the creator of everything; belief in Jesus, God's son, who was both human and divine; and belief in Jesus's miraculous life, death, Resurrection, and Ascension. It involved belief in the Holy Spirit, who was to be present on Earth until the end, when there was to be a final judgment, which the righteous were to be rewarded, and the unrighteous condemned to eternal torment. These, then, were doctrines that everyone had to agree with. You might disagree with this, that, or the other thing within those doctrines, but those doctrines had to be affirmed by everybody. That was the *regula fidei*.

This *regula fidei*, which, again, was rather amorphous, was related, in some ways, probably, to the creeds that ended up developing within early Christianity. There were early credal statements as soon as there were Christian writings. I pointed out that Paul, in 1 Corinthians, may have been quoting an earlier creed. Well, this is the earliest writer we have.

You didn't have creeds that were circulating around and being debated for their theological niceties until into the third and probably into the fourth centuries. The creeds, originally, were part of the Christian baptism ceremony. Christians were to be baptized in the name of the Father, Son, and Holy Spirit.

We have indication that these creeds were originally set up as tripartite statements of faith that were possibly said at the baptism: "Do you believe in the Father?" People being baptized would say, "Yes, I believe in the Father, the creator of all things, creator of heaven and Earth, all that is visible and invisible." They would say something like that, and then water would be poured on the head, or else the person would be dunked into the water. "Do you believe in Jesus Christ?" "Yes, I believe in Jesus Christ, his only Son, our Lord, who was begotten of the Holy Spirit, but born of the Virgin Mary." He or she would say something about Jesus, and have water poured on his or her head. "You believe in the Holy Spirit?" "Yes, I believe in the Holy Spirit." He or she would finish out the creed.

Originally, creeds were part of the ceremony, then, of Christian baptism, and were tripartite. Two creeds have come down to us today that are still recited in Christian churches, the Apostles Creed, and the Nicene Creed. Both of these have their roots back in the third century, but developed at later times. The Apostles Creed is called that because it is believed to be rooted in the teachings of the apostles, but this creed actually was not devised by the apostles. It is based upon apostolic teaching: "I believe in God the Father Almighty, the creator of heaven and earth, and in Jesus Christ, his only Son, our Lord, who was conceived of the Holy Spirit, born of the Virgin Mary, suffered under Pontius Pilate, was crucified, died, and was buried," etc. That is the Apostles Creed that is still recited today.

The Nicene Creed is a fuller creed, and is a creed that came out of the Council of Nicea, incidentally, which we will be referring to in our next lecture, when I talk about the Trinity: "We believe in one God, the Father, the Almighty, maker of heaven and Earth, and of all that is, seen and unseen," and it goes on, and spells out beliefs in "Jesus Christ, his only Son, our Lord," and belief in the "Holy Spirit, the Lord and giver of life."

These creeds were worked on over the ages, until they have come down to us today. Both of these creeds have statements that are directed against heretical forms of belief. Every statement in them is carefully crafted. When the Apostles Creed says, "I believe in God the Father Almighty, creator of heaven and earth," that is as opposed to the Gnostics, who believed that heaven and Earth was created by a subordinate deity, and "in Jesus Christ, his only Son." There was not a bunch of divine beings around. Jesus was "the only Son, our Lord." "He was conceived by the Holy Spirit," not like the Ebionites, who said that he was naturally born. No, he was of the Holy Spirit. "He was born of the Virgin Mary." She was a virgin, etc. "He suffered under Pontius Pilate." This was against those who said that Christ didn't really suffer, because he only appeared to be human. These creeds, then, were formulated in opposition to heretical views that were being spurned by the creed, so that today, when people say these creeds, they probably don't even think about what they mean. Well, you have to understand what the opposition was to make sense of these affirmations.

To sum this all up, Christianity was unique in the ancient world for its emphasis on proper belief rather than cultic action. This stress on belief led to a heightened role of doctrine, and a "correct" understanding of the tenets of the religion. These came to be refined over time, especially in opposition to other perspectives that were believed to be aberrant. These refinements then led to highly paradoxical affirmations of faith. Nowhere is this development more interesting or historically significant than in the doctrine of the Trinity, which, as I said, we will be examining in greater detail in the next lecture.

Lecture Twenty-Three
The Doctrine of the Trinity

Scope: This lecture considers the most distinctive theological development of early Christianity, the doctrine of the Trinity—that God exists in three persons, who are all equal and distinct, but who nonetheless make up only one God. We will consider the roots of this view in the books of the New Testament (where the doctrine of the Trinity is never explicitly stated) and in proto-orthodox authors of the second century, who insist that Jesus is divine and that he is distinct from God the Father, but that there is nonetheless only one God. We will also consider some of the early proto-orthodox attempts to explain the mystery of the Trinity, attempts that later came to be branded as heretical (for example, that Jesus is God the Father himself come in the flesh), and see how opposition to these views by such writers as Hippolytus and Tertullian led to the classical formulation of one God in three persons.

Outline

I. In the previous lecture, we saw how Christian doctrine became a central component of the religion in its early years and came to be refined with the passing of time into a complex and highly paradoxical set of affirmations, embodied eventually in the Christian creeds.

II. No Christian doctrine is more distinctive or historically significant than the doctrine of the Trinity. Like other doctrines that became central to the faith, however, belief in the Trinity was a historical development, not a "given" from the early years of the faith.

   A. The basic notion of the Trinity is that there are three persons in the Godhead: Father, Son, and Holy Spirit. These three are all equally God and of the same substance, but despite the fact that there are three persons, together, they comprise only one God, indivisible in nature.

   B. This doctrine does not appear to be a doctrine pronounced by the historical Jesus, Paul, or any other Christian writer during the first hundred years or so of Christianity.

C. It cannot be found explicitly stated in the earliest Christian writings. The only passage of the New Testament that declares the doctrine (1 John 5:7–8) was not originally part of the text but was added by doctrinally astute scribes at a later date (it is not found in any Greek manuscript until the 11th century).

III. The easiest way to explain the emergence of the doctrine of the Trinity is to consider developments in the understanding of Christ in the early years of Christianity.

    A. Even though there were Christians who continued to insist that Jesus was human but not divine from the beginning, there were Christians who claimed that he was, in some sense, divine.

        1. This can be seen at the very earliest stage, in the writings of Paul, especially in one passage that he appears to be *quoting* from an earlier author, Phil. 2:6–11. This belief, then, was around even before our earliest Christian writings.

        2. Other books of the New Testament (for example, Matthew and Mark) consider Jesus to be the "Son" of God but do not appear to assert that this means he was himself divine. He was God's Son in the way the kings of Israel were God's sons—his representatives on Earth (cf. 2 Sam. 7:14).

        3. But some books near the end of the New Testament period become yet more explicit that Jesus was actually himself divine, for example, the Gospel of John (cf. 1:1–3; 8:58; 10:30; 20:31).

        4. Eventually, it became common to refer to Christ as God (e.g., Ignatius Eph. 1:1; 7:2).

        5. These early writers, however, never worked out the implications of how Jesus could be God if God was God (cf. the loose statement of Ignatius Eph. 18:2).

    B. It was also thought that the Spirit of God was, in some sense, distinct from God and from Jesus (cf. John 14).

IV. Various "solutions" to the problem of how Jesus and God could both be divine were suggested by different authors.

    A. Within proto-orthodox circles, the solution had to affirm monotheism, yet accept the deity of Christ.

B. One influential solution was put forth by one of the greatest Christian thinkers and scholars of the first three centuries of Christianity, Origen of Alexandria.

    1. Origen was a genius who was raised Christian in Alexandria and, as a teenager, was appointed to be head of the famed Alexandrian school for Christian catechesis.

    2. He was an inordinately prodigious author, with over 1,000 books to his credit.

    3. And he was a deep thinker, who tried to work out for the first time in a systematic way the mysteries of the Christian faith based on the revelation found in the Scriptures.

    4. He developed a complex Christological view that affirmed that Christ was both fully divine, yet one of God's creations. He began, in fact, like all humans, as a pre-existent soul who was created to contemplate God for eternity.

    5. Other souls failed to do so, however. Only this one soul remained completely focused on God in eternity past, so much so that it became "one" with God, just as iron placed in a fire takes on all the characteristics of the fire.

    6. This is the soul that became incarnate in Christ when God sent him into the world for salvation. Christ is, thus, equal with God and of the same substance, yet distinct and, ultimately, subordinate.

    7. This solution was both creative and influential. But it was eventually condemned by theologians, because it subordinated Christ to the Father.

C. Even more influential, if less astute, was the view adopted widely by the end of the second century—even by the bishops of Rome.

    1. The view goes under a number of labels: Sabellianism (named after one of its adherents); monarchialism (named for its thesis: that there is only one monarch); or, a mocking term invented by one of its chief opponents, Patripassianism (a view that "makes the Father suffer").

    2. This is the view that Jesus really was God—God the Father come to Earth.

    3. The view allowed there to be only one God and affirmed that Jesus was God.

    4. The view was attacked, though, by numerous proto-orthodox authors, especially Hippolytus and Tertullian, because it did not allow for the separate existence of God and Christ (see especially Tertullian's *Against Praxeas*, directed against a proponent of the view).

V. The opposition to Patripassianist Christology led Tertullian and others like him to develop language that later came to form the core of Trinitarian thinking.

    A. As Hippolytus puts it, "with respect to the power, God is one; but with respect to the economy [that is, to how this power expresses itself], the manifestation is triple" (*Refutation*, 8:2).

    B. In Tertullians's formulation, God is three in degree, not condition; in form, not substance; in aspect, not power (*Against Praxeas*, 2).

    C. This Trinitarian way of thinking itself became a matter of deep reflection, as theologians began to be obsessed with the question of how and in what way Christ could be both human and divine, completely both.

        1. Did he have a human soul but a divine spirit? Did he have a divine soul instead of a human soul? Was his body really like everyone else's body? How could God have a body? Was he subordinate to the Father, as in Origen? If he was not subordinate to the Father, why was *he* the one sent, rather than the other way around?

        2. Eventually, however, the terms were worked out and written into the creeds that have come down to us today, especially the Nicene Creed, as we examined in the previous lecture.

VI. In sum, the doctrine of the Trinity developed over several centuries of theological controversy; it arose with the view that Jesus himself must be divine, while there must be one and only one God. The Spirit, too, was recognized as divine, which more or less compelled orthodox thinkers to maintain that even though there is only one God, he is manifest in three different persons who are of the same nature but are distinct in number and function, the three in one.

Essential Reading:

Bart D. Ehrman, *After the New Testament*, chapter 14.

————, *Lost Christianities*, chapter 8.

William Rusch, *Trinitarian Controversies*.

Supplementary Reading:

Jeroslav Pelikan, *The Christian Tradition*, vol. 1.

Adolf von Harnack, *History of Dogma*, vol. 1.

Questions to Consider:

1. How do you imagine Christianity would have been different if the doctrine of the Trinity had never developed?

2. Do doctrines such as the Trinity have any practical relevance to the way people live (or have lived, over the centuries)?

Lecture Twenty-Three—Transcript
The Doctrine of the Trinity

In the previous lecture, we saw how Christian doctrine became a central component of the religion in its early years, and came to be refined with the passing of time into a complex and highly paradoxical set of affirmations, embodied eventually in the Christian creeds. No Christian doctrine is more distinctive or historically significant than the doctrine of the Trinity. Like other doctrines that became central to the faith, however, belief in the Trinity was a historical development, not a given from the early years of the faith.

The basic notion of the Trinity is that there are three persons in the Godhead: Father, Son, and Holy Spirit. These three are all equally God, and of the same substance. Despite the fact that there are three persons, though, together they comprise only one God, indivisible in nature. This doctrine of the Trinity, which has become a central doctrine of Christianity, does not appear to be a doctrine pronounced by the historical Jesus, Paul, or any other Christian writer during the first 100 years or so of Christianity. Even though this became a central doctrine, then, it was not there from the beginning. This is a clear indication of how doctrine is a matter of development, as people work out the nuances and implications of their faith.

The only passage in the New Testament that explicitly declares the doctrine is a passage from a disputed verse, 1 John, chapter 5, verse 7. This is a very interesting passage, because for years, it was used as the biblical support for the doctrine of the Trinity. I should say that I don't mean by that that the doctrine of the Trinity can't be found implicitly in some passages, for people who are trying to find it there, and I am not saying that theologians cannot appeal to Scripture in support of their understanding of the doctrine of Trinity. What I am saying is that the doctrine wherein there are three persons in the Godhead, and those three are one God, cannot be found explicitly stated in any passage of Scripture. The one passage that was the exception was 1 John, chapter 5, verse 7.

1 John is a letter that was written to a community that wasn't named. The author of this book himself was not named. We call it 1 John because historically it was thought that this book was written by the same author as wrote the Gospel of John, and that was thought to be John, the son of Zebedee. In fact, this letter is anonymous, and does not claim John as its author, but then again, the Gospel of John is anonymous as well, and does

not claim John as its author. Today, there are debates among New Testament scholars as to whether 1 John was written by the same author as the Gospel of John. They are very similar in a lot of ways, in terms of their vocabulary, their writing style, their overarching concerns. I would say, though, that the majority of scholars today think that the letter of 1 John was probably written by somebody within the same community as the person who wrote the Gospel of John, but probably was a different person.

In any event, the passage we are concerned with, 1 John, chapter 5, verse 7, reads in some English Bible translations as follows: "There are three that testify in heaven: The Father, the Word, and the Holy Spirit, and these three are one. And there are three that testify on Earth: The spirit, the water, and the blood. And these three agree."

This first bit of this—that there are three in heaven who testify, the Father, the Word, and the Spirit, and these three are one—is a doctrine of the Trinity, there, in the text. The difficulty is that even though that verse is found in English Bible translations for centuries, since the King James and before, in fact, one does not find that verse in the original Greek manuscripts of the book of 1 John.

Throughout the Middle Ages, of course, the Bible of choice was the Latin Vulgate. Ultimately, parts of the Vulgate were produced by the church father Jerome in the fourth century. Jerome translated the Greek Bible into Latin for use in Western Christianity, which, of course, had Latin as its language, rather than Greek. Scholars of the church used the Latin Vulgate for centuries, until the early part of the 16th century, when people again started realizing the importance of trying to get back to the original Greek of the New Testament in the Bible—the Old Testament, Hebrew; the New Testament, Greek. They started to construct Greek New Testaments based upon the surviving Greek manuscripts.

The first scholar to publish an edition of the Greek New Testament was a famous humanist scholar from Rotterdam named Erasmus. Erasmus was the first to publish a Greek New Testament based on surviving Greek manuscripts, and when he published his New Testament, his reading of 1 John, chapter 5, verse 7 was different from the traditional reading. The traditional reading found in the Latin Vulgate was this business that there were three that testify, the heavenly Father, the Word, and the Spirit, and that the three were one. The traditional Latin reading was the reading that included the Trinity.

When Erasmus published his Greek New Testament, however, it was worded differently. When he published his Greek New Testament, it said: "There are three that testify: The spirit, the water, and the blood, and these three agree." In other words, it took out the phrasing about the three: "The Father, the Word, and the Spirit, and these three are one." Erasmus did not include that in his Greek New Testament in 1 John, chapter 5, because he didn't know of any Greek manuscript that had that wording in the text. He suspected that when the Latin Vulgate had been produced, that verse had been inserted into the text by somebody who subscribed to the doctrine of the Trinity.

Well, this caused quite a furor in the early 16th century. His edition of the New Testament was published in 1516, and theologians of the church were quite incensed, because Erasmus had taken out the one verse that referred to the Trinity, and they thought that this was a heretical undertaking. They therefore attacked Erasmus for getting rid of the Trinity.

There's a story that may be apocryphal, or may be historically right, that Erasmus responded to his critics by saying that if they could produce a Greek manuscript that had these words in it, he would put them in his next edition of the Greek New Testament, and his opponents, in response, in fact did produce a Greek New Testament. In fact, they produced a Greek manuscript with these words in it, and true to his word, then, Erasmus inserted these words in his future edition of his New Testament, so that in the new Greek version, it had the words, that "there are three that bear witness in heaven, the Father, Word, and Spirit, and these three are one."

That was the edition of the Greek New Testament from Erasmus that the King James translators used to translate the Bible into English, so that these verses, then, are found in the King James version of the Bible, although in most modern translations, scholars have recognized that, in fact, these verses were not original to the text. They were inserted later by a scribe who believed in the Trinity.

Apart from that particular verse, there is no explicit reference to the Trinity in the New Testament. There are references, of course, to the Father, Son, and the Holy Spirit. For example, in the great commission, in Matthew, chapter 28, verses 19 and 20, Jesus has been raised from the dead, and he's giving a final commission to his disciples. He says, "Make disciples of all the nations, and baptize them in the names of the Father, the Son, and the Holy Spirit." He therefore uses all three words, but he doesn't state a doctrine of the Trinity, that these three are all God, that the Father is God;

the Spirit is God; the Son is God, and these three are one. There's no statement to that effect.

The earliest writings don't have this doctrine of the Trinity, and so later scholars who believed in the doctrine of the Trinity have had to plumb the Scriptures in order to find somewhere where it may be inferred that there are three people, all of whom constitute one God. Three persons, one God.

Why did this doctrine emerge in the first place if it wasn't explicitly stated by the apostolic writings of the New Testament? The easiest way to explain the emergence of the doctrine of the Trinity is to consider the developments of the understanding of Christ in the early years of Christianity, understanding the views of Christ that developed over time.

Even though there were Christians who continued to insist that Jesus was human but not divine (as, for example, the Ebionites did), from the beginning, there were Christians who claimed that in some way or other, Jesus himself was divine. This happened very early in the formation of early theology. In fact, we can see it at the earliest stage of all in the writings of the apostle Paul. It is striking that in one of the passages of Paul, in which he appeared to be quoting an earlier source, we have a reference to Christ himself being divine.

This is a famous text from Paul's letter to the Philippians, chapter 2, verses 6 and following. I say that Paul, here, appeared to be quoting an earlier source. Many scholars think that Philippians, chapter 2, verses 6 through 11, were originally some kind of hymn or creed written about Christ that Paul quoted in this context. In many Bibles, including the one I am using here, these verses are actually put into poetic form, on the assumption that this must have been some kind of hymn that was sung to Christ, based on the way the wording is:

> Let the same mind be in you that was in Christ Jesus,
>
> who, although he was in the form of God, did not regard equality with God as something to
>
> be exploited,
>
> but he emptied himself, taking the form of a slave, being born in human likeness.

This seems to be referring to the incarnation of Jesus that, prior to becoming a human, was in the form of God, but he did not regard equality with God as something to be exploited, but he emptied himself to take the form of a slave.

This is a very early writing from early Christianity, probably produced in the early 50s of the Common Era, perhaps 20 or 25 years after Jesus's death. If Paul was quoting an earlier text here, that would mean that whoever composed this hymn thought of Jesus himself, as, in some sense, God. How could Jesus be God, though, if God is God, and there is only one God?

There are other books of the New Testament that consider Jesus to be the Son of God, but to not appear to think that Jesus himself was divine. For example, in the Gospel of Mark, Jesus is baptized, and a voice comes from heaven: "You are my beloved Son, in whom I am well pleased." Well, there it sounds like Jesus is the Son of God. If he's the Son of God, doesn't that make him a God? The son of a dog is a dog, and the son of the cat is a cat, so isn't the Son of God a God?

You might think so, but not in the biblical tradition. In the biblical tradition, the Son of God is not himself somebody who is divine. You might think of the Old Testament, for example. In a number of passages, there are references to people who are called "the Son of God." In no instance are these people, themselves, God.

For example, in the book of 1 Samuel [sic 2 Samuel], chapter 7, verse 14, God is talking to King David, and he is told that David is going to have a son, who is going to be king, and will sit on the throne: "And I will be a Father to him, and he will be my son," God said. The son of God is the son of David. Who is that? That's Solomon. 1 Samuel [sic 2 Samuel], chapter 7, verse 14. The king, King Solomon, the wisest man ever to have lived, is called "the son of God."

In the Gospels, when Jesus is called the Son of God, it appears to be a reference to this kind of idea that Jesus was chosen by God just as Solomon had been. And as a human who was chosen by God, he was in a special relationship with God, and therefore, to that extent, he was the son of God, but that did not make him God. The Philippians passage, however, seems to indicate that Jesus was, in some sense, divine prior to coming to Earth.

There are also other books that support that point of view in the New Testament, especially the Gospel of John, the Gospel of John that begins: "In the beginning was the Word, and the Word was with God, and the Word was God.

"The Word was God"? Who was the Word? Later on, we find out: "The Word became flesh, and dwelt among us, and we have beheld his glory as the only begotten before the Father."

"The Word became flesh." Who is the Word that became flesh? Jesus. Jesus was God's Word that became a human being in the Gospel of John. This Word that became Jesus was in existence with God from the very beginning, and in fact, was himself God. That's why in the Gospel of John, Jesus could say things such as: "I and the Father are one." At the end of the Gospel, Thomas could see Jesus and proclaim: "My Lord and my God."

Jesus, in some sense, was portrayed as divine in the Gospel of John, just as he was portrayed, in some sense, as divine, in the book of Philippians.

Eventually, after the New Testament period, it became quite common to refer to Jesus as himself being God. For example, in the writings of Ignatius, which we have considered on several occasions, Ignatius sometimes talked about Jesus as being divine himself. We have seen his letter to the Ephesians, chapter 7, verse 2. He talked about Jesus being the "one physician of flesh, yet spiritual born, yet unbegotten, God incarnate, that Christ is God himself in the flesh."

Somewhat earlier in Ignatius's letter to the Ephesians, he tells the Ephesians: "You are imitators of God, and it was God's blood that stirred you up once more to do the sort of thing you do naturally, and have now done to perfection."

"God's blood"? What was he referring to? He was referring to the death of Jesus. Since Jesus was himself divine, his blood was the blood of God.

Moreover, not only was Jesus thought of as, in some sense, divine, there was also the business of the Holy Spirit, who is referred to throughout scripture in various places, sometimes talked about as the "spirit of God." Jesus himself talked about the spirit that is coming into the world, that will be the new comforter, to replace him, Jesus, as the previous comforter, and in some sense, performing the same function that Jesus himself fulfilled among God's people.

We have Jesus, who was portrayed as divine, the spirit of God, who was being portrayed as divine, and yet, you have only one God. How can you have one God, and yet, have three persons in one God? Why don't you have three Gods?

There are various solutions to this problem. I should emphasize that Christians themselves were insistent that there could only be one God. Christians differentiated themselves from various pagans precisely by the fact that they were monotheists, who knew quite well, from the Jewish Bible, that there was only one God. God the Father was the God. There was no other God. Yet, they were calling Jesus "God," and the spirit "God." How could this be?

There were a number of attempts early on to try and solve this problem. You don't find any attempts to solve the problem within the New Testament. Why not? My guess is that the New Testament authors simply either didn't realize that was a problem, or they had other things on their minds before they wanted to solve the problem of the divine mystery of how Jesus and God could both be God if there were only one God.

As time went on, however, people started to think more and more about it. Within the proto-orthodox circles, the solution to the problem had to continue to affirm monotheism. Proto-orthodox Christians insisted on remaining monotheistic, and yet, at the same time, they needed a solution that would explain the deity of Christ himself, as to how Christ himself could be divine, and then ultimately, the deity of the Holy Spirit as well. How did it work?

Well, there were a number of solutions, as I pointed out. I want to talk about one particularly important solution that ended up not making it, a solution that at the time was considered to be perfectly acceptable, and orthodox, but that with the passage of time, came to be condemned as heretical. That's one of the interesting features of Christian theology; as time passed on, solutions that at one time appeared to be completely orthodox, and later times, appeared to be heresies.

The solution I want to talk about was a solution given by one of the most brilliant authors of early Christianity, and arguably the greatest genius of the first three centuries of Christendom, a person named Origen, from the city of Alexandria, Egypt.

Origen was a very interesting figure. He was a wunderkind as a young child, quite a child prodigy in the church of Alexandria, an intellectual genius. As a teenager, just in his teens, he was appointed to be a head of the famous Alexandrian Christian school, which was a kind of school of higher learning for Christians in the city of Alexandria. Origen was broadly trained in the classics and in literature, and applied his massive intellect to problems of Christian theology.

He was an inordinately prodigious author who allegedly wrote somewhat over 1,000 books. How can somebody write over 1,000 books? Origen could do it because he had a patron who recognized his intellectual genius and provided him with all the tools needed in order to crank out the publications. Origen would have had no trouble in our current climate of "publish or perish." He did have unusual help, though. This patron was a man in Alexandria named Ambrose. Ambrose provided him with a whole array of secretaries. There were people who took down his worded dictation, and another crew who were calligraphers, who prepared his writings for publication. Then, they would copy and distribute them, so that all he had to do was dictate his brilliant thoughts, and somebody else would write them down and ready them for publication. There were other people with the same resources, though, who didn't write 1,000 books. He was quite an amazing fellow.

Origen was not somebody who thought lightly about things. In fact, he was an incredibly deep thinker, who was trying for the first time in a systematic way to work out the mysteries of the Christian faith based upon the revelation found in the Scriptures, and so, he was a scriptural theologian who used the Scriptures to try to understand the things the Scriptures might imply, but not spell out, including some understanding of how Christ could be God, and God could be God, yet, there only being one God.

Origen developed a complex Christological view, a complex view of Christ that affirmed that Christ was fully divine, and yet, since God the Father was the creator of all, Christ was one of God's creations. How could he be one of God's creations, if he himself was fully divine? Origen worked out a way for that to have happened.

Origen maintained that Christ began, as did all humans, and all beings, whether human beings, angels, or demons, every spiritual being, as a pre-existent disembodied mind that God had created. God, in the eternity past, created a whole array of minds, and everybody, all of these spirits, were created in order to contemplate God forever. Everybody, all of these pre-existent minds, these disembodied minds, were created in order to contemplate God. Some of them decided to rebel against God. They had free will, and could do that. They did so, including the devil and his demons, who fell from the divine realm.

Others simply could not sustain contemplation of God for eternity, and they also fell and became human beings, souls in human bodies. They are here in the world in order to be trained so that they can once again return to their heavenly home to contemplate God. There was only one mind that stayed affixed to God permanently. This one mind was so wrapped up in its contemplation of God, so fixed on God himself, that this one became one with God, just as when you take a piece of iron, and put the piece of iron in the fire. If you leave it there long enough, the piece of iron will become so hot it will assume all the characteristics of the fire that it is put into.

So, too, with this soul. It was fixed on God, contemplating God, and so wrapped up in its contemplation of God that it took on all of the characteristics of God, so much so that when you saw this soul, you would see God.

This soul is the soul that became incarnate in Christ when God sent him into the world for salvation. Christ is thus equal with God, and of the same substance as God, because he fused, became one with God, and yet he is distinct from God, because he was a mind, that at some point in the past, was created, and ultimately, then, Christ is subordinate to God. Thus, Christ is both divine and separate from God, yet, there is only one God, and Jesus is the same as that God.

This solution was both creative and influential, but it was eventually condemned by theologians, because ultimately, it subordinated Christ to the Father. Even though Christ is one with God in the system, ultimately, Christ is subordinate to the Father, because the Father is the one who is God, Christ is just kind of borrowing his divinity from God. Thus, this was eventually condemned as a heresy, and Origen himself was condemned as a heretic in the fifth century, because of this doctrine and his idea that ultimately, all things will return to God, even the devil, because, as Origen believed, God was ultimately sovereign, and God would ultimately manifest as a sovereignty over the Earth. That meant that everything would have to confess God in the end, including even the devil. Some people didn't like that, and they declared Origen a heretic.

Even more influential, if less astute, were the views adopted widely by the end of the second century, even by some of the bishops of Rome. This other view is not nearly as sophisticated as Origen's, in the early third century, and goes under a number of labels. Sometimes it is called Sabellianism, named after one of its adherents, a guy named Sabellius. It is also called modalism, or monarchialism; its thesis is that there is only one monarch, and is therefore called monarchialism. This is the view the Jesus himself really was God, that Jesus was God the Father, who came to the Earth for the salvation of the world, that Jesus and God are one, because Jesus really was God the Father here on Earth, so that God in heaven was God the Father, and Jesus on Earth was God on Earth. Only one God appears in three modes of existence: The Father, Son, and Spirit, three modes of existence. That's why it is sometimes called modalism, with three modes of existence, but only one God. Just as I can be a father, son, and brother all at the same time, God can also be Father, Son, and Spirit at the same time, according to this view.

This was a very popular view, because it allowed for there to only be one God, and allowed Jesus to be God, even though Jesus was God and God was God. Even though it made sense to a lot of people, though, it came to be attacked, especially by prominent proto-orthodox authors like Hippolytus in Rome, we have looked at, and Tertullian. It came under attack by people such as Tertullian because it didn't allow for the separate existence of both God and Christ. Opponents would ask, "Why is it that Scripture says that God sent his Son, instead of saying that God sent himself, if Jesus and God the Father were the same person?"

How can the same person be his own father and his own son at one and the same time? To whom is Jesus talking when he prays? Is he talking to himself? How can Jesus talk about going to his Father, if he is the Father? Is it really conceivable that God the Father was killed, that he was crucified?

This last issue became a rallying point for the opponents of this Sabellian view, or this modalist view. The opponents accused the supporters of this view of thinking that the Father had suffered, and so coined the term "Patripassionist" for those who held this perspective; "Patripassionism" meaning a view that God the Father, "Pater," suffered, "passion," or "passionist."

It was especially in opposition to the Patripassionist Christology that Tertullian, Hippolytus, and others began to develop language that came to form the core of Trinitarian thinking. As Hippolytus put it: "With respect to the power of God as one, with respect to the economy," (that is, how the power manifests itself) "the manifestation is triple; three persons, one God." Or, as Tertullian put it: "God is three in degree, not condition. He is three in form, not substance. He is three in aspect, not power." Obviously, these people are using very nuanced terms to try and explain themselves.

This Trinitarian way of thinking itself became a matter of deep reflection, as theologians began to be obsessed with the question of how, and in what way, Christ could be both human and divine. How did it work? Did Jesus have a human soul, but a divine spirit? Did he have a divine soul instead of a human soul? Did he really have a body like everybody else, or was he somehow subordinated to God the Father? If he was not subordinate, why was he sent instead of God the Father? People had to work out the implications for these various views. They eventually did work them out, and these became manifest in the various creeds that have come down to us, the Nicene Creed, for example, as we looked at in the previous lecture.

To sum this up, the doctrine of the Trinity developed over several centuries of theological controversy. It arose with the view that Jesus himself must have been divine, while there must be one and only one God. The Spirit, too, was recognized as divine, which more or less compelled orthodox thinkers to maintain that even though there was only one God, he was manifest in three different persons who were of the same nature, of the same substance, but distinct in number and function: the three in one. That's the doctrine of the Trinity.

Lecture Twenty-Four
Christianity and the Conquest of Empire

Scope: This concluding lecture brings together the various strands we
have explored throughout the course and considers the character of
Christianity at the beginning of the fourth century. We will return
here to the conversion of the Roman emperor Constantine and
discuss the significance of this conversion for the fortunes of later
Christianity. As we know, it moved from being a persecuted
minority to having "most favored status" among the religions of
the empire, leading to massive conversions and, eventually, to
Christianity's status as the official religion of the state. These
developments had enormous consequences for the history of
Western civilization, as the Christian church was then positioned
to become the dominant religious, political, social, cultural, and
economic institution of Europe and the New World.

Outline

I. Throughout these lectures, we have traced significant developments in
    Christianity from the days of Jesus in the first century A.D. to the
    conversion of Constantine in the early fourth. As we come now to the
    conclusion of our course, I would like to take stock of where we are.

    A. By the early fourth century, Christianity had almost completely
        separated off from Judaism, the religion of Jesus and his apostles.
        1. Although it started as a sect within Judaism, it was widely
            rejected among Jews and soon became a separate religion that
            went on the counterattack against its Jewish opponents.
        2. By the second century, Christians had already begun to adopt
            harshly anti-Judaic rhetoric, accusing Jews of misinterpreting
            their own Scriptures, rejecting their own Messiah, spurning
            their own God; Jews were considered Christ-killers and a
            people fallen from grace.
        3. This anti-Judaic polemic was heightened by the need felt by
            Christians to embrace the Jewish Scriptures as their own to
            establish the credibility of their religion as ancient in a world
            that valued antiquity. To claim the Scriptures, however, meant
            taking them from the Jews.

B. By the early fourth century, non-Jewish Christianity had become a major world religion.

    1. Already by the middle of the first century, missionaries, such as Paul, had spread the religion to major urban areas of the Mediterranean.

    2. Growth was steady over the years, affected through conversions of family members, friends, and neighbors of converts. It appears to have grown at about the rate of 40 percent every decade.

    3. Its missionary effectiveness was facilitated by its exclusivistic claims: Those who joined this religion had to reject their previous one (this was not the case for other religions in the empire, except for Judaism, which was not, by and large, a missionary religion). This means that Christianity destroyed other religions while advancing its own.

    4. By the early fourth century, possibly five to seven percent of the population of the empire was Christian.

C. By the early fourth century, Christianity had a long history of local and official opposition, persecution, and martyrdom.

    1. In the vast majority of cases, the persecutions were sporadic and local, instigated by mobs offended by the Christian refusal to worship the gods and by reports of flagrant immorality.

    2. There were several instances, however, in which emperors had become involved in persecution (Nero, Marcus Aurelius, Decius).

D. By the early fourth century, Christianity had undergone significant theological development.

    1. There had been numerous theological controversies over God, Christ, the material world, salvation, and many other issues.

    2. Most of the major "heresies" of earlier days, however, had been effectively suppressed by the fourth century (Ebionites, Marcionites, Gnostics).

    3. Christianity had, by this time, developed a core of sacred Scriptures (even if the canon was not fixed in final form), a church hierarchy, set liturgical practices, and important creedal statements, including a widespread belief that Jesus was somehow both God and man and the concomitant acceptance of some notion of the Trinity, the details of which would be worked out by theologians of the fourth and fifth centuries.

II. Despite all this impressive progress, a good case can be made that it was the conversion of Constantine himself that proved to be the single most important event of Christianity's first 300 years, a climactic moment on the one hand and the beginning of something entirely new on the other.

A. Constantine's conversion was one of the most significant events in all of Western civilization.

1. Had it not happened, the vast majority of Christians throughout history (there are some two billion today, the largest world religion) would have remained pagan.

2. As a result, the history of Western civilization that we know through the Middle Ages, to the Renaissance, the Reformation, and into modern times would never have occurred.

3. If Constantine had not converted, neither would have the Roman Empire. And that would have changed everything.

B. No 10-year period was more important for the fortunes of Christianity than 303–313 C.E.

1. In 303 C.E., the pagan emperor of the eastern part of the empire, Diocletian, ordered a persecution of Christians, matched to some degree by a persecution in the western part of the empire by his colleague, the emperor Maximian.

2. Several imperial edicts were issued that called for the burning of Christian books, the demolition of Christian churches, the removal of class privileges for Christians, and eventually, the imprisonment of high-ranking Christian clergy.

3. In 304, a further edict required all Roman subjects to perform sacrifices to the gods; noncompliance meant death or forced labor.

4. This "Great Persecution," as it is called, lasted on and off for nearly a decade, well beyond the retirement of Diocletian and Maximian in 305 C.E.

5. But the persecution failed to force the majority of Christians to recant.

6. For a variety of reasons, official toleration for Christians was pronounced in both the western and eastern parts of the

empire by 313. People throughout the empire were granted freedom of religious choice and the property of the Christians was restored.

C. The senior emperor at that time was Constantine.

    1. In 312, Constantine had begun to attribute his military and political ascendancy to the God of the Christians and to identify himself, as a result, as a Christian.

    2. Once his base of power was secure, Constantine became quite active in church affairs, dealing with various controversies in an attempt to keep the church united. Some historians think that Constantine saw the Christian church, with its belief in *one* God, as a way to bring unity to the empire itself.

    3. In 325 C.E., Constantine called the Council of Nicea—the first so-called "ecumenical council" of the church, that is, the first council at which bishops from around the world were brought together to establish a consensus on major points of faith and practice.

    4. All these bishops agreed with the major theological positions hammered out by their proto-orthodox forebears. The council devised a creed that became the heart of what we today call the Nicene Creed.

D. As a result of the favors Constantine poured out on the church, conversion to the Christian faith soon became popular.

    1. By the end of the century, it appears to have been the religion of choice of fully half the empire.

    2. After Constantine, every emperor except one was Christian.

    3. Near the end of the fourth century, Theodosius I (emperor, 379–395 C.E.) made Christianity (specifically Roman Christianity, with the bishop of Rome having ultimate religious authority) the official religion of the state, opposed the surviving pagan religions, and eventually banned pagan sacrificial practices.

    4. More conversions naturally followed, until Christianity became *the* religion to be handed down to the Middle Ages and onward.

E. None of this would have happened without Constantine's "conversion."

1. In some ways, then, this conversion made Christianity the most powerful religious, historical, cultural, social, economic, and political force in the history of Western civilization, destined to change billions of lives.
2. And it continues to change and affect lives in our own day, not just in the West but in places as far flung as Eastern Europe, Korea, South America, and developing countries, in fact, throughout the world.
3. This is a far cry from its small and insignificant beginnings in the teachings of a lower-class Jewish peasant in a remote corner of the Roman world. Maybe this religion is best seen as a mustard, the smallest of all seeds, but when placed in the ground, an enormous bush grows so that the birds of the air can make nests in its branches.

Essential Reading:

James Carroll, *The Sword of Constantine*.

Bart D. Ehrman, *Lost Christianities*, chapter 13.

Robin Lane Fox, *Pagans and Christians*.

Supplementary Reading:

Ramsay MacMullen, *Christianizing the Roman Empire*.

Rodney Stark, *The Rise of Christianity*.

Questions to Consider:

1. In your judgment, if Constantine had not converted, is it possible that Christianity still would have taken over the empire?
2. What would be different about our lives if the majority of people in the West were not Christian (either by profession or heritage) but pagan?

Lecture Twenty-Four
Christianity and the Conquest of Empire

Throughout these lectures, we have traced significant developments in Christianity from the days of Jesus in the first century A.D., to the conversion of Constantine in the early fourth century. As we come now to the conclusion of our course, I would like to take stock of where we are.

By the early fourth century, Christianity had almost completely separated off from Judaism, the religion of Jesus and his apostles. Although it started out as a sect of Judaism, with Jesus himself and then his disciples, it was so widely rejected among Jews that it soon became a separate religion that went on counterattack against its Jewish opponents. Nonetheless, we should remember and keep firmly in our minds that Christianity started off as Jewish. Jesus himself was Jewish. His disciples understood him to be the Jewish Messiah, sent from the Jewish God to the Jewish people in fulfillment of the Jewish Law.

Since most non-Christian Jews could not see Jesus as the Messiah, though—the Messiah who was to be a great and powerful figure, who was to lead Israel to victory over its enemies, or the Messiah as a great cosmic figure sent to overthrow the forces of evil—since Jesus obviously was not that sort of person, most Jews rejected Jesus. Since they rejected Jesus as the Messiah, and Christians accepted Jesus as the Messiah, there came a natural split. This led to antagonism and animosity.

By the second Christian century, Christians had already begun to adopt partially anti-Jewish rhetoric, accusing Jews of misinterpreting their own scriptures, of rejecting their own Messiah, of spurning their own God. Jews were considered and called "Christ killers" and "a people fallen from grace." You may remember the heightened rhetoric of Melito of Sardis, who wrote his Easter homily directed against Jews, asking why they had killed the one who had called them, asking why they had killed their own God, accusing them of deicide.

This anti-Judaic polemic was heightened by the need felt by Christians to embrace the Jewish Scriptures as their own, to establish the credibility of their own religion, the Christian religion, as ancient in a world that valued antiquity. You may, therefore, recall the Epistle of Barnabas, where Barnabas maintained that in fact the Old Testament was not a Jewish book at all, even though it is the Jewish Scriptures, the Hebrew Scriptures—not for Barnabas—for Barnabas, the Old Testament was in fact a Christian book, not a Jewish book.

Why did Barnabas claim this? For the same reason other Christians were claiming the Old Testament. Because if they didn't have the Old Testament, they couldn't claim antiquity for their religion, and without antiquity, they had no standing in the ancient world (there, any new development in philosophy or religion was immediately suspect). Christians, then, had to claim the ancient Scriptures as their own, and they did so by pointing to the prophecies in the Scriptures, prophecies that looked forward to Christ, so that Christ, according to the Christians, was anticipated in the Jewish Scriptures.

Claiming the Jewish Scriptures as their own, however, meant that Christians had to take these Scriptures away from the Jews, and this led to heightened tensions between non-Christian Jews and Christians who were either Jew or Gentile. By the early fourth century, then, Christianity had almost completely separated off from Judaism, even though it began as a Jewish sect.

By the early fourth century, non-Jewish Christianity had become a world religion. Already by the middle of the first century, missionaries such as Paul had spread the religion to major urban areas of the Mediterranean. The religion started off as quite small, simply the followers of Jesus following his crucifixion and the reports of his Resurrection in Jerusalem.

It's hard to know how many people started out believing in Jesus. According to the Book of Acts, there were perhaps 20 or so, or up to 120, who were the initial believers. Soon, though, other people converted to believe that Jesus was the Messiah. Paul himself converted on the basis of the vision of Jesus that he had after Jesus's death. Even though Paul started out as a persecutor of the Christian church, he soon became its leading apostle.

Other people converted as well, and several people besides Paul became missionaries to places around the Mediterranean. The reason for going to the urban areas is obvious. Even though Jesus himself started out as a rural preacher, a rural prophet going to small villages and towns, the early Christians want to convert as many people as they could as quickly as possible, because the end was coming soon, and so there was an urgency in the mission of Paul and others.

It's difficult to know how many people were converted in these early decades and centuries, but it does appear that there was a steady growth rate over the years, as conversions were affected among family members, friends, and neighbors of other converts. It appears that this religion was spread by word of mouth through the networking of people who were associated with one another. It appears to have grown at about the rate of 40 percent every decade. In other words, every ten years, the Christians seemed to have grown by 40 percent in number.

The missionary effectiveness of this religion was facilitated significantly by a unique characteristic of Christianity, namely, that Christians made exclusivistic claims for themselves. They claimed that their religion was right and every other religion was wrong. In order to join this religion, one had to reject one's previous religious attachments; so that if one was a pagan, one had to stop worshiping whichever gods s/he had worshipped previously, had to reject the knowledge of these other gods, and believe that there was only one God worthy of worship, the God of the Jews, whose Son, Jesus, had come and died for the sins of the world.

Since Christians were exclusivistic, claiming that they alone were right and all the others were wrong, it meant that any time a pagan converted to Christianity, paganism lost one of its members, so that Christianity destroyed other religions in its wake. This was completely unlike any other religion in the empire. If there was a new religion that started up, that of course, claimed to be old, in some city or town, if a new temple to Zeus sprang up, and people decided that they wanted to worship in the temple, anyone who decided that they wanted to worship Zeus in the new temple would not have had to give up being pagan in order to worship this god for the first time. Pagans never lost pagans when people converted to a different form of religion, because nobody completely converted by giving up their other religion.

Not so with Christianity. Because of its exclusivistic claims, Christianity destroyed religions as it increased its own. By the early fourth century, possibly five to seven percent of the population of the empire was Christian, so that from beginnings of 25 to 100 followers of Jesus, within 300 years it had grown to a religion that had three to four million people following it. By the early fourth century, then, non-Jewish Christianity and Christianity itself had become a major world religion.

By the early fourth century, Christianity had a long history of local and official opposition, persecution, and martyrdom. In the vast majority of cases, the persecutions were sporadic and local, instigated by mobs who were offended by Christians' refusal to worship the gods, and by reports of flagrant immorality. We have seen this in the Martyrdom of Polycarp, one of our early martyrological texts that we have looked at at some length.

It appears in the Martyrdom of Polycarp, and in these other martyrological texts, that it was not the Roman officials who instigated persecution against the Christians. Instead, it was the mobs. Why would mobs fear the Christians? We have seen that in part it was because people expected that the gods would reward those who honored them through the sacrifices in their temples, and through other acts of worship, but the gods were to be feared. When they were ignored, they would bring catastrophe upon the people, and so when there were floods, famine, disasters, or pestilence, the reason for these was because the gods had been offended.

Why were they offended? Because people were not worshipping them in the proper way. What people did not worship the gods? The Christians. Therefore, when disasters hit, Christians had to look out, because persecution could be right around the corner. We saw this in Polycarp, and in our other texts.

There were several instances, however, in which we saw that emperors had become involved in persecution, the first of which was the emperor Nero. He persecuted the Christians not for being Christian, but because they were being accused of arson, for burning the city of Rome. It appears that in this particular case, Nero himself was responsible for the burning of Rome, so that Christians were not actually being persecuted for being Christian so much as they were scapegoats for Nero himself.

There were later emperors, though, who were directly involved in the persecution of Christians on rare occasions, including Marcus Aurelius, an otherwise good emperor who in the 170s, apparently authorized the persecution of the Christians in Lyons and Vienne, in Gaul.

It was not until the mid-third century, however, that any emperor was actively involved in trying to wipe out Christianity, and that was the persecution under the emperor Decius, who in the year 249, required every person in the empire to perform a sacrifice to the pagan gods, so as to guarantee that the gods would be worshipped in the proper way, and thereby weed out the Christians, who of course refused to perform the sacrifices. For the most part, however, up until the beginning of the fourth century, persecutions were sporadic and local, caused at the grass-roots level, rather than because of the emperors.

By the early fourth century, Christianity had undergone significant theological developments, as we have seen. There had been numerous theological controversies over God, Christ, Scripture, the material world, salvation, and many other issues. Most of the major heresies of the earlier days of

Christianity, however, such as the Ebionites, Marcionites, Gnostics, and most other heresies had been effectively suppressed by the fourth century.

During their own time, in the early second century and throughout the second century, each of these heresies had a large following. In some parts of early Christianity, if we go along with the views of Walter Bauer, these alternative views were, in fact, the majority, and possibly the original form of Christianity, perhaps in Egypt, or possibly in Syria, for example. Eventually, however, all of these other forms of Christianity were wiped out, until the proto-orthodox had established a majority hold on Christianity, could claim itself as orthodox, and then, through people such as Eusebius, could rewrite the history of the engagements between the heresies and the orthodoxies.

As proto-orthodoxy developed into orthodoxy, and as it triumphed over other forms of the religion, it developed into traditional forms of Christianity that we are familiar with today. This kind of traditional Christianity that emerged from proto-orthodoxy included a kind of religion that had a core of sacred Scriptures, even if the canon was not fully fixed yet. By the time of the fourth century, most Christians were proto-orthodox and understood a kind of core of Scriptures that were canonical, the canon coming to be fixed, then, in later years.

This traditional form of Christianity had an organized church hierarchy, where each church had a bishop and a group of presbyters or elders, and some deacons. Churches in larger urban areas, such as Antioch or Rome, had bishops who were bishops over churches throughout the area. Moreover, this traditional form of Christianity had set liturgical practices, including worship services and the practices of baptism and Eucharist.

Moreover, and possibly most importantly, this traditional form of Christianity embodied important credal statements, including a widespread belief that Jesus was somehow both God and man, and the concomitant acceptance of some notion of the Trinity, the details of which were going to be worked out by theologians of the fourth and fifth centuries. Nonetheless, by the fourth century, most Christians who were coming out of the proto-orthodox tradition maintained that there was a Trinity of some kind, three persons who comprised one God. By the early fourth century, then, Christianity had undergone a significant and important theological development.

Despite all of this impressive progress from the days of Jesus and his apostles to the beginning of the fourth century, a good case can be made that it was the conversion of Constantine, in the early fourth century, that proved to be the single most important event of Christianity's first 300 years, a climactic moment on the one hand, and the beginning of something entirely new on the other.

Constantine's conversion, by all accounts, was one of the most significant events in all of Western civilization. Had it not happened, had Constantine not converted to Christianity, the vast majority of Christians throughout history—there are some two billion in the world today—may well have remained pagan. We, ourselves, had Constantine not converted, can well imagine that the majority of people living in the West today, would still be pagan, had Constantine not converted.

As a result, obviously, the history of Western civilization itself, through the Middle Ages, to the Renaissance, to the Protestant Reformation, and on into modern times, would never have occurred, or if they had occurred, would have been radically different from the way they did occur, if, in fact, Constantine had not converted. If Constantine had not converted, neither would have the Roman Empire, and that would have changed everything. It isn't possible to overstate the importance of the Roman emperor, in the early fourth century, converting to worship Christ, and the God of Jesus Christ, instead of worshiping the pagan gods.

I think it's safe to say that there is no 10-year period that is more important for the fortunes of Christianity than the years 303 to 313 A.D. There was no 10-year period that was more important for the fate of Christianity, and for the fate of our world as we know it.

In 303 A.D., the pagan emperor of the eastern part of the empire—by this time, the empire was split into an eastern part, and a western part of the Roman Empire—was named Diocletian. In the year 303 A.D., Diocletian ordered the persecution of Christians. This was the first really major persecution since Decius, in the year 249 (this was 50 years later). Diocletian ordered a persecution of Christians that was matched, to some degree, by a persecution in the western part of the empire by his colleague, his co-emperor, Maximian.

There were several imperial edicts, sent out from the emperor, that were issued, and that called for the burning of Christian books, the demolition of Christian churches, the removal of class privileges for Christians, and eventually, the imprisonment of high-ranking Christian clergy. You can see that the emperors were going for the jugular. They were after the things that made Christianity Christianity, that made the Christian church possible. Burning Christian books meant burning books that Christians considered to be Scripture, burning canonical books. If you didn't have these canonical books, how were you supposed to know God's will? The emperors knew what these books were all about, and so they tried to burn them.

Some people have argued, by the way, that the burning of books under Diocletian was one of the things that motivated Christians to decide on which books should actually be part of the canon, because of the Roman soldiers came knocking on your door, and they said, "We want your sacred authorities," you may have had to decide which books you were going to hand over, and which ones you would not. You may have been willing to hand over The Shepherd of Hermas, but would you really want to hand over the Gospel of John? You would therefore have had to decide which ones of those were canonical authorities. It's a theory that some people pronounce, that the persecution of Diocletian, and the burning of the books, in fact, helped finalize the Christian canon.

They were demolishing Christian churches, so the people had no place to worship except in the home. In removing the class privileges of Christians and imprisoning high-ranking Christian clergy, of course, this also cut back on the possibilities of Christians who were no longer high-ranking, and their own clergy were no longer available for advice and exhortation, etc.

In 304, a further edict required all Roman subjects to perform sacrifices to the gods. Everybody in the empire had to perform the sacrifice. Refusal to comply, to perform the sacrifice, meant death or forced labor in the salt mines, etc. This meant that there was quite an incentive to perform the sacrifice, even if it was in bad faith.

This persecution started in 303-304, and sometimes is called the "Great Persecution." This is because it was the most systematic attempt to wipe out Christianity in the ancient world. The persecution lasted on and off for nearly a decade. Diocletian and Maximian, as co-emperors, actually retired from their imperial posts in the year 305, so that they were only around for the first two years of the persecution, but it went on for another eight years.

Even though it was implemented to be a systematic persecution, it was not systematically enforced, and as it turns out, this persecution failed to lead to Christians recanting throughout the empire. In other words, there were a lot of Christians who simply refused to recant. For a variety of reasons, official toleration for Christians was pronounced in both the western and eastern parts of the empire by 313, ten years later. This was a famous instance called the Edict of Milan, which was an edict that rescinded the orders of persecution.

The Edict of Milan was put out by the two co-emperors, Constantine and Licinius. Constantine, by this time, was associating with Christianity. Licinius was his co-emperor. They published an edict in the city of Milan in the year 313, which allowed people to follow whatever religion they wanted to follow. This, in effect, was granting freedom of worship to the Christians, so that people throughout the empire, east and west, were granted freedom of religious choice. Additionally, the property of the Christians that had previously been confiscated was restored.

Constantine was the senior of the two emperors, and as I have pointed out, his conversion is usually dated to 312, the year prior to the publication of the Edict of Milan. I have talked about his conversion in a previous lecture. We have several accounts of Constantine's conversion, and it is difficult to know historically what actually happened.

Eusebius, the church historian writing in the fourth century, claimed to have gotten the account of the conversion directly from Constantine himself, who apparently claimed that prior to going to battle against an opposing general of the Roman armies (there was a kind of civil war going on that Constantine was involved with before he was the emperor, and he was nervous about this coming battle), he realized that he needed divine help in order to win this battle, and he had a vision in the daytime of a cross in the sky that had the words "By this conquer" on it, meaning, as he found out later by a dream interpreter, that the cross would be the way to victory.

That night, disturbed by the vision, he went to sleep, and had a vision of Christ himself, who told him what he had to do in order to have victory. He put this sign of the cross, which included the first two letters of the name "Christ" in Greek, the chi-rho (XP) on the cross. So there is a cross with a XP through it, and he put this on the shields of his warriors, and became the symbol of the battle he was to fight. As it turned out, he won the battle and attributed his victory to Christ. From that point on, he began to worship Christ.

There are disputes about the authenticity of Constantine's conversion. People have pointed out that even after this time, Constantine minted some coins in which the sun god was placed, and so some people think that he continued to maintain the pagan worship of the sun. People have also pointed out that Constantine was not baptized until he was on his deathbed, so that maybe he was not fully committed to Christianity.

Some people think that Constantine was actually using Christianity as a way to unite his empire, that Christianity, with its exclusivistic claims and belief in one God would be quite useful for an emperor who wanted to have one empire under one God, so that this was more of a political move than a religious conversion. Other people think that it was, in fact, a genuine conversion, and that it simply had a positive political payoff.

Either way, it became clear that once his base of power was secure following these civil wars, Constantine became quite active in church affairs. He wasn't somebody who just wanted to appeal to Christianity. He wanted to be actively involved in Christianity, and he dealt with various controversies within Christianity in order to help keep the church united. That, of course, would make sense if the church was having theological disputes and was not unified itself. It is obviously not a very good unifying force for the empire.

Most particularly, in the year 325, Constantine called Council of Nicea. It was called the Council of Nicea because it met in the city of Nicaea. This was the first ecumenical council of the church, that is, the first council where the bishops from major cities around the world were brought together in order to establish a consensus on major points of faith and practice. The Council of Nicea in 325 was a very important time, in part because this was the council out of which the creed emerged that was eventually called the Nicene Creed.

The immediate reason for the council was that there was a particular controversy concerning Christ. A theologian from Alexandria named Arius maintained that Christ was divine, and he maintained something like the doctrine of the Trinity, but he thought that Christ was a subordinate God who had been created, that God the Father originally existed by himself, but he created Christ as a divine being in eternity past, so that Christ was subordinate to God. He was of a similar nature to God, but he was not himself fully divine. He was subordinate to God.

The Council of Nicea was called together to debate this issue, and at Nicaea it was decided that, in fact, this was a heresy, that Christ was not subordinate to God, but that Christ was equal with God even though he wasn't identical. From this came the doctrine of the Trinity that we referred to in the previous lecture.

Constantine called this council, got the bishops to agree to a certain Christological point of view, hoping for the unity of the church, because the unity of the church depended on the unity of the empire.

From the time of his conversion, Constantine poured out numerous favors on the church, and as a result, conversion to Christianity became popular. By the end of the fourth century, it appears that Christianity was the religion of choice of fully half the empire. And as I pointed out earlier, every emperor after Constantine except for one, his nephew Julian, was a Christian, and Julian only ruled for a few years.

Near the end of the fourth century, Theodosius I, who was emperor from 379 to 395, made Christianity, specifically Roman Christianity, with the bishop of Rome having the ultimate religious authority, the official religion of the state. Moreover, Theodosius was quite straightforward in opposing the surviving pagan religions, he eventually banned pagan sacrificial practices. Naturally, more conversions followed until Christianity became the religion to be handed down through the Middle Ages and onward.

None of this would have happened without Constantine's conversion. In some ways, then, it was this conversion that made Christianity most powerful religious, cultural, historical, social, economic, and political force in the history of Western civilization, destined to change billions of lives, and it continues to change and affect lives in our own day, not just in the West, but in places as far-flung and Eastern Europe, Korea, South America, and developing countries, in fact, throughout the world.

This is a far cry from its small and insignificant beginnings in the teachings of a lower-class Jewish peasant in a remote corner of the Roman world. Maybe the beginnings of this religion in the first century, though, are best seen as a mustard seed, the smallest of all seeds, says Jesus, but when placed in the ground, an enormous bush grows, so that the birds of the air can make nests in its branches.

The seed was planted during the days of Jesus, and from there it grew in small fits and starts. Over the decades, though, it slowly started putting forth its branches. By the end of the third century, it had grown into a sizable bush. With the conversion of Constantine, it experienced an unexpected growth spurt, so that by the end of the fourth century, it was set to take over the world of its day, and to determine the course of Western civilization and history, down to modern times, when it still exercises enormous influence over us all. Thank you.

Timeline

333–323 B.C. .... Conquests of Alexander the Great.

63 B.C. .... Conquest of Palestine by the Romans.

44 B.C. .... Assassination of Julius Caesar.

40–4 B.C. .... Herod, king of the Jews.

27 B.C.–A.D. 14 .... Octavian Caesar Augustus as emperor.

4 B.C.? .... Jesus's birth.

A.D. 14–37 .... Emperor Tiberius.

A.D. 26–36 .... Pilate as Governor of Judea.

A.D. 30? .... Jesus's death.

A.D. 33? .... Conversion of Paul.

A.D. 37–41 .... Emperor Caligula.

A.D. 41–54 .... Emperor Claudius.

A.D. 54–68 .... Emperor Nero.

A.D. 50–60 .... Pauline Epistles.

A.D. 50?–110 .... Ignatius of Antioch.

A.D. 62–113 .... Pliny the Younger.

A.D. 65? .... Gospel of Mark.

A.D. 66–70 .... Jewish Revolt and destruction of the Temple.

A.D. 69–79 .... Emperor Vaspasian.

A.D. 70–156 .... Polycarp of Smyrna.

A.D. 79–81 .... Emperor Titus.

A.D. 80–85? .... Gospels of Matthew and Luke, Book of Acts.

A.D. 81–96 .... Emperor Domitian.

A.D. 90–95? .... Gospel of John.

A.D. 95? .... Book of Revelation.

A.D. 98–117 .... Emperor Trajan.

A.D. 100–160 .... Justin Martyr.

A.D. 100–160? .... Marcion.

A.D. 110–130? .... Gospels of Peter and Thomas.

A.D. 130–200 .... Irenaeus.

A.D. 135? .... Epistle of Barnabas.

A.D. 150–? .... Clement of Alexandria.

A.D. 160–225 .... Tertullian.

A.D. 170–? .... Hippolytus of Rome.

A.D. 185–251 .... Origen of Alexandria.

d. A.D. 190 .... Melito of Sardis.

d. A.D. 203 .... Perpetua.

A.D. 249–251 .... Emperor Decius.

A.D. 260–340 .... Eusebius.

A.D. 284–305 .... Emperor Diocletian.

A.D. 285–337 .... Constantine (emperor, 306–337).

A.D. 300–375 .... Athanasius.

A.D. 303–312 .... The "Great Persecution."

A.D. 312? .... "Conversion" of Constantine.

A.D. 315–403 .... Epiphanius.

A.D. 325 .... Council of Nicea.

A.D. 346–395 .... Theodosius I (emperor, 379–395).

Glossary

3 Corinthians: Part of the apocryphal Acts of John, a letter allegedly by Paul to the Corinthians warning against *docetic* teachers and emphasizing that Jesus was a real flesh-and-blood human being and that there could be a future resurrection of the body.

adoptionism: The view that Jesus was not divine but was a flesh-and-blood human being who had been adopted by God to be his Son at his baptism

Alexander the Great: The great military leader of Macedonia (356–323 B.C.) whose armies conquered much of the lands around the Mediterranean, including Egypt, Palestine, and Persia, and who was responsible for the spread of Greek culture (Hellenism) throughout the lands he conquered.

apocalypticism: A worldview held by many ancient Jews and Christians that maintained that the present age is controlled by forces of evil, but that these will be destroyed at the end of time, when God intervenes in history to bring in his Kingdom, an event thought to be imminent.

apologists: Group of second- and third-century Christian intellectuals who wrote treatises defending Christianity against charges leveled against it.

apology: Literally, "defense"; used as a technical term for a reasoned defense of the faith against its opponents.

apostle: From a Greek word meaning "one who is sent." In early Christianity, the term designated emissaries of the faith who were special representatives of Christ. See **disciple**.

Apostles' Creed: An orthodox creed that affirms the essential elements of the faith; based on a creed that was formulated in Rome, probably sometime in the third century.

autograph: The original manuscript of a document, from a Greek word that means "the writing itself."

canon: From a Greek word that literally means "ruler" or "straight edge." The term is used to designate a recognized collection of texts; the New Testament canon is, thus, the collection of books that Christians have traditionally accepted as authoritative.

cult: A reference to any ritualistic practices meant to honor God or the gods.

Didymus Judas Thomas: The alleged author of the Coptic Gospel of Thomas, whose exploits are narrated in the Acts of Thomas; in these traditions, he is said to be the twin brother of Jesus.

docetism: The view that Jesus was not a human being but only "appeared" to be; from a Greek word that means "to seem" or "to appear."

Ebionites: A group of second-century adoptionists who maintained Jewish practices and Jewish forms of worship.

Epistle of Barnabas: Letter (falsely) attributed to Paul's companion Barnabas, which attempts to show the superiority of Christianity to Judaism, arguing that the Old Testament is a Christian, rather than a Jewish, book.

Gentiles: Designation for non-Jews.

Gnosticism: A group of ancient religions, closely related to Christianity, that maintained that sparks of a divine being had become entrapped in the present, evil world and could escape only by acquiring the appropriate secret *gnosis* (Greek for "knowledge") of who they were and of how they could escape. This *gnosis* was generally thought to have been brought by an emissary descended from the divine realm.

Gospel of Peter: A Gospel mentioned by Eusebius as containing a docetic Christology, a fragment of which was discovered in a monk's tomb in 1886; the fragment contains an alternative account of Jesus's trial, Crucifixion, and Resurrection, notable for its anti-Jewish emphases and its legendary qualities (including a tale of Jesus actually emerging from his tomb on Easter morning).

Gospel of Thomas: The most famous document of the Nag Hammadi library; it contains 114 sayings of Jesus, many of them similar to the sayings of the New Testament, others of them quite different, in that they appear to presuppose a Gnostic understanding of the world.

Greco-Roman world: The lands around the Mediterranean from roughly the time of Alexander the Great (c. 300 B.C.) to the time of the Roman emperor Constantine (c. A.D. 300).

heresiologist: An opponent of heresy; one who engages in literary polemics against heretical groups.

heresy: Any worldview or set of beliefs deemed by those in power to be deviant; from a Greek word that means "choice" (because "heretics" have "chosen" to deviate from the "truth"; see **orthodoxy**).

liturgy: From the Greek word for "service," used to refer to any communal act of worship, including, for Christianity, the rituals of baptism and the Eucharist.

manuscript: Any handwritten copy of a literary text.

Marcionites: Followers of Marcion, the second-century Christian scholar and evangelist, later labeled a heretic for his docetic Christology and his belief in two Gods, the harsh legalistic God of the Jews and the merciful loving God of Jesus—views that he claimed to have found in the writings of Paul.

Melito of Sardis: Bishop of a city in Asia Minor in the mid-second century; author of a Passover homily that accuses Jews of the death of Jesus.

Nag Hammadi: Village in Upper (South) Egypt, near the place where a collection of Gnostic writings, including the Gospel of Thomas, was discovered in 1945.

Nicea, Council of : The first major council of bishops from around the Christian world, called by the emperor Constantine in 325 C.E. in the city of Nicea. The council was to resolve theological disputes in the church, especially in light of Arianism; at its conclusion, the council issued a creed that eventually developed into the Nicene Creed.

Nicene Creed: Creed that developed out of the Council of Nicea, which affirms that Jesus is "of the same substance" as the Father, while being a distinct being from him.

orthodoxy: Literally, "right opinion"; a term used to designate a worldview or set of beliefs acknowledged to be true by the majority of those in power. For its opposite, see **heresy**.

paganism: Any of the polytheistic religions of the Greco-Roman world; an umbrella term for ancient Mediterranean religions other than Judaism and Christianity.

patripassianism: View of the relationship of God and Christ, widespread in the second century, in which Christ was God the Father himself, become flesh. The designation was invented by Tertullian as a term of derogation, meaning "those who make the Father suffer." Also known as Sabellianism, after a prominent advocate of the view.

patristic writings: Writings of the orthodox church fathers (Latin: *patres*), starting with the period after the New Testament.

Proto-orthodox Christianity: A form of Christianity endorsed by some Christians of the second and third centuries (including the Apostolic Fathers), which promoted doctrines that were declared "orthodox" by the victorious Christian party in the fourth and later centuries, in opposition to such groups as the Ebionites, the Marcionites, and the Gnostics.

pseudepigrapha: Literally, "false writings"; commonly used of ancient non-canonical Jewish and Christian literary texts, many of which were written pseudonymously.

pseudonymity: The practice of writing under a "false name," evident in a large number of pagan, Jewish, and Christian writings from antiquity.

Roman Empire: All the lands (including Palestine) that had been conquered by Rome and were ruled, ultimately, by the Roman emperor, starting with Caesar Augustus in 27 B.C. Before Augustus, Rome was a republic, ruled by the Senate.

sabellianism: See **patripassianism**.

Secret Book of John: Also known as the Apocryphon of John, one of the Gnostic books discovered among the Nag Hammadi library, in which John, the son of Zebeddee, is shown the secrets of how the divine realm, the material world, and humans came into being.

trinity: Key doctrine of orthodox Christianity, which maintained that the godhead consists of three persons, Father, Son, and Holy Spirit, who are all equally God, even though there is only one God.

Biographical Notes

Athanasius: Athanasius was a highly influential and controversial bishop of Alexandria throughout the middle half of the fourth century. Born around 300 A.D., he was active in the large and powerful Alexandrian church already as a young man, appointed as deacon to the then bishop Alexander. He served as secretary at the important Council of Nicea in 325 C.E., which attempted to resolve critical issues concerning the nature of Christ as fully divine, of the same substance as God the Father, and co-eternal with the Father.

As bishop of Alexandria from 328 to 375, Athanasius was a staunch defender of the Nicene understanding of Christ and a key player in the development of the orthodox doctrine of the Trinity, in which there were three distinct persons (Father, Son, and Spirit) who were nonetheless one God, all of the same substance. This defense created enormous difficulties for Athanasius in the face of powerful opposition, to which he reacted with a show of force (even violence). He was sent into exile on several occasions during his bishopric, spending nearly 16 years away from Alexandria while trying to serve as its bishop.

Author of numerous surviving works, Athanasius is also significant for his role in determining which books should be accepted in his churches as sacred scripture. In 367 A.D., in his 39th annual "Festal Letter," which like all the others, set the date for the celebration of Easter and included pastoral instruction, he indicated that the 27 books that we now have in the New Testament, and only those 27, should be regarded as canonical. This decree helped define the shape of the canon for all time and helped lead to the declaration of other books, such as the Gnostic Gospels and the like, as heretical.

Athenagoras: Not much is known about the second-century Christian apologist Athenagoras, because he is scarcely mentioned in the writings of other church fathers. The few references to him that survive indicate that he was a Greek philosopher who lived in Athens. His best known work is his "Apology ['Defense'] of Christianity," addressed to the emperors Marcus Aurelius and Commodus, probably written in 177 C.E. In it, Athenagoras defends Christians against charges of atheism and crass immorality involving incestuous orgies and ritual cannibalism and tries to demonstrate the superiority of the Christian faith to all others. Among his notable contributions to Christian theology is his indication that Christians worship three, who are: God the Father, Son, and Holy Spirit. Eventually, such reflections led to the formation of the classical doctrine of the Trinity.

Barnabas: We are not well informed about the historical Barnabas. He is mentioned both by the apostle Paul (Gal. 2:13; 1 Cor. 9:6) and the Book of Acts (Acts 9:27; 11:22–26) as one of Paul's traveling companions. It appears that he was originally a Hellenistic Jew who converted to faith in Christ, then became, like Paul, a traveling missionary who spread the faith. The Book of Acts goes so far as to consider him one of the apostles (Acts 14:4, 14).

The Epistle of Barnabas discussed in this course is attributed to him, but modern scholars are reasonably sure that he could not have written it. The book appears to have been written some time around 130 or 135 A.D., some 60 years or so after the historical Barnabas would have died. The book was attributed to him, then, by Christians who wanted to advance its authoritative claims as being rooted in the views of one of the most important figures from the early years of Christianity.

Walter Bauer: Walter Bauer was an influential German theological scholar, whose scholarly work made a permanent impact on the field of early Christian studies. Born in 1877, he had university positions at Marburg, Breslau, and finally, Göttingen, where he spent the majority of his long career. He died in 1960.

Bauer is probably most well known for a Greek *lexicon* ("dictionary") of the New Testament and other early Christian writings that he edited and, after further revision, is still the standard work in the field and is called by his name. For this course, he is most important for his classic book *Orthodoxy and Heresy in Earliest Christianity*, in which he set out to dismantle the classical, Eusebian understanding of the relationship of orthodoxy and heresy. Looking at an enormous range of ancient sources and subjecting them to careful and minute analysis, sometimes with inquisitorial zeal, Bauer maintained that orthodoxy was *not* always the oldest and largest form of Christianity. Instead, what later came to be called heresy was, in many regions of Christendom, the oldest form of the faith and that, in many places, it was difficult to draw hard lines between what was heretical and what was orthodox. In his view, what later came to be crystallized into orthodoxy was the form of Christianity prominent in the early years in Rome; because of its administrative skill and material wealth, the Roman church was able to cast its influence onto other churches of the Mediterranean, until eventually, its understanding of the faith became universal. Once this version of Christianity became dominant, its representatives (such as Eusebius) rewrote the history of the disputes, contending that their perspective had been dominant from the beginning.

Clement of Alexandria: Clement is a shadowy figure from the early days of the Alexandrian church. Born probably around 150 A.D., possibly in Athens, he appears to have come to Alexandria, Egypt, to pursue his theological training with leading Christian thinkers of his day. Tradition indicates that while there, he became the head of the catechetical school (which provided rudimentary training in the faith for Christian converts), but he fled Alexandria in 202 A.D. during a persecution there.

Clement is the author of several surviving works, including an important apology for Christianity, a book on Christian living and manners, and a book called the *Miscellanies*, which sketches out some of his most important philosophical and theological views.

Constantine the Great: Constantine was the first emperor, some three centuries after the birth of Jesus, to accept Christianity, to bring to an end its persecution, and to begin to bestow favors on the church that ultimately led to its triumph over the pagan religions of Rome. Born in 285 A.D., Constantine was, by the early fourth century, one of Rome's principal generals and became involved in a complicated set of power struggles over the ultimate rulership of Rome. According to his own account, delivered to Eusebius, the father of church history and Constantine's biographer, when Constantine marched against his rival Maxentius in Rome in 312, he had a vision of the cross and the words "in this, conquer." He took this as a divine sign and, having successfully overcome his opponent in battle, began openly to favor the Christian religion.

His real commitment to Christianity is open to question, because he continued to evidence devotion to pagan deities, as well. But he certainly brought an end to persecutions and, once he had consolidated his power, bestowed numerous benefits on the church that made it clearly advantageous for others among the empire's upper classes to convert. From being a small minority of possibly five to eight percent of the empire's population at the beginning of the fourth century (demographic numbers are nearly impossible to reach with any certainty), by the end of the century, Christians made up nearly half the populace and the faith became the "official" religion of the state—in large part as a result of Constantine's conversion. Constantine died in 337, after receiving baptism on his deathbed.

Epiphanius: Epiphanius was the bishop of Salamis (on Cyprus) in the second half of the fourth century (315–403 A.D.). Known as a rigorous supporter of monasticism, he is most famous for his virulent attack on anything that struck him as heretical. His best preserved work is called the *Panarion*, which means "medicine chest." In it, he intends to provide the orthodox antidote for the bites of the serpents of heresy.

The book contains detailed accounts (some of them fabricated) and refutations of 80 different heresies that Epiphanius had come across during his ardent search for falsehood in the church (20 of the heresies are actually pre-Christian sets of false teaching). For some of the lesser known Gnostic groups, Epiphanius is our principle source of information; unfortunately, given his lack of intellectual restraint, many of his claims appear to be unreliable.

Eusebius: Eusebius of Caesarea is one of the most important figures in the history of the early church. Born around 260 A.D., he was trained by some of the leading Christian scholars of his time and was to become the first author to produce a full history of Christianity up to his own day, in a book called the *Ecclesiastical (or Church) History*. Eusebius was quite active in the politics of the church and empire; ordained bishop of the large and important church of Caesarea in 315, he was active at the Council of Nicea and the theological disputes in its aftermath, originally opposing but later accepting the creedal statements about Christ that were to become orthodox. He died around 340 A.D.

Eusebius was a prolific writer, but it was his *Ecclesiastical History* in particular that made a huge impact on subsequent generations—down to our own day. This chronological sketch of early Christianity provides us with the majority of our information about the spread of Christianity throughout the Roman world, the persecution of the early Christians, the conflicts between what Eusebius considered to be orthodoxy and heresies, the development of church offices and structures, and so on. Of particular value in this 10-volume work is Eusebius's frequent citation, often lengthy, of his actual sources; through his account, then, we have access to the writings of his Christian predecessors that otherwise have been lost to history. Thus, even though Eusebius puts his own slant on the history that he tells, it is possible to use the sources that he cites to gain significant insight into the conflicts and developments that transpired in the Christian church of the first three centuries up to his own day.

Hippolytus: Hippolytus was a controversial figure in the Roman church in the early third century, best known today for his 10-volume work against heresies (the second and third volumes of which are lost). Born around 170 A.D., Hippolytus became a prominent figure in the church in Rome, often taking strong stands against movements within the church that he considered heretical. In fact, he is the first known *anti-pope*, that is, one who allowed himself to be elected as the true pope on the grounds that the reigning pope (in this case, a man named Callistus; pope from 217–222) was a heretic (holding a Sabellianist Christology that equated Jesus and God the Father) and had no right to claim the papal office. Probably because of his schismatic activities (and partly because he wrote in Greek, rather than Latin), Hippolytus was largely forgotten in the Western church until modern times, when some of his writings were discovered.

The most important writings are (a) the *Refutation of All Heresies*, which explains the various heresies of the Christian church and tries to show how each of them is rooted, not in the Christian revelation, but in secular (and, therefore, erroneous) philosophical traditions, and (b) the *Apostolic Traditions*, which describes and prescribes the ecclesiastical structure and liturgical practices of the church in Rome at the beginning of the third century.

Ignatius: Ignatius is one of the most interesting figures from the early second century. We know little of his life, except that he was bishop of the major church in Antioch, Syria; was arrested for Christian activities; and was sent to Rome under armed guard to face execution by being thrown to the wild beasts in the Roman arena. En route to his martyrdom, Ignatius wrote seven surviving letters to churches that had sent representatives to greet him. In these letters, he warns against false teachers, urges the churches to strive for unity, stresses the need for the churches to adhere to the teachings and policies of the one bishop residing over each of them, and emphasizes that he is eager to face his violent death so that he might be a true disciple of Christ.

One of the letters that he wrote was to the bishop of the city of Smyrna, Polycarp, who may have been the one who collected the other letters together. Within a couple of centuries, Christian authors forged other letters allegedly by Ignatius; throughout the Middle Ages, these forgeries were circulated with the authentic letters and were not recognized for what they were until scholars undertook an assiduous examination of them in the 17th century.

Irenaeus: Irenaeus was an important theologian and heresiologist of the late second century. Born probably around 130 A.D., he may have been raised in the city of Smyrna and educated, eventually, at Rome. He ended up in the Christian church of Lyon, Gaul (modern-day France), where he was made bishop around 178 A.D. He died around the year 200 A.D.

Irenaeus is our best patristic source for the Gnostic sects of the second century. His well-known book is a five-volume attack on heresy, which he entitled *Refutation and Overthrow of What Is Falsely Called Gnosis*, frequently called simply *Against Heresies*. In it, he gives considerable detail concerning various heretical groups (not simply Gnostics) and, based on his understanding of Scripture and using a full panoply of rhetorical ploys and stratagems, refutes them one by one. This book was used as a source for many of the later heresiologists, including Tertullian and Epiphanius.

Jesus: We do not know when Jesus was born, but if it was during the reign of King Herod of Israel, as recorded in the Gospels of Matthew and Luke, then it must have been sometime before 4 B.C., the date of Herod's death. Jesus was raised in a Jewish home in the small village of Nazareth in Galilee, the northern part of what is now Israel. As an adult, he engaged in an itinerant preaching ministry in largely rural areas of Galilee; there is no record of him visiting any large cities until his fateful journey to Jerusalem at the end of his life. His message was comparable to that found in the prophets of the Hebrew Bible: The people of Israel must repent or they will be faced with judgment. Jesus, however, gave this message an apocalyptic twist, as did many other religious Jews of his day. The coming judgment would be of cosmic proportions and brought by an emissary from heaven, the Son of Man, who would overthrow the forces of evil and establish God's Kingdom on Earth. When this happened, there would be a serious reversal of fortunes: Those in power now would be destroyed, and those who suffered and were oppressed would be exalted. People needed to prepare for this historical cataclysm by turning back to God and keeping his Law, especially as interpreted by Jesus himself.

Despite Jesus's reputation as a healer and exorcist, he was not viewed favorably by Jewish leaders. At the end of his life, he came to Jerusalem during a Passover feast, caused a disturbance in the Temple, and raised the ire and fears of the ruling party, the Sadducees, who were intent on keeping the peace and avoiding any riots during such tumultuous times. They had Jesus arrested and turned him over to the Roman governor, Pontius Pilate, who ordered him crucified as a troublemaker. Scholars dispute the precise year of his death, but it must have been some time around 30 A.D.

Justin Martyr: Justin was an important figure in the mid-second–century church of Rome. Born of pagan parents (c. 100 A.D.), evidently in Samaria, he undertook secular philosophical training before converting to Christianity when he was about 30. He began to teach the philosophical superiority of Christianity to secular learning, first in Ephesus, then in Rome, where he established a kind of Christian philosophical school in mid-century.

Justin is the first prominent Christian *apologist*, that is, one who defended the Christian faith against the charges of its cultured (pagan) despisers and strove to show its intellectual and moral superiority to anything that the pagan (or Jewish) world could offer. Three of his major works survive, usually known as his *First Apology* (a defense of Christianity addressed to Emperor Antoninus Pius and his sons, including Marcus Aurelius, around 155 A.D.), his *Second Apology* (addressed to the Roman Senate around 160 A.D.), and his *Dialogue with Trypho*, an account of his conversion and subsequent debate with a (possibly fictitious) Jewish rabbi, Trypho, over the superiority of Christianity to Judaism, based largely on an exposition of key passages in the Old Testament.

Justin's defense of Christianity led to political opposition; he was martyred on charges of being a Christian around 165 C.E.

Marcion: Marcion was one of the most infamous "heretics" of the second century. Tradition indicates that he was born and raised in Sinope, on the southern shore of the Black Sea, where as a young man, he acquired considerable wealth as a shipping merchant. His father was allegedly the bishop of the Christian church there, who excommunicated his son for his false teachings. In 139 A.D., Marcion went to Rome, where he spent five years developing his theological views, before presenting them to a specially called council of the church leaders. Rather than accepting Marcion's understanding of the gospel, however, the church expelled him for false teaching. Marcion then journeyed into Asia Minor, where he proved remarkably successful in converting others to his understanding of the Christian message. *Marcionite* churches were in existence for centuries after his death, which took place around 160 A.D.

Marcion's understanding of the gospel was rooted in his interpretation of the writings of the apostle Paul, whose differentiation between the "Law" (of the Old Testament) and the "Gospel" (of Christ) Marcion took to an extreme, claiming that the old and new were fundamentally different, so much so that they represented the religions of different Gods. Marcion, in other words, was a *ditheist*, who thought that the Old Testament God—who had created the world, called Israel to be his people, and gave them his Law—was a different god from the God of Jesus, who came into the world in the "appearance" of human flesh (because he was not actually part of the material world of the creator-God) to save people from the just but wrathful God of the Jews. Marcion's views were based on his canon of Scripture—the first canon known to be formally advanced by a Christian—which did not, obviously, contain anything from the Old Testament, but comprised a form of the Gospel of Luke and 10 of Paul's letters (all those currently in the New Testament except 1 and 2 Timothy and Titus).

Melito of Sardis: Little is known of the life of Melito, apart from the facts that he was bishop of the city of Sardis near the end of the second century (died around 190 A.D.); that, at some point in his life, he made a pilgrimage to the Christian sites of the holy land; and that he was a staunch advocate of proto-orthodox Christianity. The one literary work of his to survive, discovered in the 20th century, is a homily apparently delivered at an Easter celebration, in which Melito explicates the Old Testament account of the Passover in a way that shows that the Passover Lamb represents Christ. In Melito's view, because Christ has fulfilled the foreshadowings and predictions of the Jewish Scriptures, the laws of the Jews are no longer in force. The old has passed away with the appearance of the new.

In the course of this highly rhetorical exposition, Melito takes the occasion to lambaste the people of Israel for rejecting their own Messiah, and his language at times is vitriolic in its anti-Judaic claims. This sermon represents the first known instance of a Christian charging the Jewish people with *deicide*, "the murder of god."

Origen: Origen was the most brilliant and prolific Christian author of the first three centuries. A lengthy account of his life is provided by Eusebius, in Book 6 of his *Ecclesiastical History*. Born in 185 A.D. in Alexandria, Egypt, of Christian parents, Origen was trained by some of the leading scholars of his day. Tradition claims that after a severe persecution in Alexandria in 202 A.D., in which his father was martyred, the highly precocious Origen was appointed to be head of the catechetical school, which trained Christian converts in the rudiments of the faith. But he periodically came into conflict with the bishop of the Alexandrian church, named Demetrius, and eventually (in 230 A.D.), left Alexandria to settle in Caesarea, where he devoted himself to teaching, research, and writing. He was imprisoned during the persecution of the Roman emperor Decius in 250 A.D. and died two years later as a result of prolonged torture.

Origen's literary output was immense, aided by a literary patron, Ambrose, who provided him with extensive secretarial help (stenographers, copyists, and so on). He is thought to have produced nearly 2,000 volumes, including biblical commentaries, volumes of homilies, theological treatises, polemical tractates (against heresies), apologies, and practical and pastoral works. Most of his works are lost, but those that survive still fill many volumes. As a theologian, Origen developed many ideas that later became highly debated in disputes over the Trinity, the person of Christ, and the nature of the soul; as a biblical scholar, he developed and refined methods of interpretation—including the extensive use of figurative modes of exegesis—that proved highly influential in interpretive methods used down through the Middle Ages.

Paul: Paul was a Hellenistic Jew born and raised outside of Palestine. We do not know when he was born, but it was probably sometime during the first decade A.D. Through his own letters and the encomiastic account found in the Book of Acts, we can learn something of his history. He was raised as a strict Pharisaic Jew and prided himself on his scrupulous religiosity. At some point in his early adulthood, he learned of the Christians and their proclamation of the crucified man Jesus as the Messiah; incensed by this claim, Paul began a rigorous campaign of persecution against the Christians, only to be converted himself to faith in Jesus through some kind of visionary experience.

Paul then became an ardent proponent of the faith and its best known missionary. He saw his call as a missionary to the Gentiles and worked in major urban areas in the regions of Asia Minor, Macedonia, and Achaia to establish churches through the conversion of former pagans. A distinctive aspect of his message was that all people, Jew and Gentile, are made right with God through Jesus's death and Resurrection and by no other means; the practical payoff was that Gentiles did not need to become Jewish in order to be among the people of the Jewish God—in particular, the men did not need to become circumcised.

We know about Paul principally through the letters that he wrote to his churches when problems arose that he wanted to address. There are seven letters in the New Testament that indisputably come from his hand; six others claim him as an author, but there are reasons to doubt these claims. According to the Book of Acts, Paul was eventually arrested for socially disruptive behavior and sent to Rome to face trial. An early tradition outside of the New Testament indicates that Paul was martyred there, in Rome, during the reign of the emperor Nero, in A.D. 64.

Perpetua: Perpetua was a martyr during the persecutions in Carthage, North Africa, in 203 C.E. She was a young Roman matron, mother of an infant, and daughter of a pagan father who attempted to have her recant of her Christian faith at her trial. His efforts were spurned by his daughter, who insisted on paying the ultimate price for her faith.

We know about Perpetua's sufferings and imprisonment, because she kept a diary after her arrest. Among the many fascinating features of the record are her accounts of four dreams, two of which concerned a younger (non-Christian) brother who had died of cancer and was in the place of punishment before her prayers brought his release, and two others that anticipate her own death in the arena.

The narrative of her martyrdom itself was added in another hand; it describes in graphic detail the events surrounding the hunting games in the arena in which she and her Christian companions, including her slave Felicitas, were killed by wild beasts.

Polycarp: Polycarp was the bishop of Smyrna, in Asia Minor, for most of the first half of the second century. Born around 70 C.E., he was martyred as a Christian in 156 C.E.; the account of his arrest, trial, and execution (by being burned at the stake) are preserved for us in a firsthand report written in a letter by fellow Christians in Smyrna. This is the first detailed account of a martyrdom outside the New Testament to survive from ancient Christianity.

Some 45 years before his death, Polycarp had received a letter from Ignatius of Antioch, which still survives; Ignatius indicates that he had stayed in Smyrna en route to his own martyrdom in Rome and had come to know and respect the bishop there. In addition, we have a letter (or more likely, two letters, later spliced together) written by Polycarp himself to the Christians of Philippi, addressing ethical and theological issues that had arisen in their church.

Although not an original thinker, Polycarp was one of the most well known and important proto-orthodox leaders of the early and mid-second century. Later legend indicates that he had once been a companion of the apostle John and later became the teacher of Irenaeus; the latter claim may be accurate, but there appears to be little credible evidence for the former.

Tertullian: Tertullian, from Carthage (North Africa), was one of the most influential authors of early Christianity. Much of his life is shrouded in obscurity, but it appears that he was born into a relatively affluent family of pagans around 160 A.D. and received extensive training in (pagan) literature and rhetoric. He converted to Christianity some time in his mid-30s, then became an outspoken, even vitriolic, proponent of the Christian faith, writing numerous works defending the faith against its cultured despisers (*apologies*), scathing criticisms of heretics and their beliefs, and severe tractates concerning Christian morality. At some point in his life, he joined a group of schismatics known to history as the Montanists (named after their founder, Montanus), an ethically rigorous, ascetic group that anticipated the imminent end of the world as we know it.

A bitter opponent of both Gnostics and Marcionites, Tertullian is one of our best sources of information concerning what these groups, especially the latter, believed. His five-volume attack on Marcion, for example, still survives and is our principal means of access to Marcion's life and teaching.

Theodosius I: Theodosius "the Great" was Roman emperor during the turbulent years of 379–395. Although active as a military leader, he is most important for this course for the role he played in the Christian church. In 380, he published an edict declaring that the "true" understanding of the faith was to be that promulgated by the bishop of Rome; the following year, he called a church council (the Council of Constantinople) that condemned competing understandings of the faith (*Arianism*, which disputed the understanding of the Creed of Nicea that Christ was "of the same substance" as the Father). Theodosius eventually published legislation that made pagan cultic practices illegal. In effect, then, it was under the reign of Theodosius and as a result of the assertion of his authority that Christianity became the "official" state religion of Rome.

Bibliography

Bauer, Walter. *Orthodoxy and Heresy in Earliest Christianity*. Tr. Robert Kraft, et. al., ed. Robert Kraft and Gerhard Krodel. Philadelphia: Fortress, 1971. One of the most important books of the 20th century on the history of early Christianity. Bauer argues against the classical understanding of orthodoxy and heresy by maintaining that what was later called *heresy* was, in many regions of early Christendom, the oldest and largest form of Christian belief.

Blackman, E. C. *Marcion and His Influence*. London: S.P.C.K., 1948. A clear and useful study of the life and teachings of the second-century philosopher-theologian Marcion and the impact he made on early Christianity.

Bradshaw, Paul. *The Search for the Origins of Christian Worship: Sources and Methods for the Study of Early Liturgy*. 2nd ed. Oxford/New York: Oxford University Press, 2002. One of the most thorough studies of the original forms of Christian liturgy available.

Bruce, F. F. *The Canon of Scripture*. Downers Grove, IL: Intervarsity Press, 1988. An overview of the formation of the Christian Bible, both "Old" and New Testaments, by a classically trained British scholar.

Burtchaell, James. *From Synagogue to Church: Public Services and Offices in the Earliest Christian Communities*. Cambridge: Cambridge University Press, 1992. A useful study of the development of Christian church offices from their roots in the Jewish synagogue.

Carroll, John. *Constantine's Sword: The Church and the Jews. A History*. Boston: Houghton Mifflin, 2001. A terrific and widely popular account of Jewish-Christian relations, beginning with Jesus, moving to the modern period, but focusing on the significance of Constantine's conversion for understanding the history of anti-Judaism in Western civilization.

Cartlidge, David R., and David L. Dungan, eds. *Documents for the Study of the Gospels*, 2nd ed. Philadelphia: Fortress, 1994. Presents a valuable selection of ancient literary texts that are closely parallel to the New Testament Gospels, providing a good overview of important aspects of Jewish and pagan religiosity in the Greco-Roman world.

Chadwick, Henry. *The Early Church*. Rev. ed. New York: Penguin, 1993. A useful introductory overview of the history of early Christianity, by one of the world's eminent church historians. Ideal for beginning students.

Chesnut, Glenn F. *The First Christian Histories: Eusebius, Socrates, Sozomen, Theodoret, and Evagrius.* 2nd rev. ed. Macon, GA: Mercer, 1986. An important study of the character (and biases) of the earliest historians of Christianity, our sources for the majority of our information about the early church.

Droge, Arthur. *Moses or Homer: Early Christian Interpretations of the History of Culture.* Tübingen: J.C.B. Mohr (Paul Siebeck), 1989. An intriguing study of the early Christian apologists and their assertion that the Christian faith could claim greater antiquity than pagan religions in a world that respected antiquity.

Dunn, James. *The Theology of Paul the Apostle.* Grand Rapids, MI: Eerdmans, 1998. A broad-ranging sketch of Paul's major theological views, by a well-known British scholar

————. *Unity and Diversity in the New Testament: An Inquiry into the Nature of Earliest Christianity.* 2nd ed. Philadelphia: Trinity Press International, 1990. An extremely useful sketch of the major elements of diversity in the New Testament writings, along with reflections on features of these texts that bind them all together.

Ehrman, Bart D. *After the New Testament: A Reader in Early Christianity.* New York: Oxford, 1999. A collection of some of the most important early Christian writings from the second and third centuries, in quality English translations, dealing with a range of issues covered in this course, including persecution and martyrdom, Jewish-Christian relations, apostolic pseudepigrapha, the formation of canon, and the development of Christian theology. All in all, probably the best companion volume for the course.

————. *Lost Christianities: The Battles for Scripture and the Faiths We Never Knew.* New York: Oxford University Press, 2004. A study of the wide ranging diversity of Christianity in the second and third centuries, of the sacred texts (many of them forged) produced and revered by different Christian groups of the period, and of the struggles that led to the emergence of "orthodox" Christianity before the conversion of Constantine. For popular audiences.

————. *Lost Scriptures: Books That Did Not Make It into the New Testament.* New York: Oxford University Press, 2004. A collection of non-canonical Gospels, Acts, Epistles, and Apocalypses available in the second and third centuries, in readable English translations with brief introductions. For popular audiences.

————. *The New Testament and Other Early Christian Writings: A Reader.* New York: Oxford, 1998. A collection of all of the writings by the early Christians from within the first century after Jesus's death (that is, written before 130 A.D.), both canonical and non-canonical. It includes several of the texts discussed in this course. Ideal for beginning students.

————. *The Orthodox Corruption of Scripture: The Effect of Early Christological Controversies on the Text of the New Testament.* New York: Oxford University Press, 1993. A study of the ways scribes were influenced by doctrinal disputes in the early church and of how they modified their texts of the New Testament to make them conform more closely with their own theological views. Best suited for more advanced students.

Elliott, J. K. *The Apocryphal New Testament: A Collection of Apocryphal Christian Literature in an English Translation.* Oxford: Clarendon, 1993. An excellent one-volume collection of non-canonical Gospels, Acts, Epistles, and Apocalypses, in a readable English translation with brief introductions.

Ferguson, Everett. *Church and State in the Early Church.* New York: Garland, 1993. A collection of important articles dealing with the relationship of the early church and the Roman Empire, including important articles by St. Croix and Sherwin-White on the reasons for the persecution of Christians.

————, ed. *Worship in Early Christianity.* New York: Garland, 1993. A collection of important articles on various aspects of worship in the early church.

————. *Encyclopedia of Early Christianity.* 2nd ed. New York: Garland, 1998. A useful reference tool with brief articles on every aspect of early Christianity and up-to-date bibliographies. Suitable for beginning students and scholars alike.

Fredriksen, Paula. *From Jesus to Christ: The Origins of the New Testament Images of Jesus.* New Haven: Yale University Press, 1988. An important and widely used study of the earliest Christian views of Jesus and of the ways they developed as Christianity moved away from its Jewish roots.

————. *Jesus of Nazareth, King of the Jews: A Jewish life and the Emergence of Christianity.* New York: Knopf, 1999. A lively sketch of the life and teachings of Jesus that takes seriously the Jewish world in which he lived and pays close attention to the problems posed by our surviving sources.

Frend, W. H. C. *Martyrdom and Persecution in the Early Church*. Oxford: Blackwell, 1965. This classic is the best full-length study of Christian persecution and martyrdom during the first three centuries A.D., which tries to understand Christian views of martyrdom in light of the martyrdoms in the Jewish tradition.

―――. *The Rise of Christianity*. Philadelphia: Fortress, 1984. A full introductory discussion of the major issues involved with the history of the first six centuries of Christianity, packed with important information, names, and dates.

Gager, John. *The Origins of Anti-Semitism: Attitudes toward Judaism in Pagan and Christian Antiquity*. New York: Oxford, 1983. A seminal study of anti-Jewish attitudes and activities in the Roman world, especially in early Christianity.

Gamble, Harry. *The New Testament Canon: Its Making and Meaning*. Philadelphia: Fortress, 1985. A clearly written and informative overview of the formation of the canon that shows how, why, and when Christians chose the current 27 books to include in their sacred Scriptures of the New Testament.

Grant, Robert M. *Greek Apologists of the Second Century*. Philadelphia: Westminster, 1988. A survey of all the Christian apologists writing in Greek during the second century, focusing on their major themes and the sources of their ideas. For more advanced students.

―――. *Jesus after the Gospels: The Christ of the Second Century*. Louisville: Westminster/John Knox, 1990. An intriguing discussion of different understandings of Christology among a variety of early Christian groups in the decades after the New Testament was written.

―――. *Marcion: The Gospel of the Alien God*. Tr. John E. Steely and Lyle D. Bierma. Durham, NC: Labyrinth Press, 1990. The classic study of the life and teachings of the second-century philosopher-theologian Marcion.

Hengel, Martin. *Between Jesus and Paul: Studies in the History of Earliest Christianity*. London, SCM Press, 1983. A collection of essays on important aspects of the development of Christian thought during its earliest years, before the writing of the books of the New Testament.

Hennecke, Edgar, and Wilhelm Schneemelcher, eds. *New Testament Apocrypha*, 2 vols. Trans. by A. J. B. Higgins, et. al. Ed. by R. McL. Wilson. Philadelphia: Westminster Press, 1991. English translations of all the early non-canonical writings preserved from Christian antiquity, with detailed scholarly introductions; an indispensable resource for advanced students.

Klijn, A. F. J. *Jewish Christian Gospel Tradition*. Leiden: E.J. Brill, 1992. An authoritative discussion of the Jewish-Christian Gospels of the Ebionites, Nazareans, and Hebrews, including English translations of the remains of these texts.

Macmullen, Ramsey. *Christianizing the Roman Empire*. New Haven: Yale University Press, 1984. A succinct and learned account of how Christianity managed to convert pagans to faith in Jesus in the first several centuries of the church, emphasizing the role of "miracles" in the Christian mission.

Meeks, Wayne, ed. *The Writings of St. Paul*. New York: Norton, 1972. An annotation of the Pauline editions that includes a number of classical essays on key problems and issues in the study of Paul's writings (including ones by F. Nietzche and George Bernard Shaw).

———. *The First Urban Christian: The Social World of the Apostle Paul*. New Haven: Yale University Press, 1983. An impressive and influential study of Paul, not from the perspective of the theology of his writings, but in light of what can be known of the social world in which he lived, worked, and wrote.

Meier, John. *A Marginal Jew: Rethinking the Historical Jesus*, vol. 1. New York: Doubleday, 1991. An authoritative discussion of the historical Jesus (three volumes are available to this point) by a highly knowledgeable and sensible scholar.

Metzger, Bruce. *The Canon of the New Testament*. Oxford: Clarendon, 1987. The most thorough and informative account of the formation of the New Testament canon, by one of the world's eminent scholars of early Christianity.

Musurillo, H., ed. *The Acts of the Christian Martyrs*. Oxford: Clarendon, 1972. An intriguing collection of 28 accounts of Christian martyrdoms in English translation, taken from eyewitness sources of the second to fourth centuries.

Norris, Richard. *The Christological Controversy*. Philadelphia: Fortress, 1983. A useful presentation of some of the major texts from antiquity involving the controversies over the nature and person of Christ.

Pagels, Elaine. *The Gnostic Gospels*. New York: Random, 1976. An enormously popular and provocative account of the views of some of the early Gnostics in relation to emerging Christian orthodoxy.

Pelikan, Jeroslav. *The Christian Tradition*, vol. 1. Chicago: University Press, 1971. An authoritative discussion of the theology and theologians of early Christianity in the first centuries of the church.

Perkins, Judith. *The Suffering Self: Pain and Narrative Representation in the Early Christian Era*. London/New York: Routledge, 1995. An intriguing investigation of early Christian understandings of pain, suffering, and persecution in light of a broader cultural shift in the understanding of the self in the early centuries of Christianity; one's bodily suffering became a celebrated mark of self-identity.

Robinson, James, ed. *The Nag Hammadi Library in English*, 3rd ed. New York: Harper & Row, 1988. A convenient English translation of the documents discovered at Nag Hammadi, with brief introductions.

Roetzel, Calvin. *The Letters of Paul: Conversations in Context*, 3rd ed. Atlanta: John Knox, 1991. One of the best available introductory discussions of the Pauline Epistles, which includes an examination of the issues of authorship and date, as well as a sketch of the major themes of each letter.

―――. *The World That Shaped the New Testament*. 2nd ed. Louisville: John Knox Press, 2002. A nice overview of the Jewish and Greco-Roman worlds from which Christianity emerged, by a scholar of the New Testament; good for beginning students.

Rudolph, Kurt. *Gnosis: The Nature and History of Gnosticism*. Tr. R. McL. Wilson. San Francisco: Harper & Row, 1987. Still the best book-length introduction to ancient Gnosticism.

Ruether, Rosemary. *Faith and Fratricide: The Theological Roots of Anti-Semitism*. New York: Seabury, 1974. A controversial discussion by a prominent feminist theologian of the early Christian attitudes toward Jews and Judaism, which maintains that anti-Semitism is the necessary corollary of Christian belief in Jesus as the Messiah.

Rusch, William G. *The Trinitarian Controversy*. Philadelphia: Fortress, 1980. A presentation of key texts in the ancient controversies involved with the doctrine of the Trinity.

Sanders, E. P. *The Historical Figure of Jesus*. London: Penguin, 1993. One of the best introductions available to the life and teachings of the historical Jesus. It is well-suited for beginning students.

―――. *Judaism Practice and Belief, 63 B.C.E.–66 C.E.* London/Philadelphia: SCM Press/Trinity Press International, 1992. A full, detailed, and authoritative account of what it meant to be a Jew immediately before and during the time of the New Testament, by one of the great New Testament scholars of our generation.

Sandmel, Samuel. *Anti-Semitism in the New Testament?* Philadelphia: Fortress, 1978. A clear and interesting discussion, from the perspective of a prominent Jewish scholar of the New Testament, of whether parts of the New Testament should be viewed as anti-Semitic.

Schweitzer, Albert. *The Quest of the Historical Jesus.* New York: Macmillan, 1968. The classic study of the major attempts to write a biography of Jesus up to the first part of the 20th century (the German original appeared in 1906). It is also one of the first and perhaps the most important attempt to portray Jesus as a Jewish apocalypticist.

Segal, Alan. *Paul the Convert: The Apostolate and Apostasy of Saul the Pharisee.* New Haven: Yale University Press, 1990. An intriguing assessment of the teachings and theology of Paul in light of the Judaism of his day, focusing on the role and significance of his "conversion" to become a follower of Jesus; written by an important scholar of ancient Judaism.

Setzer, Claudia. *Jewish Responses to Early Christians: History and Polemics, 30–150 C.E.* Minneapolis: Fortress Press, 1994. A nice overview of how Jews reacted to Christians during the first 120 years of Jewish-Christian relations. Good for beginning students.

Shelton, Jo-Ann, ed. *As the Romans Did: A Source Book in Roman Social History.* New York/Oxford: Oxford University Press, 1988. A highly useful anthology of ancient texts that deal with every major aspect of life in the Roman world, including religion.

Siker, Jeffrey. *Disinheriting the Jews: Abraham in Early Christian Controversy.* Louisville: Westminster/John Knox Press, 1991. An important study of how such Christian authors as Paul and Justin used the figure Abraham, father of the Jews, in their attacks on Jewish understandings of Scripture and salvation.

Simon, Marcel. *Verus Israel: A Study of the Relations between Christians and Jews in the Roman Empire (135–425).* Tr. H. McKeating. New York: Oxford, 1986. A standard study of Jewish-Christian relations in the early centuries of the church.

Stark, Rodney. *The Rise of Christianity: A Sociologist Reconsiders History.* Princeton: Princeton University Press, 1996. A widely read account of the spread of early Christianity throughout the Roman Empire that considers, in particular, sociological explanations for its success. For popular audiences.

Torjesen, Karen Jo. *When Women Were Priests: Women's Leadership in the Early Church and the Scandal of Their Subordination in the Rise of Christianity*. San Francisco: HarperSanFrancisco, 1993. A discussion of the leadership roles played by women in the earliest stages of Christianity and an account of how women's voices eventually came to be silenced over time. Good for popular audiences.

Turcan, Robert. *The Cults of the Roman Empire*. Oxford: Blackwell, 1996. This is a superb introduction to some of the major religious cults in the Roman Empire from roughly the time of early Christianity (and before).

Vermes, Geza. *Jesus the Jew: A Historian's Reading of the Gospels*. New York: Macmillan, 1973. A readable but very learned study of Jesus in light of traditions of other Jewish "holy men" from his time, written by a prominent New Testament scholar at Oxford.

von Campenhausen, H. *The Formation of the Christian Bible*. Tr. J. A. Baker. Philadelphia: Fortress, 1972. An important and erudite study of the formation of the New Testament canon, for more advanced students.

————. *Ecclesiastical Authority and Spiritual Power in the Church of the First Three Centuries*. Stanford: Stanford University Press, 1969. A classical study by an important German scholar of the formation of church structure over the formative periods of Christianity. For advanced students.

von Harnack, Adolf. *History of Dogma*, vol. 1. Tr. from the 3rd ed. by Neil Buchanan. New York: Dover, 1961 (German original, 1900). A classic and invaluable sketch of the development of Christian theology during the early centuries of the church, by one of the most erudite historians of Christianity of modern times.

Wilken, Robert. *The Christians as the Romans Saw Them*. New Haven: Yale University Press, 1984. A popular and clearly written account of the mainly negative views of Christians held by several Roman authors. It is particularly suitable for beginning students.

Williamson, G. A. *Eusebius: The History of the Church from Christ to Constantine*. Rev. and ed. Andrew Louth. London: Penguin, 1989. A handy and accessible English translation of Eusebius's classic work, the *Church History*.

Notes

Notes

Notes

Notes

Notes

Notes